HOUGHTON MIFFLIN BOSTON

Program Authors

William Badders
Director of the Cleveland Mathematics and Science Partnership
Cleveland Municipal School District
Cleveland, Ohio

Douglas Carnine, Ph.D.
Professor of Education
University of Oregon
Eugene, Oregon

James Feliciani
Supervisor of Instructional Media and Technology
Land O' Lakes, Florida

Bobby Jeanpierre, Ph.D.
Assistant Professor, Science Education
University of Central Florida
Orlando, Florida

Carolyn Sumners, Ph.D.
Director of Astronomy and Physical Sciences
Houston Museum of Natural Science
Houston, Texas

Catherine Valentino
Author-in-Residence
Houghton Mifflin
West Kingston, Rhode Island

Content Consultants

Dr. Robert Arnold
Professor of Biology
Colgate University
Hamilton, New York

Dr. Carl D. Barrentine
Associate Professor Humanities and Biology
University of North Dakota
Grand Forks, North Dakota

Dr. Steven L. Bernasek
Department of Chemistry
Princeton University
Princeton, New Jersey

Dennis W. Cheek
Senior Manager
Science Applications International Corporation
Exton, Pennsylvania

Dr. Jung Choi
School of Biology
Georgia Tech
Atlanta, Georgia

Prof. John Conway
Department of Physics
University of California
Davis, California

Printed in the U.S.A.

ISBN-13: 978-0-618-49224-4
ISBN-10: 0-618-49224-0

3 4 5 6 7 8 9-DW-16 15 14 13 12 11 10 09 08 07 06

Content Consultants

Dr. Robert Dailey
Division of Animal and Veterinary Sciences
West Virginia University
Morgantown, West Virginia

Dr. Thomas Davies
IODP/USIO Science Services
Texas A & M University
College Station, Texas

Dr. Ron Dubreuil
Department of Biological Sciences
University of Illinois at Chicago
Chicago, Illinois

Dr. Orin G. Gelderloos
Professor of Biology
University of Michigan - Dearborn
Dearborn, Michigan

Dr. Michael R. Geller
Associate Professor, Department of Physics
University of Georgia
Athens, Georgia

Dr. Erika Gibb
Department of Physics
Notre Dame University
South Bend, Indiana

Dr. Fern Gotfried
Pediatrician
Hanover Township, New Jersey

Dr. Michael Haaf
Chemistry Department
Ithaca College
Ithaca, New York

Professor Melissa A. Hines
Department of Chemistry
Cornell University
Ithaca, New York

Dr. Jonathan M. Lincoln
Assistant Provost & Dean of Undergraduate Education
Bloomsburg University
Bloomsburg, Pennsylvania

Donald Lisowy
Wildlife Conservation Society
Bronx Zoo
Bronx, New York

Dr. Marc L. Mansfield
Department of Chemistry and Chemical Biology
Stevens Institute of Technology
Hoboken, New Jersey

Dr. Scott Nuismer
Department of Biological Sciences
University of Idaho
Moscow, Idaho

Dr. Suzanne O'Connell
Department of Earth and Environmental Sciences
Wesleyan University
Middletown, Connecticut

Dr. Kenneth Parsons
Assistant Professor of Meteorology
Embry-Riddle Aeronautical University
Prescott, Arizona

Betty Preece
Engineer and Physicist
Indialantic, Florida

Dr. Chantal Reid
Department of Biology
Duke University
Durham, North Carolina

Dr. Todd V. Royer
Department of Biological Sciences
Kent State University
Kent, Ohio

Dr. Kate Scholberg
Physics Department
Duke University
Durham, North Carolina

Dr. Jeffery Scott
Department of Earth, Atmospheric, and Planetary Sciences
Massachusetts Institute of Technology
Cambridge, Massachusetts

Dr. Ron Stoner
Professor Emeritus, Physics and Astronomy Department
Bowling Green State University
Bowling Green, Ohio

Dr. Dominic Valentino, Ph.D.
Professor, Department of Psychology
University of Rhode Island
Kingston, Rhode Island

Dr. Sidney White
Professor Emeritus of Geology
Ohio State University
Columbus, Ohio

Dr. Scott Wissink
Professor, Department of Physics
Indiana University
Bloomington, Indiana

Dr. David Wright
Department of Chemistry
Vanderbilt University
Nashville, Tennessee

UNIT
A
Plants and
Animals

Unit B Environments and Energy

Treasures From Earth

Patterns in the Sky

Matter and Energy

Motion and Forces

Features

Unit A

Investigate Activities

Reading in Science

Focus On

Unit B

Investigate Activities

Reading in Science

Focus On

Unit C

Investigate Activities

Reading in Science

Focus On

Investigate Activities

Reading in Science

Focus On

UNIT
E

Investigate Activities

Reading in Science

Focus On

UNIT
F

Investigate Activities

Reading in Science

Focus On

How Your Book Is Organized

The Nature of Science

In the front of your book you will learn about how people explore science.

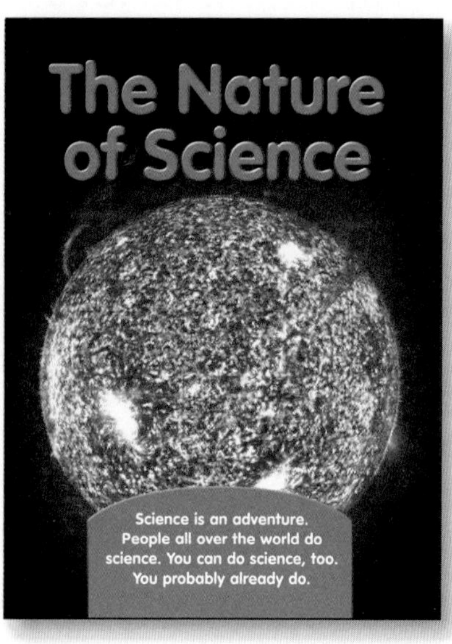

Units

The major sections of your book are units.

Unit Title tells you what the unit is about.

Find more information related to this unit from the creators of Cricket magazine, on the EduPlace web site.

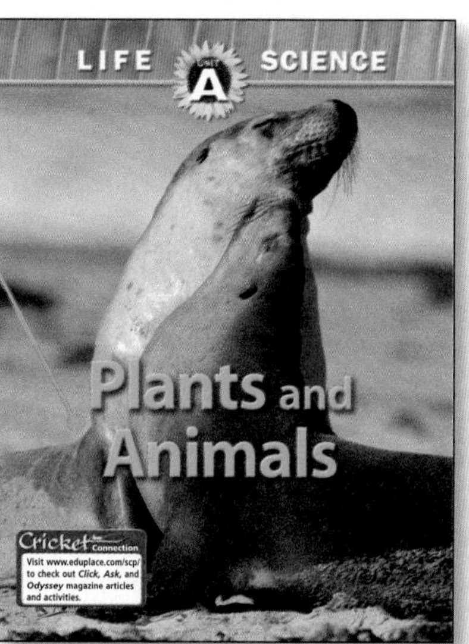

Reading in Science gives you something to think and talk about.

Chapters are parts of a unit. This tells you what the chapters are about.

You can read these on your own.

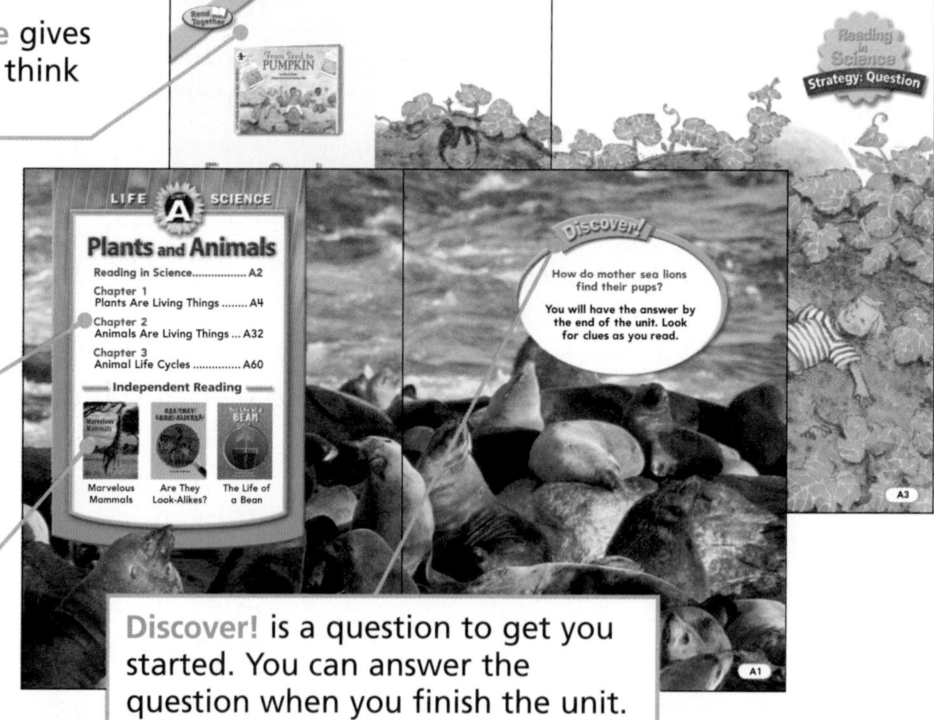

Discover! is a question to get you started. You can answer the question when you finish the unit.

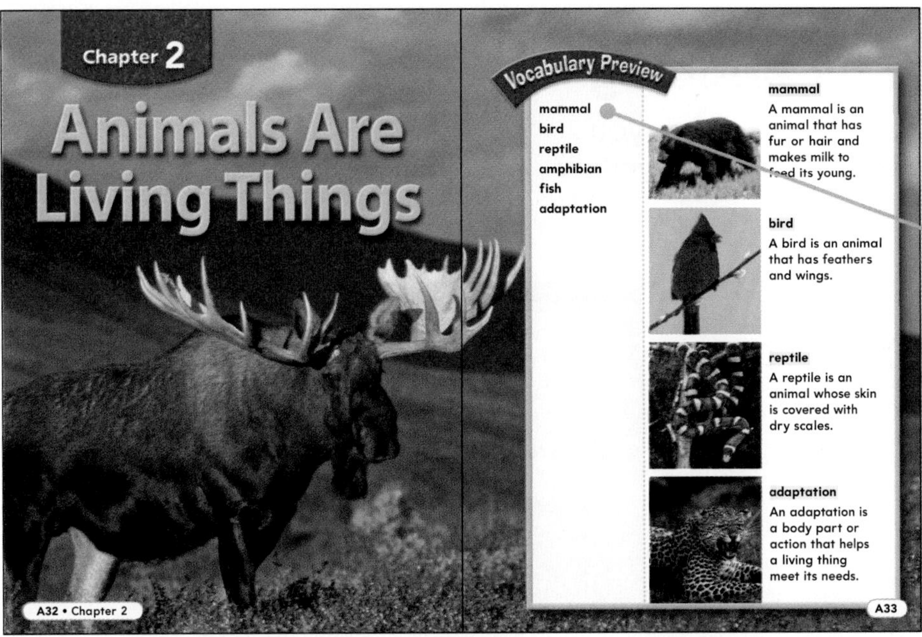

Chapter Vocabulary shows the vocabulary you will learn and gets you started.

Every lesson in your book has two parts.

Part 1: Investigate Activity

Science and You helps you think about the lesson.

Inquiry Skill shows the main inquiry skill for the activity and helps you use it.

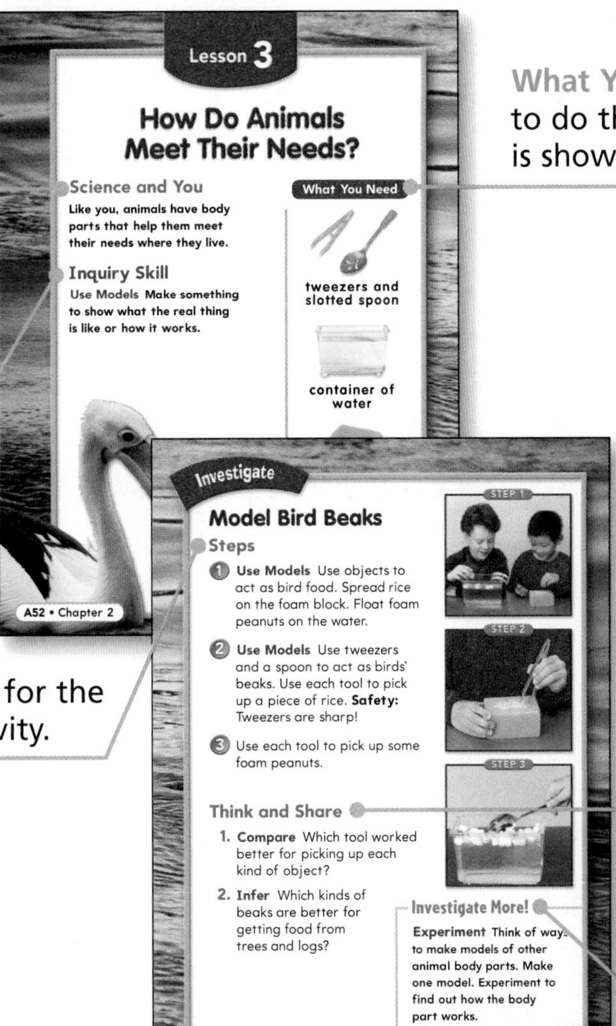

What You Need to do the activity is shown here.

Steps to follow for the Investigate activity.

Think and Share lets you check what you have learned.

Investigate More lets you do more on your own.

Part 2: Learn by Reading

Vocabulary lists the new science words you will learn. In the text dark words with yellow around them are new words.

Main Idea is underlined to show you what is important.

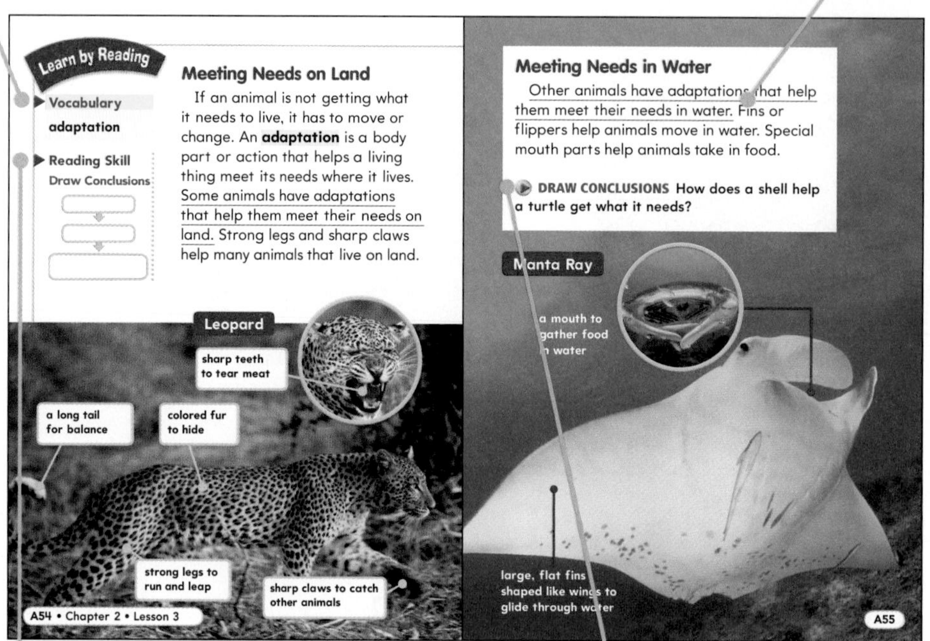

Reading Skill helps you understand the text.

Reading Skill Check has you think about what you just read.

Lesson Wrap-Up

After you read, check what you have learned.

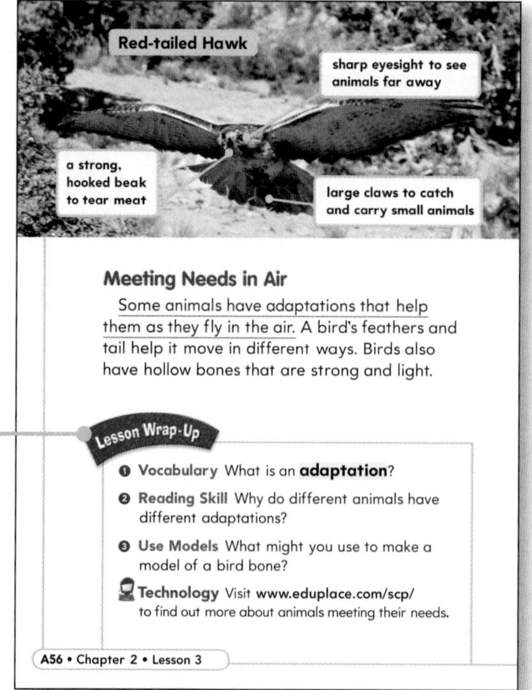

Focus On

Focus On lets you learn more about an important topic. Look for Biography, Technology, Literature, Readers' Theater—and more.

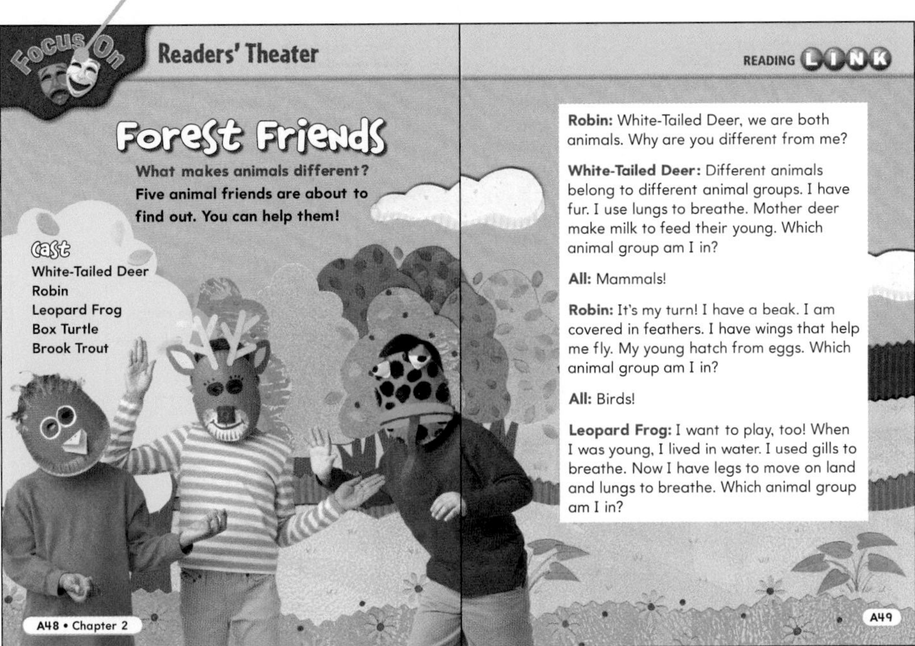
Focus On

Readers' Theater

READING LINK

Forest Friends

What makes animals different? Five animal friends are about to find out. You can help them!

Cast
White-Tailed Deer
Robin
Leopard Frog
Box Turtle
Brook Trout

Robin: White-Tailed Deer, we are both animals. Why are you different from me?

White-Tailed Deer: Different animals belong to different animal groups. I have fur. I use lungs to breathe. Mother deer make milk to feed their young. Which animal group am I in?

All: Mammals!

Robin: It's my turn! I have a beak. I am covered in feathers. I have wings that help me fly. My young hatch from eggs. Which animal group am I in?

All: Birds!

Leopard Frog: I want to play, too! When I was young, I lived in water. I used gills to breathe. Now I have legs to move on land and lungs to breathe. Which animal group am I in?

A48 • Chapter 2

A49

Links

Connects science to other subject areas.

You can do these at school or at home.

LINKS for Home and School

Math **Pet Survey**

Ask classmates which kind of animal makes the best pet. Record data in a bar graph.

Best Pets

Kind of Animal: mammal, bird, reptile, amphibian, fish

Number of Children: 0 1 2 3 4 5 6 7 8 9 10

1. Which kind of animal do children think makes the best pet?
2. How many children think that a reptile makes the best pet?

Music **Animal Groups**

In groups, write new words to the song "Old MacDonald Had a Farm." Write words for each animal group. Practice your songs, and perform them for the class.

And on his farm he had some mammals E-I-E-I-O. With some fur here and some hair there.

A57

Review and Test Prep

These reviews help you to know you are on track with your learning. Here you will practice and apply your new skills.

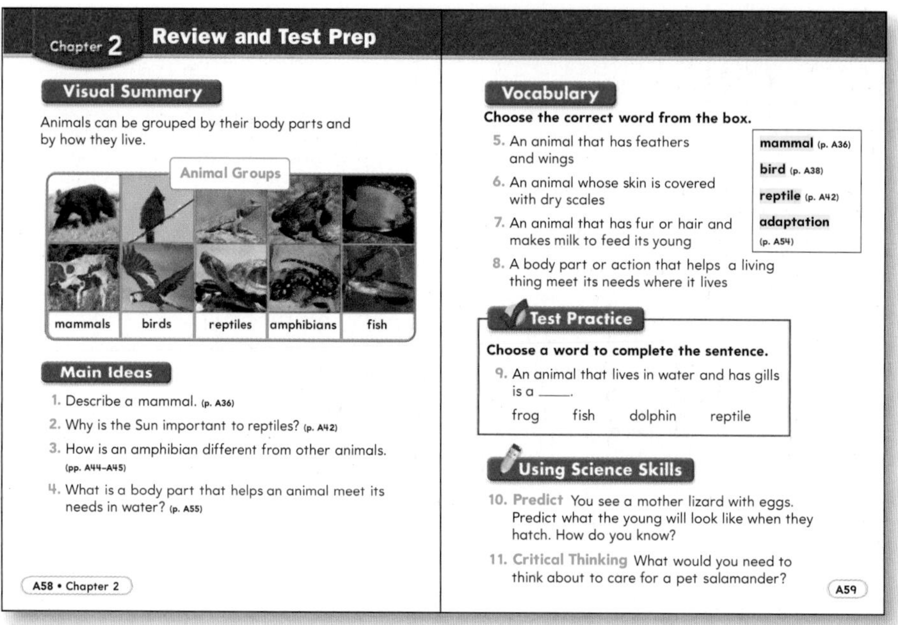

Unit Wrap-Up

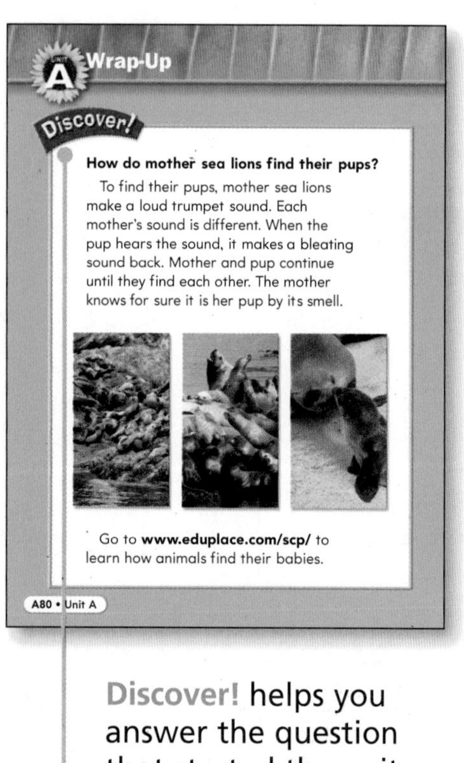

Discover! helps you answer the question that started the unit.

References

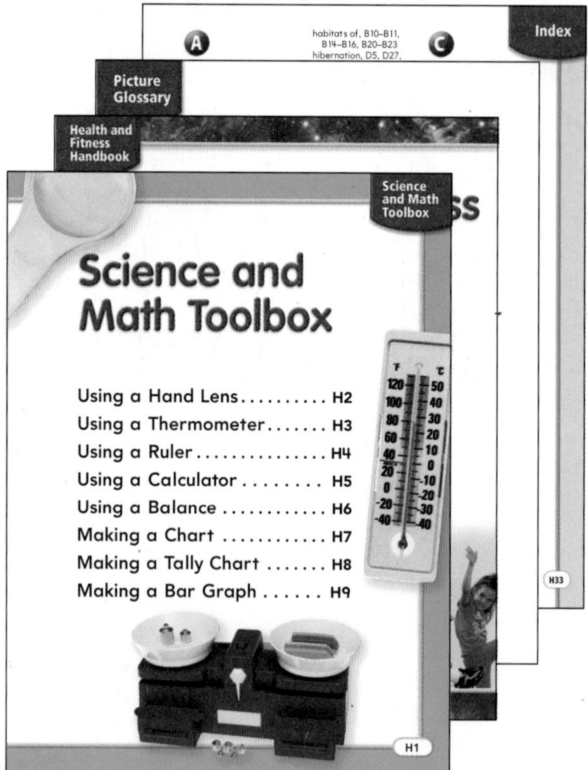

The back of your book includes sections you will refer to again and again.

Science is an adventure. People all over the world do science. You can do science, too. You probably already do.

National Science Education Standards

Science Content Standards

Grades K–4.A. ABILITIES NECESSARY TO DO SCIENTIFIC INQUIRY

- Ask a question about objects, organisms, and events in the environment.
- Plan and conduct a simple investigation.
- Employ simple equipment and tools to gather data and extend the senses.
- Use data to construct a reasonable explanation.
- Communicate investigations and explanations.

Grades K–4.A. UNDERSTANDINGS ABOUT SCIENTIFIC INQUIRY

- Scientific investigations involve asking and answering a question and comparing the answer with what scientists already know about the world.
- Scientists use different kinds of investigations depending on the questions they are trying to answer. Types of investigations include describing objects, events, and organisms; classifying them; and doing a fair test (experimenting).
- Simple instruments, such as magnifiers, thermometers, and rulers, provide more information than scientists obtain using only their senses.
- Scientists develop explanations using observations (evidence) and what they already know about the world (scientific knowledge). Good explanations are based on evidence from investigations.
- Scientists make the results of their investigations public; they describe the investigations in ways that enable others to repeat the investigations.
- Scientists review and ask questions about the results of other scientists' work.

Grades K–4.E. ABILITIES OF TECHNOLOGICAL DESIGN

- Identify a simple problem.
- Propose a solution.
- Implementing proposed solutions.
- Evaluate a product or design.
- Communicate a problem, design, and solution.

The Nature of Science

You Can...

Do What Scientists Do

Meet Fernando Caldeiro, the astronaut. His friends call him Frank. He is training to go into space. When he is not training, he tests computer programs used to run the space shuttle. Before Mr. Caldeiro became an astronaut, he tested new jets. He also worked on space shuttle rockets.

Frank Caldeiro is floating in a jet that gives the feeling of low gravity. This jet is one tool scientists use to learn more about space.
The jet's nickname is the "vomit comet." Can you guess why?

Many Kinds of Investigations

Astronauts carry out many investigations in space. Sometimes they observe Earth and take photos. Other times they do experiments. They may test how plants or animals react to low gravity. They share what they find out with other scientists.

Astronauts learn to fly the space shuttle in machines called simulators. They also learn to use space shuttle tools to collect information.

You Can...

Think Like a Scientist

Everyone can do science.
To think like a scientist you have to:

- ask a lot of questions.
- find answers by investigating.
- work on a team.
- compare your ideas to those of others.

What is this lizard doing? Is it sleeping? Is it waiting for insects to fly by? Or, is it doing something else?

Use Critical Thinking

When you know the difference between what you observe and what you think about your observation, you are a critical thinker. A fact is an observation that can be checked to make sure it is true. An opinion is what you think about the facts. When you ask someone, "How do you know that?" you are asking for facts.

The lizard lies under the heat lamp for a while. Then it gets food. **I wonder if it must warm up before it can move around?**

I read that a lizard's body temperature falls when the air cools. It warms itself by lying in the sun.

Science Inquiry

You can use **scientific inquiry** to find answers to your questions about the world around you. Say you have seen crickets in the yard.

Observe It seems like crickets chirp very fast on some nights, but slowly on other nights.

Ask a question I wonder, does the speed of cricket chirping change with temperature?

Form an idea I think crickets chirp faster when it's warmer.

Experiment I will need a timer and a thermometer. I will count how many times a cricket chirps in 2 minutes. I will do this when the air temperature is warmer and when the air temperature is cooler.

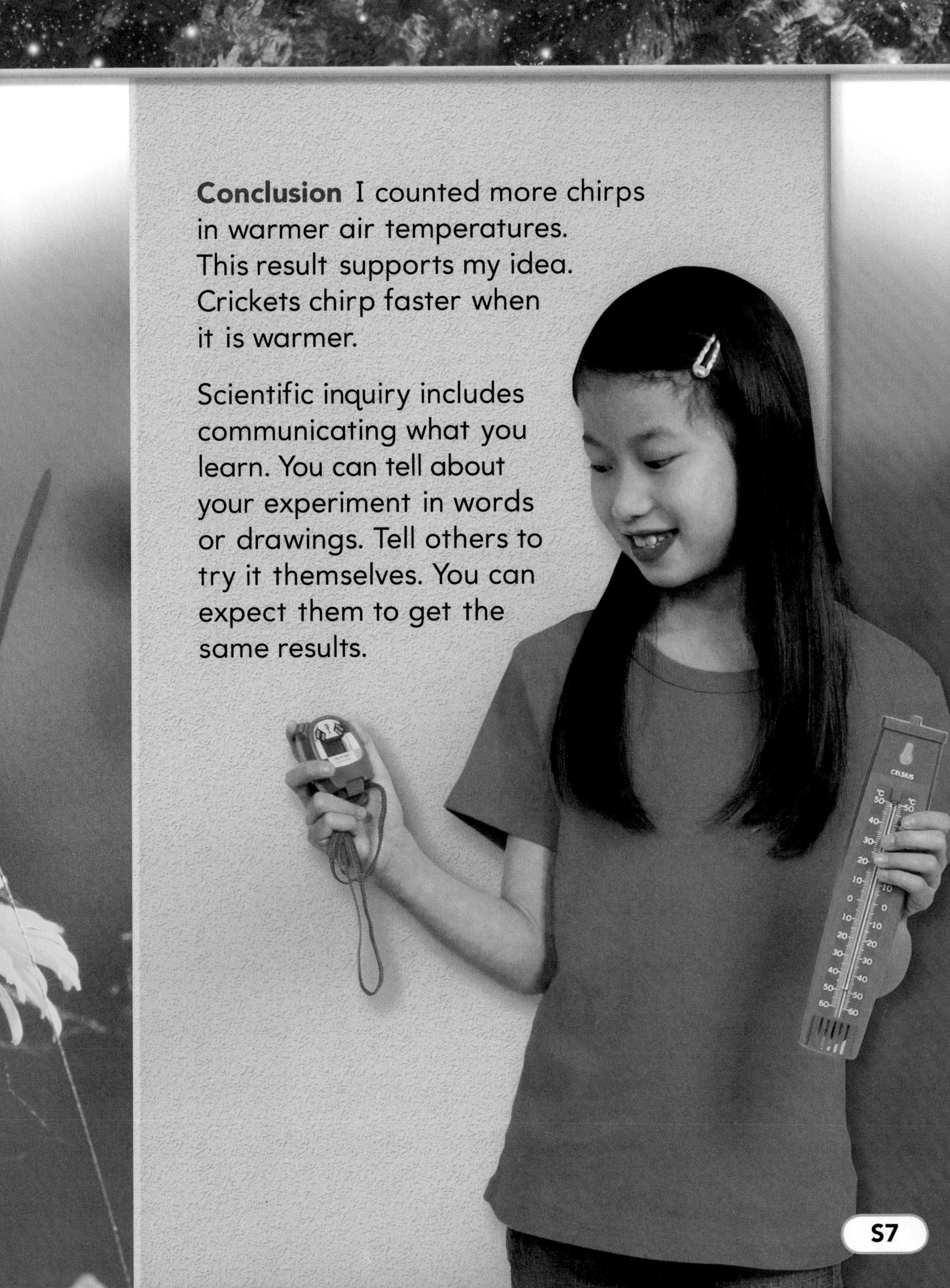

Conclusion I counted more chirps in warmer air temperatures. This result supports my idea. Crickets chirp faster when it is warmer.

Scientific inquiry includes communicating what you learn. You can tell about your experiment in words or drawings. Tell others to try it themselves. You can expect them to get the same results.

Inquiry Process

Here is a process that some scientists follow to answer questions and make new discoveries.

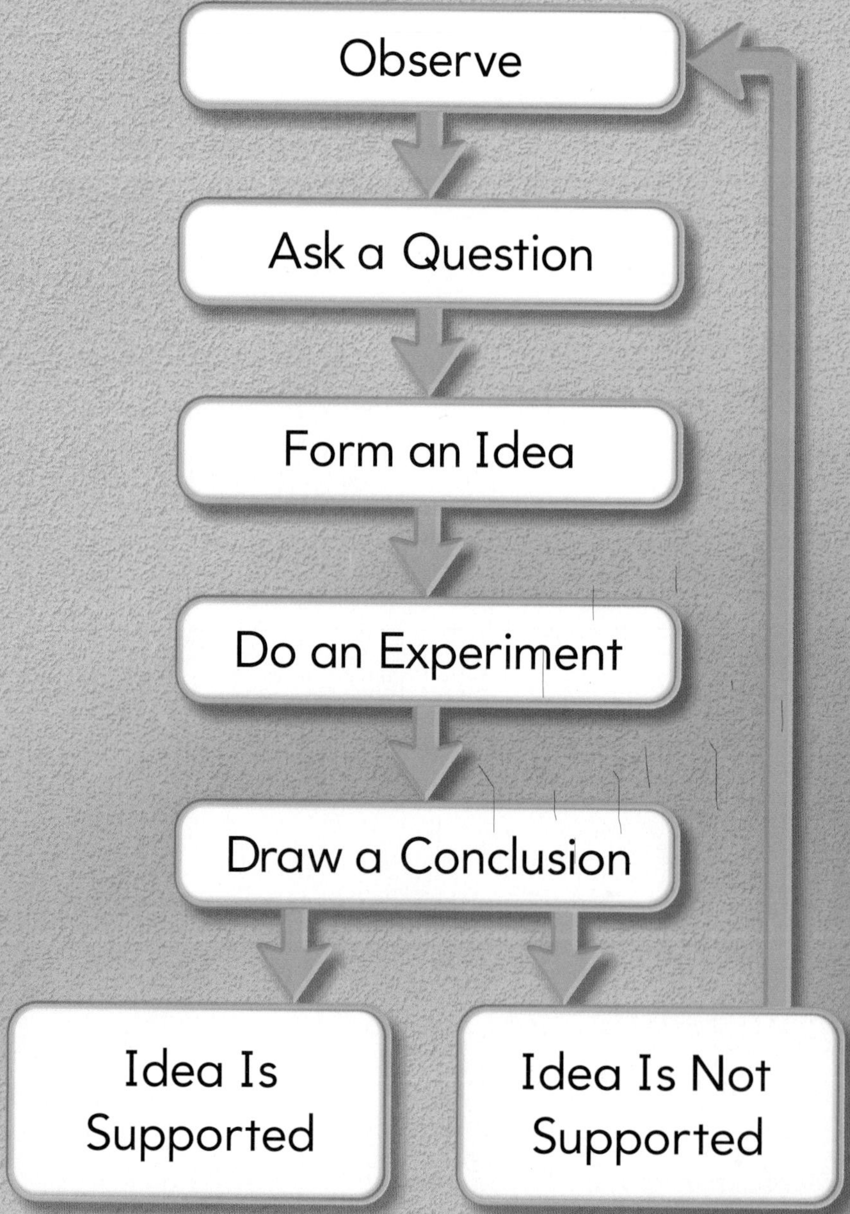

Observe

Ask a Question

Form an Idea

Do an Experiment

Draw a Conclusion

Idea Is Supported

Idea Is Not Supported

Try it Yourself!

Experiment With Bouncing Balls

Both balls look the same. However, one ball bounces and the other one does not.

1. What questions do you have about the balls?
2. How would you find out the answers?
3. Write an experiment plan. Tell what you think you will find out.

You Can...

Be an Inventor

Lloyd French has enjoyed building things and taking them apart since sixth grade.

Mr. French invents robots. They are used as tools to make observations in places where people cannot easily go. One of his robots can travel to the bottom of the ocean. Another robot, called Cryobot, melts through thick layers of ice—either in Antarctica or on Mars. Cryobot takes photos as it moves through the ice.

"If you want to be a scientist or engineer, it helps to have a sense of curiosity and discovery."

What Is Technology?

The tools people make and use are all **technology**. A pencil is technology. A cryobot is technology. So is a robot that moves like a human.

Scientists use technology. For example, a microscope makes it possible to see things that cannot be seen with just the eyes. Measurement tools are used to make their observations more exact.

Many technologies make the world a better place to live. But sometimes solving one problem causes others. For example, airplanes make travel faster, but they are noisy and pollute the air.

A Better Idea

"I wish I had a better way to _____". How would you fill in the blank? Everyone wishes they could do something more easily. Inventors try to make those wishes come true. Inventing or improving an invention takes time and patience.

Kids have been riding on scooters for many years. These newer scooters are faster. The tires won't get flat. They are also easier to carry from place to place.

How to Be an Inventor

1. **Find a problem.** It may be at school, at home, or in your community.
2. **Think of a way to solve the problem.** List different ways to solve the problem. Decide which one will work best.
3. **Make a sample and try your invention.** Your idea may need many materials or none at all. Each time you try it, record how it works.
4. **Improve your invention.** Use what you learned to make your design better.
5. **Share your invention.** Draw or write about your invention. Tell how it makes an activity easier or more fun. If it did not work well, tell why.

You Can...

Make Decisions

Plastic Litter and Ocean Animals

It is a windy day at the beach. A plastic bag blows out of sight. It may float in the ocean for years.

Plastic litter can harm ocean animals. Sometimes sea turtles mistake floating plastic bags for jellyfish, their favorite food. The plastic blocks the stomach, and food cannot get in. Pelicans and dolphins get tangled up in fishing line, six-pack rings, and packaging materials. Sometimes they get so tangled that they cannot move.

Deciding What to Do

How can ocean animals be protected from plastic litter?

Here's how to make your decision. You can use the same steps to help solve problems in your home, in your school, and in your community.

Learn	**Learn about the problem. You could talk to an expert, read a science book, or explore a web site.**
List	**Make a list of actions you could take. Add actions other people could take.**
Decide	**Decide which action is best for you or your community.**
Share	**Explain your decision to others.**

Science Safety

Know the safety rules of your classroom and follow them. Read and follow the safety tips in your science book.

- **Wear safety goggles when your teacher tells you.**
- **Keep your work area clean. Tell your teacher about spills right away.**
- **Learn how to care for the plants and animals in your classroom.**
- **Wash your hands when you are done.**

LIFE UNIT A SCIENCE

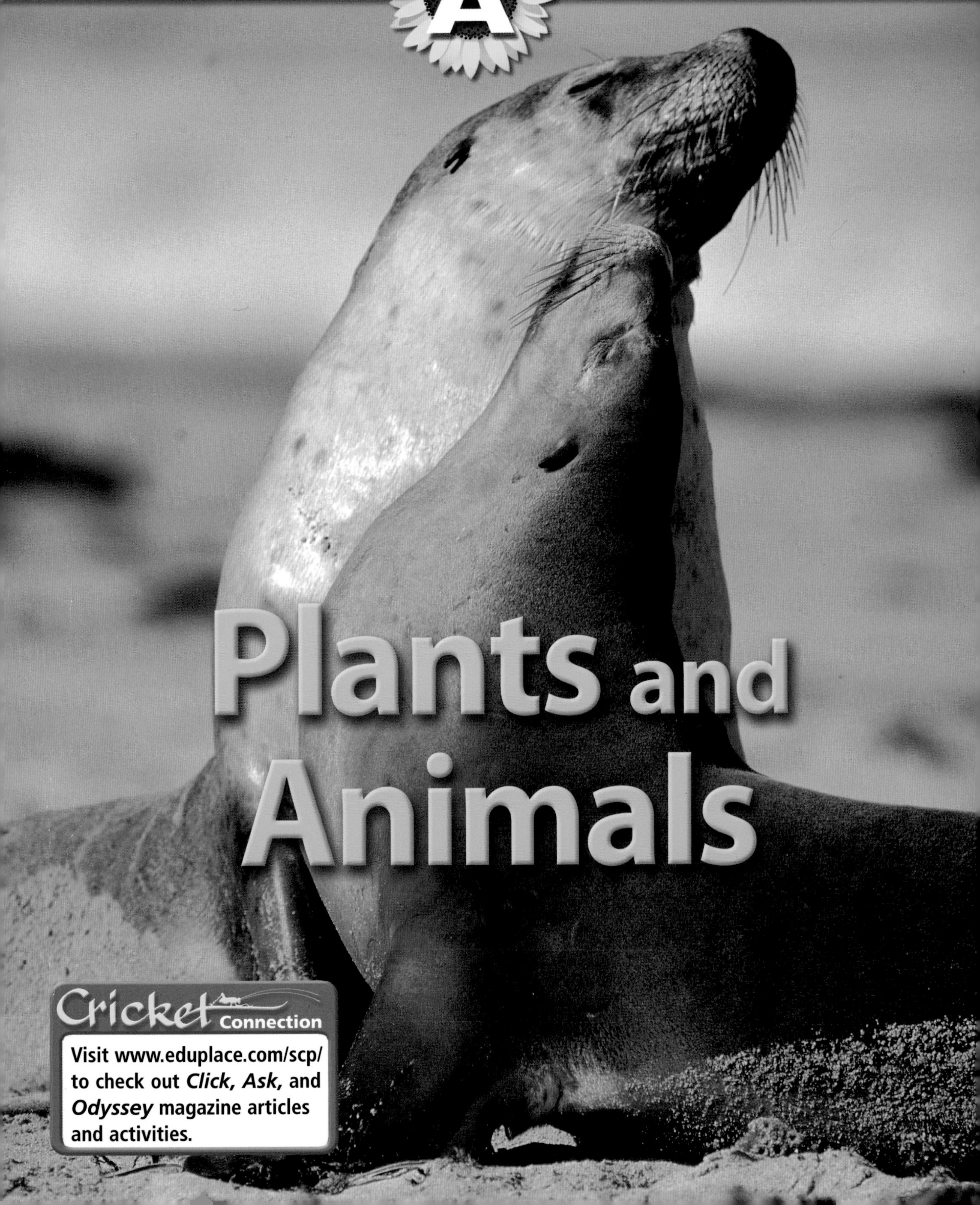

Plants and Animals

Cricket Connection

Visit www.eduplace.com/scp/ to check out *Click, Ask,* and *Odyssey* magazine articles and activities.

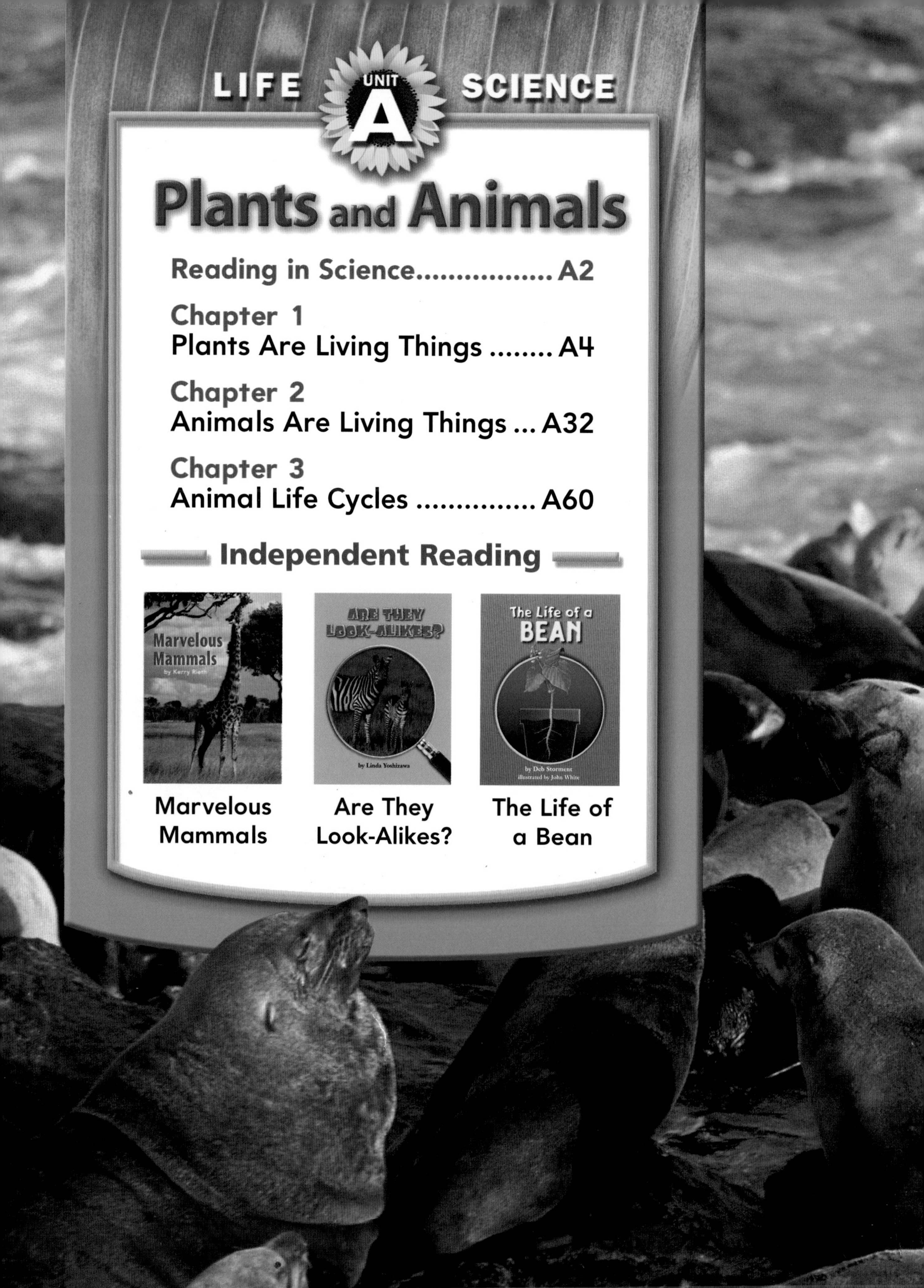

LIFE UNIT A SCIENCE

Plants and Animals

Independent Reading

Marvelous Mammals

Are They Look-Alikes?

The Life of a Bean

Discover!
How do mother sea lions find their pups?
Think about this question as you read. You will have the answer by the end of the unit.

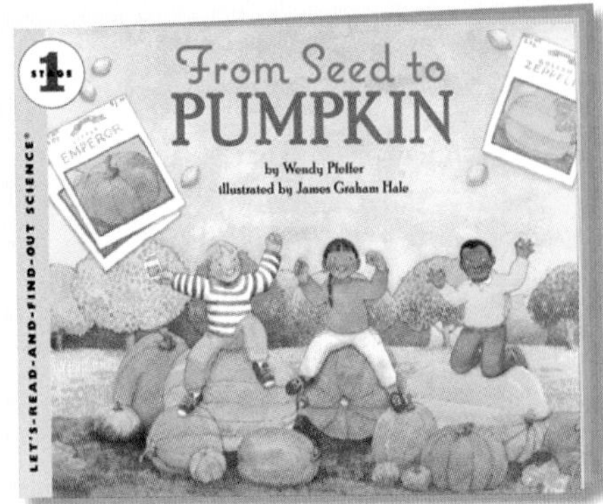

From Seed to PUMPKIN

by Wendy Pfeffer
illustrated by
James Graham Hale

Pumpkin plants don't stand up tall. As the stems grow longer, they sprawl all over the ground. Before long, twisted, tangled vines cover the pumpkin patch.

Reading in Science
Strategy: Question

Chapter 1

Plants Are Living Things

Vocabulary Preview

living thing
shelter
nutrient
flower
fruit
seed
cone
taproot
fibrous root
life cycle
seedling

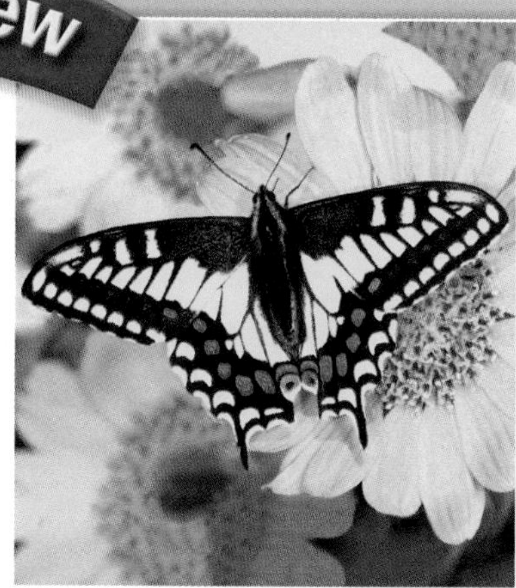

living thing

A living thing is something that grows and changes.

flower

A flower is the plant part where fruit and seeds form.

taproot

A taproot is a root that has one main branch.

seedling

A young plant that grows from a seed is called a seedling.

Lesson 1

How Are the Needs of Living Things Different?

Science and You

Knowing about the needs of living things can help you care for them better.

Inquiry Skill

Record Data Make a chart to show what you observe.

What You Need

plant

classroom pet

word cards and scissors

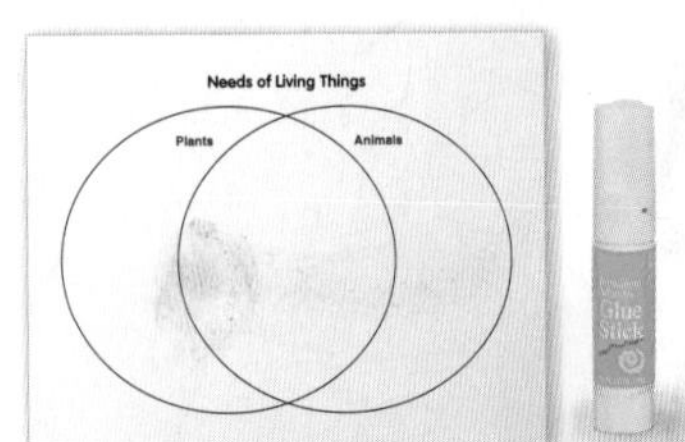

recording chart and glue

Investigate

Record Needs

Steps

1. **Observe** Watch a plant and an animal. Think about how to care for each of them.

2. Cut out the word cards. **Safety:** Scissors are sharp! Think about which things animals need and which things plants need.

3. **Record Data** Place the word cards on a chart to show what plants and animals need. Discuss with a partner. Then glue the word cards in place.

STEP 1

STEP 2

STEP 3

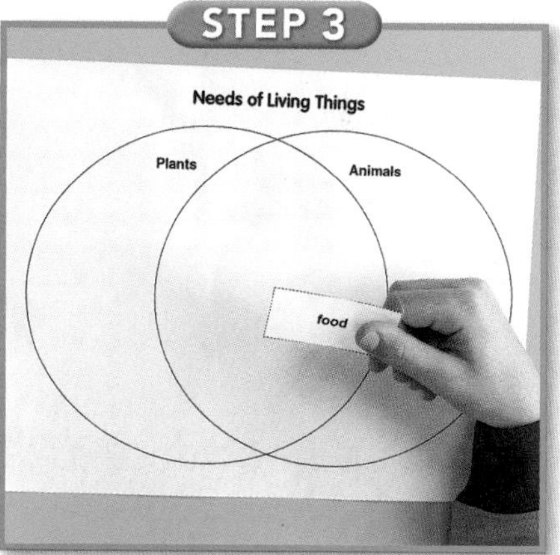

Think and Share

1. What do both plants and animals need?
2. How are the needs of plants and animals different?

Investigate More!

Solve a Problem Suppose that plants in a community garden are dying. What can you and other people do to help them live?

Learn by Reading

Vocabulary

living thing

shelter

nutrient

Reading Skill

Main Idea and Details

Living Things Have Needs

A **living thing** is something that grows and changes. Living things make other living things that are like themselves. Plants and animals are living things.

All living things need air, food, water, and space. Larger plants and animals need more air, food, water, and space than smaller plants and animals.

Big trees need more water and space than small flowers.

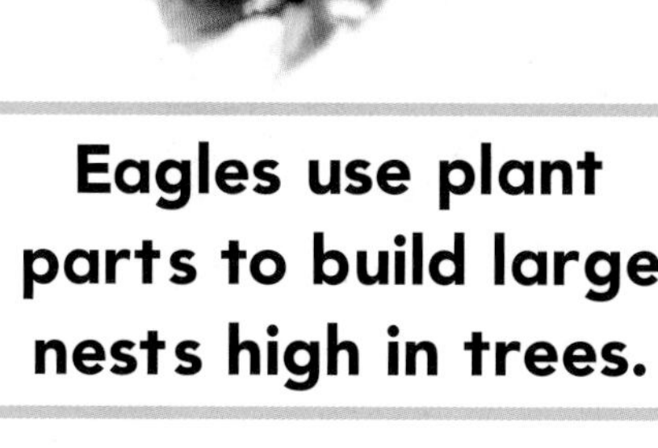

Eagles use plant parts to build large nests high in trees.

Animals also need shelter. A **shelter** is a place where a living thing can be safe. A bigger living thing needs a bigger shelter than a smaller living thing.

Many animals use plants for shelter. Some animals use a hole in a tree. Others find shelter at the base of a tree under roots or leaves.

Some animals find shelter in water or under rocks and logs. These places protect the animal from danger.

MAIN IDEA How are the needs of large and small living things different?

A hummingbird lays eggs in a small nest.

What Plants Need

Plants cannot move from place to place as animals do. Plants must get all the things they need in the place where they grow. Plants that do not get what they need may die. Like all living things, plants need air, food, water, sunlight, and space. The sunflowers in the field are getting what they need to live.

This plant is not getting enough water.

Plants also need sunlight. Sunlight helps plants grow. Plants do not get food in the same way as other living things. Plants make their own food. They use sunlight, air, water, and nutrients.

A **nutrient** is a material in soil that helps a plant live and grow. Plants also get water from the soil. Plants use the food that they make to grow and change.

MAIN IDEA **How do plants use sunlight?**

Lesson Wrap-Up

1. **Vocabulary** What are **nutrients**?
2. **Reading Skill** What do plants need to live?
3. **Record Data** What are two ways that you can record data?

Technology Visit **www.eduplace.com/scp/** to find out more about living things.

Lesson 2

How Do Plants Meet Their Needs?

Science and You

Like you, plants have parts that help them get what they need.

Inquiry Skill

Infer Use what you observe and know to tell what you think.

What You Need

celery stalk

jar of water

food coloring

knife and hand lens

Investigate

Moving Water

Steps

1. Use a knife to cut off the end of a celery stalk. **Safety:** A knife is sharp!

2. Add food coloring to the jar of water and stir. Put the celery into the colored water.

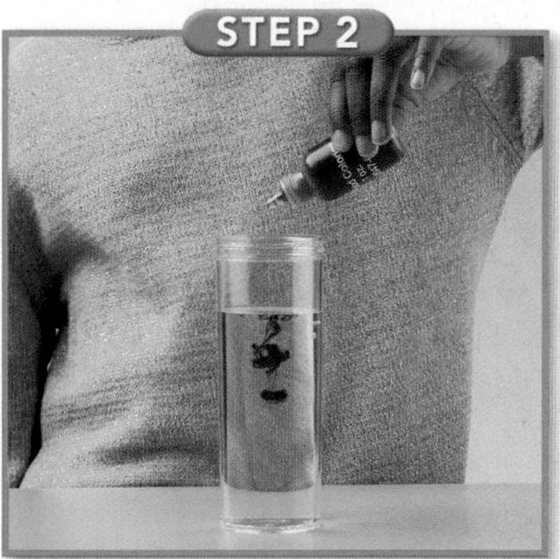

3. **Observe** Wait two hours. Then look at the celery. Use a hand lens to see if the celery has changed.

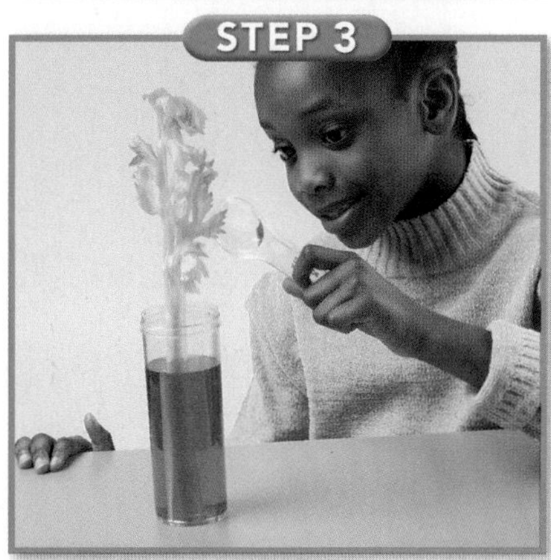

Think and Share

1. What happened to the celery stalk?
2. **Infer** How do you think a plant gets water?

Investigate More!

Experiment You have a white flower. How can you find out if what happened to the celery leaves can happen to flowers?

Learn by Reading

Vocabulary

flower

fruit

seed

Reading Skill

Compare and Contrast

Plant Parts

A plant has many parts. A plant's parts help it grow, change, and make new plants.

Some parts help a plant make new plants. A **flower** is the plant part where fruit and seeds form. A **fruit** is the part of a flower that grows around a seed. A **seed** is the part from which a new plant grows.

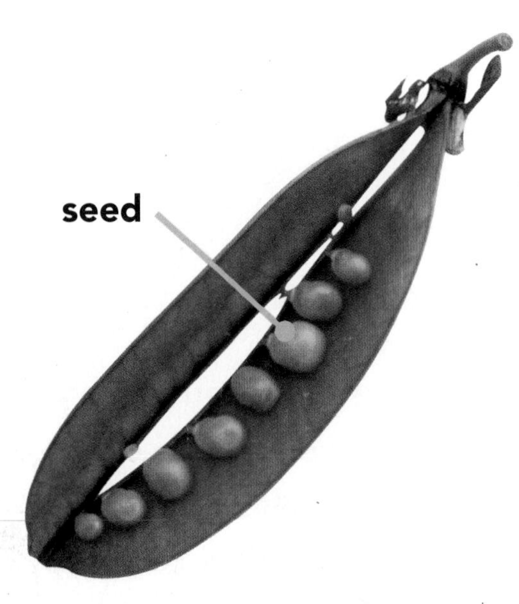

Some parts help a plant get food. The picture of a dandelion shows how a plant uses its roots, stem, and leaves to get what it needs to make food. Then the parts help move the food through the plant.

COMPARE AND CONTRAST How are roots and leaves different?

A bee gets food from this plant and helps the plant make seeds.

A rosebush has a stem with thorns to keep away some animals.

How Plants Use Their Parts

All plants have roots, stems, and leaves. But the parts are not the same on every plant. Parts of plants are different to help plants get what they need in different places.

◀ A Venus flytrap gets nutrients from insects that it traps in its leaves. This helps it live in places with poor soil.

The trunk of a tree is a stem. It grows tall to help leaves get sunlight. The waxy stem of a cactus stores water. Thorns on some stems protect the plants from animals.

Some plants have roots that spread out in the soil to get water from a large area. Long roots help a weeping willow tree live in many kinds of places.

The long stem of a water lily connects the roots at the bottom of the pond to the leaf at the surface.

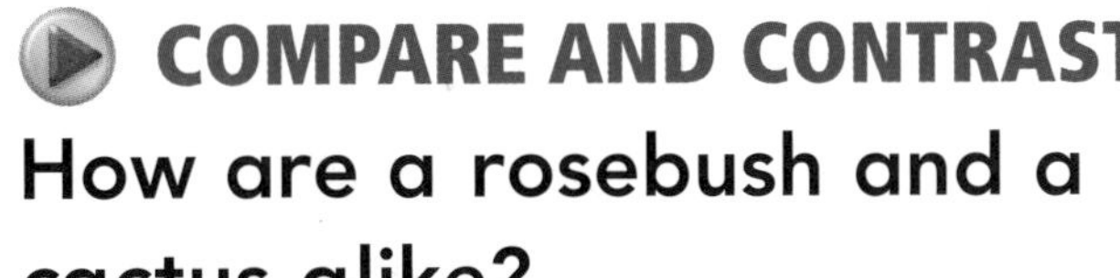

COMPARE AND CONTRAST
How are a rosebush and a cactus alike?

Lesson Wrap-Up

1. **Vocabulary** What is a **seed**?
2. **Reading Skill** How are all plants alike?
3. **Infer** What will happen to this cut flower? Tell why.

Technology Visit **www.eduplace.com/scp/** to find out more about plants.

Lesson 3

How Can Plants Be Grouped?

Science and You

Knowing how plants can be grouped can help you take care of them.

Inquiry Skill

Classify Sort objects into groups to show how they are alike.

What You Need

index cards

crayons

paper and glue

Investigate

Group Plants

Steps

1. **Observe** Go outdoors with your class. Observe different kinds of plants.

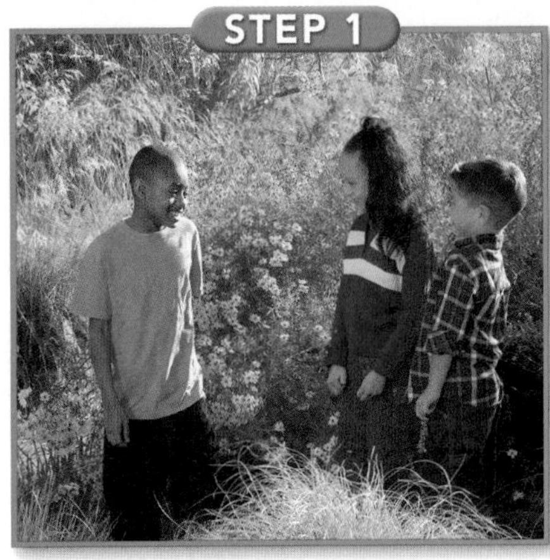

2. **Record Data** Draw each plant on an index card.

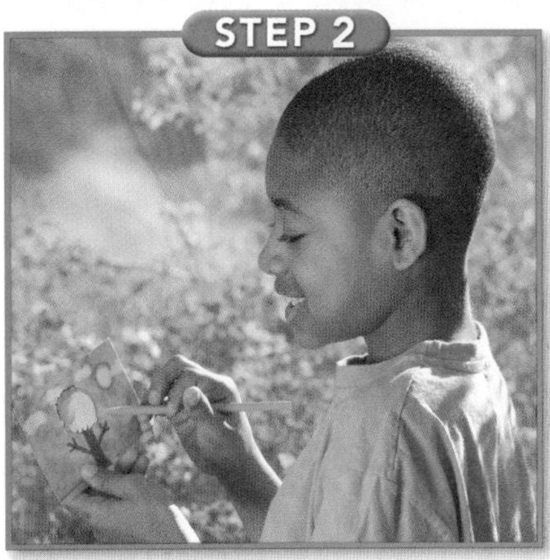

3. **Classify** Look at how the plants you drew are alike and different. Sort the plant pictures into two groups.

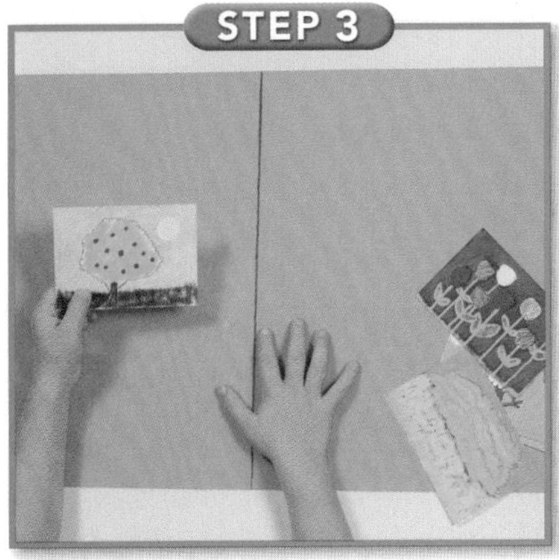

4. Write the name of each group. Glue the pictures in each group to the paper.

Think and Share

1. How are the plants in one of your groups alike?
2. **Compare** How are the plants in the two groups different?

Investigate More!

Work Together Work with a partner. Think about ways to group plants by how they change during the year. Tell how the plants in the groups are different.

Learn by Reading

▶ Vocabulary

cone

taproot

fibrous root

▶ Reading Skill

Categorize and Classify

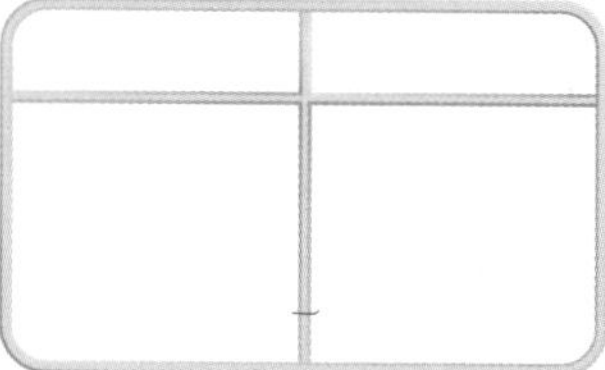

Ways to Group Plants

There are thousands of different plants. Scientists group the many kinds of plants by their parts.

Plants can be grouped by whether they have flowers or cones. A flower is the part where the fruit and seeds form in some plants.

A **cone** is a part of a nonflowering plant where seeds form. The cone protects the seed while it is forming.

Plants can be grouped by their stems. Many flowers and vegetables have soft, green stems. Many bushes and trees have hard, woody stems. We eat the stems of some plants, such as broccoli and celery.

Plants can be grouped by their leaves. Many trees, small plants, and vegetables have broad, flat leaves. Many trees with cones, such as pine, fir, and spruce trees, have needlelike leaves.

CLASSIFY Name a plant that has a hard, woody stem.

taproot

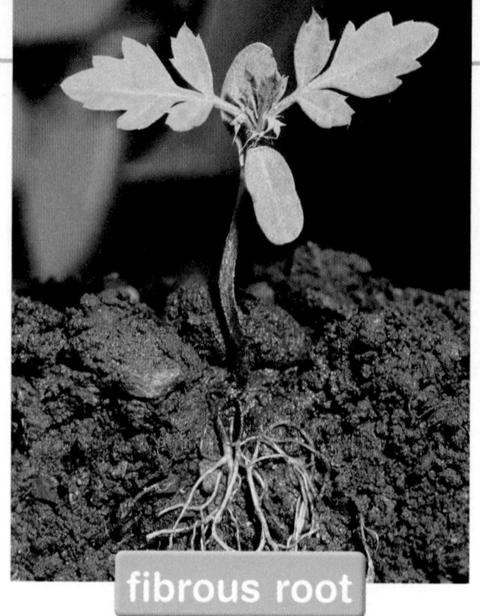
fibrous root

Kinds of Roots

Plants can be grouped by their roots. A **taproot** is a root that has one main branch. A **fibrous root** is a root that has many thin branches. We eat some roots, such as carrots.

CLASSIFY Which kind of root has one main branch?

Lesson Wrap-Up

1. **Vocabulary** What is a **fibrous root**?
2. **Reading Skill** What is one way that plants can be grouped?
3. **Classify** How can you group plants by their leaves?

Technology Visit **www.eduplace.com/scp/** to find out more about grouping plants.

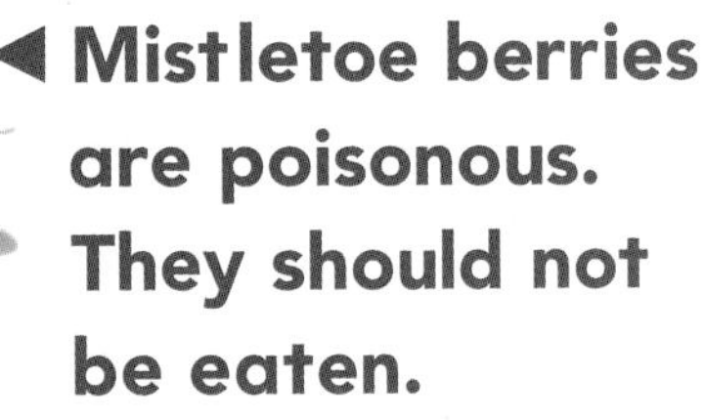

◀ Mistletoe berries are poisonous. They should not be eaten.

Unsafe Plants

Plants can be grouped by whether or not they are poisonous. A poisonous plant can harm or kill another living thing. Poison ivy and poison oak make an oil that causes rashes. Leaves from a rhubarb plant are poisonous. They cannot be eaten. Berries of some plants are poisonous. Never eat plant parts before checking with an adult.

poison ivy ▶

poison oak ▶

Sharing Ideas

1. **Write About It** How does poison ivy cause a rash?
2. **Talk About It** What can you do to stay safe from poisonous plants?

Lesson 4

How Do Plants Change During Their Life Cycles?

Science and You

You know why seeds are important when you know about plant life cycles.

Inquiry Skill

Compare Tell how objects or events are alike and different.

What You Need

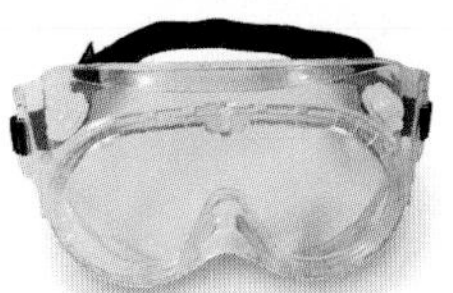

goggles

seeds

cup and soil

water and ruler

Investigate

Grow a Plant

Steps

STEP 1

1. Choose one kind of seed. Look at the picture on the packet. Plant several seeds in soil. Water as needed. **Safety:** Wear goggles!

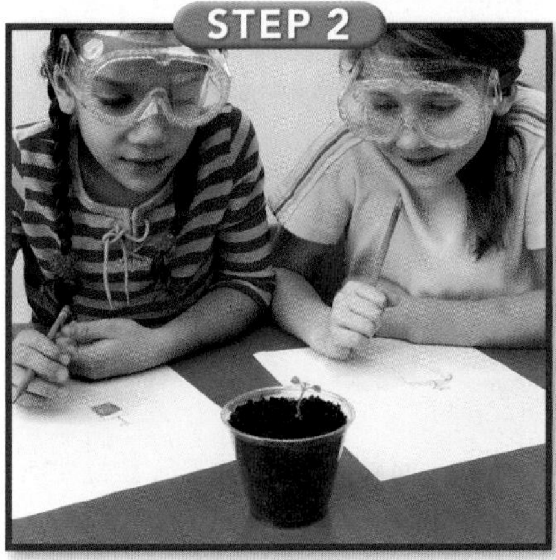
STEP 2

2. **Observe** Observe and draw your plants every day.

STEP 3

3. **Measure** Use a ruler to measure how tall the plants are. Record the height next to each drawing.

Think and Share

1. How did the plants change after one week?
2. **Compare** After two weeks, how are your plants the same as the plant pictured on the seed packet? How are they different?

Investigate More!

Experiment Mix different kinds of seeds in a cup. Then plant the seeds. Guess what kind of plant each seed will grow to be. Observe how they grow.

Learn by Reading

Vocabulary

life cycle

seedling

Reading Skill

Sequence

Plant Life Cycles

All living things grow, change, and finally die. The series of changes that a living thing goes through as it grows is its **life cycle**.

Different kinds of plants have different life cycles. Most plants start from a seed. When the seed gets what it needs, it sprouts. A young plant that grows from a seed is called a **seedling**.

Seeds fall into soil. They need warmth and water to sprout.

A seedling grows. The roots grow down. The stem grows up.

The plant changes as it grows. The adult plant makes flowers.

The seedling grows and changes. It grows more stems and leaves. It grows flowers or cones that make new seeds. New plants can grow from these seeds. These plants will look like the adult plant from which they came. The cycle of growing and changing starts again.

SEQUENCE When does a young plant sprout?

Flowers make fruit. Seeds grow inside the fruit.

The adult plant dies. The seeds may scatter. They may grow into new plants.

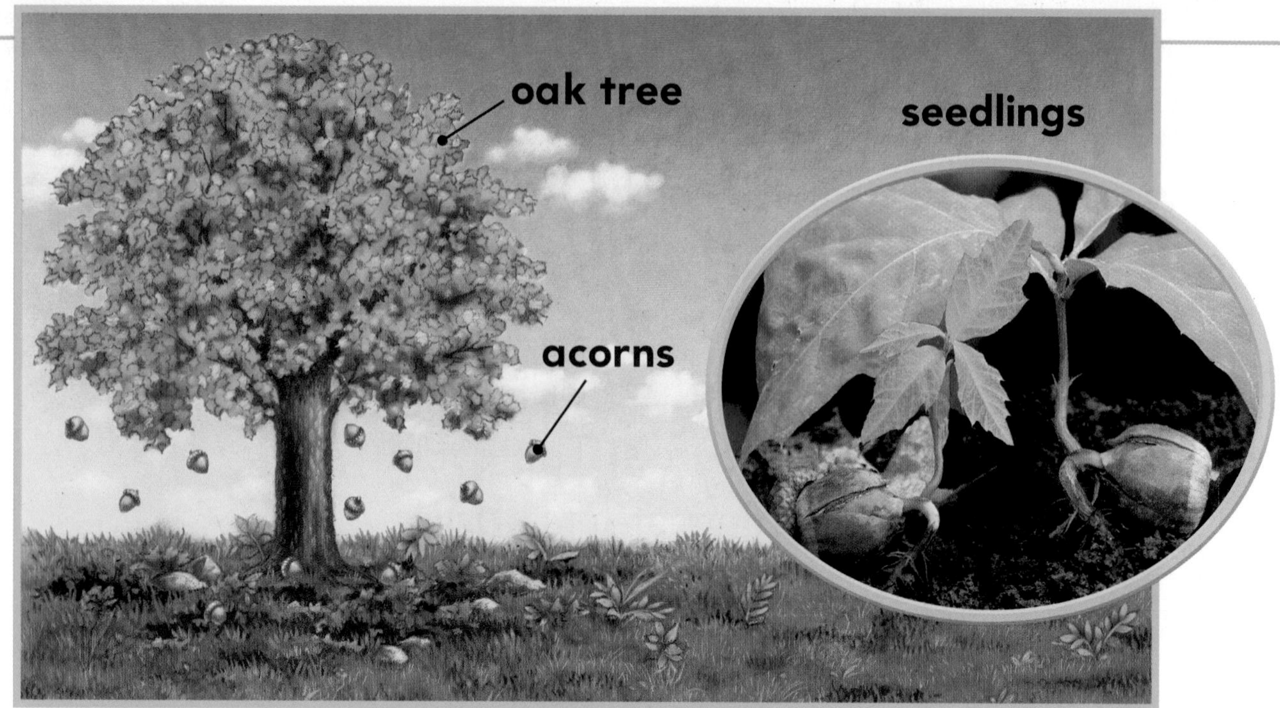

The Same but Different

Acorns are the fruit of an oak tree. When acorns fall to the ground, the seeds inside may grow new plants. The seedlings are all the same kind of tree. But each seedling may be a little bit different in size or shape.

Lesson Wrap-Up

1. **Vocabulary** What is a **seedling**?
2. **Reading Skill** After a plant dies, what happens to the seeds that have formed?
3. **Compare** How is a seedling different from an adult plant?

Technology Visit **www.eduplace.com/scp/** to find out more about plant life cycles.

LINKS for Home and School

Math Make a Fruit Graph

With classmates, observe a fruit. Cut the fruit in half. Measure it with a ruler. Record the measurement. Then count the number of seeds in your fruit. Make a class bar graph to show your results.

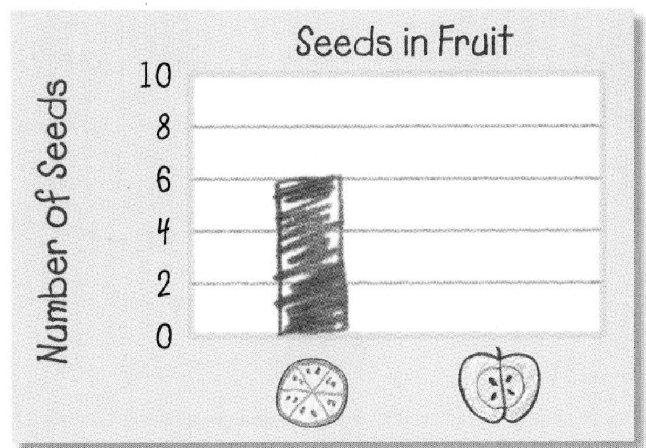

Art Make a Game

Draw picture cards that show stages in a plant's life cycle. Mix your cards with those of your classmates. Play a game of "Go Fish." When you collect a set of pictures, put them in the correct order.

Review and Test Prep

Visual Summary

Plants use their parts to get what they need and to make new plants.

Plant Parts

roots	stems	leaves	flowers	cones
take in water and nutrients from soil	carry water and nutrients to plant parts	take in air and sunlight to make food	where fruit and seeds form	where seeds form in non-flowering plants

Main Ideas

1. What four things do all living things need? **(p. A8)**
2. How does a flower help a plant? **(p. A14)**
3. What is one way in which plants can be grouped? **(pp. A20–A22)**
4. What is the series of changes that a plant goes through as it grows? **(p. A26)**

Vocabulary

Choose the correct word from the box.

shelter (p. A9)
nutrient (p. A11)
seed (p. A14)
seedling (p. A26)

5. A material in soil that helps a plant live and grow
6. The part from which a new plant grows
7. A place where a living thing can be safe
8. A young plant that grows from a seed

Test Practice

Choose a word to complete the sentence.

9. A _____ is the part of a flower that grows around a seed.

   stem   fruit   trunk   leaf

Using Science Skills

10. **Compare** How is a taproot different from a fibrous root?
11. **Critical Thinking** How can you tell when a plant near your home is not getting what it needs?

Chapter 2

Animals Are Living Things

Vocabulary Preview

mammal
bird
reptile
amphibian
fish
adaptation

mammal

A mammal is an animal that has fur or hair and makes milk to feed its young.

bird

A bird is an animal that has feathers and wings.

reptile

A reptile is an animal whose skin is covered with dry scales.

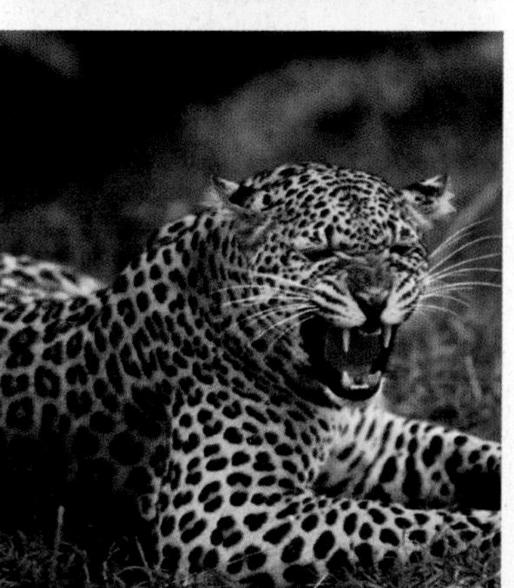

adaptation

An adaptation is a body part or action that helps a living thing meet its needs.

Lesson 1

What Are Mammals and Birds?

Science and You

Knowing about different kinds of animals can help you group them.

Inquiry Skill

Predict Use what you know and observe to tell what you think will happen.

What You Need

feather

hand lens

dropper

water in a cup

Investigate

Explore Feathers

Steps

1. **Observe** Look at a feather. Use a hand lens. Draw what you see.

2. **Predict** Predict what will happen when you put water on the feather. Record your prediction.

3. **Observe** Put two drops of water on the feather. Observe what happens. Record your observations.

STEP 1

STEP 2

STEP 3

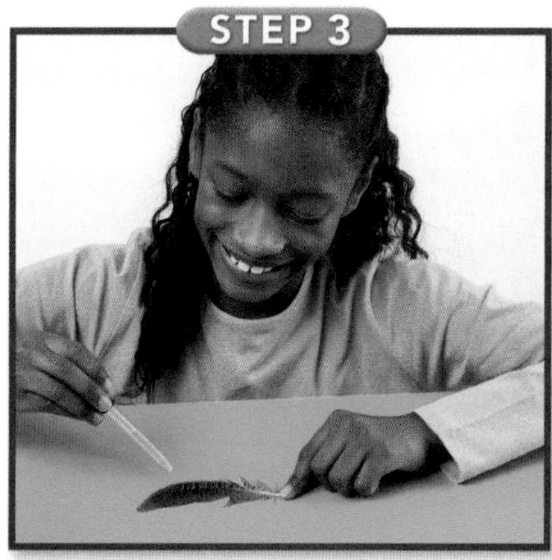

Think and Share

1. How does your prediction compare to what you observed?

2. **Infer** What is one way that feathers help a bird?

Investigate More!

Ask Questions What are ways that fur helps animals? Finish the question. How can fur help an animal ________?

Learn by Reading

Vocabulary

mammal

bird

Reading Skill

Categorize and Classify

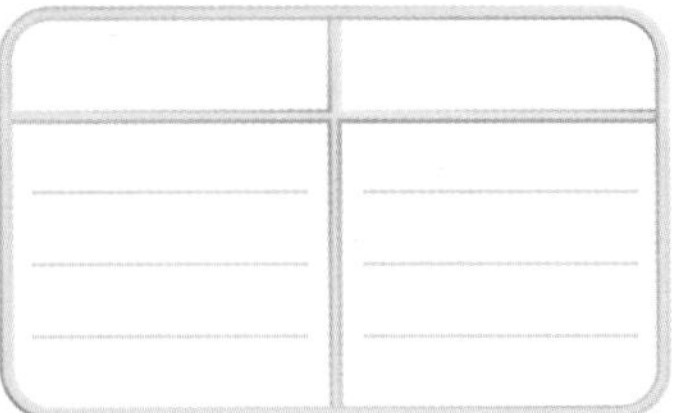

Mammals

Animals can be grouped by their body parts and by how they live. A **mammal** is an animal that has fur or hair and makes milk to feed its young. Most mammals grow inside the mother and then are born alive. All mammals use lungs to breathe. When the air temperature changes, a mammal's body temperature does not change.

This bear's fur helps keep it warm and dry.

Some mammals are unusual. Dolphins and whales live in the ocean. They have flippers instead of legs. They use their flippers and tails to swim. A bat is a mammal that uses wings to fly.

CLASSIFY What kind of animal has fur or hair and makes milk to feed its young?

Young mammals depend on their parents to take care of them.

A whale comes out of the ocean to breathe air with its lungs.

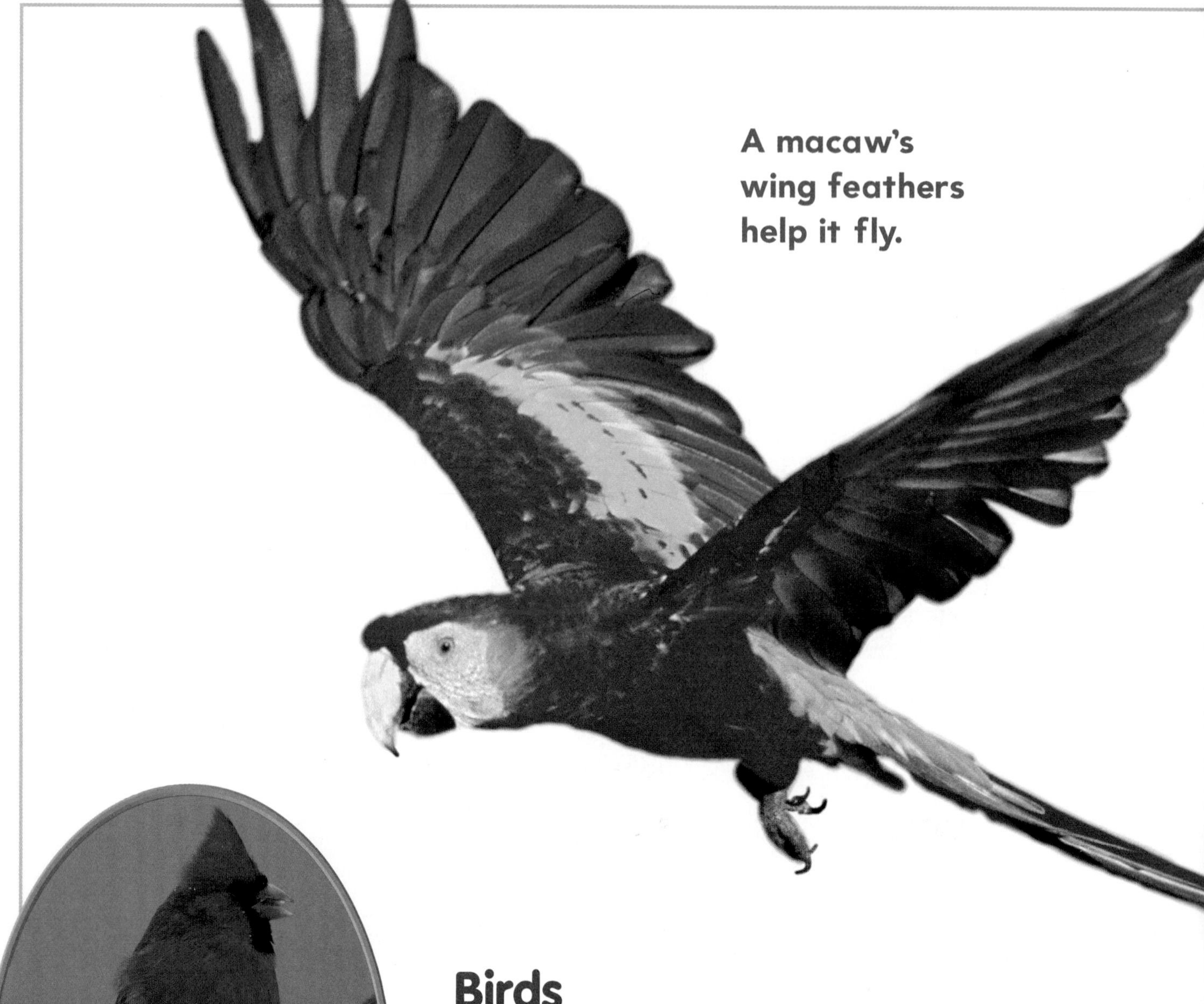

A macaw's wing feathers help it fly.

The shape of the cardinal's beak helps it crack seeds.

Birds

A **bird** is an animal that has feathers and wings. Feathers keep a bird warm and dry and help it fly. A bird has two legs and a beak. It uses lungs to breathe. Young birds hatch from eggs with hard shells. Most birds care for their young until the young can get their own food.

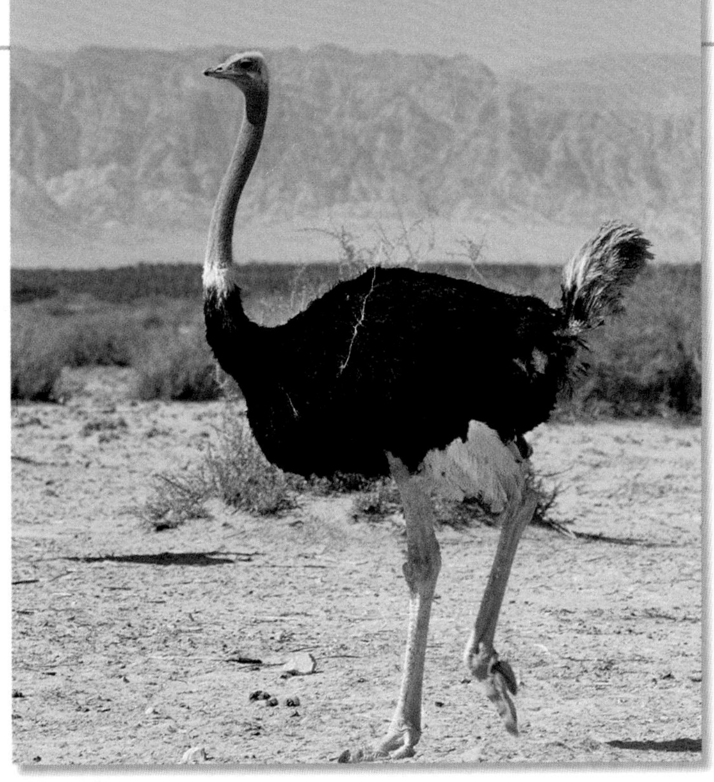

An ostrich uses its wings for balance as it runs.

Some birds are unusual. Ostriches and penguins are birds that cannot fly. A penguin uses its wings to help it swim.

CLASSIFY What kind of animal has feathers and wings?

Lesson Wrap-Up

1. **Vocabulary** What is a **mammal**?
2. **Reading Skill** To which animal group does a duck belong?
3. **Predict** A whale has been under water for a long time. Predict what will happen.

Technology Visit **www.eduplace.com/scp/** to find out more about mammals and birds.

Lesson 2

What Are Reptiles, Amphibians, and Fish?

Science and You

You can see many kinds of reptiles, amphibians, and fish at a pet store.

Inquiry Skill

Compare Tell how objects or events are alike and different.

What You Need

animal cards

Reptiles, Amphibians, and Fish

Animal	Where It Lives	Body Covering	Body Parts It Uses to Move	How It Moves

animal chart

Investigate

Compare Animals

Steps

STEP 1

1. **Observe** Look at the animal cards. Notice how each animal looks. Think about how each animal moves.

STEP 2

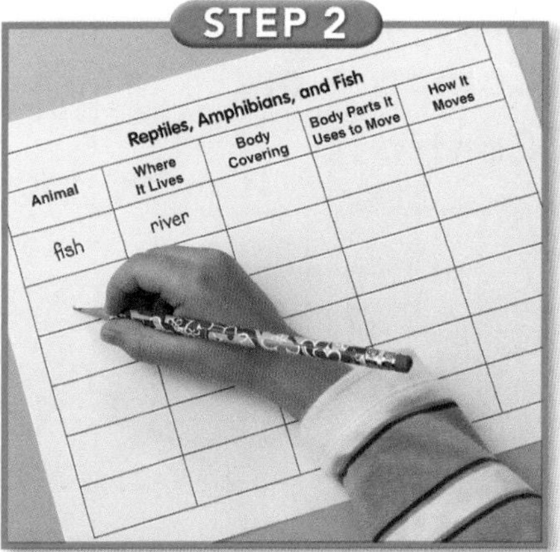

2. **Record Data** Write each animal name on the chart. Then complete the chart for each animal.

STEP 3

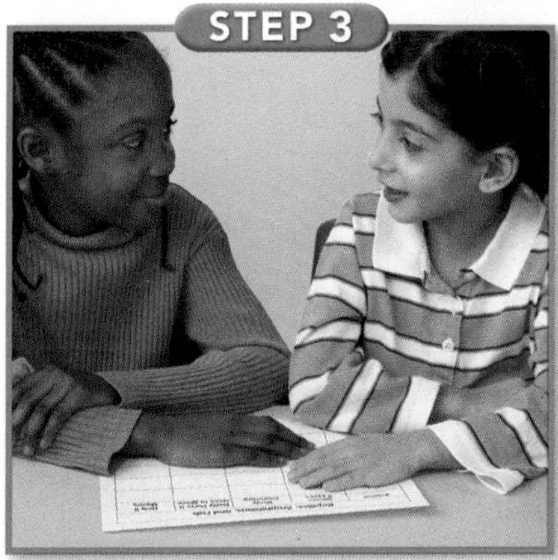

3. **Compare** Look at your chart. Talk with a partner about how these animals are alike and different.

Think and Share

1. What are some ways you can group these animals?
2. **Infer** Why are fish not found in the desert?

Investigate More!

Work Together Work with a partner to make a list of animals. Decide how you could sort the animals into groups. Share your sorting rule with the class.

Learn by Reading

Vocabulary

reptile

amphibian

fish

Reading Skill

Compare and Contrast

Reptiles

Lizards, turtles, crocodiles, and snakes are reptiles. A **reptile** is an animal whose skin is covered with dry scales. All reptiles use lungs to breathe, and most have four legs.

Reptiles get heat from the Sun and other warm things. When the air temperature changes, a reptile's body temperature also changes.

A lizard uses the Sun's heat to warm its body.

Most reptiles lay eggs. Young reptiles hatch from the eggs. From the time they are hatched, young reptiles look much like their parents. A young reptile can care for itself as soon as it hatches.

Reptiles have body parts that help them meet their needs. Crocodiles use their strong tails to move in water. Some lizards have patterns on their skin that help them hide from danger.

How are snakes different from other reptiles?

COMPARE AND CONTRAST
How are all reptiles alike?

A turtle's hard shell helps keep it safe from other animals.

Amphibians

An **amphibian** is an animal that lives part of its life in water and part of its life on land. Frogs, toads, and salamanders are amphibians. They have smooth, moist skin.

Most amphibians lay eggs in water. The young begin their lives in water and use gills to breathe. Most adult amphibians use lungs to breathe. Most young amphibians look different from their parents. The body of an amphibian changes as it grows into an adult.

COMPARE AND CONTRAST How are young and adult amphibians different?

Frogs

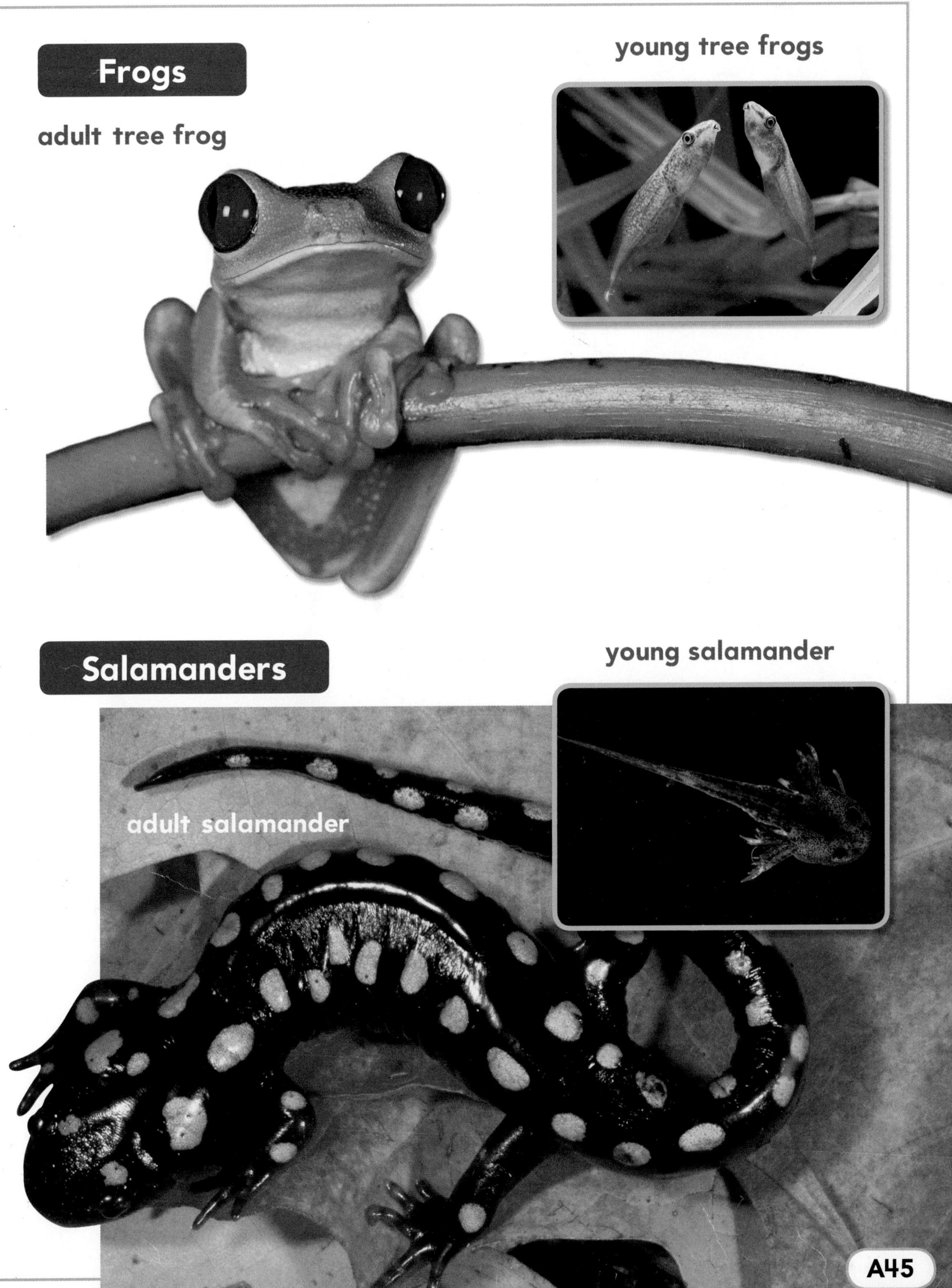

Salamanders

Fish

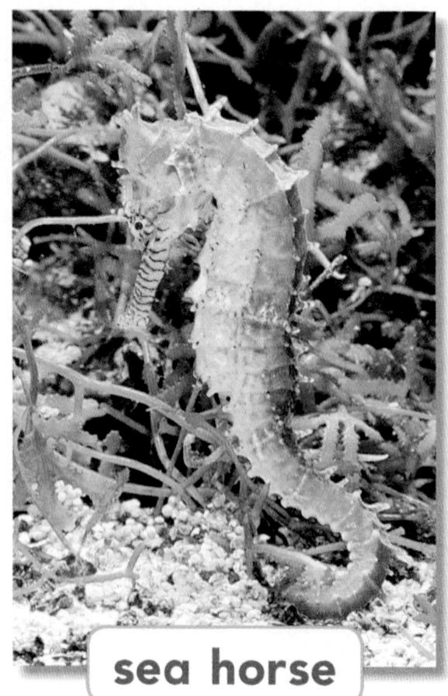
sea horse

A **fish** is an animal that lives in water and has gills. Its gills take in oxygen from the water. Most fish are covered with scales and have fins. Fins and tails help fish move. Young fish hatch from eggs.

clarion angelfish

sailfish

Fish live in water all of their lives. Freshwater fish live in ponds, streams, or lakes. Rainbow trout and catfish are freshwater fish. Saltwater fish live in the ocean. Sailfish, sea horses, and most angelfish are saltwater fish.

rainbow trout

COMPARE AND CONTRAST **How is a catfish different from a sailfish?**

catfish

Lesson Wrap-Up

1. **Vocabulary** Tell three things that you know about **fish**.
2. **Reading Skill** How is a fish different from an amphibian?
3. **Compare** How is a reptile like a fish?

Technology Visit **www.eduplace.com/scp/** to find out more about reptiles, amphibians, and fish.

Forest Friends

What makes animals different?

Five animal friends are about to find out. You can help them!

White-Tailed Deer
Robin
Leopard Frog
Box Turtle
Brook Trout

Robin: White-Tailed Deer, we are both animals. Why are you different from me?

White-Tailed Deer: Different animals belong to different animal groups. I have fur. I use lungs to breathe. Mother deer make milk to feed their young. Which animal group am I in?

All: Mammals!

Robin: It's my turn! I have a beak. I am covered in feathers. I have wings that help me fly. My young hatch from eggs. Which animal group am I in?

All: Birds!

Leopard Frog: I want to play, too! When I was young, I lived in water. I used gills to breathe. Now I have legs to move on land and lungs to breathe. Which animal group am I in?

All: Amphibians!

White-Tailed Deer: Box Turtle, give us hints about which animal group you are in.

Box Turtle: Hmm. I have skin covered with dry scales. I use lungs to breathe. I warm my body with the Sun's heat. Which animal group am I in?

All: Reptiles!

Leopard Frog: Hey, Brook Trout, stop splashing in that stream and come play with us! Give us some clues about your animal group.

Brook Trout: Okay. I use gills to breathe. I have fins that help me swim. I am covered in scales. Which animal group am I in?

All: Fish!

Robin: So, some of us have fur, and some have feathers.

Box Turtle: Some have legs, and some have fins.

White-Tailed Deer: Some have lungs. Some have gills.

Brook Trout: But we are all animals.

Sharing Ideas

1. **Write About It** Choose two animals. List clues about each animal's group next to each name.
2. **Talk About It** Give hints about a different animal. Have classmates guess the group to which the animal belongs.

Lesson 3

How Do Animals Meet Their Needs?

Science and You

Like you, animals have body parts that help them meet their needs where they live.

Inquiry Skill

Use Models Make something to show what the real thing is like or how it works.

What You Need

tweezers and slotted spoon

container of water

foam block

objects to pick up

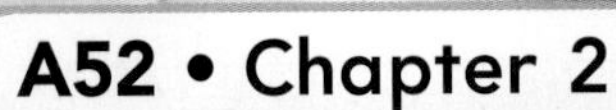

Investigate

Model Bird Beaks

Steps

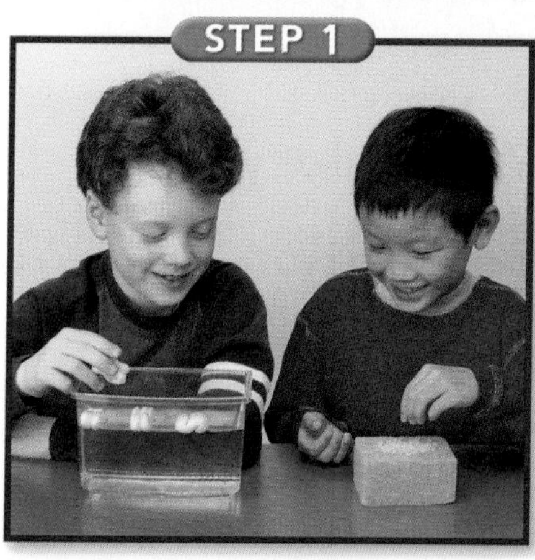

1. **Use Models** Use objects to act as bird food. Spread rice on the foam block. Float foam peanuts on the water.

2. **Use Models** Use tweezers and a spoon to act as birds' beaks. Use each tool to pick up a piece of rice. **Safety:** Tweezers are sharp!

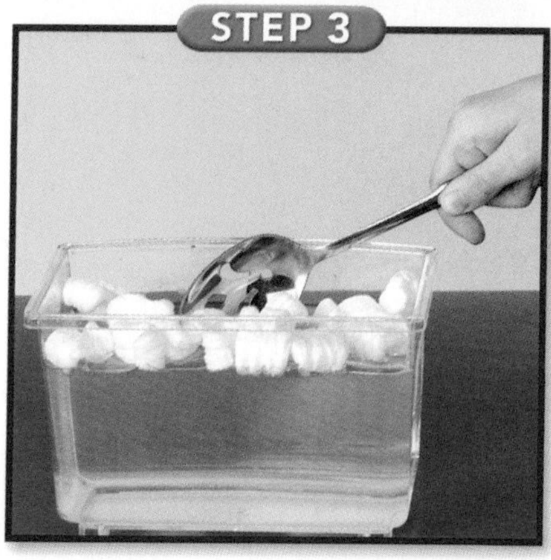

3. Use each tool to pick up some foam peanuts.

Think and Share

1. **Compare** Which tool worked better for picking up each kind of object?
2. **Infer** Which kinds of beaks are better for getting food from trees and logs?

Investigate More!

Experiment Think of ways to make models of other animal body parts. Make one model. Experiment to find out how the body part works.

Learn by Reading

Vocabulary

adaptation

Reading Skill

Draw Conclusions

Meeting Needs on Land

If an animal is not getting what it needs to live, it has to move or its body needs to change. An **adaptation** is a body part or action that helps a living thing meet its needs where it lives. Some animals have adaptations that help them meet their needs on land. Strong legs and sharp claws help many animals that live on land.

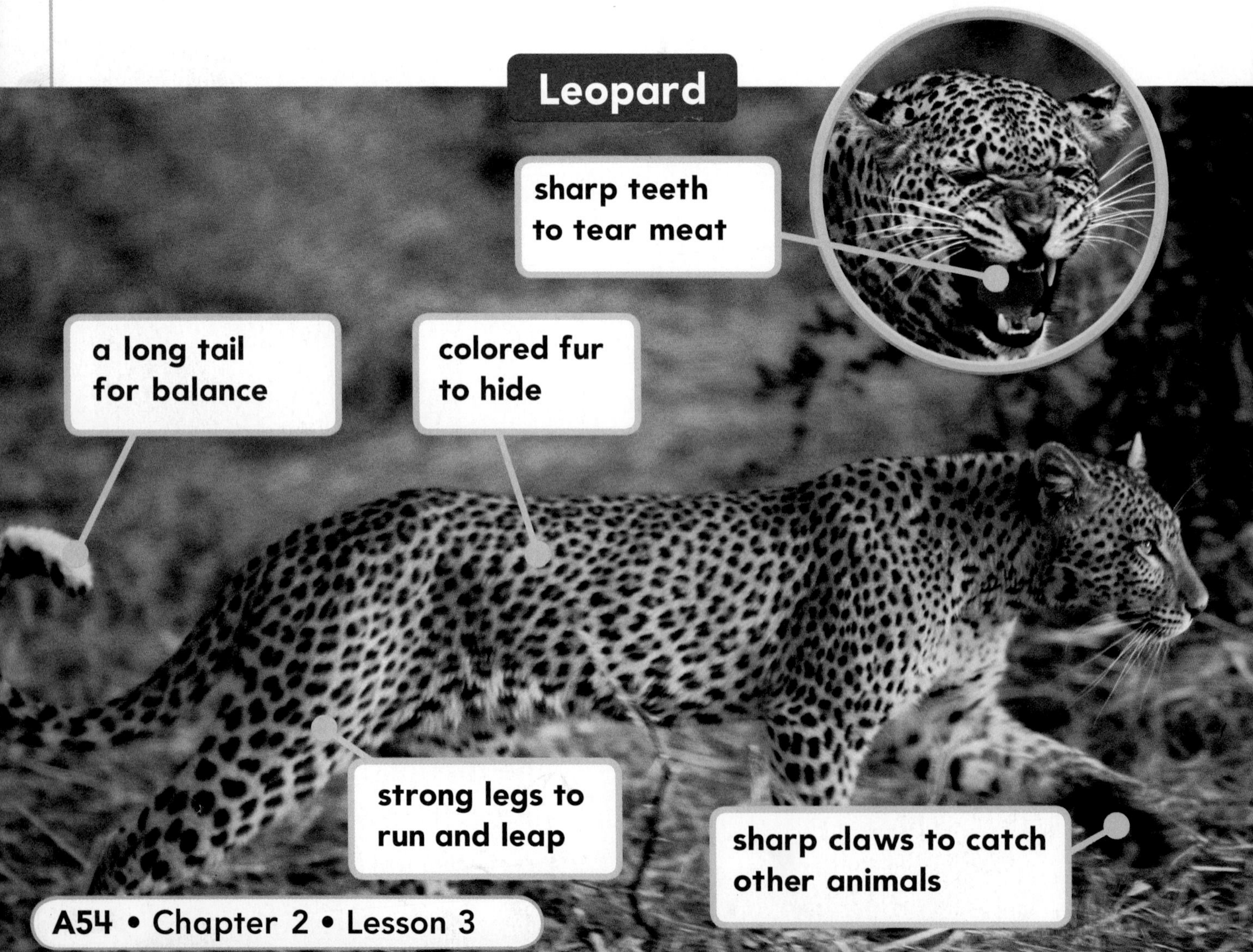

Meeting Needs in Water

Other animals have adaptations that help them meet their needs in water. Fins or flippers help animals move in water. Special mouth parts help animals take in food.

DRAW CONCLUSIONS **How does a shell help a turtle get what it needs?**

Manta Ray

a mouth to gather food in water

large, flat fins shaped like wings to glide through water

Meeting Needs in Air

Some animals have adaptations that help them as they fly in the air. A bird's feathers and tail help it move in different ways. Birds also have hollow bones that are strong and light.

Lesson Wrap-Up

1. **Vocabulary** What is an **adaptation**?
2. **Reading Skill** Why do different animals have different adaptations?
3. **Use Models** What might you use to make a model of a bird bone?

Technology Visit **www.eduplace.com/scp/** to find out more about animals meeting their needs.

LINKS for Home and School

Math Pet Survey

Ask classmates which kind of animal makes the best pet. Record data in a bar graph.

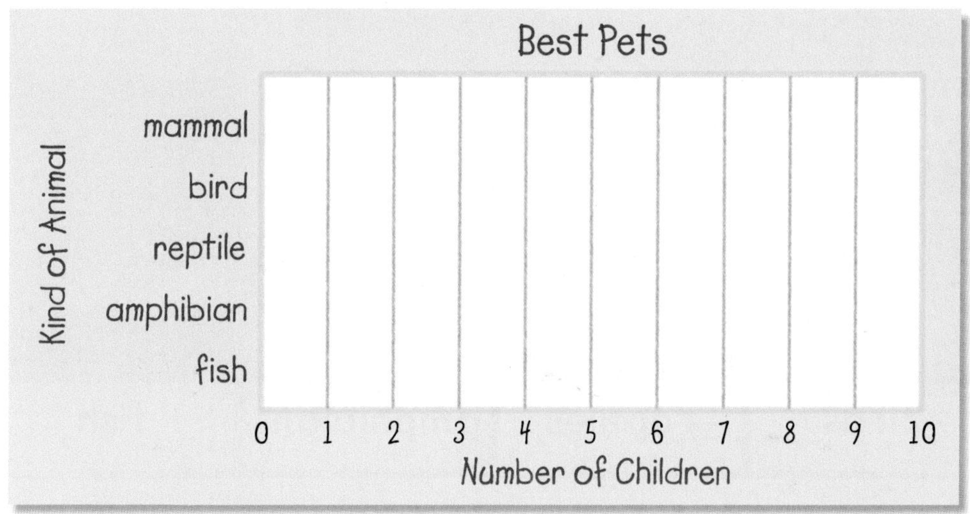

1. Which kind of animal do children think makes the best pet?
2. How many children think that a reptile makes the best pet?

Music Animal Groups

In groups, write new words to the song "Old MacDonald Had a Farm." Write words for each animal group. Practice your songs, and perform them for the class.

And on his farm he had some mammals E-I-E-I-O. With some fur here and some hair there.

Chapter 2 Review and Test Prep

Visual Summary

Animals can be grouped by their body parts and by how they live.

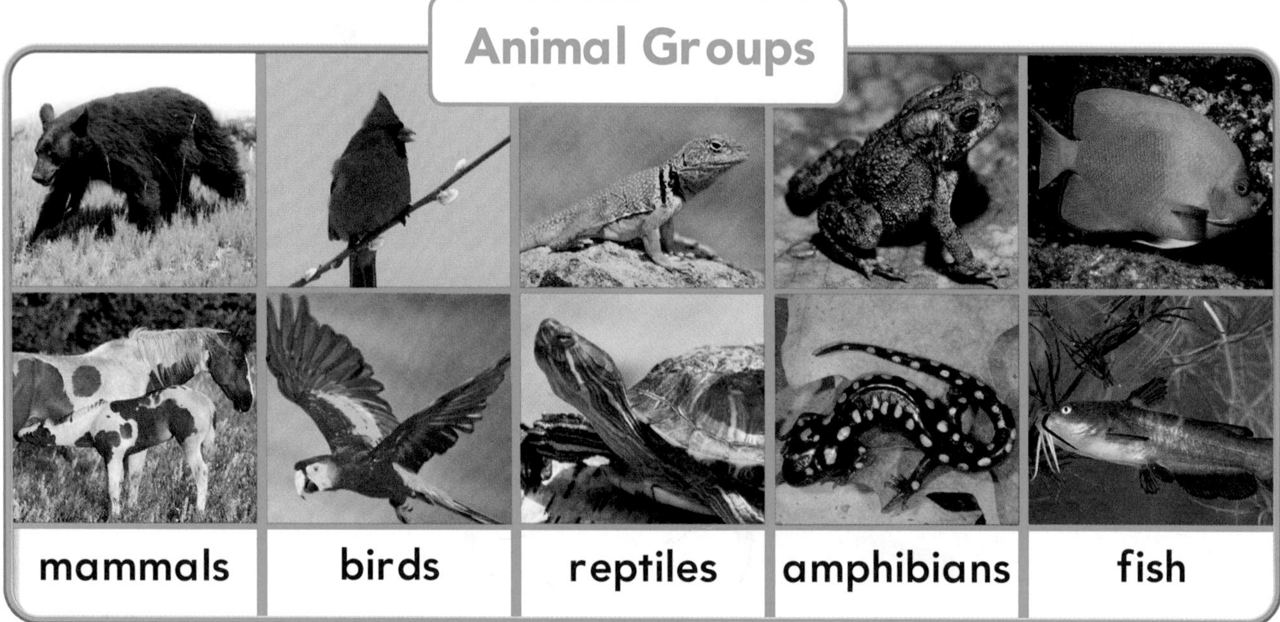

Main Ideas

1. Describe a mammal. **(p. A36)**
2. Why is the Sun important to reptiles? **(p. A42)**
3. How is an amphibian different from other animals? **(pp. A44–A45)**
4. What is a body part that helps an animal meet its needs in water? **(p. A55)**

Vocabulary

Choose the correct word from the box.

mammal (p. A36)
bird (p. A38)
reptile (p. A42)
adaptation (p. A54)

5. An animal that has feathers and wings
6. An animal whose skin is covered with dry scales
7. An animal that has fur or hair and makes milk to feed its young
8. A body part or action that helps a living thing meet its needs where it lives

Test Practice

Choose a word to complete the sentence.

9. An animal that lives in water and has gills is a ____.

frog fish dolphin reptile

Using Science Skills

10. **Predict** You see a mother lizard with eggs. Predict what the young will look like when they hatch. How do you know?

11. **Critical Thinking** What would you need to think about to care for a pet salamander?

Chapter 3

Animal Life Cycles

Vocabulary Preview

reproduce
offspring
larva
pupa

reproduce

When living things reproduce, they make more living things of the same kind.

offspring

Offspring are the group of living things that come from the same living thing.

larva

A larva that hatches from an egg is wormlike.

pupa

A pupa is the stage between larva and adult when an insect changes form.

Lesson 1

Which Baby Animals Look Like Their Parents?

Science and You

Knowing which animals look like their parents helps you know what some baby animals will look like when they get older.

Inquiry Skill

Classify Sort objects into groups to show how they are alike.

What You Need

animal cards

Investigate

Match Animals

Steps

1. **Observe** Look at the animal pictures. Name the animals.

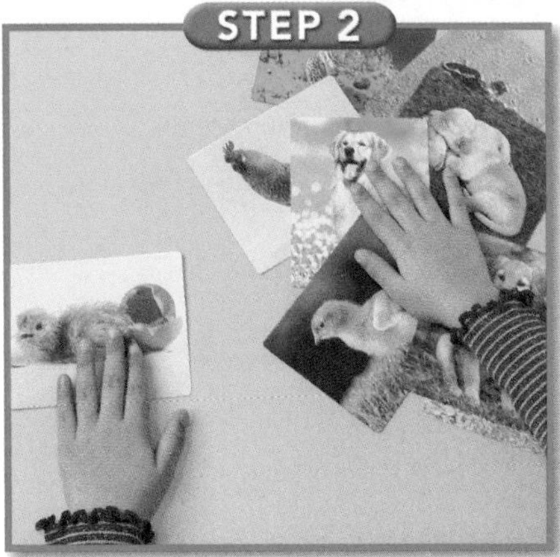

2. **Classify** Think about how the animal pictures are alike and different. Sort the pictures. Make a group for each kind of animal.

3. Order each group. Put the baby animal first and the adult animal last.

Think and Share

1. **Compare** How are the baby and adult in each group alike?
2. How do animals change from babies to adults?

Investigate More!

Work Together With a partner, think of an animal. Talk about how the animal looks as a baby. Make cards to show how the animal grows and changes.

Learn by Reading

▶ Vocabulary

reproduce

offspring

▶ Reading Skill

Compare and Contrast

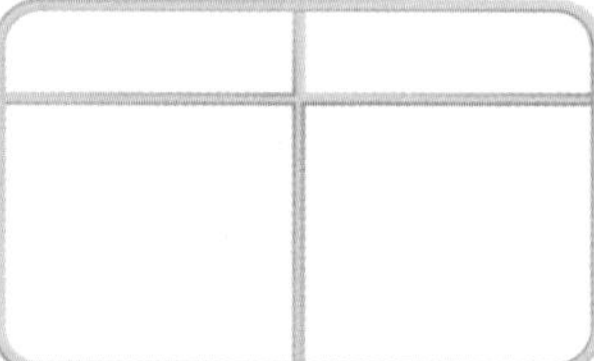

Changes in Living Things

All living things grow, change, and reproduce. When living things **reproduce**, they make more living things of the same kind. Nonliving things cannot reproduce.

All living things come from other living things. **Offspring** are the group of living things that come from the same living thing. A child is the offspring of his or her mother and father. Kittens are the offspring of adult cats.

Kittens in a litter are alike in some ways and different in others.

How are the members of this family alike and different?

Living things have offspring that are the same kind but have differences. Brothers and sisters in the same family are alike in some ways. They are also different in some ways. Kittens are all young cats. Yet kittens that are born together in the same litter can have fur of different colors.

COMPARE AND CONTRAST How are cat offspring alike and different?

Life Cycle of a Bird

A mother bird lays eggs. A chick grows inside each one.

A chick hatches from an egg. A parent feeds it.

Life Cycle of a Mouse

A mother mouse gives birth to baby mice.

The mother's body makes milk. The babies drink the milk.

Familiar Life Cycles

Different kinds of animals grow in different ways. The steps of their life cycles are different. Birds, mammals, fish, and reptiles have young that look like their parents.

COMPARE AND CONTRAST How are birds, mammals, fish, and reptiles alike?

The chick gets new feathers as it grows.

The young bird grows to be an adult. It can reproduce.

The mice grow more fur. They get bigger.

When a mouse is fully grown, it can reproduce.

Lesson Wrap-Up

1. **Vocabulary** What do living things do when they make more living things of the same kind?
2. **Reading Skill** How is the life cycle of a bird different from that of a mouse?
3. **Classify** How are brothers and sisters in a family alike?

Technology Visit **www.eduplace.com/scp/** to find out more about animal life cycles.

Maria Sibylla Merian

Scientist, Nature Artist

Maria Sibylla Merian lived in Europe about 300 years ago. She began drawing pictures of plants and animals when she was a child. As an adult, Merian observed living things as they grew. She painted pictures of plants and animals at different steps of their life cycles.

Merian painted life cycles of animals on plants.

Merian traveled to study and draw pictures of plants and animals in different parts of the world. Many of her pictures were printed in books. The pictures taught others about the living things Merian had observed. Many years later, some of Merian's paintings were shown on United States postage stamps.

Sharing Ideas

1. **Write About It** How can drawing a picture of something you observe help you learn about it?
2. **Talk About It** Why is it important for scientists to share what they learn with others?

Lesson 2

Which Baby Animals Look Unlike Their Parents?

Science and You

Knowing how some animals change will help you understand that a caterpillar and a moth are the same animal.

Inquiry Skill

Use Data **Use what you observe and record to learn more about something.**

What You Need

Triops tank

Triops eggs

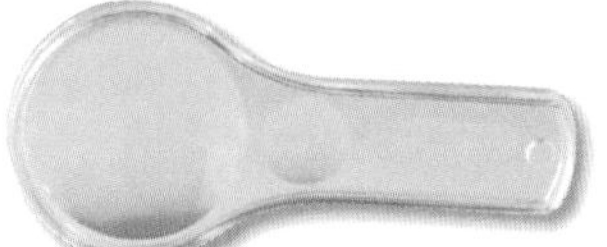

hand lens

ruler

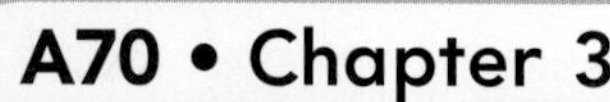

Investigate

Triops Changes

Steps

1. Gently pour the Triops eggs into a tank of water. **Safety:** Wash your hands!

2. **Observe** Use a hand lens to observe the Triops each day. Record what they look like.

3. **Measure** When a Triops is three days old, measure its length. Repeat each day for five days.

STEP 1

STEP 2

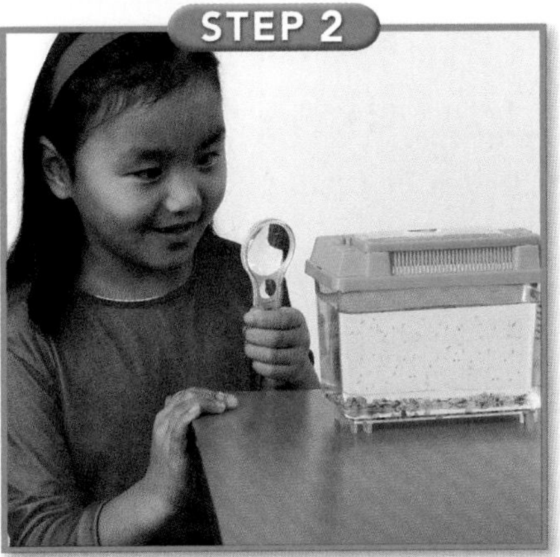

STEP 3

Length of Triops	
Day 1	about ________ cm
Day 2	about ________ cm
Day 3	about ________ cm
Day 4	about ________ cm
Day 5	about ________ cm

Think and Share

1. **Use Data** How did the Triops change over time?
2. **Infer** How is a baby Triops different from its parents?

Investigate More!

Ask Questions Talk with classmates about the Triops. Then finish the question. How does a Triops __________?

Learn by Reading

Vocabulary

larva

pupa

Reading Skill

Sequence

Frog Life Cycle

Some young animals look very different from their parents. These animals change form as they grow to be adults.

Most amphibians change form as they grow. When they become adults, they will look like their parents.

Life Cycle of a Frog

A frog lays its eggs in water.

A tadpole hatches from an egg. It has gills, a tail, and no legs.

Over many weeks, a tadpole's back legs grow. Its skin gets thicker.

A frog is an amphibian. When frogs hatch from eggs, they have body parts that help them live in water.

Later, frogs grow parts that will help them live on land. Parts that they needed to live in water disappear. When frogs become adults, they look like their parents.

SEQUENCE What happens after parts for living on land form?

Lungs grow and gills disappear. The tail will soon disappear.

An adult frog can reproduce.

Butterfly Life Cycle

Butterflies belong to an animal group called insects. Most insects change form as they grow. A **larva** that hatches from an egg is wormlike. It looks very different from its parent.

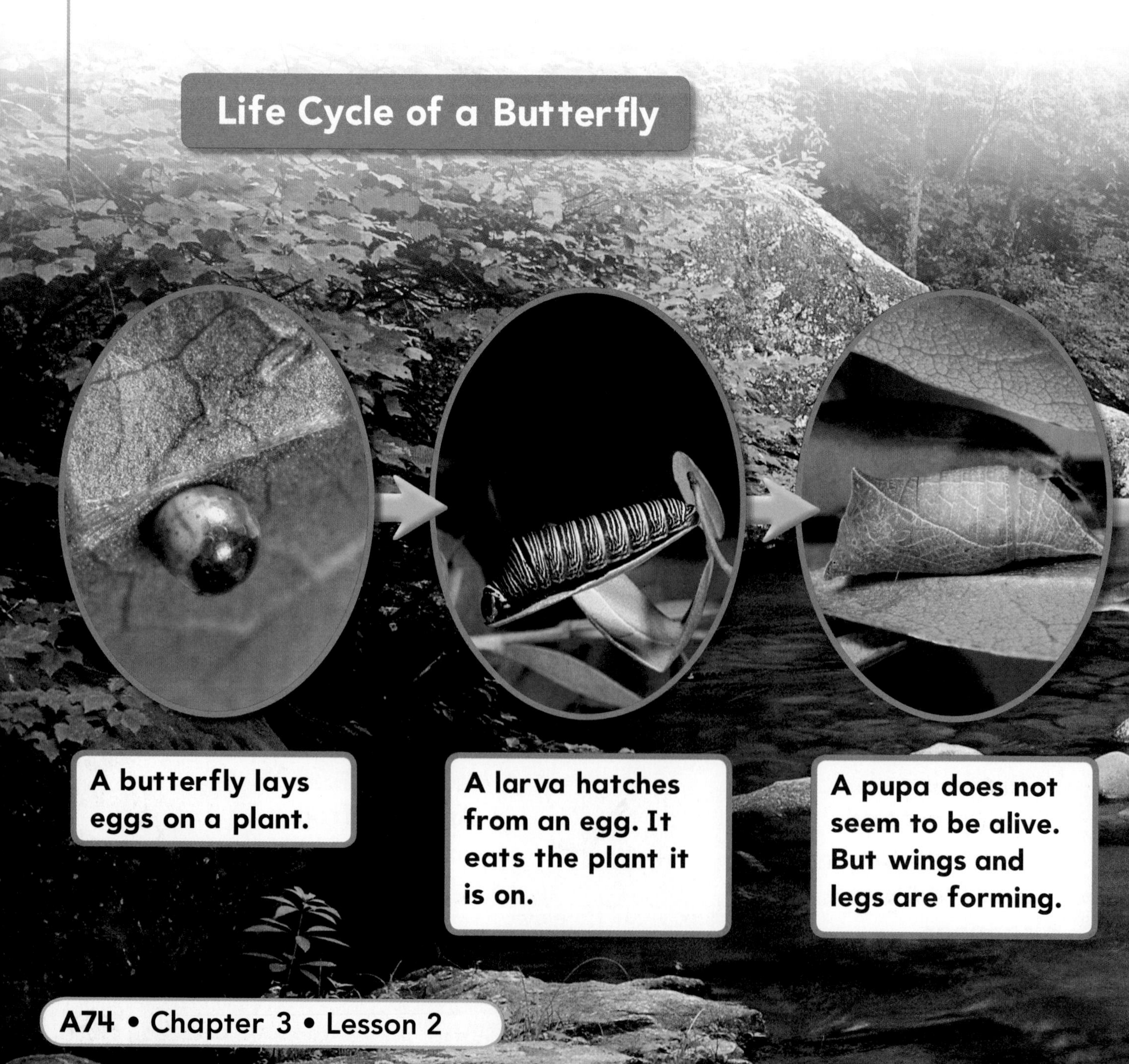

A butterfly lays eggs on a plant.

A larva hatches from an egg. It eats the plant it is on.

A pupa does not seem to be alive. But wings and legs are forming.

A larva grows and sheds its skin many times. Then it turns into a pupa. A **pupa** is the stage between larva and adult when an insect changes form. A pupa does not eat.

COMPARE AND CONTRAST How is a butterfly life cycle different from a person's life cycle?

The change is finished. The pupa has become a butterfly.

A butterfly lives for several weeks. It lays eggs, and a new life cycle begins.

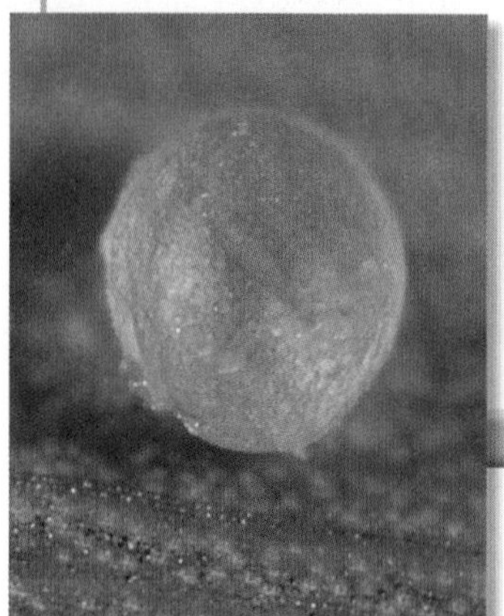

A dragonfly lays eggs in or near water.

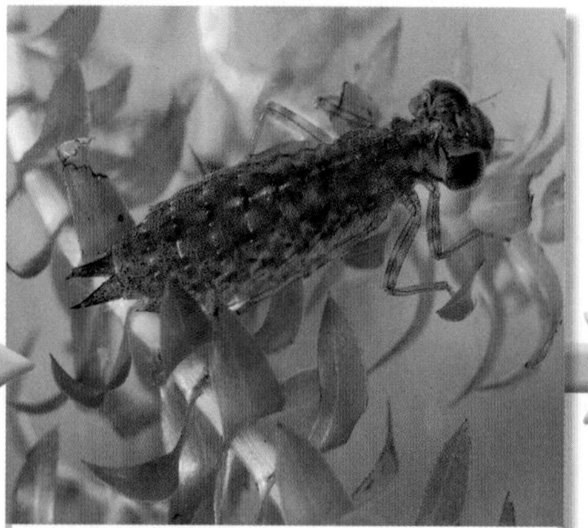

A larva breathes with gills. It sheds its skin as it grows.

The larva comes out of the water as an adult dragonfly.

Dragonfly Life Cycle

A dragonfly is another kind of insect that changes form during its life cycle. It begins life in water. As a dragonfly changes form, it grows parts that help it live on land and fly through the air.

Lesson Wrap-Up

1. **Vocabulary** What is a **larva**?
2. **Reading Skill** What happens to a butterfly larva after it sheds its skin many times?
3. **Use Data** How is data that you collect useful?

Technology Visit **www.eduplace.com/scp/** to find out more about animals that change form.

LINKS for Home and School

Math Animal Lengths

The chart shows about how many centimeters long animals are at birth and when grown. Cut yarn to show the lengths. Use a different color for each animal.

Animal Lengths

Animal	Length at birth	Length when grown
Garter Snake	13	40
Hammerhead Shark	69	600
Sea Otter	46	152

1. Which animal is the longest at birth?
2. Which animal is the longest when grown?

Language Arts Life Cycle Adventure

Think about what happens in each stage of a frog's life cycle. Write an adventure story about a frog's life. Tell it from the frog's point of view. Make a drawing to go with your story.

Review and Test Prep

Visual Summary

All living things grow, change, and reproduce. Some baby animals look like their parents. Others change form as they grow.

Main Ideas

1. How might offspring of the same parents be alike and different? **(pp. A64–A65)**
2. Which kinds of animals have young that look like their parents? **(p. A66)**
3. What are three animals that change form as they grow? **(pp. A72–A76)**
4. How is a dragonfly's life cycle different from a butterfly's life cycle? **(p. A76)**

Vocabulary

Choose the correct word from the box.

reproduce (p. A64)
offspring (p. A64)
larva (p. A74)
pupa (p. A75)

5. The stage between larva and adult when an insect changes form
6. The group of living things that come from the same living thing
7. A worm-like thing that hatches from an egg
8. When living things make more living things of the same kind

Test Practice

Choose a word to complete the sentence.

9. The series of changes that a living thing goes through as it grows is its ____.

   offspring   life cycle   parents   pupa

Using Science Skills

10. **Classify** What are two animals that do not change form as they grow?
11. **Critical Thinking** How are the life cycles of a frog and a butterfly different?

How do mother sea lions find their pups?

To find their pups, mother sea lions make a loud trumpet sound. Each mother's sound is different. When the pup hears the sound, it makes a bleating sound back. Mother and pup continue until they find each other. The mother knows for sure it is her pup by its smell.

Go to **www.eduplace.com/scp/** to learn how animals find their babies.

LIFE UNIT B SCIENCE

Environments and Energy

Cricket Connection

Visit www.eduplace.com/scp/ to check out *Click, Ask,* and *Odyssey* magazine articles and activities.

Environments and Energy

Independent Reading

Down by the Stream

River Otter

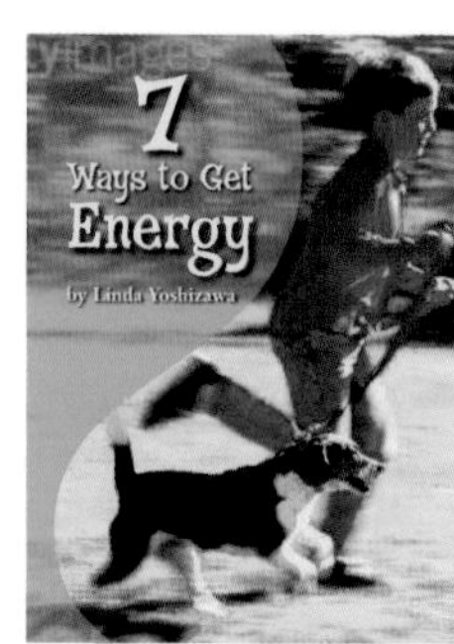

7 Ways to Get Energy

Discover!
Why are flamingos pink?
Think about this question as you read. You will have the answer by the end of the unit.

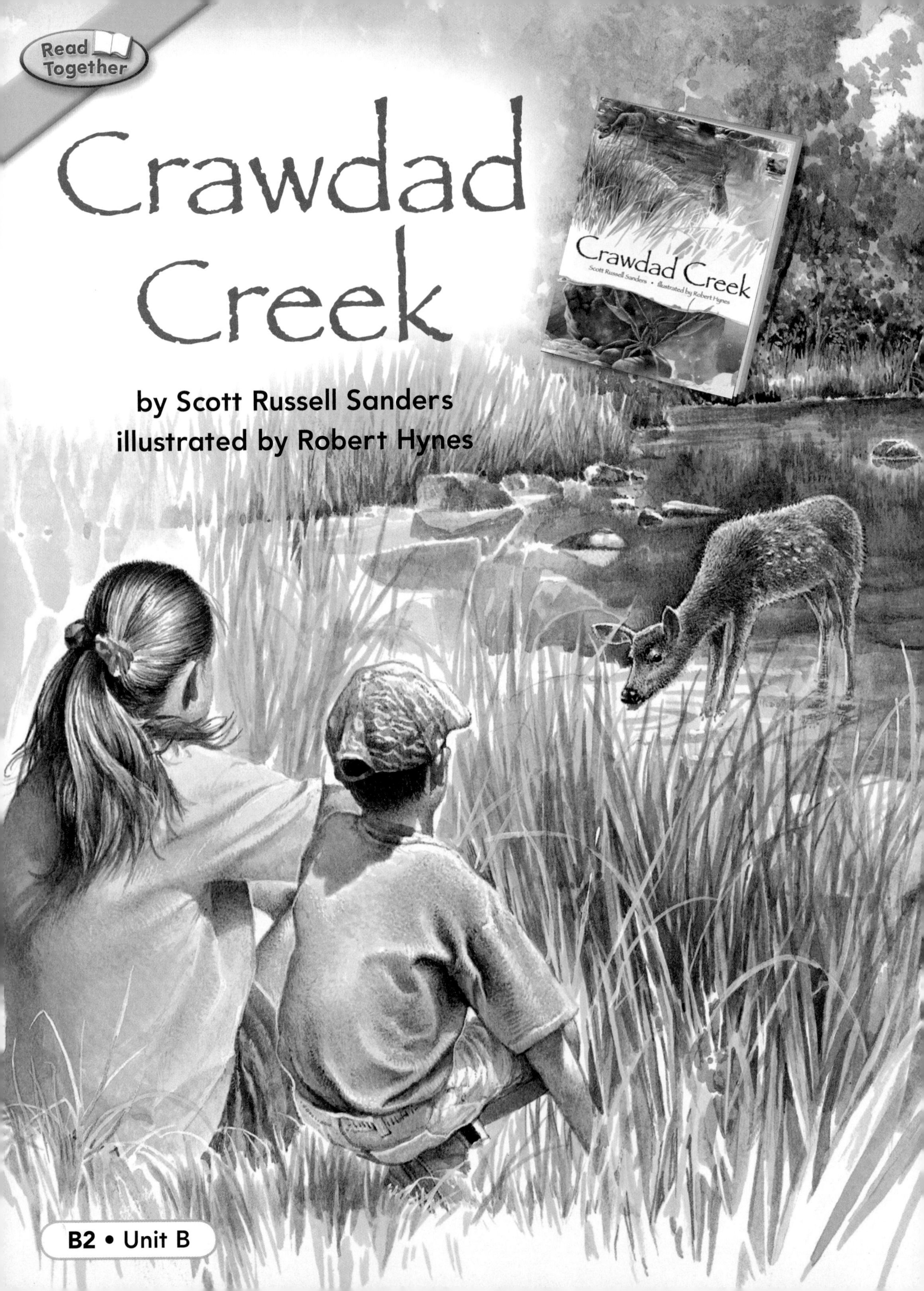

Crawdad Creek

by Scott Russell Sanders
illustrated by Robert Hynes

In the warm evenings, just before going in to bed, we sat very still beside Crawdad Creek, hoping to see the animals that made the tracks. And sure enough, we saw deer coming down to drink, saw rabbits nibbling and muskrats swimming, even saw raccoons grubbing for mussels in the water.

Chapter 4

Environments

Vocabulary Preview

environment
habitat
stream
woodland
resource
drought

habitat

The part of an environment where a plant or an animal lives is its habitat.

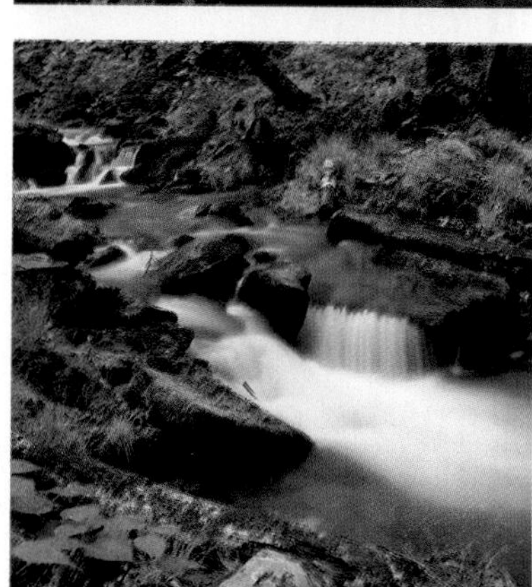

stream

A stream is a small river.

woodland

A woodland is a place with many trees and bushes.

drought

A long time with little or no rain is a drought.

Lesson 1

What Makes Up an Environment?

Science and You

You can help living things survive when you know about environments.

Inquiry Skill

Classify Sort organisms or objects into groups to show how they are alike.

What You Need

hand lens

drawing paper

crayons

Investigate

Living or Nonliving

Steps

1. **Observe** Look around a small rock or log for a living thing. Think about what it uses to meet its needs.

2. **Classify** Look up close. Decide whether each thing it uses is living or nonliving.

3. **Record Data** Make a chart like the one shown. Draw each thing you see in the correct place on the chart.

4. **Communicate** Show your chart to others. Talk about what you observed.

STEP 1

STEP 2

STEP 3

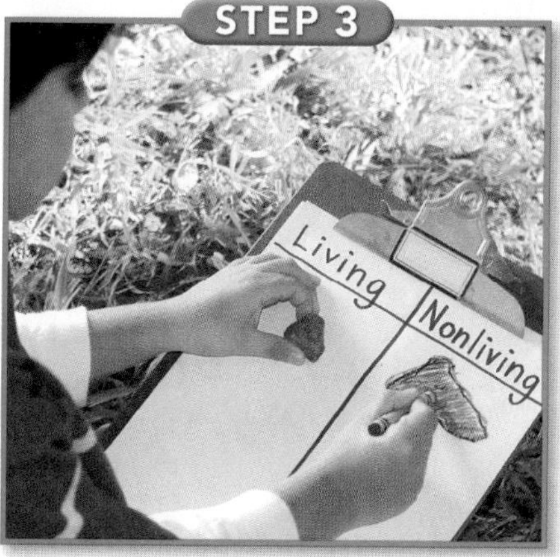

Think and Share

1. Did your living thing use more living or nonliving things to meet its needs?

2. **Compare** How are the nonliving things alike?

Investigate More!

Ask Questions Make a list of questions about the living things that you observed. Think of ways to find answers to your questions.

Learn by Reading

▶ Vocabulary

environment

habitat

▶ Reading Skill

Main Idea and Details

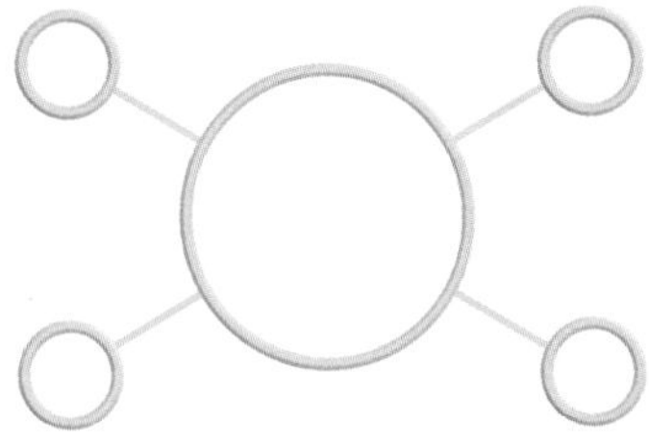

Different Environments

All the living and nonliving things around a living thing make up an **environment**. Plants and animals are the living things. Soil, water, rocks, and air are some of the nonliving things.

The world has many kinds of environments. Different plants and animals live in each one. They adapt to the environment where they live.

Alpine Tundra

The alpine tundra is cold and dry. The plants grow low to the ground to be safe from the wind.

Rain Forest

A rain forest is a warm, wet forest with many kinds of plants.

An environment can be hot or cold. It can be wet or dry. Some environments have many trees and other plants. Other environments have very few plants.

MAIN IDEA **What are three different kinds of environments?**

Prairie

The prairie is hot in summer and cold in winter.

Meeting Needs

Living things will survive only if they get what they need. So different plants and animals live in different environments. The part of an environment where a plant or an animal lives is its **habitat**.

In hot, desert habitats, animals find shade under rocks or under the ground. They look for food at night, when it is cooler. Many desert animals get water from the foods they eat.

In what kind of habitat does a fish need to live?

Spotted skin helps the lizard blend in with its desert environment.

The thick stem of a cactus holds water.

◀ Hooves help mountain goats climb rocky slopes in the tundra.

Plants and animals have parts that help them live in their habitats. Some parts help them stay safe. Other parts help them get food and water.

A large beak helps a macaw crack open nuts it finds in the rain forest. ▼

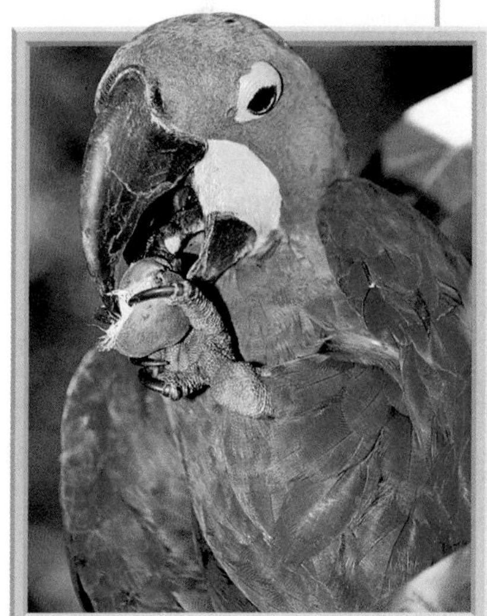

MAIN IDEA **Why do different plants and animals live in different places?**

Lesson Wrap-Up

1. **Vocabulary** What is a **habitat**?
2. **Reading Skill** How do parts of plants and animals help them in their habitats?
3. **Classify** Name two living things and two nonliving things in a desert.

Technology Visit **www.eduplace.com/scp/** to find out more about habitats.

Lesson 2

What Is a Stream Habitat?

Science and You

Knowing about a stream habitat helps you know what living things you might find there.

Inquiry Skill

Use Models You can use models to find out more about real things.

What You Need

large pan

clay

rocks and pebbles

water

Investigate

Make a Stream

Steps

1. **Use Models** Use clay to make a stream in a pan. Flatten the clay to make the bottom of the stream. Make walls of clay for the banks of the stream.

2. Put rocks and pebbles in the bottom of the stream.

3. **Observe** Slowly pour water in one end of the stream. Observe how the water moves.

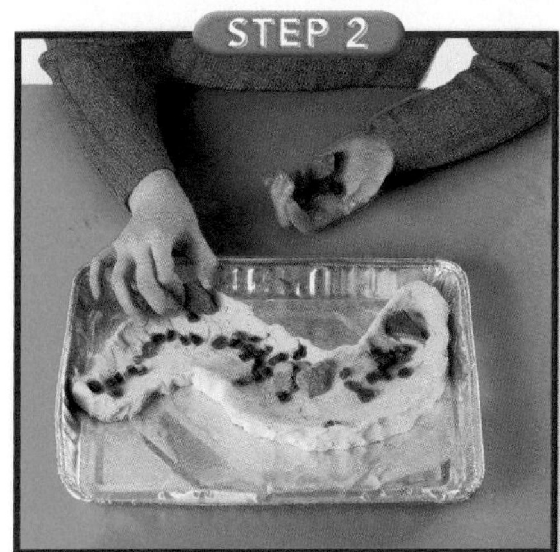

Think and Share

1. **Communicate** Describe the nonliving parts of a stream habitat.
2. **Infer** How might living things meet their needs in a stream habitat?

Investigate More!

Experiment Plan ways to change how the water moves in your model stream. Record what happens each time. Share your results.

Learn by Reading

Vocabulary

stream

Reading Skill

Draw Conclusions

A Stream Habitat

A **stream** is a small river. A stream and the area around it make up a stream habitat.

Many living and nonliving things are found in and around a stream. A stream habitat has plants and animals. It has air, water, rocks, and dirt. The water moves fast in some parts of the stream and more slowly in other parts.

Water helps plants grow in and around a stream.

Many living things meet their needs in a stream habitat. Plants and animals use water from the stream. They use the air around the stream. Fish move through the water. They eat plants and insects that live in the stream.

DRAW CONCLUSIONS **What nonliving things in a stream habitat do animals use?**

Raccoons use their senses to find crayfish and frogs along the banks of a stream.

Rocks provide a place for small animals to hide.

Life in a Stream

Living things in a stream habitat have adaptations to meet their needs. Plants that float have roots that hang in the water. A fish uses fins to swim. It uses gills to get air from the stream. A dragonfly uses its sense of sight to hunt for flying insects. A heron uses its long legs to walk in shallow water.

DRAW CONCLUSIONS **How does a turtle's shell help it in a stream habitat?**

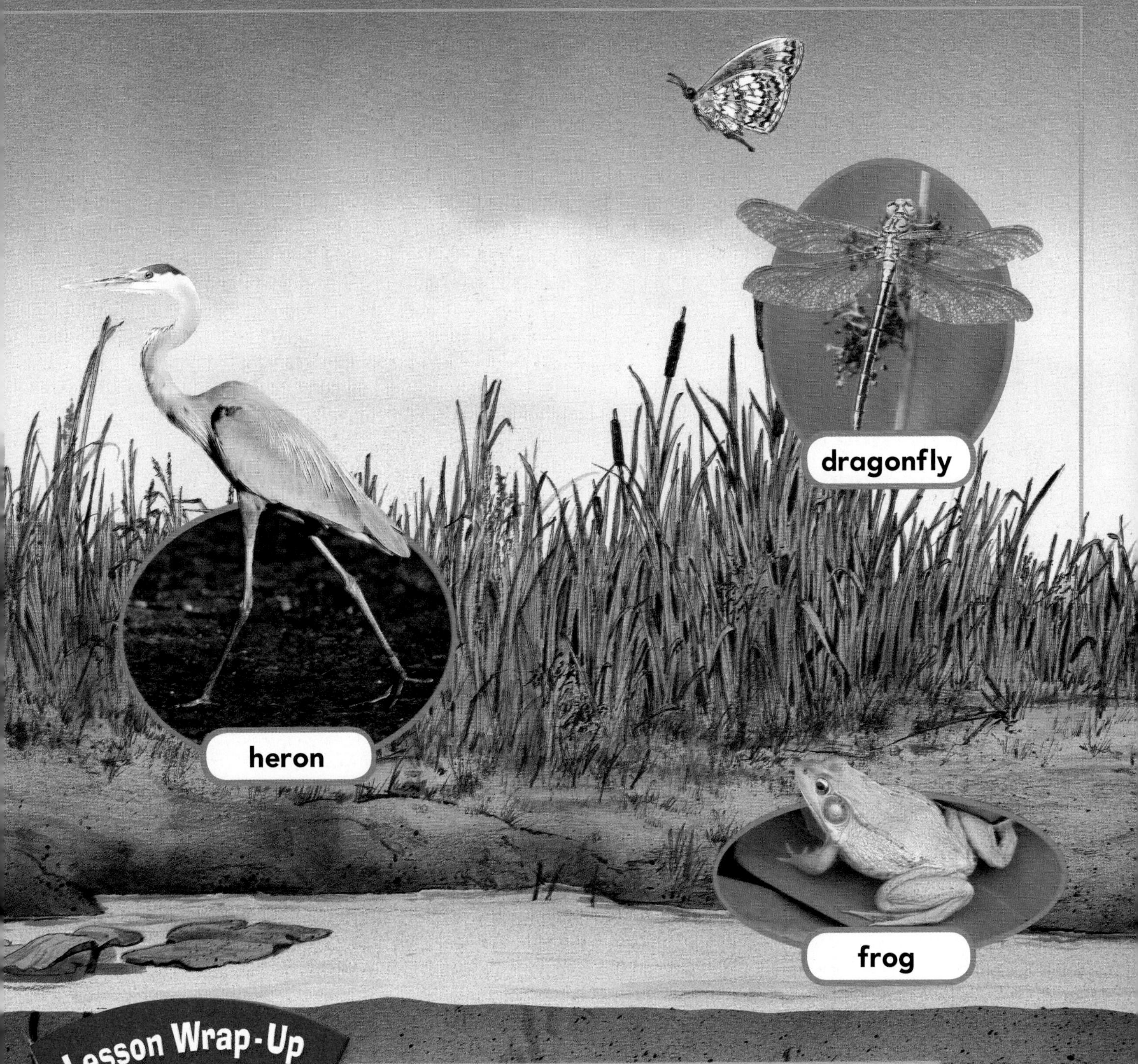

Lesson Wrap-Up

1. **Vocabulary** What is a **stream**?
2. **Reading Skill** How does a frog's color help it live in a stream habitat?
3. **Use Models** How is using a model helpful?

Technology Visit **www.eduplace.com/scp/** to find out more about stream habitats.

Lesson 3

What Is a Woodland Habitat?

Science and You

Knowing about a woodland habitat helps you understand the importance of trees.

Inquiry Skill

Use Models You can use models to find out more about real things.

What You Need

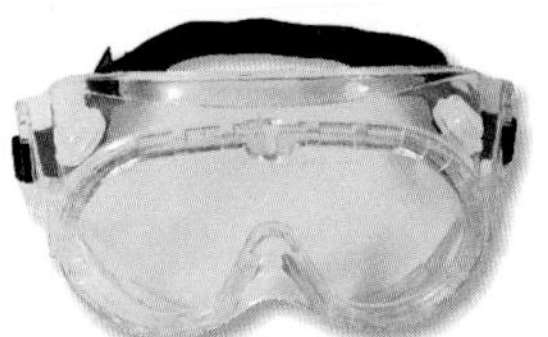

goggles

2 cups and tape

gravel, soil, and a spoon

moss or a fern and water

Investigate

Woodland Model

Steps

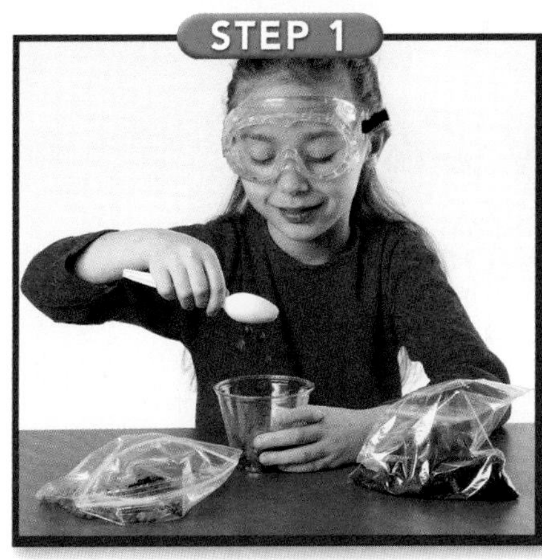

1. **Use Models** Make a model of a woodland. Put some gravel in the bottom of a cup. Add soil until the cup is half full. **Safety:** Wear goggles!

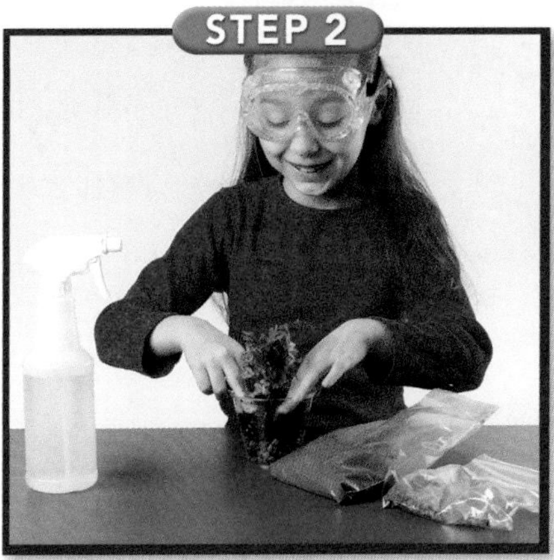

2. Spray the soil with water. Plant moss or a fern.

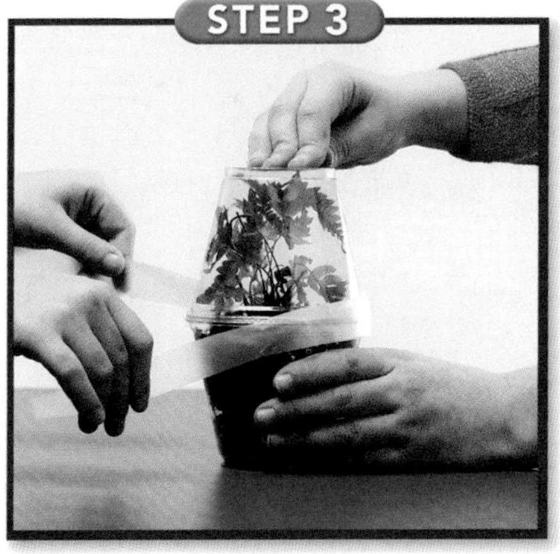

3. Put an empty cup on top of the first cup. Tape the cups together.

4. **Record Data** Put your model in dim light. Record the changes you see each day.

Think and Share

1. **Infer** Why do you think a woodland model should be kept in dim light?
2. **Predict** What changes do you think will happen over time?

Investigate More!

Experiment How might bright light affect your woodland model? Make and carry out a plan. Share what you observe.

Learn by Reading

Vocabulary

woodland

resource

Reading Skill

Compare and Contrast

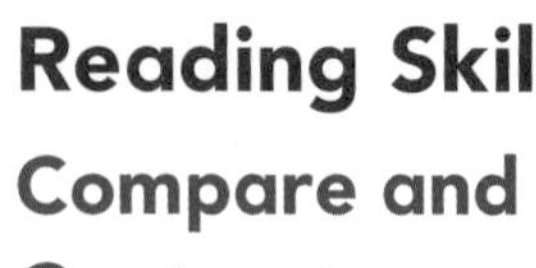

A Woodland Habitat

A **woodland** is a place with many trees and bushes. Living things in a woodland have adaptations to help them survive. Small plants that live under tall trees can grow with less sunlight. Woodland animals use these plants for food and shelter.

Many woodland animals have body parts for climbing or flying to the tops of trees. The brown coloring of many woodland animals helps them to hide.

COMPARE AND CONTRAST How are small plants different from tall trees in a woodland?

fox

hawk
squirrel
deer
pheasant
skunk
snake

Trees Are Resources

A **resource** is something that plants and animals use to live. A tree is a resource for woodland plants and animals. A tree can give living things food and shelter.

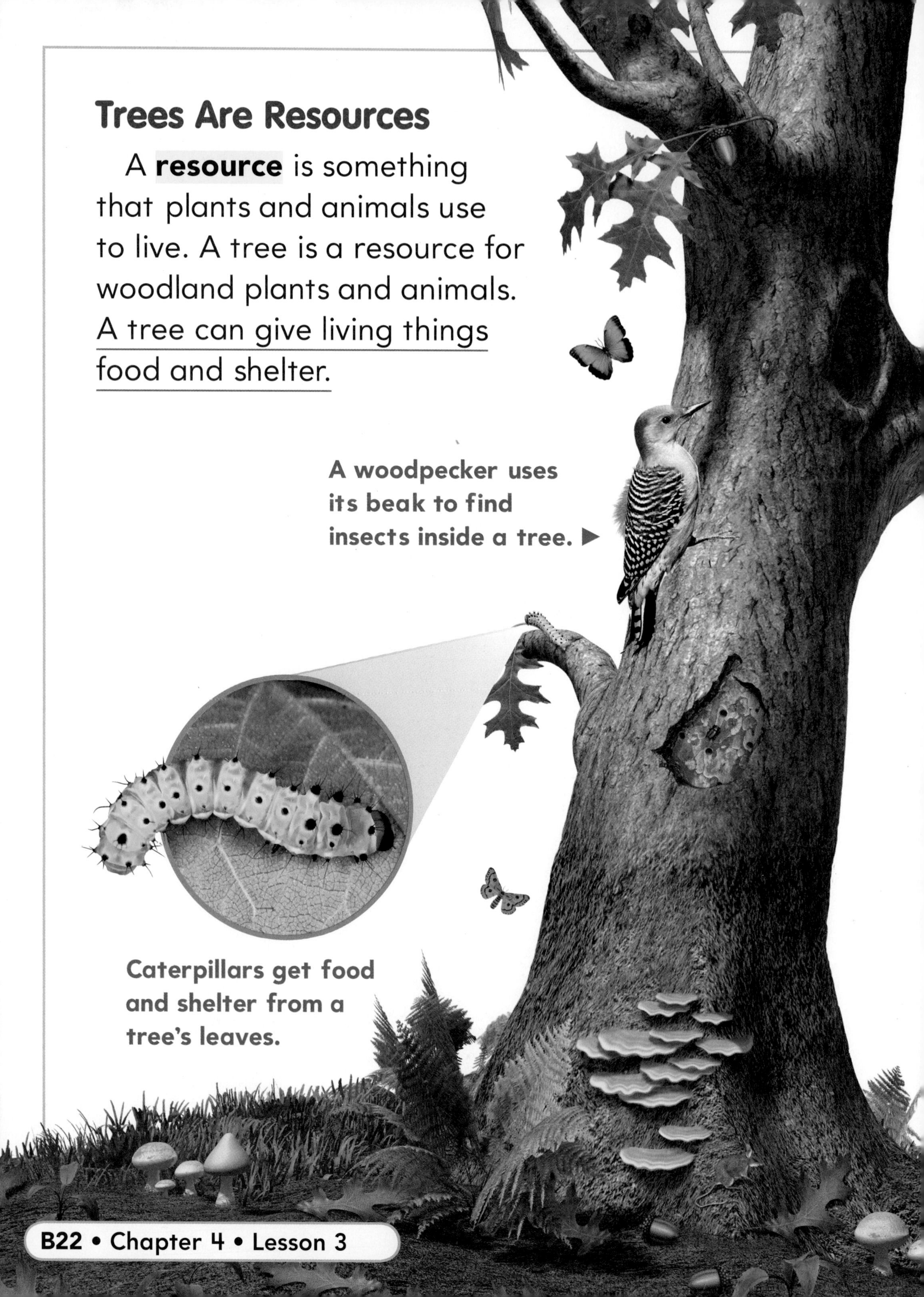

A woodpecker uses its beak to find insects inside a tree. ▶

Caterpillars get food and shelter from a tree's leaves.

Both an owl and a squirrel use a tree for shelter.

Animals use all parts of a tree. They use the roots, leaves, and nuts for food. Some animals build nests in tree branches. Others live on leaves or under the bark.

COMPARE AND CONTRAST How do squirrels and caterpillars use trees in the same way?

Lesson Wrap-Up

1. **Vocabulary** What is a **resource**?
2. **Reading Skill** Compare how a fox and a hawk are adapted to live in a woodland.
3. **Use Models** What does a model show?

Technology Visit **www.eduplace.com/scp/** to find out more about woodland habitats.

Creating Habitats

Aquariums and zoos have habitats made by people. Workers study living things in the real habitats. Then they build the habitats indoors.

The Tennessee Aquarium has indoor woodland and stream habitats. The streams are made of long tanks of water. Computers keep the woodland air cool and wet. They also control the flow of water in the streams.

A pointed glass roof at the Tennessee Aquarium lets in sunlight. ▼

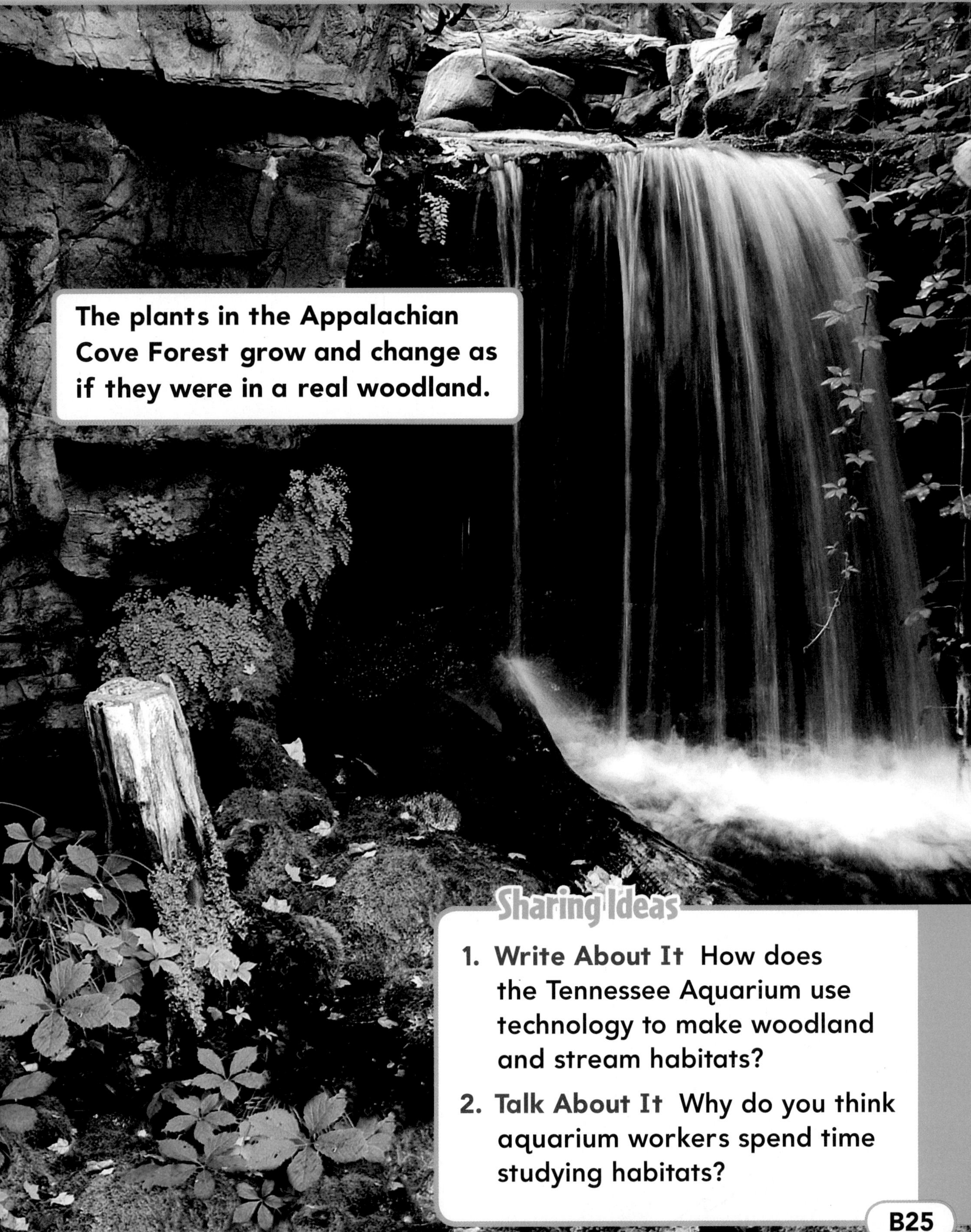

The plants in the Appalachian Cove Forest grow and change as if they were in a real woodland.

Sharing Ideas

1. **Write About It** How does the Tennessee Aquarium use technology to make woodland and stream habitats?
2. **Talk About It** Why do you think aquarium workers spend time studying habitats?

Lesson 4

How Do Environments Change?

Science and You

You can help care for environments by knowing how they change.

Inquiry Skill

Predict Use what you know and observe to tell what you think will happen.

What You Need

2 cups of grass

tray

water

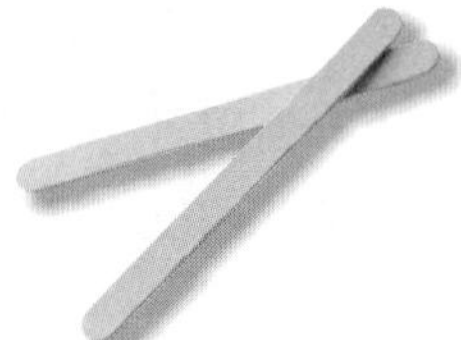

2 craft sticks

Investigate

Predict Change

Steps

1. Write **Water** on one stick. Write **No Water** on the other stick. Label each cup of grass. Water only the grass labeled **Water**.

2. **Predict** Place the cups on a tray in a sunny window. Tell how you think each cup of grass might change after five days.

3. Continue to water only the grass labeled **Water** each day for five days. Record your results.

STEP 1

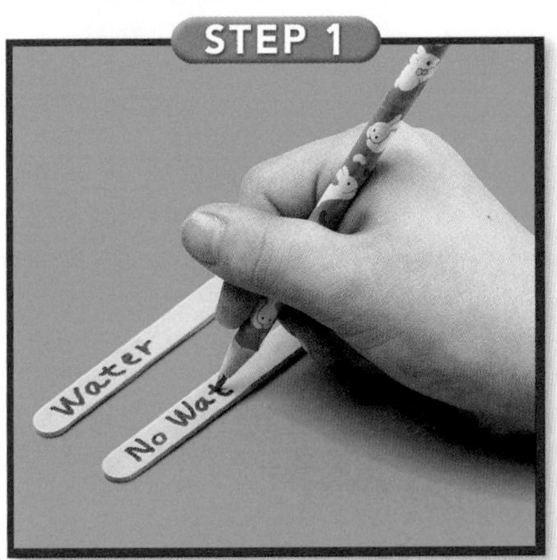

STEP 2

STEP 3

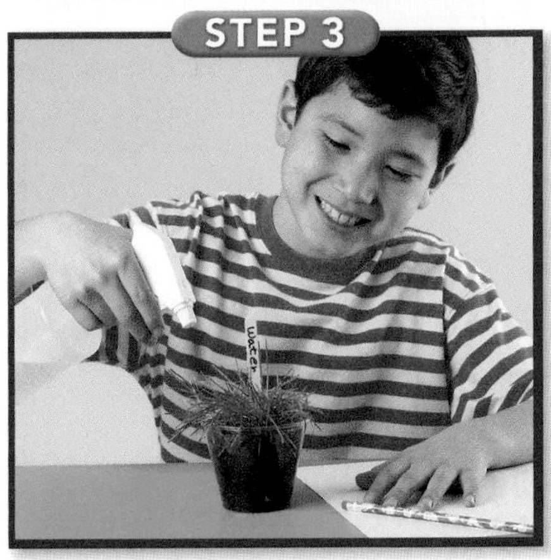

Think and Share

1. **Infer** How did each cup of grass change? Tell why.

2. **Compare** How did your results compare to your prediction?

Investigate More!

Experiment Plan a way to find out what happens when a plant gets too much water. Carry out your plan. Share the results with your classmates.

Learn by Reading

Vocabulary

drought

Reading Skill

Cause and Effect

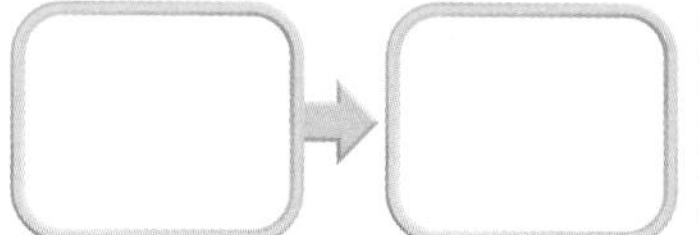

Nature Changes Environments

Things that happen in nature can change an environment. The changes can be slow or fast. They can be harmful or helpful. Forest fires harm trees. But the fires help some seeds grow into new trees.

Too much rain can cause a flood. A long time with little or no rain is a **drought**. Without water, plants cannot grow. Animals do not get enough to eat and drink. Plants and animals might die.

effect of drought ▶

Plants also can change an environment. New plants might block sunlight needed by other plants. Animals that depend on these plants must find other things to eat.

Some animals might harm the resources of other animals. The animals then must find new homes or new kinds of food. Other animals might help the environment by making new habitats.

CAUSE AND EFFECT How can a drought change an environment?

▲ **Kudzu is a vine that can kill trees by blocking the sunlight.**

A beaver builds a dam, and a pond forms behind it. The pond is a new home for many animals.

Animals Adapt to Change

People can change an environment by building in places where plants and animals live. Animals can learn to adapt to their changed habitats. Instead of finding food in a woodland, an animal might find food in household trash.

This skunk has learned to meet its needs in a changed environment.

Lesson Wrap-Up

1. **Vocabulary** What is a time of little rain called?
2. **Reading Skill** What can cause an environment to change?
3. **Predict** What might happen to a vegetable garden if no rain fell for a long time?

Technology Visit **www.eduplace.com/scp/** to find out more about how environments change.

LINKS for Home and School

Math Use a Bar Graph

Ms. Park's class observed the trees near their school. The graph shows how many different trees they saw.

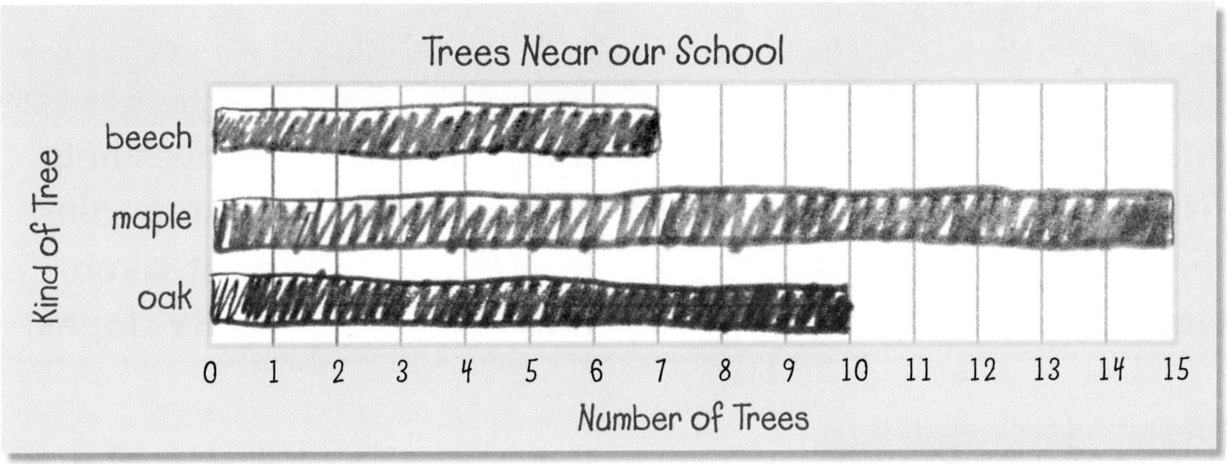

1. How many oak and beech trees are there altogether?

2. How many more maple trees are there than beech trees?

Social Studies Make a Poster

Think about how you meet your needs in your habitat. Make a poster to show how you meet one of those needs.

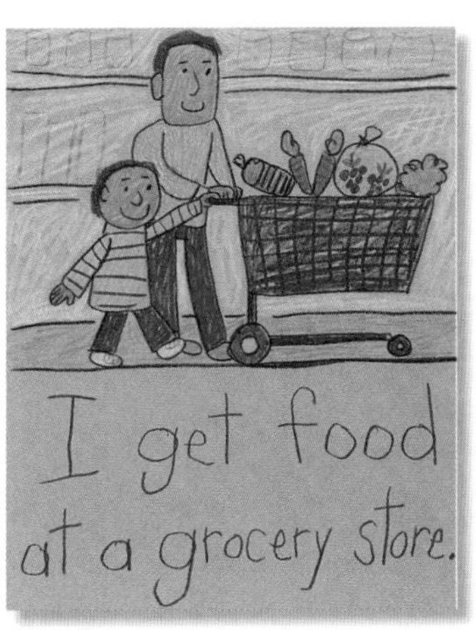

Review and Test Prep

Visual Summary

Animals have features that help them live in their environments.

Stream	Woodland	Desert	Tundra
Fins help a fish swim through water.	Claws help a squirrel climb trees.	Spots help a lizard blend in with its habitat.	Hooves help a mountain goat climb rocky slopes.

Main Ideas

1. Describe what makes up an environment. (p. B8)
2. How do fish use a stream to meet their needs? (pp. B14–B16)
3. How do animals use trees to meet their needs? (pp. B22–B23)
4. What events in nature can change an environment? (pp. B28–B29)

Vocabulary

Choose the correct word from the box.

habitat (p. B10)
woodland (p. B20)
resource (p. B22)
drought (p. B28)

5. A long time with little or no rain
6. A place with many trees and bushes
7. The part of an environment where a plant or an animal lives
8. Something that plants and animals use to live

Test Practice

Choose a word to complete the sentence.

9. A _____ is a small river.

shelter woodland drought stream

Using Science Skills

10. **Classify** Draw a picture of three animals in a stream habitat. Draw another picture of three animals in a woodland habitat. Compare your drawings.

11. **Critical Thinking** Why do people need to be careful about where they build new buildings?

Chapter 5

Energy Needs

Vocabulary Preview

energy
food chain
food web
healthful food
healthful meal

energy

Energy is the ability to do things.

food chain

A food chain is the order in which energy passes from one living thing to another.

healthful food

A healthful food is a food that is good for your body.

healthful meal

A healthful meal is a meal with foods from the different food groups.

Lesson 1

How Do Plants and Animals Get Energy?

Science and You

Knowing about food chains helps you understand how living things depend on their environments.

Inquiry Skill

Use Models You can use models to find out more about real things.

What You Need

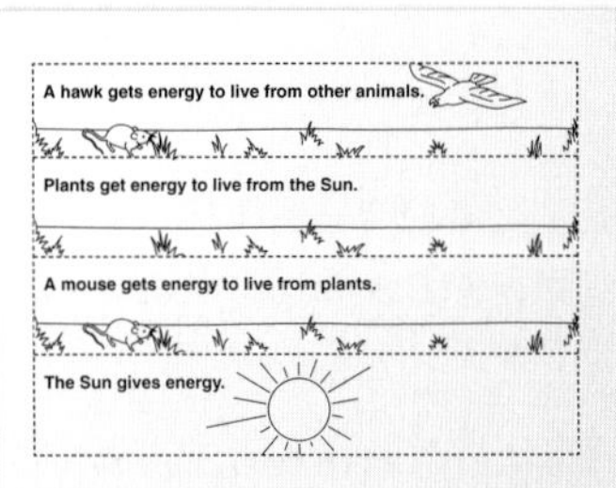

food chain strips

scissors

glue

Investigate

Make a Food Chain

Steps

1. Cut along the dotted lines to make food chain strips. **Safety:** Scissors are sharp!

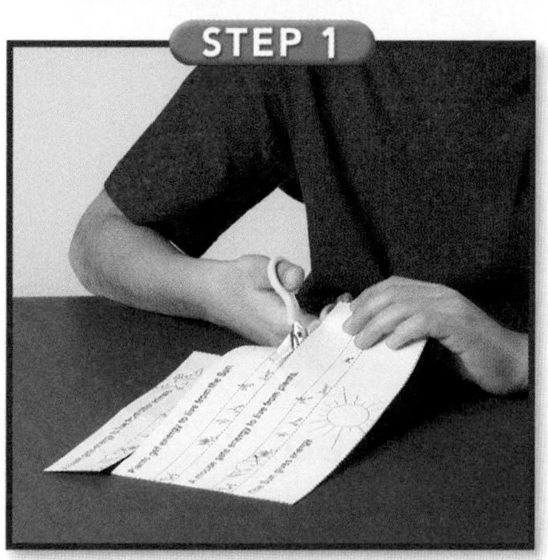
STEP 1

2. Find the strip with the Sun. Glue the ends together to make a loop.

STEP 2

3. **Use Models** Add loops in the correct order to make a food chain. Use the clues on the strips.

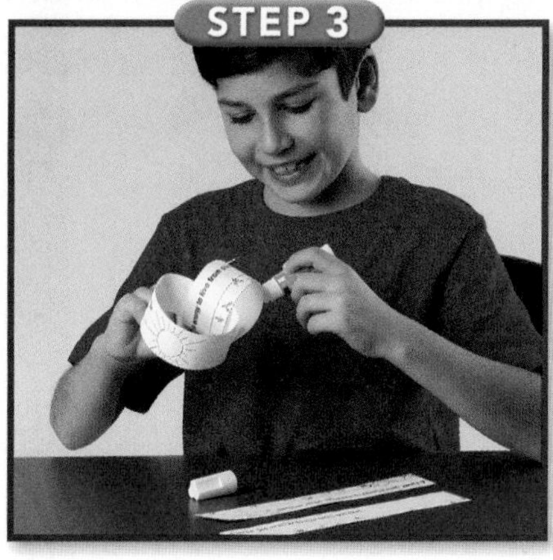
STEP 3

4. **Communicate** Talk with a partner. Tell how each link connects to the next link.

Think and Share

1. Why did your food chain model start with the Sun?
2. Why does a hawk need plants to live?

Investigate More!

Ask Questions Ask about what some other animals eat. Use what you learn to make a new food chain.

Learn by Reading

Food and Energy

Vocabulary

energy
food chain
food web

Reading Skill
Sequence

When you run, play a game, or clean your room, you use energy. **Energy** is the ability to do things. Living things get the energy they need from food.

Remember that plants are living things. Plants use sunlight to make their own food. The food gives them energy to grow and change.

Young wasps get energy by eating part of a hornworm.

Animals are living things, too. Animals get energy to grow and change from the food they eat. Different animals eat different kinds of food. Some animals eat only plants. Some eat only other animals. Some animals eat both plants and other animals.

SEQUENCE What do animals do to get energy?

Giraffes eat only plants. ▶

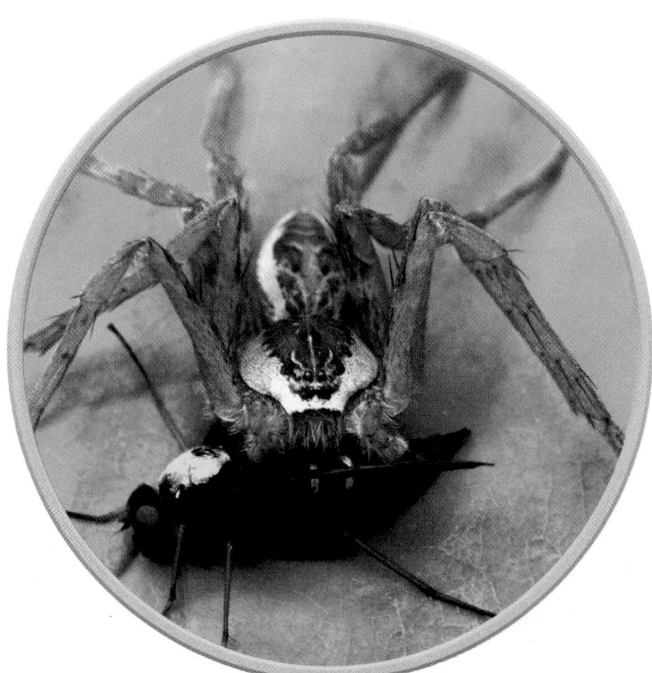

▲ Spiders hunt and eat insects.

Food Chains

A chain is made of parts that are linked in some way. Plants and animals are linked by the energy they use to live. A **food chain** shows the order in which energy passes from one living thing to another.

Almost all food chains start with the Sun. Most plants get energy by turning sunlight into food. The arrows show the direction that energy moves in each food chain.

SEQUENCE With what do most food chains begin?

1 **Grass gets energy from the Sun.**

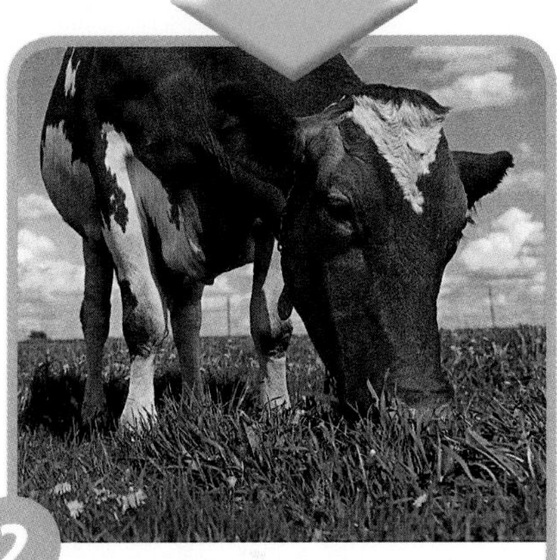

2 **A cow eats the grass.**

3 **A child drinks milk that came from the cow.**

3 **A large fish eats the small fish.**

Food Webs

Many food chains can be found at the same time in one environment. A **food web** shows how different food chains are related. The picture shows a food web made up of some desert food chains.

One part of a food web may change. When this happens, the lives of other living things in the web can change, too.

SEQUENCE Tell the order in which energy moves from the Sun to a rattlesnake.

Lesson Wrap-Up

1. **Vocabulary** What is **energy**?
2. **Reading Skill** What is one way that energy moves from the Sun to a hawk?
3. **Use Models** What does a food chain show?

Technology Visit **www.eduplace.com/scp/** to find out more about food chains and food webs.

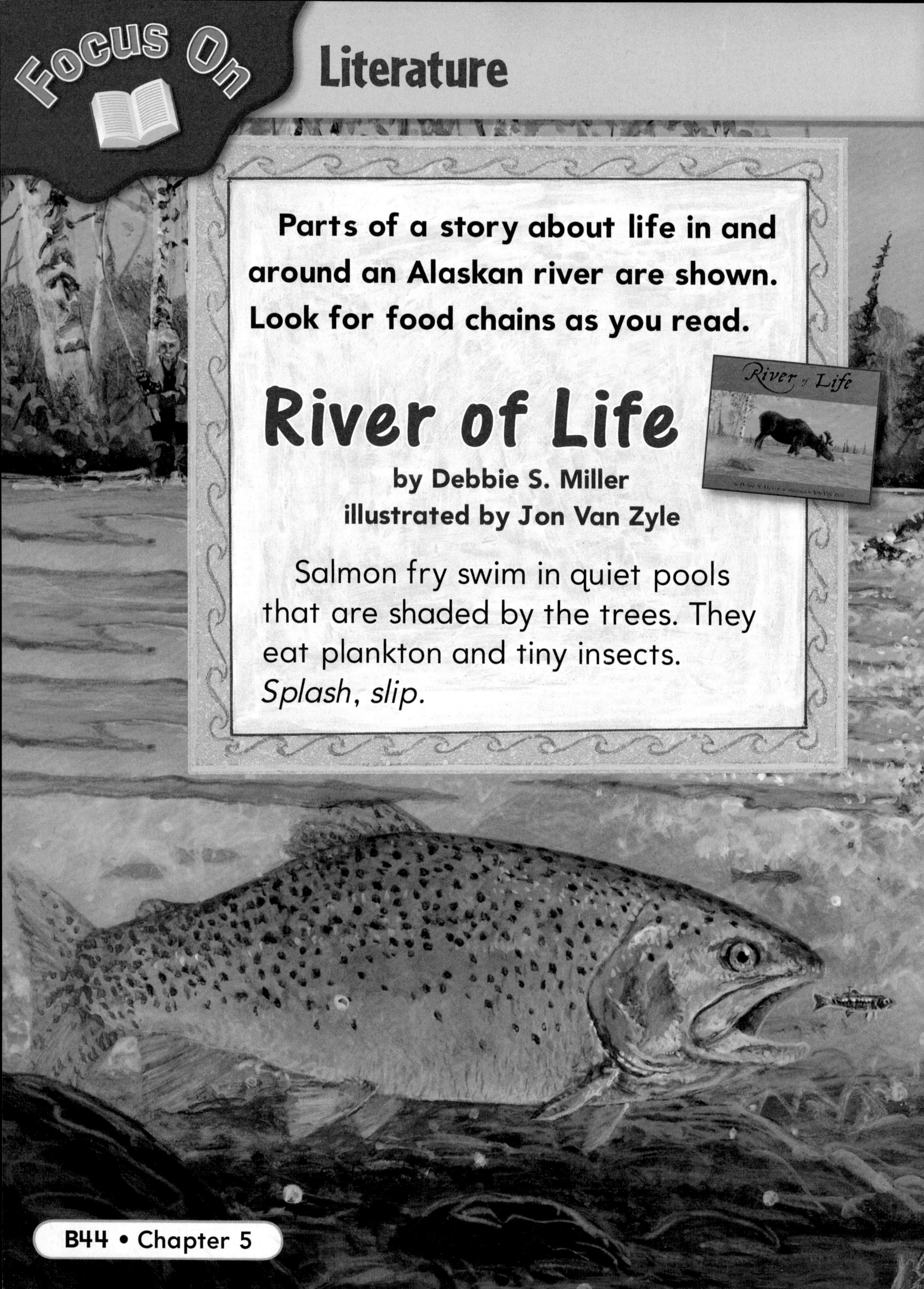

Parts of a story about life in and around an Alaskan river are shown. Look for food chains as you read.

River of Life

by Debbie S. Miller
illustrated by Jon Van Zyle

Salmon fry swim in quiet pools that are shaded by the trees. They eat plankton and tiny insects. *Splash*, *slip*.

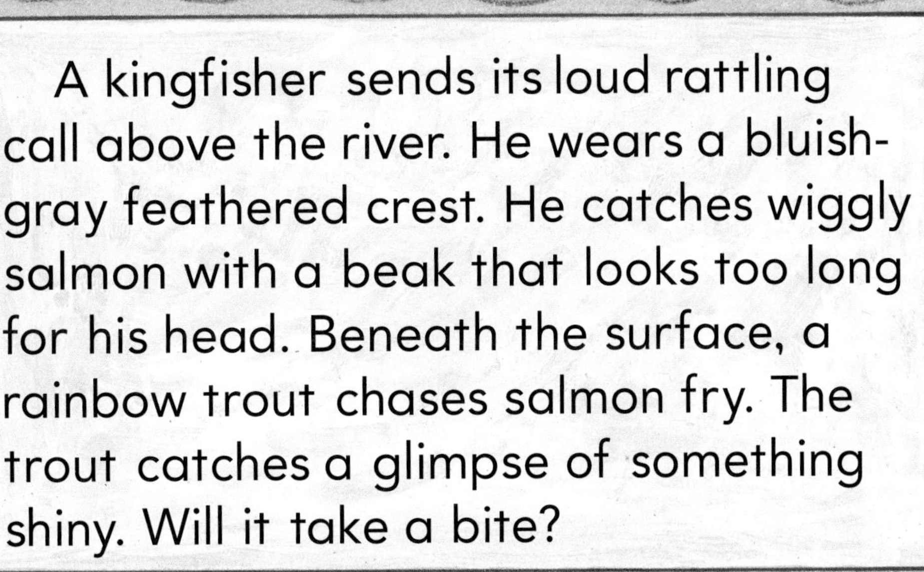

A kingfisher sends its loud rattling call above the river. He wears a bluish-gray feathered crest. He catches wiggly salmon with a beak that looks too long for his head. Beneath the surface, a rainbow trout chases salmon fry. The trout catches a glimpse of something shiny. Will it take a bite?

Sharing Ideas

1. **Write About It** Draw a food chain or food web described in the story. Be sure to label its parts.
2. **Talk About It** What animals might eat trout from the river?

Lesson 2

How Do People Get Energy?

Science and You

Eating the right kinds of foods helps you play, learn, and grow.

Inquiry Skill

Classify Sort objects into groups to show how they are alike.

What You Need

food ads

paper

scissors

glue

Investigate

Classify Foods

Steps

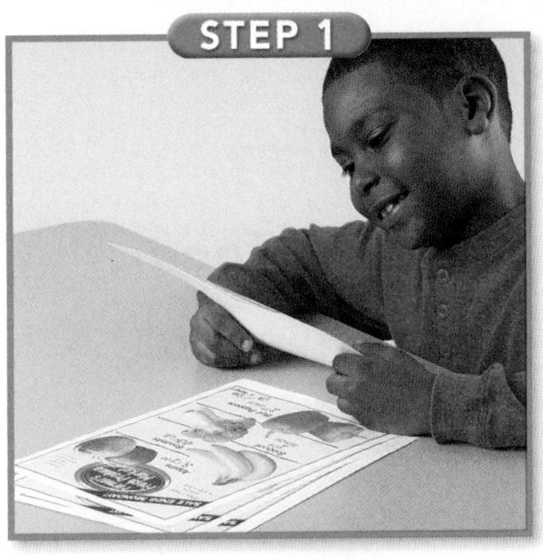

STEP 1

1. **Compare** Look at food ads. Look for foods that are alike. Look for foods that are different.

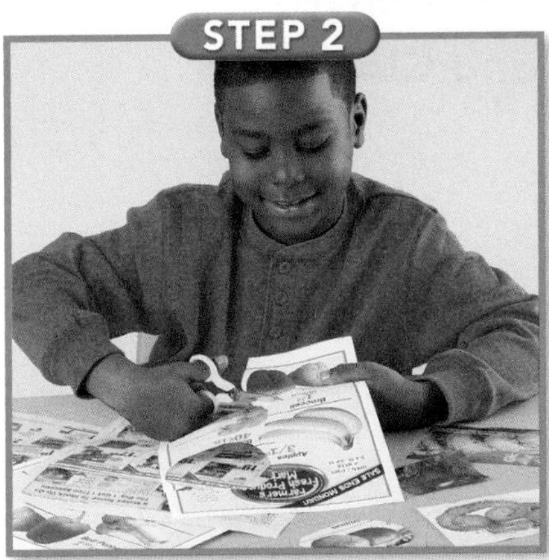

STEP 2

2. Cut out pictures of 10 different foods. **Safety:** Scissors are sharp!

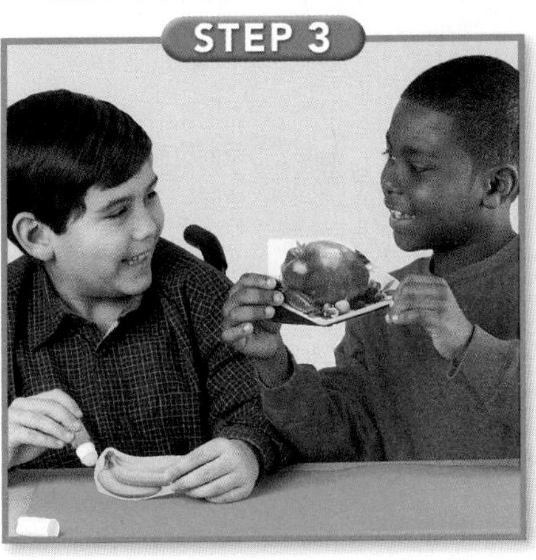

STEP 3

3. **Classify** Fold a sheet of paper into four parts. Sort the pictures into four groups. Glue each group to a different part of the paper.

Think and Share

1. **Communicate** Tell how you sorted the foods.
2. What other ways could the foods be sorted?

Investigate More!

Work Together Survey classmates to find out what foods they do not like. Discuss as a group how the foods named in the survey are alike.

Learn by Reading

Vocabulary

healthful food

healthful meal

Reading Skill

Categorize and Classify

People Get Energy from Food

People are living things that need food, air, water, and shelter. Food gives people the energy needed to do everyday things.

Foods come from different places. Think about foods you see at a market or grocery store. They all come from somewhere else.

Farmers grow vegetables in soil.

Farmers gather eggs from chickens.

A farmer grows vegetables and a fisher catches fish. A grocer buys the vegetables and fish from the farmer and the fisher. Then the grocer sells these foods to the shoppers.

CLASSIFY Where might grocers get the food they sell?

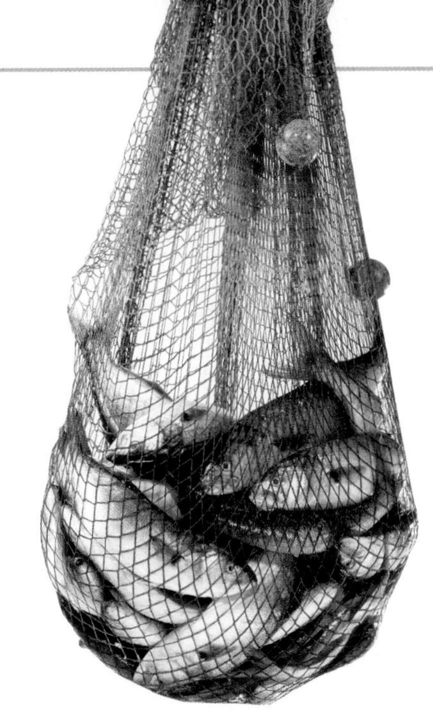

▲ Fish come from rivers, lakes, and oceans.

Where do the vegetables in this market come from? ▼

Food Choices

Some foods are better for you than others. A **healthful food** is a food that is good for your body. Healthful foods give your body energy and vitamins. Healthful foods can be sorted into groups. Eating healthful foods from each group helps your body be its best.

Foods such as candy and other sweets are not as good for you. These foods will not help your body be its best. Be sure to eat healthful foods most of the time.

CLASSIFY Which foods help your body be its best?

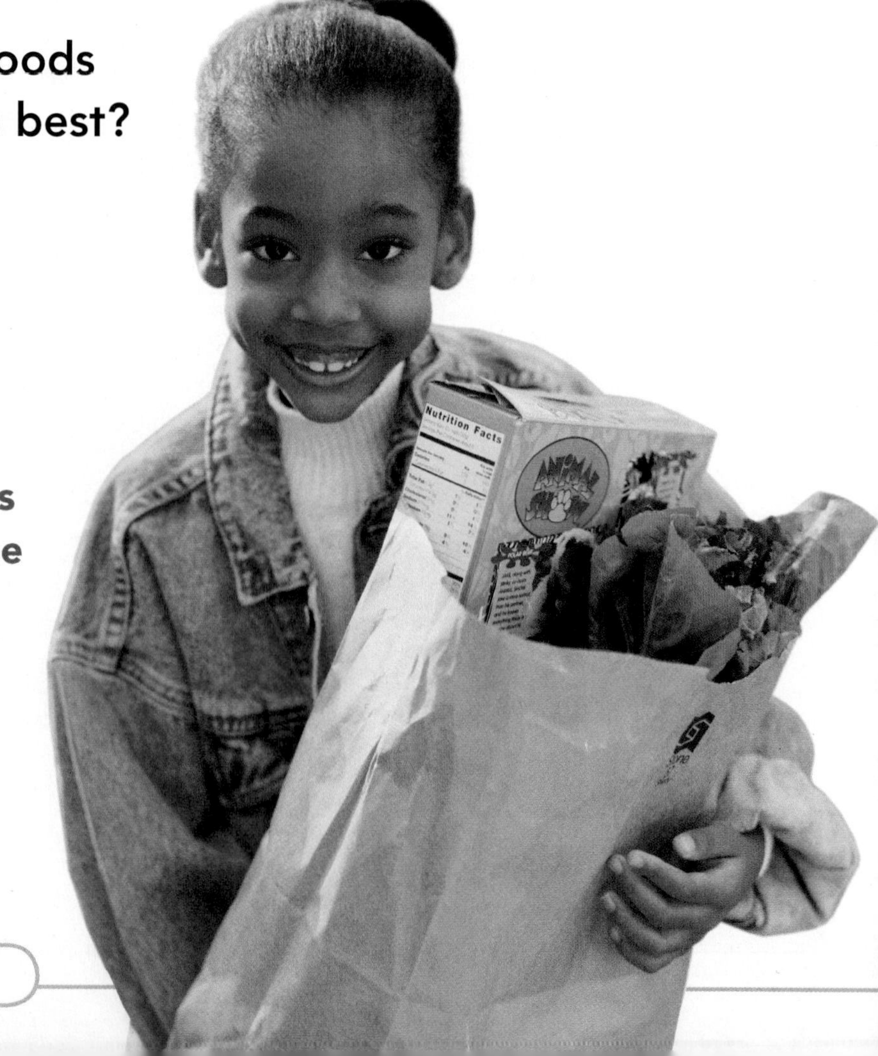

In which food groups do the cereal and the lettuce belong?

grains: bread, cereal, rice, pasta

milk: milk, cheese, yogurt

meat and beans: meat, chicken, fish, eggs, beans, nuts

vegetables

fruits

Healthful Meals

It is important to eat healthful foods at each meal and as snacks. A **healthful meal** is a meal with foods from the different food groups.

Lesson Wrap-Up

1. **Vocabulary** What is an example of a **healthful food**?
2. **Reading Skill** Name two foods that come from a farm.
3. **Classify** Which two foods belong in the same group?

Technology Visit **www.eduplace.com/scp/** to find out more about food and energy.

LINKS for Home and School

Math Read a Chart

This chart shows the favorite healthful foods of children in a second-grade class.

Healthful Foods	
Favorite Food	Number of Children
apples	5
carrots	1
pasta	3
cheese	4

1. Cheese is the favorite food of how many?
2. How many children have a favorite food that is a fruit or vegetable?

Language Arts Food Chain Book

Make a picture book about a food chain. Find out about a food chain on your own, or use one of these food chains.

fruit, fly, spider, lizard
leaf, caterpillar, frog, snake
arrow worm, herring, salmon, shark

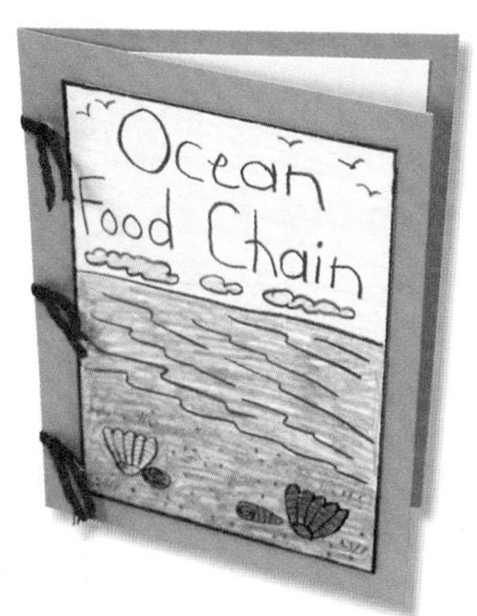

Chapter 5

Review and Test Prep

Visual Summary

Living things need energy from food to live.

Plants make their own food.

Some animals eat plants.

Some animals eat other animals.

People eat plants or animals.

Main Ideas

1. Describe how plants and animals get energy. **(pp. B38–B39)**
2. What starts each food chain? **(p. B41)**
3. How is a food chain different from a food web? **(pp. B40–B43)**
4. How do people meet their need for energy? **(p. B48)**

Vocabulary

Choose the correct word from the box.

energy (p. B38)
food chain (p. B40)
healthful food (p. B50)
healthful meal (p. B52)

5. A food that is good for your body
6. The ability to do things
7. Meal with foods from the different food groups
8. The order in which energy passes from one living thing to another

Test Practice

Choose a word to complete the sentence.

9. A _____ shows how different food chains are related.

food group   food web   market   meal

Using Science Skills

10. **Classify** List three foods that belong in the same group. Tell why.

11. **Critical Thinking** What might happen to a food web if all of the plants died?

Why are flamingos pink?

Flamingos are pink because of a food chain. Flamingos eat animals called crustaceans. Crustaceans eat algae. Algae contain nutrients that can cause things to be pink. When a flamingo eats the crustaceans, it takes in these nutrients. This causes the flamingo's feathers to turn pink.

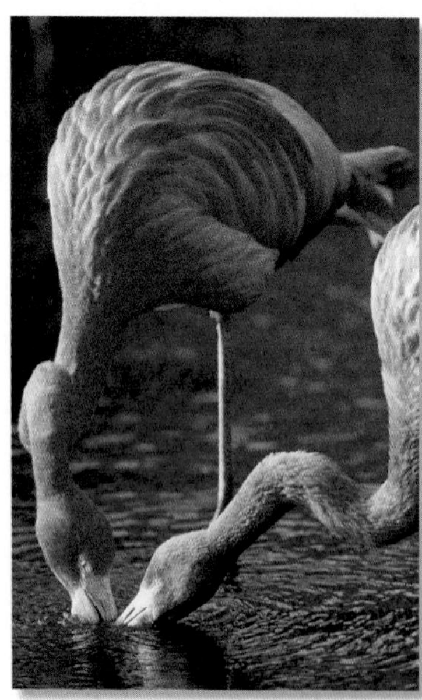

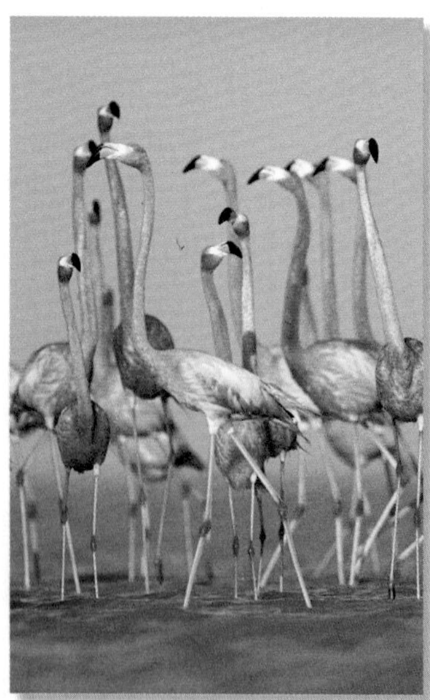

Go to **www.eduplace.com/scp/** to study more animal food chains.

EARTH SCIENCE

UNIT C

Treasures from Earth

Cricket Connection

Visit www.eduplace.com/scp/ to check out *Click, Ask,* and *Odyssey* magazine articles and activities.

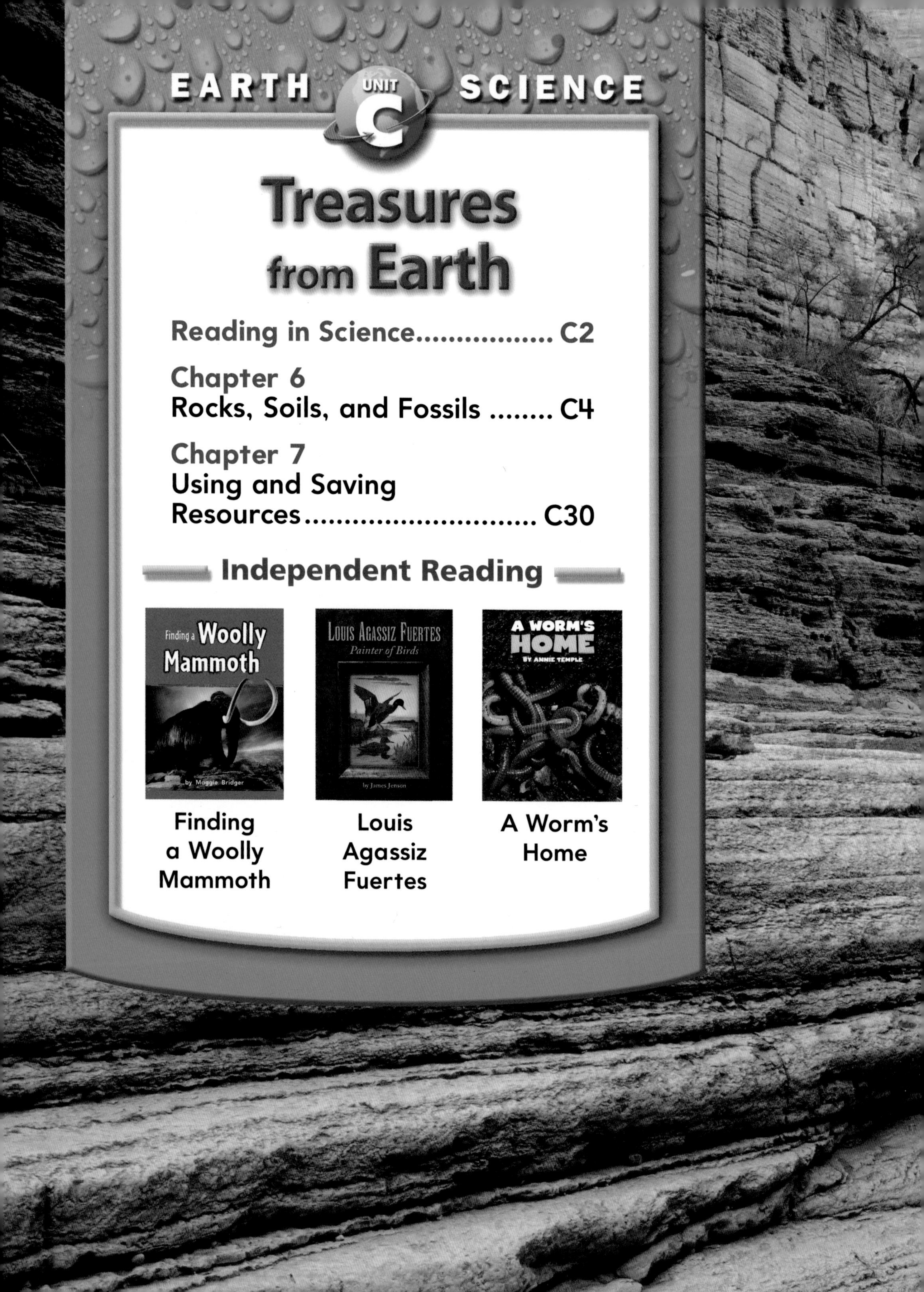

EARTH UNIT C SCIENCE

Treasures from Earth

Independent Reading

Finding a Woolly Mammoth

Louis Agassiz Fuertes

A Worm's Home

Discover!
When can you see through rocks?
Think about this question as you read. You will have the answer by the end of the unit.

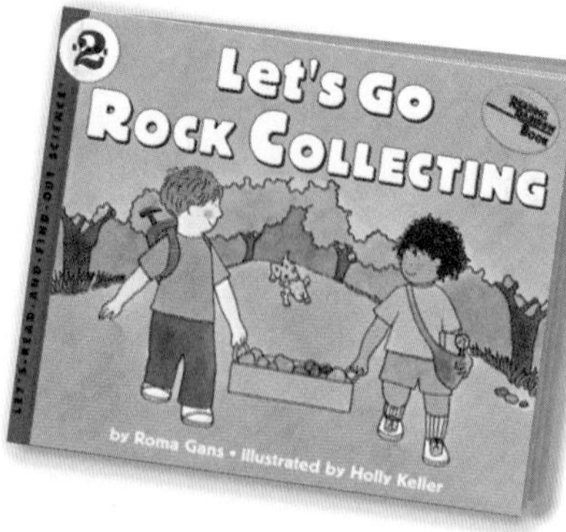

Let's Go Rock Collecting

by Roma Gans
illustrated by Holly Keller

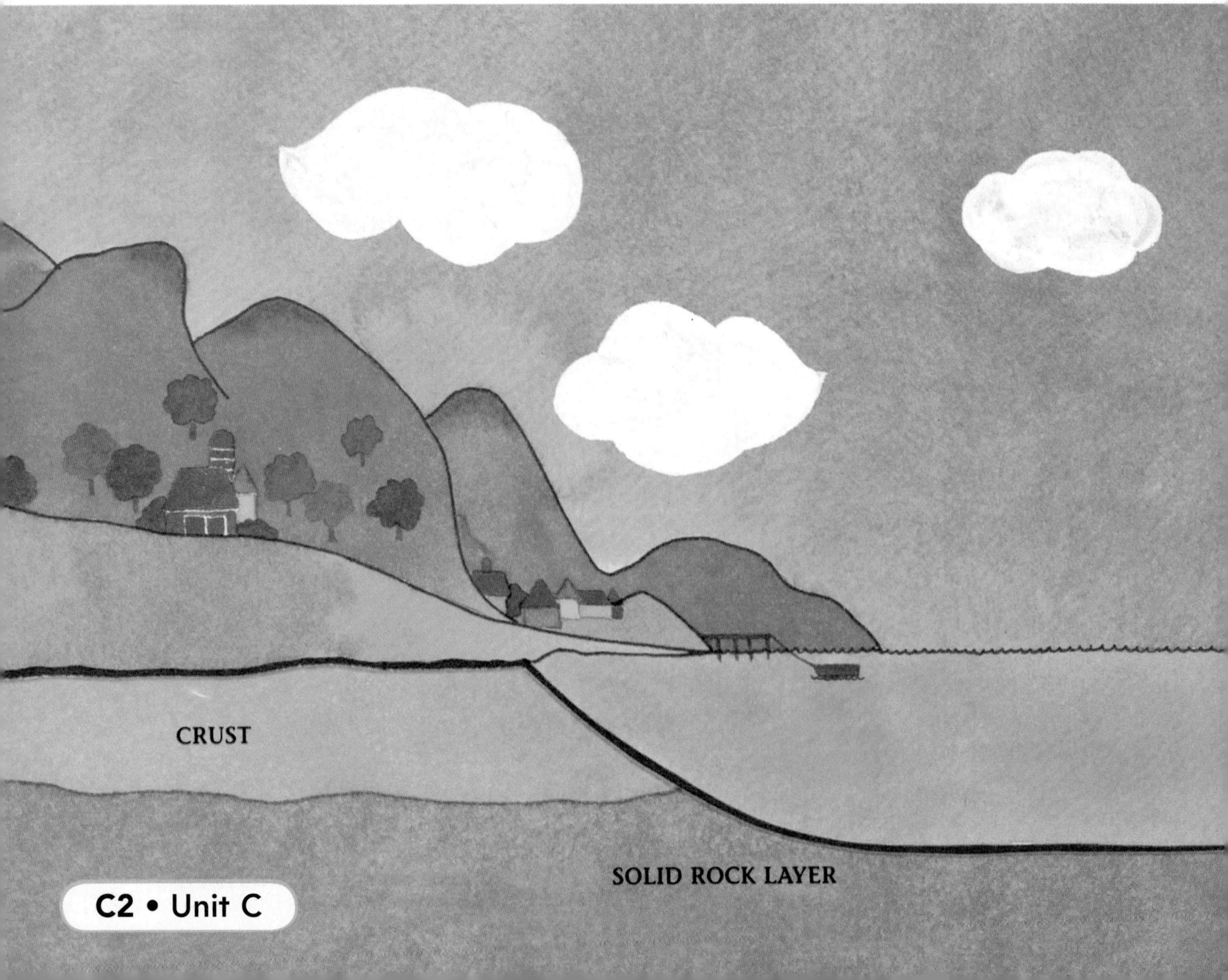

CRUST

SOLID ROCK LAYER

Reading in Science

Strategy: Predict

Rocks cover the whole earth. No matter where you live, you live on rock.

There is rock under city streets and country farms. And there is rock under every ocean, lake, and river.

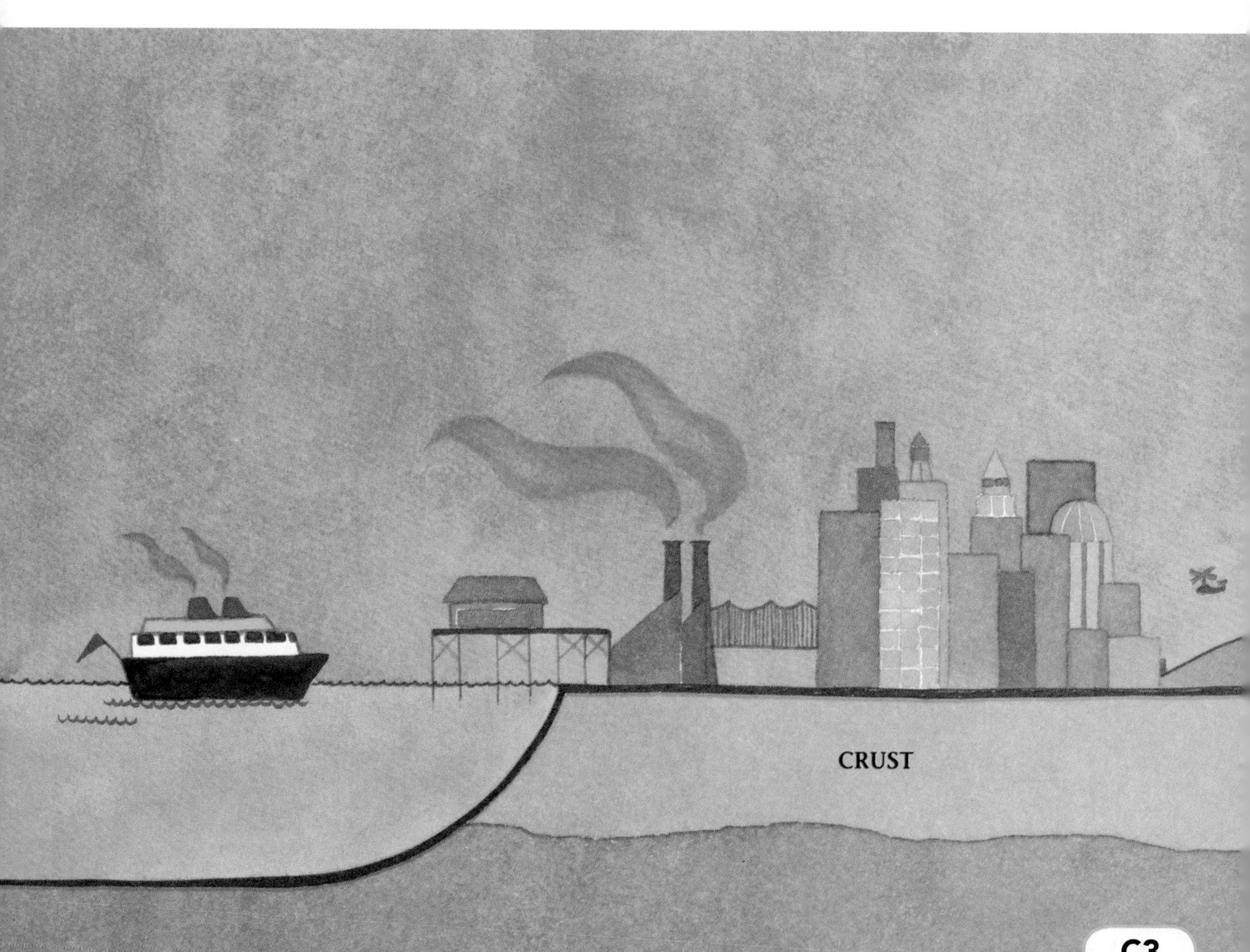

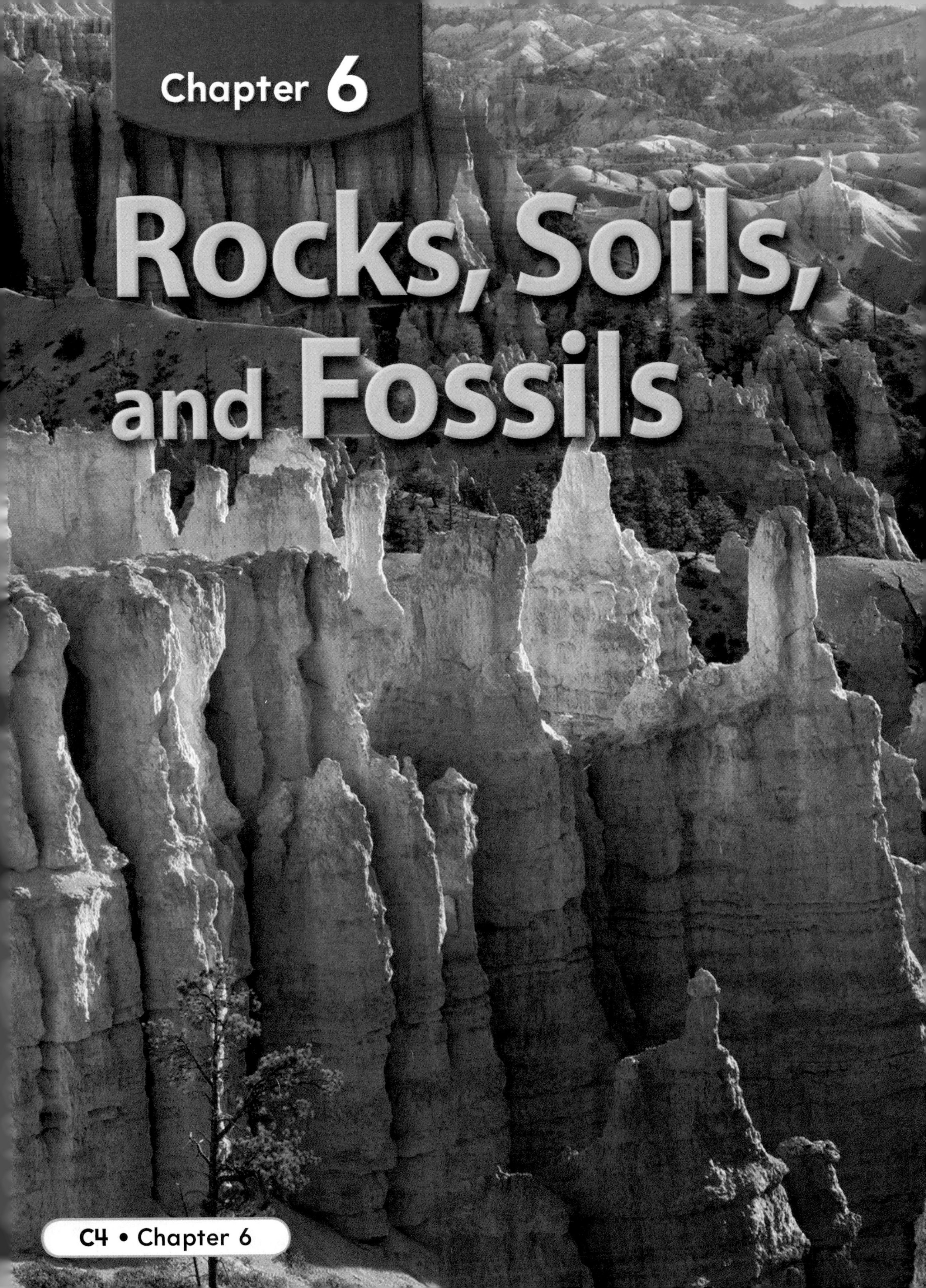

Chapter 6

Rocks, Soils, and Fossils

Vocabulary Preview

mineral
rock
soil
humus
weathering
erosion
gravity
fossil
imprint

rock

A rock is a solid made of one or more minerals.

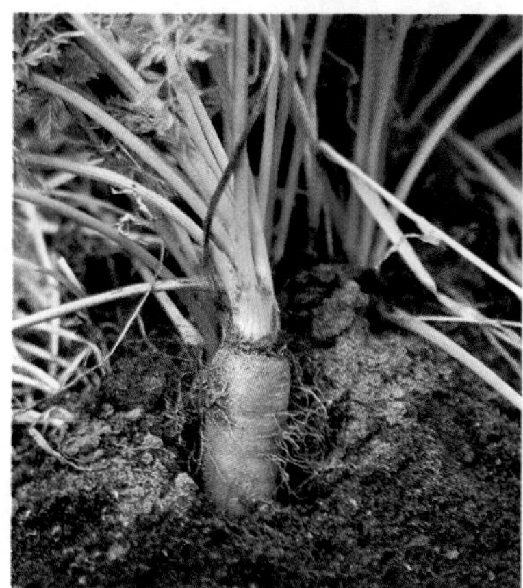

soil

Soil is the loose material that covers Earth's surface.

weathering

Weathering is the wearing away and breaking apart of rock.

fossil

A fossil is something that remains of a living thing from long ago.

Lesson 1

What Makes Up Rocks and Soils?

Science and You

Knowing about rocks and soils helps you know how they can be used.

Inquiry Skill

Communicate Share information with others.

What You Need

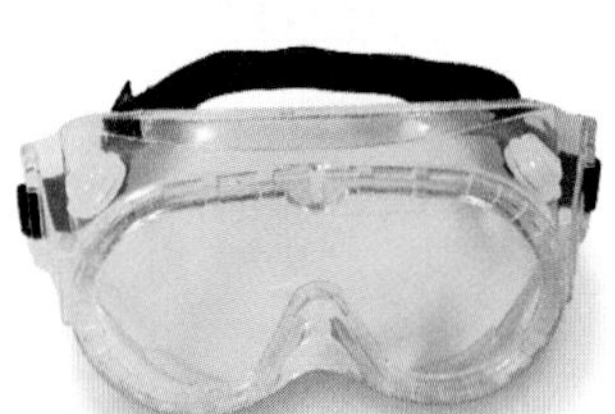

goggles

rock samples

soil samples

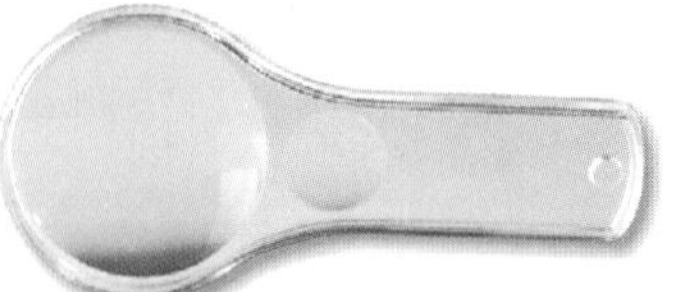

hand lens

Investigate

Compare Samples

Steps

1. **Observe** Use a hand lens. Look at the rock samples. Notice their color. Feel them. **Safety:** Wear goggles!

2. **Record Data** Draw each rock. Write how each one looks and feels.

3. Repeat steps 1 and 2 with the soil samples. **Safety:** Wash your hands!

4. **Communicate** Share your data with a classmate. Talk about what you observed.

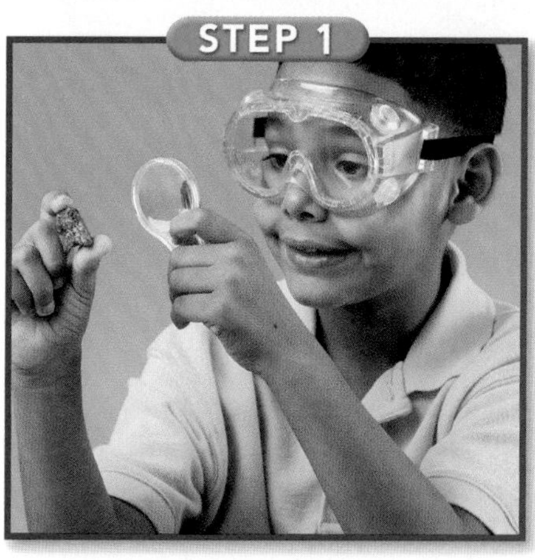

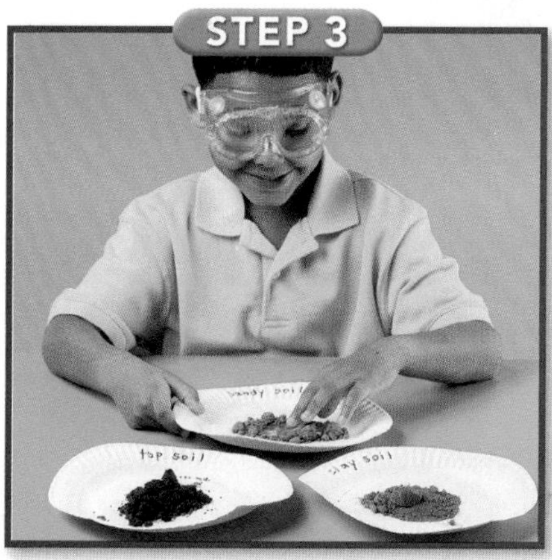

Think and Share

1. **Compare** How are the rocks alike and different? How are the soils alike and different?

2. How are rocks different from soils? How are rocks like soils?

Investigate More!

Be an Inventor Think of a new way that a rock could be used in your home. Try out your idea. Explain how it works.

Learn by Reading

Vocabulary

mineral

rock

soil

humus

Reading Skill

Compare and Contrast

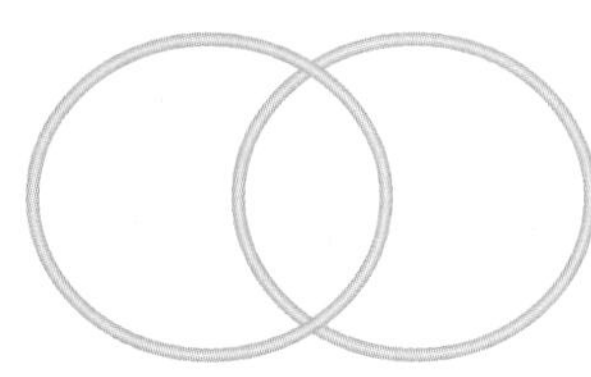

Rocks

Earth is made up of land and water. The surface of Earth is made of different kinds of solid materials. A **mineral** is a nonliving solid found in nature. There are many kinds of minerals.

Minerals join in different ways to form different kinds of rocks. A **rock** is a solid made of one or more minerals.

What parts of Earth's surface do you see?

Each kind of rock is different from other rocks. Some rocks are dark colors. Others are light colors. Some rocks are very hard. Others are softer. Rocks can be big or small.

Different kinds of rocks are used in different ways. People often carve softer rocks into statues. They use hard rocks to make buildings and tabletops. Minerals from some rocks are used in jewelry.

COMPARE AND CONTRAST How are different kinds of rocks used differently?

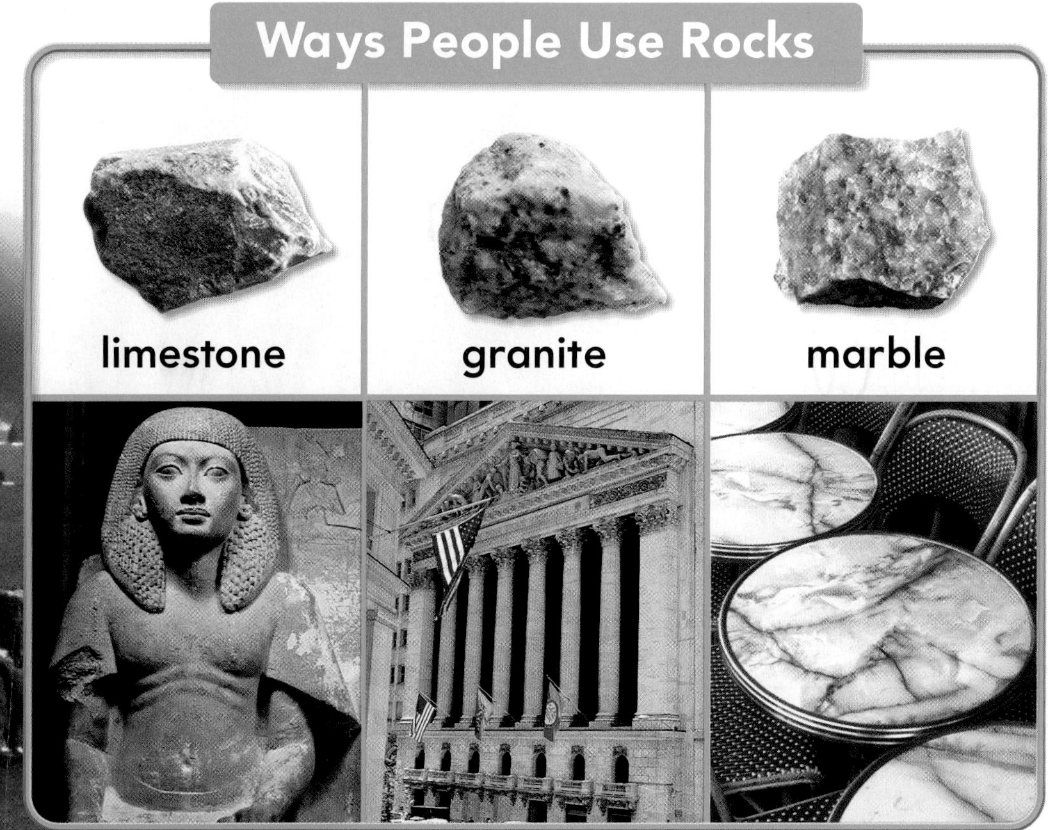

Soils

Soil is the loose material that covers Earth's surface. Soil contains bits of rock, humus, air, and water. **Humus** is tiny bits of dead plants and animals in soil. Humus contains nutrients, or materials that help a plant grow well.

Layers of Soil

Top Layer
This layer is rich in humus. Plants grow here.

Middle Layer
This layer has less humus. Small rocks collect here.

Bottom Layer
Tree roots can grow down into this layer of larger rocks.

clay soil

sandy soil

topsoil

Soil is important to all living things. Plants get the water and nutrients they need from soil. In turn, animals get energy from plants. Some kinds of soil are better than others for the growth of certain kinds of plants.

COMPARE AND CONTRAST How are the three layers of soil different?

Lesson Wrap-Up

1. **Vocabulary** What is a **mineral**?
2. **Reading Skill** How are rocks different from soils?
3. **Communicate** Why is soil important to all living things?

Technology Visit **www.eduplace.com/scp/** to find out more about rocks and soils.

George Washington Carver

Agriculturist

George Washington Carver was a scientist who found ways to improve crops for farmers.

Cotton plants grow well in the soil of the southern United States. Farmers planted cotton in the same fields for years. The plants took nutrients away from the soil. Over time, few nutrients were left.

Carver told farmers about rotating crops. He said that planting a different crop would put nutrients back in the soil. Farmers grew peanuts in their fields. The next year, the soil had the nutrients to grow cotton again.

Some farmers rotate these three different crops over a four-year cycle.

cotton field

Sharing Ideas

1. **Write About It** Why do some farmers rotate crops?
2. **Talk About It** How could you find out which crops grow best in the soil where you live?

Lesson 2

How Do Rock and Soil Change?

Science and You

Knowing what causes changes can help you understand why rocks have different shapes.

Inquiry Skill

Work Together You can work with a team to share ideas and still think for yourself about what you observe.

What You Need

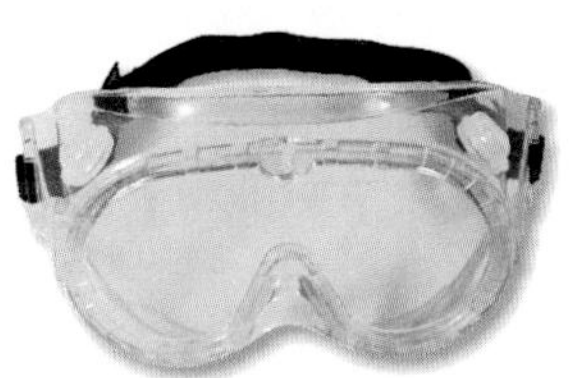

goggles

sand and topsoil

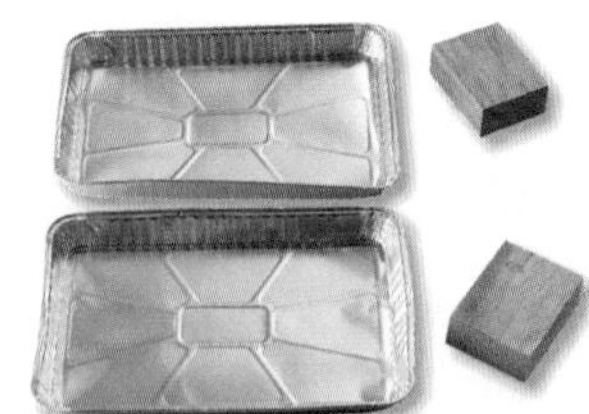

2 pans and 2 blocks

2 cups of water

Investigate

Change the Land

Steps

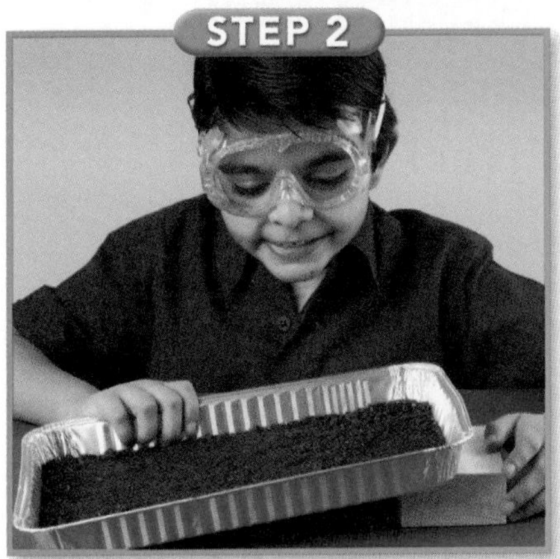

1. Put topsoil in one pan and the same amount of sand in the other pan. **Safety:** Wear goggles!
2. **Use Models** Put a block under one end of each pan to model two hillsides.
3. Slowly pour water down each hill at the same time.
4. **Observe** Watch as the water flows down the hillsides. Look for differences. **Safety:** Wash your hands!

Think and Share

1. **Communicate** What differences did you see as the water flowed through each pan?
2. **Infer** Would topsoil or sand stay longer on a hillside in a rainstorm? Tell why.

Investigate More!

Work Together During the year, record changes you see to the school grounds. Talk about what you think caused the changes.

Learn by Reading

Vocabulary

weathering

erosion

gravity

Reading Skill

Cause and Effect

Weathering

Earth's surface is always changing. Some changes, such as weathering, can be slow. **Weathering** is the wearing away and breaking apart of rock. Wind, water, and plants can cause weathering. Rock can break into smaller pieces over and over again. Then the little bits of rock can become part of soil.

CAUSE AND EFFECT What are three causes of weathering?

Wind and water caused parts of this rock to wear away.

▲ This rock was broken apart by ice.

Water moved across these rocks. Their edges are now rounded. ▼

Roots grew into cracks in this rock. The roots split the rock into pieces.

Erosion

Another change to Earth's surface is erosion. **Erosion** is the carrying of weathered rock and soil from place to place. Water, wind, and gravity can cause erosion. **Gravity** is a pull toward the center of Earth.

Gravity causes water to run downhill. Water moving downhill in a river can move rocks and soil. Frozen water in the form of a glacier can slowly move rock and soil down a mountain.

CAUSE AND EFFECT What causes erosion?

Ocean waves crash onto the shore. Some land is pulled away as the waves move back to the ocean.

Strong gusts of wind pick up sandy soil and move it to new places. ▶

Lesson Wrap-Up

1. **Vocabulary** What is **erosion**?
2. **Reading Skill** How can plants cause weathering?
3. **Work Together** Why is sharing ideas with others helpful?

Technology Visit **www.eduplace.com/scp/** to find out more about weathering.

Lesson 3

What Are Fossils?

Science and You

If you look carefully at some kinds of rocks, you might find a fossil.

Inquiry Skill

Infer Use what you observe and know to tell what you think.

What You Need

plate

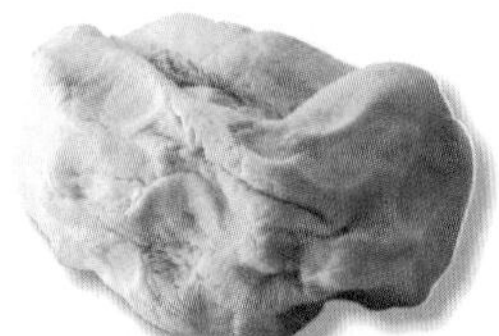
salt dough

objects from nature

Investigate

Make Imprints

Steps

1. Flatten some dough on a plate.

2. **Use Models** Choose two objects. Press each object into the dough to make an imprint.

3. **Infer** Trade plates with a classmate. Infer which object was used to make each imprint.

Think and Share

1. **Communicate** Tell what clues helped you decide which object made each imprint.
2. What can you learn about an object by looking at only an imprint?

Investigate More!

Work Together Look for imprints near your school. Share ideas about what made the imprints.

Learn by Reading

Vocabulary

fossil

imprint

Reading Skill

Sequence

How Fossils Form

Scientists learn about once-living things by studying fossils. A **fossil** is something that remains of a living thing from long ago. Fossils form in different ways.

Some fossils are imprints. When a living thing presses down in soft mud, it leaves a shape in the mud. Over time the mud turns to rock. The shape of a living thing found in rock is an **imprint.**

How Casts Form

1 A living thing dies and is buried in mud. The mud turns to rock.

2 The hard part of the living thing breaks down. Its imprint is left in rock.

Some fossils are hard parts of animals, such as bones or teeth. After the animals died, layers of mud covered them. The soft parts rotted away. Over millions of years, the hard parts turned to rock. These are some of the fossils that people find today.

SEQUENCE How does a bone become a fossil?

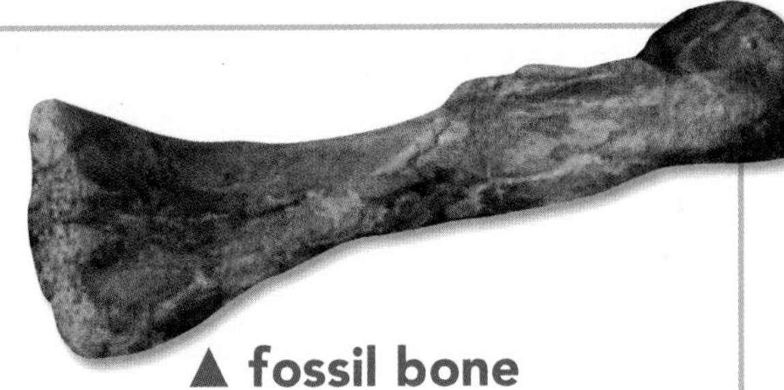

▲ fossil bone

▲ leaf imprint

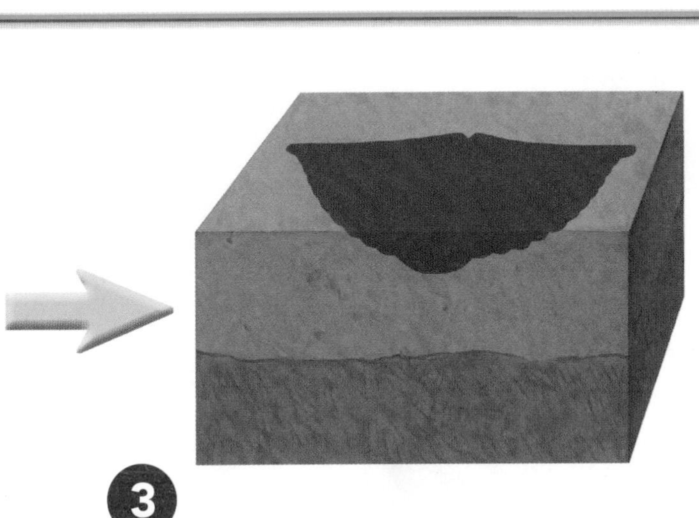

3

If mud or minerals fill the imprint, a cast forms.

Learning from Fossils

Fossils give clues about plants and animals that lived long ago. Some of those plants and animals, such as dinosaurs, no longer live on Earth.

Fossil bones give information about the size of an animal. Fossil teeth show whether an animal ate plants or meat. Imprints and casts show how a plant or an animal looked. Tracks show how an animal moved from place to place.

COMPARE AND CONTRAST What can different fossils tell us about animals?

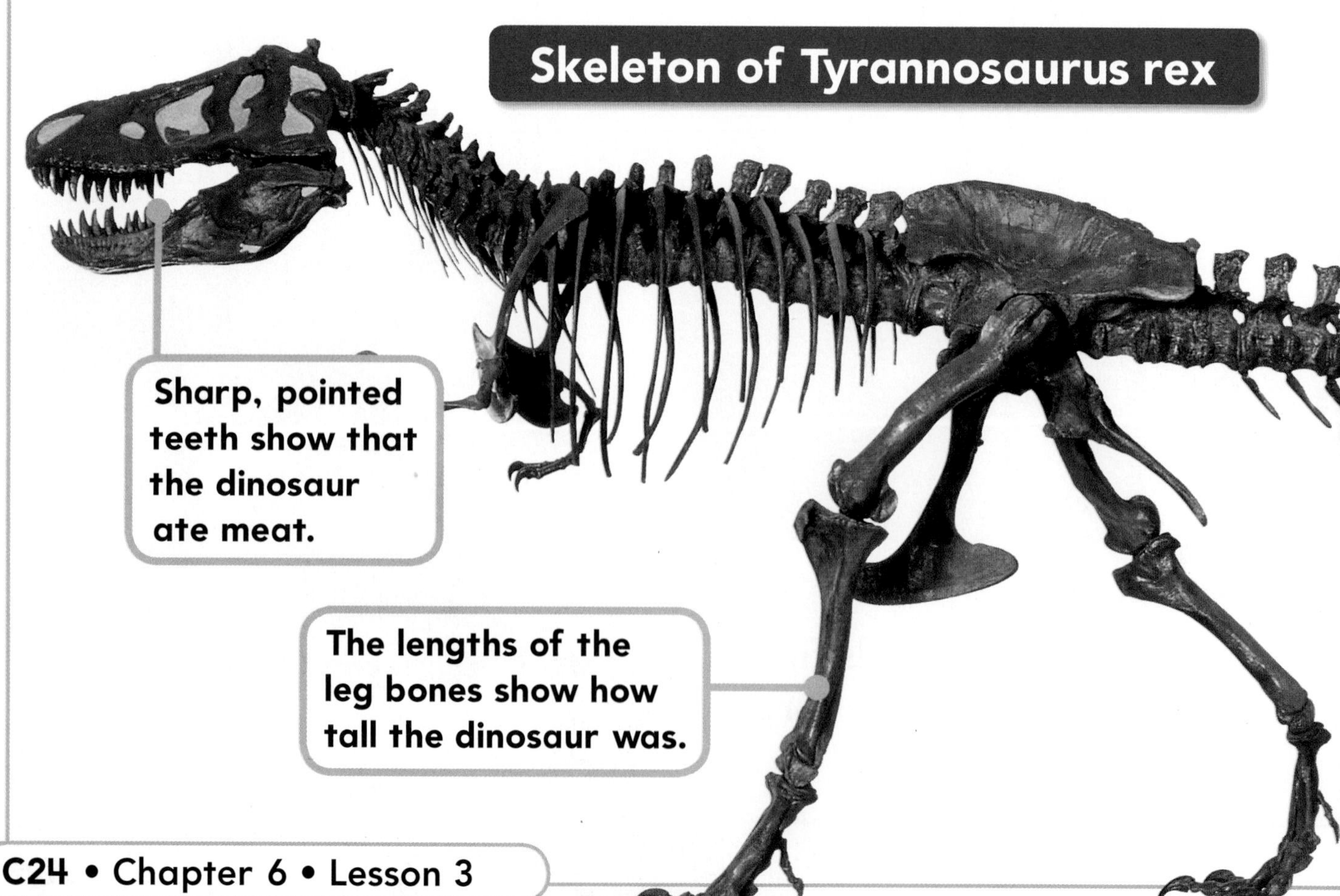

How might an artist know what a dinosaur looked like?

Footprints give clues about the weight and speed of the dinosaur.

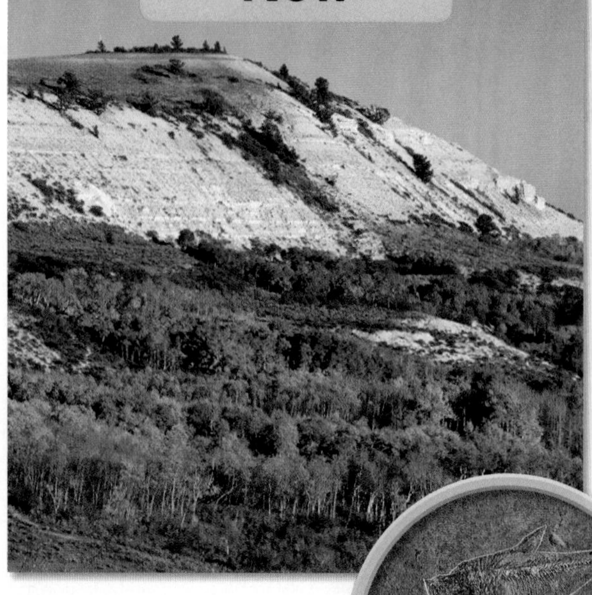

The land where these fossils were found was probably once under water. ▶

Clues to Earth's Past

Scientists study fossils to learn how places on Earth have changed over time. A fish lives in water. When a fossil of a fish is found on land, scientists can infer that the land was once covered by water.

Lesson Wrap-Up

1. **Vocabulary** What is a **fossil**?
2. **Reading Skill** How does a fossil imprint form?
3. **Infer** What can you infer from this fossil tooth?

Technology Visit **www.eduplace.com/scp/** to find out more about fossils.

LINKS for Home and School

Math Read a Bar Graph

The graph shows the lengths of four dinosaurs.

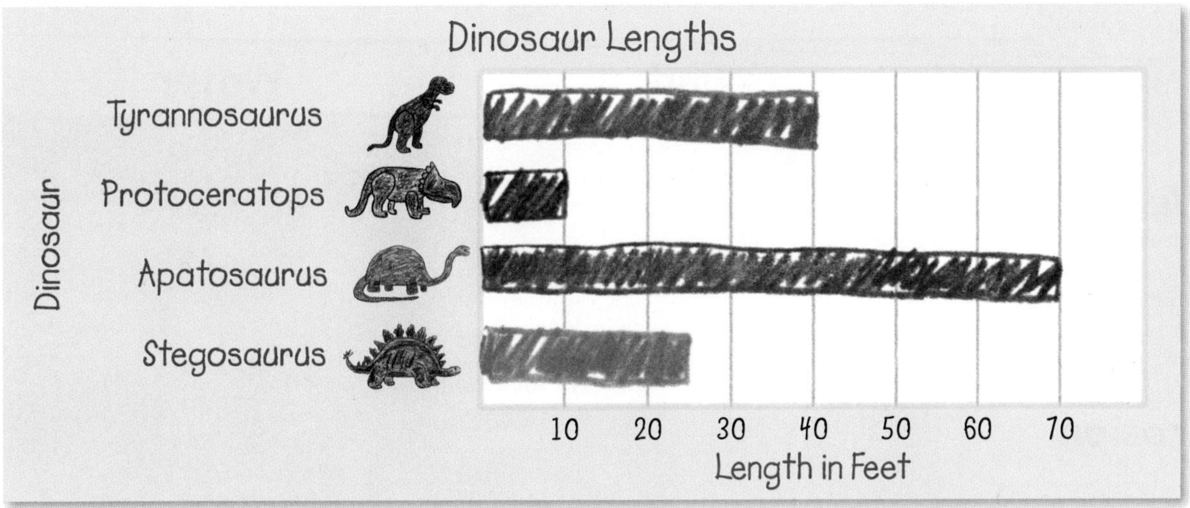

1. List the dinosaurs from shortest to longest.
2. About how many protoceratops lined up would equal the length of a tyrannosaurus?

Social Studies Land and Water

This picture shows a view of Earth from space. Compare it to a world map.

1. Find and name Earth's seven continents.
2. Find and name Earth's four oceans.

Review and Test Prep

Visual Summary

Earth's surface changes because of weathering and erosion.

Causes of Weathering and Erosion

Cause	Wind	Water
Weathering		
Erosion	 SAND	

Main Ideas

1. Tell about two of the solids that the surface of Earth is made of. **(p. C8)**
2. Why is humus in soil important? **(p. C10)**
3. How does weathering change Earth's surface? **(p. C16)**
4. Why do scientists study fossils? **(pp. C24–C26)**

Vocabulary

Choose the correct word from the box.

rock (p. C8)
soil (p. C10)
humus (p. C10)
erosion (p. C18)

5. The carrying of weathered rock and soil from place to place
6. Tiny bits of dead plants and animals in soil
7. A solid made of one or more minerals
8. The loose material that covers Earth's surface

Test Practice

Choose a word to complete the sentence.

9. _____ is a pull toward the center of Earth.

Weathering Mineral Soil Gravity

Using Science Skills

10. **Infer** What can you infer about a rock that has smooth edges?

11. **Critical Thinking** What could scientists tell about a desert if they found an imprint of a large leaf there?

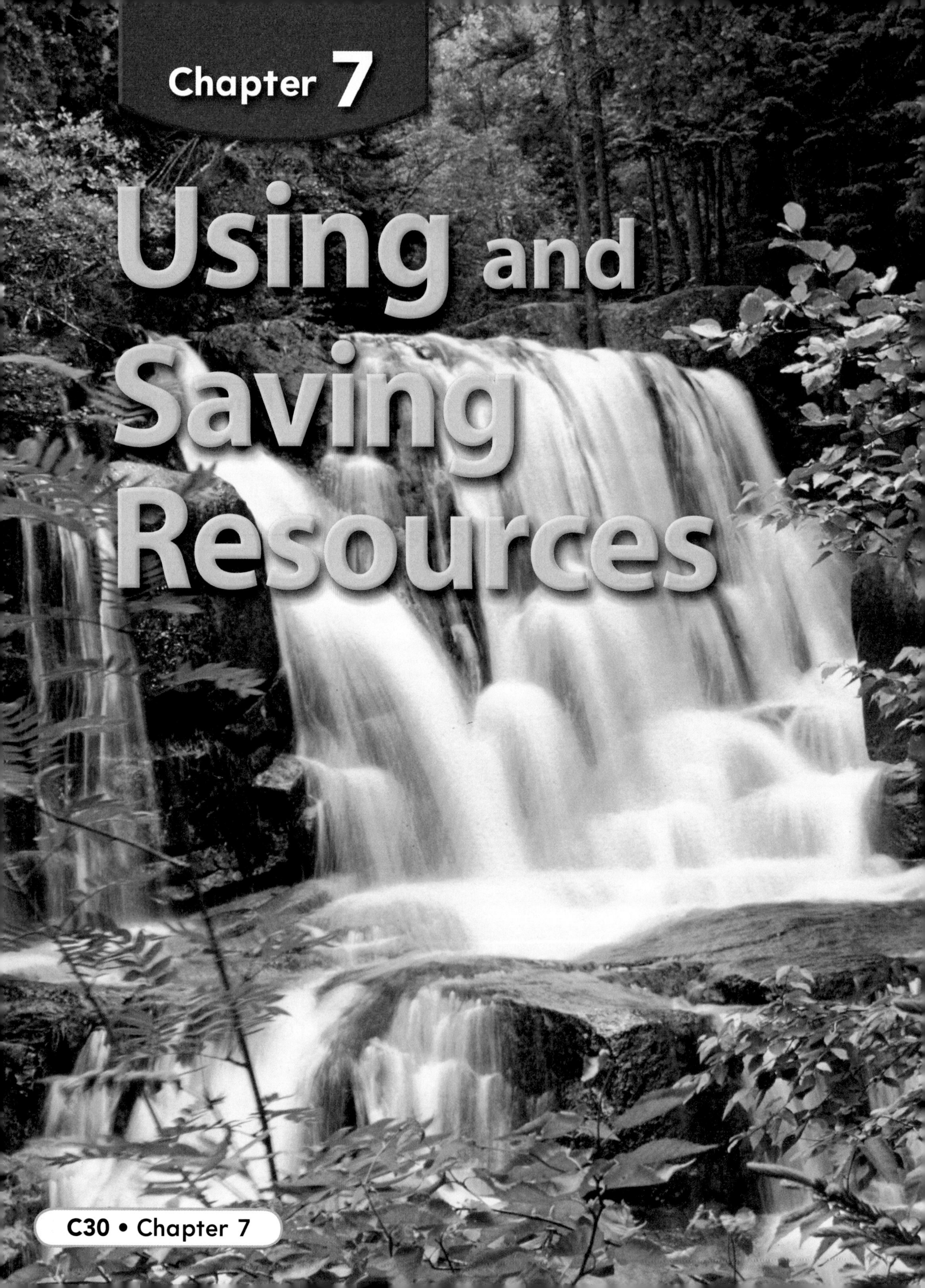

Chapter 7

Using and Saving Resources

Vocabulary Preview

natural resource
pollution
litter
conserve
recycle
reuse

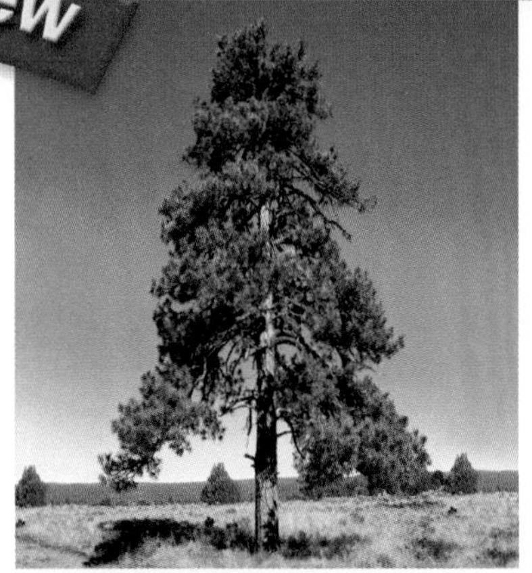

natural resource

A natural resource is something found in nature that people need or use.

pollution

Pollution is waste that harms the land, water, or air.

recycle

When you recycle, you collect items made of materials that can be used to make new items.

reuse

When you reuse something, you use it again and again.

Lesson 1

What Resources Do People Use?

Science and You

Knowing how to save natural resources can help you enjoy them.

Inquiry Skill

Observe Use your senses to find out about something.

What You Need

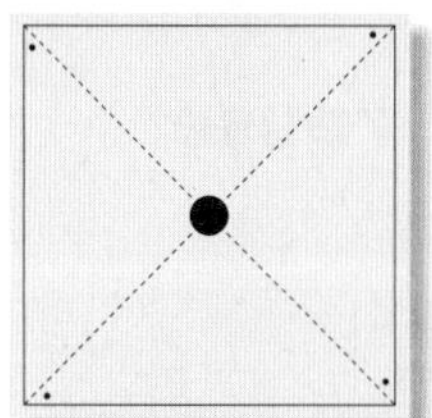

pinwheel pattern

scissors

pencil

pushpin

Investigate

Make a Pinwheel

Steps

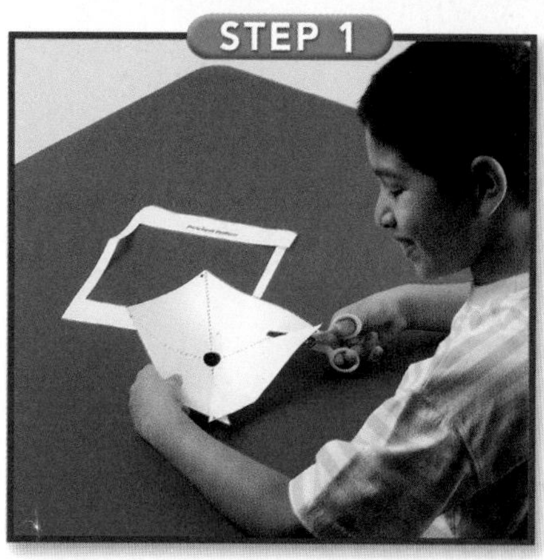
STEP 1

STEP 2

STEP 3

1. Cut along the solid lines of the pinwheel pattern. Then cut along the dashed lines stopping at the center circle. **Safety:** Scissors and pushpins are sharp!

2. Put a pushpin through the four dots and the center circle. Then put it into the eraser of a pencil.

3. **Observe** Blow lightly on the pinwheel. Then blow hard on it. Observe what happens.

Think and Share

1. **Infer** What made the pinwheel spin?

2. **Compare** How did the pinwheel move differently each time you blew? Tell why.

Investigate More!

Experiment Plan and try other ways to make the pinwheel spin. Observe how fast it spins each time. Share your results.

Learn by Reading

Vocabulary

natural resource

Reading Skill

Categorize and Classify

Natural Resources

A **natural resource** is something found in nature that people need or use. Air, water, soil, and rocks are some natural resources.

People get water from rivers and lakes to use for drinking, washing, and cooking. They use soil for growing food. Sometimes people use rocks to build their homes.

How does your family use water?

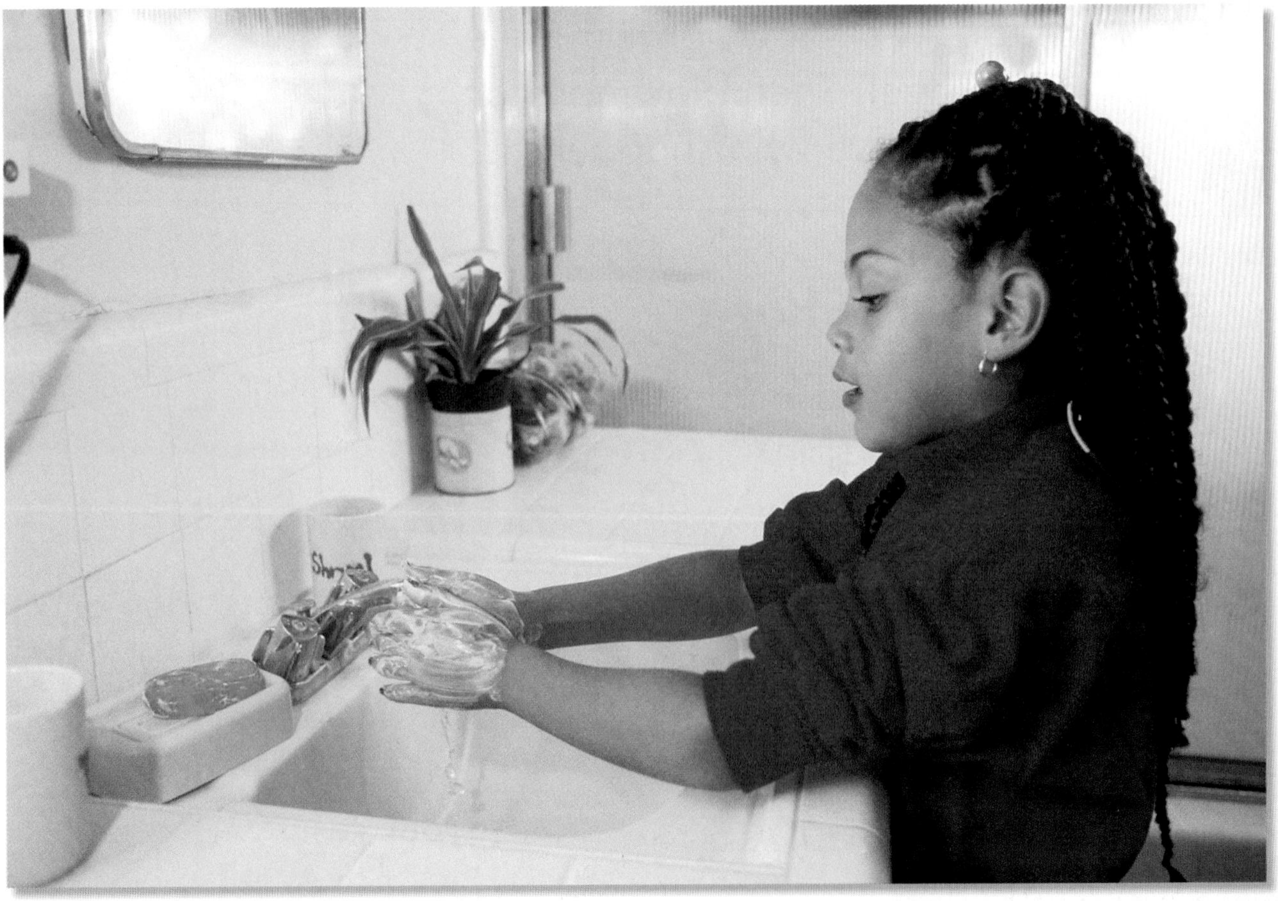

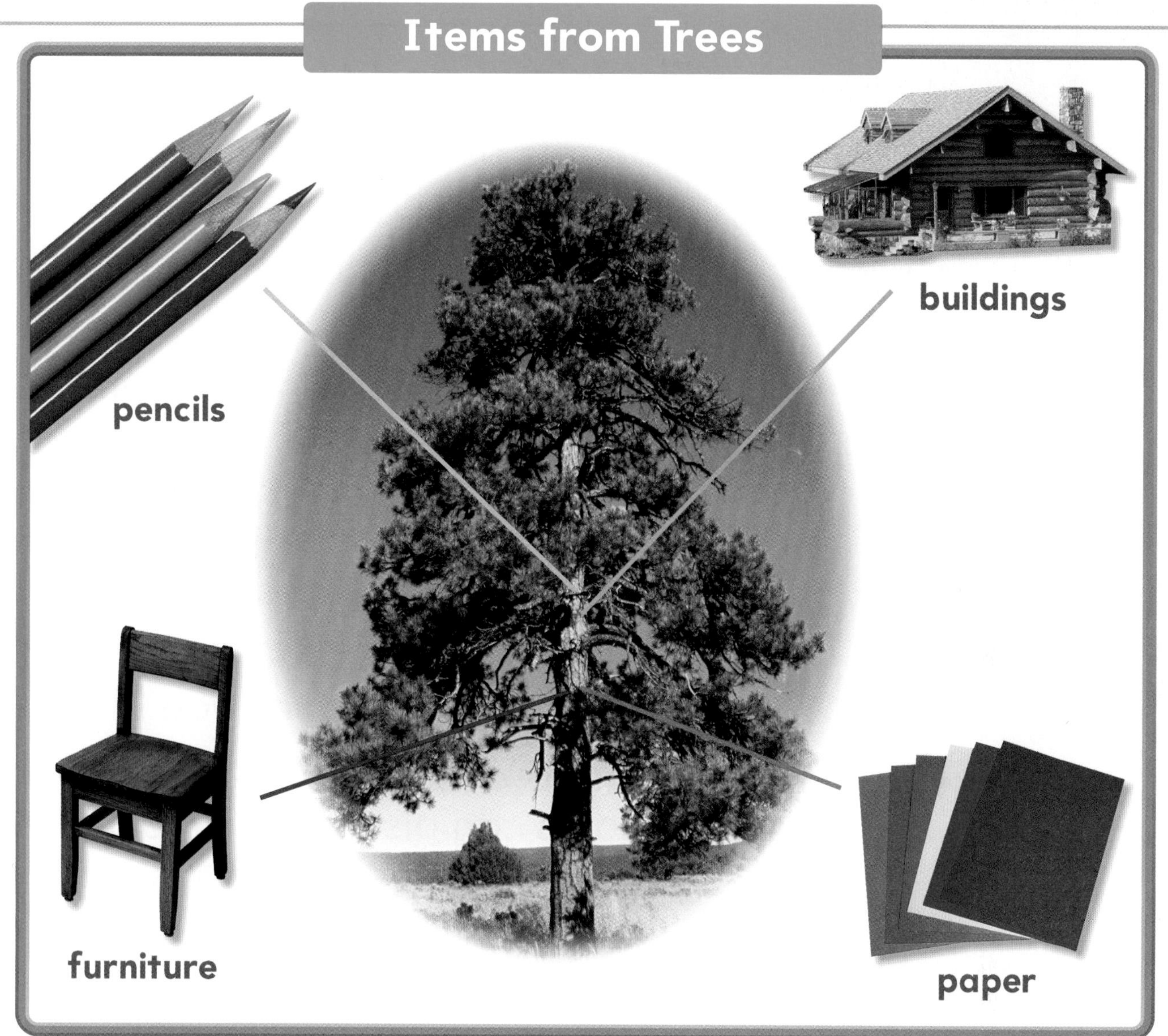

Trees and other plants are natural resources, too. People get many foods and medicines from plants. People also use trees for many things. New trees need to be planted to replace the ones that are cut down. This will help make sure that there will be enough trees to meet our needs.

CLASSIFY What are three natural resources?

Electricity and Heat

People use some natural resources to make electricity and heat. Most machines that make electricity are powered by steam. Burning coal makes this steam.

▲ Hoover Dam

Wind and moving water can also power machines that make electricity. The blades of a wind turbine spin in the same way that a pinwheel spins when you blow on it. Moving water that collects in dams can also power machines that make electricity.

▼ wind turbines on a wind farm

Some people collect sunlight in a solar collector. The light is changed to heat. The heat warms water in pipes. Then the water warms the air in the house.

▲ solar collector

Wood, oil, coal, and gas are kinds of fuel. When they are burned, they give off heat. The heat is used to warm homes and to cook food.

▲ gas stove

CLASSIFY Which resources make heat?

Lesson Wrap-Up

1. **Vocabulary** What is a **natural resource**?
2. **Reading Skill** Which resources help make electricity?
3. **Observe** On which part of a house would you be likely to see solar collectors? Tell why.

Technology Visit **www.eduplace.com/scp/** to find out more about natural resources.

People and Resources

What are resources? Find out with the Scott family.

Cast

Mom

Dad

Grandma

Jon

Beth

Grandma: I have tomatoes from my garden for our salad.

Dad: Salad will taste great with the pasta I am cooking.

Mom: Beth, your costume for tonight's school play is ready.

Jon: What is the play about?

Beth: It's called **People and Resources**.
I play an ear of corn that is used to make cornbread and tortillas.

Jon: An ear of corn? Mom, do I have to go?

Mom: Yes, Jon. The play will help you understand how people use natural resources.

Jon: I know all about natural resources.

Beth: Really? How are we using natural resources right now?

Jon: Let's start with plants. Our salad is made from plant parts. The pasta is made from flour that came from parts of a plant.

Dad: Not bad. Not bad at all.

Jon: The cloth in Beth's costume is made from parts of a plant. Even the pages of a book are made from plant parts.

Grandma: Don't stop! You're on a roll.

Jon: Dad is cooking with gas. Gas is a natural resource that is burned to make heat.

Beth: Don't forget about the water that Dad is using in the pasta pot.

Mom: I guess you do know about natural resources. But there is still a very good reason to go to the play.

Jon: What's that?

Grandma: To show you care about your little sister!

Jon: Okay, I'll go. It should be a very **corny** evening.

Sharing Ideas

1. **Write About It** What would your life be like without plants? Write a story about it.
2. **Talk About It** What other natural resources do you use in your home?

Lesson 2

How Do People Change the Environment?

Science and You

Picking up litter is a positive change that you can make in an environment.

Inquiry Skill

Experiment When you experiment, you choose the items you will need and plan the steps you will follow.

What You Need

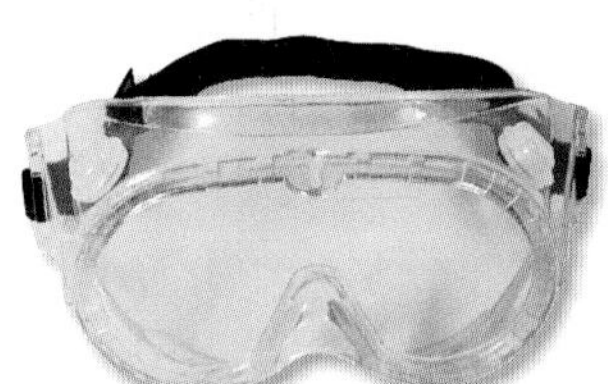

goggles

2 funnels and 2 filters

2 jars and water

2 soil samples and 2 spoons

Investigate

Look for Pollution

Steps

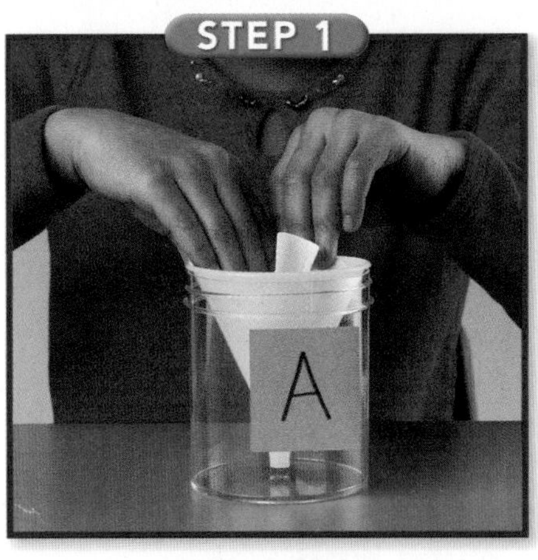

1. Place a funnel in each jar, and then put a filter in each funnel.

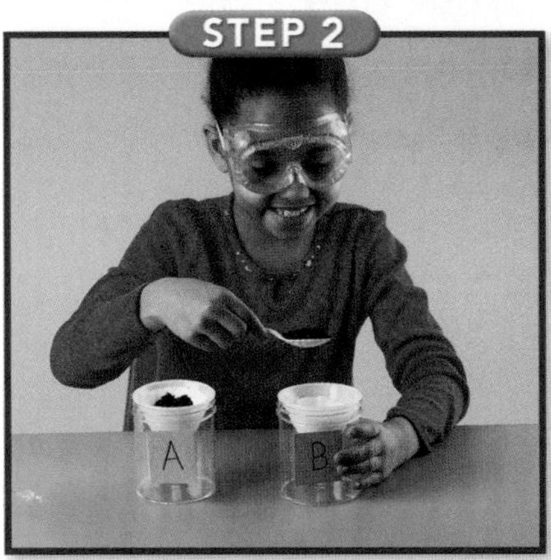

2. **Use Models** Put a spoonful of soil A in jar A. Put a spoonful of soil B in jar B. The jars are environments. **Safety:** Wear goggles!

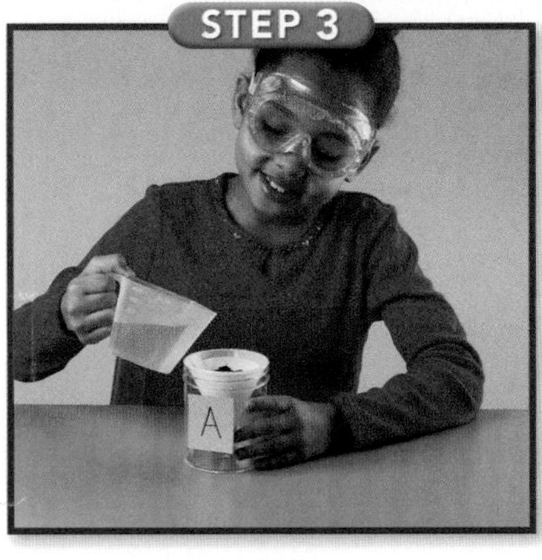

3. **Compare** Pour some water onto the soil in each jar. The water is rain. Tell how each environment changes.

Think and Share

1. **Communicate** Which soil do you think might be polluted? Tell why.
2. **Infer** Can soil pollution always be seen? How do you know?

Investigate More!

Experiment Predict what will happen if you pour colored water into the soil in jar B. Try it. Tell about your results.

Learn by Reading

Vocabulary

pollution

litter

Reading Skill

Cause and Effect

People Make Changes

When people use natural resources, they cause changes in the environment. Rivers change when people build dams to collect water. Forests change when people cut down trees to build houses and roads.

Some trash that you throw away goes to a landfill. A landfill is a low area of land where trash is buried. Some landfills are getting too full.

▼ landfill

▲ changing the forest

People can cause harm to their environment with pollution. **Pollution** is waste that harms the land, water, or air. Pollution also can harm plants and make people and animals sick.

Pollution has many causes. Gases from cars and factories cause air pollution. Oil and other harmful waste spilled in water cause water pollution. **Litter**, or trash on the ground, causes land pollution.

▲ water pollution

CAUSE AND EFFECT What are three causes of pollution?

Positive Changes

People can make changes that help their environment. Riding a bike or walking instead of driving a car can help prevent air pollution. Picking up litter can help prevent land and water pollution. It also can protect plants and animals. Planting trees can help the land. It can give some animals shelter.

CAUSE AND EFFECT **What are some effects of picking up litter?**

Planting a community garden can help the environment.

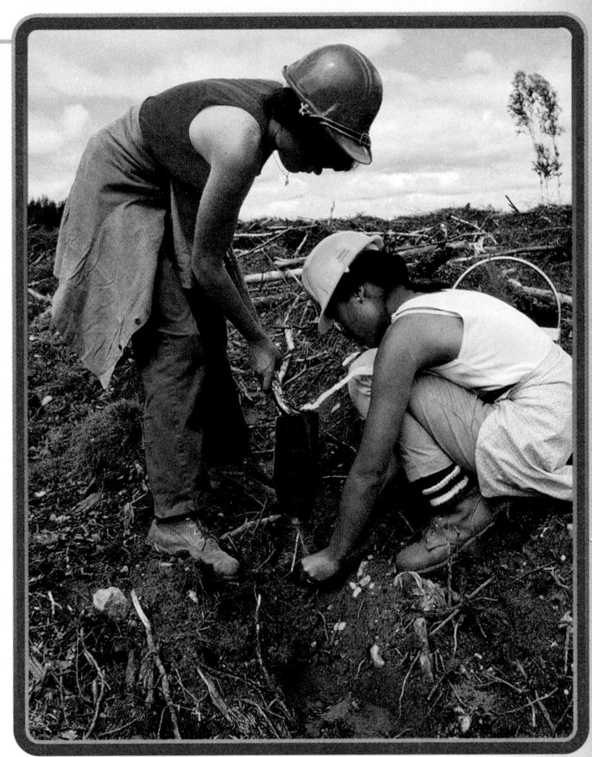

People can plant seedlings to replace trees after a fire.

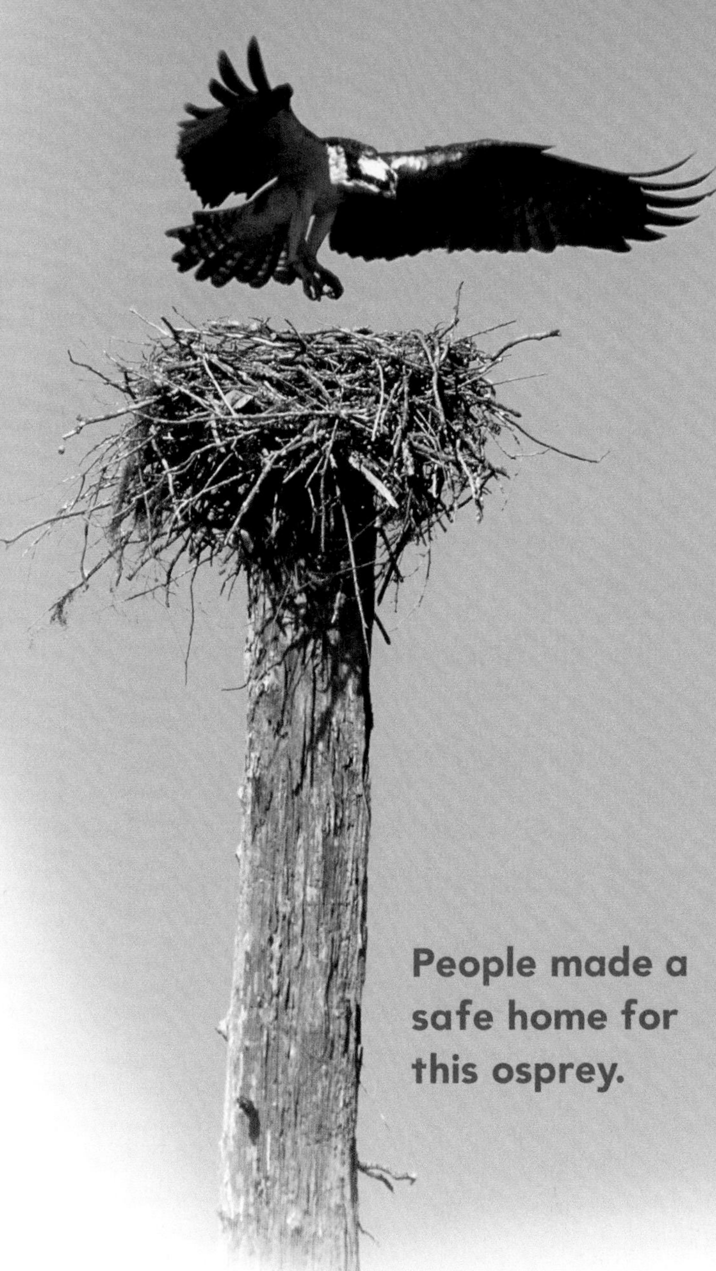

People made a safe home for this osprey.

Lesson Wrap-Up

1. **Vocabulary** What is the name for trash on the ground that causes land pollution?
2. **Reading Skill** What are some things that people do that harm the environment?
3. **Experiment** What are two things that you do when you experiment?

Technology Visit **www.eduplace.com/scp/** to find out more about pollution.

Lesson 3

How Can People Save Resources?

Science and You

You can help save resources by using things again.

Inquiry Skill

Use Numbers Use numbers to describe and compare events.

What You Need

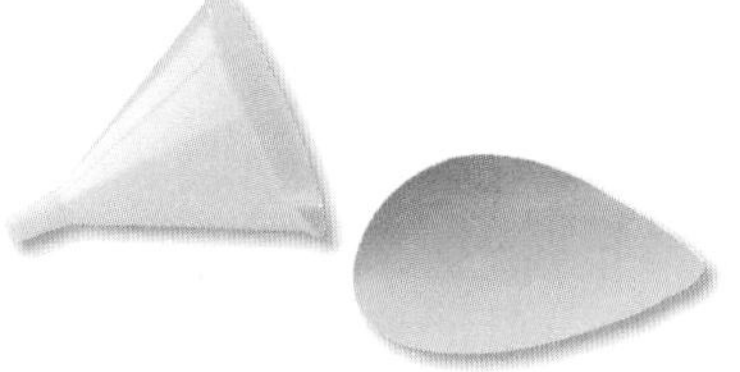

funnel and filter

graduated cylinder and water

pan

stopwatch

Investigate

Wasted Water

Steps

1. **Use Models** Put a filter in a funnel. Put the funnel in the top of a cylinder. The funnel is a model of a leaky faucet.

2. Stand the cylinder in a pan. Pour some water into the funnel. Wait one minute.

3. **Measure** Remove the funnel. Measure the amount of water in the cylinder. Record the measurement.

STEP 1

STEP 2

STEP 3

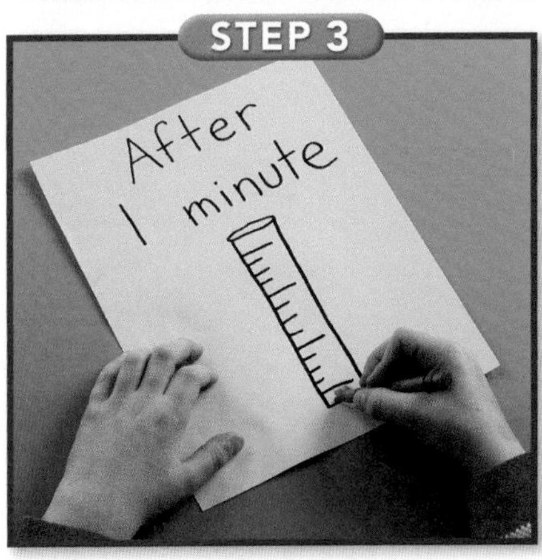

Think and Share

1. **Compare** Share your results with others. How were the results alike or different? Tell why.

2. **Use Numbers** How much water would your leaky faucet waste in 5 minutes?

Investigate More!

Solve a Problem Find out how water is wasted at school. Make a list of ways that the school can waste less water. Share your ideas with the class.

Learn by Reading

Vocabulary

conserve

recycle

reuse

Reading Skill

Draw Conclusions

Conserving Resources

People can conserve Earth's natural resources. When you **conserve** something, you use less of it to make it last longer. Some resources, like gas and oil, cannot be replaced once they have been used. So, people should conserve these resources whenever they can.

Recycling can also help save resources. When you **recycle**, you collect items made of materials that can be used to make new items.

DRAW CONCLUSIONS What might happen if people use too much oil?

When you recycle, less trash goes into a landfill. ▶

Conserving at Home

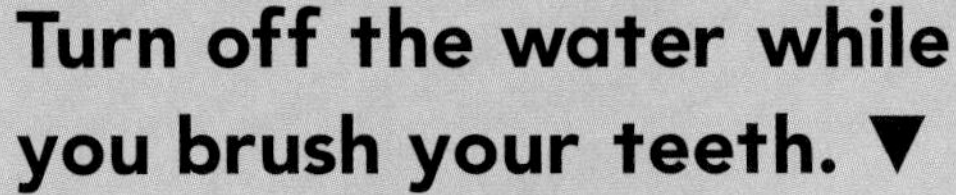

Turn off the water while you brush your teeth. ▼

Turn off lights when you leave a room. ▼

Wash full loads of clothes. ►

Reusing Resources

You can help the environment by reusing items. When you **reuse** something, you use it again and again.

There are many ways that you can reuse resources. You can pack your lunch in the same lunchbox every day. You can use a paper bag to wrap a gift. You can use a plastic bottle to make a bird feeder.

Old tires can be reused on a playground.

Lesson Wrap-Up

1. **Vocabulary** How do you **conserve** resources?
2. **Reading Skill** How does wearing a sweater at home help you conserve resources?
3. **Use Numbers** Why is using numbers helpful when talking about conserving resources?

Technology Visit **www.eduplace.com/scp/** to find out more about conserving resources.

LINKS for Home and School

Math Read a Chart

Mr. Ruiz's class recycled trash in school. The chart shows how many items they collected.

Trash We Collected	
Kind of Trash	Number of Items
Cardboard Boxes	3
Sheets of Paper	31
Plastic Bottles	24

1. Which kind of trash was collected most?
2. How many items did the class collect in all?

Language Arts Thank-you Letter

Find out who in your town keeps the streets clean and the parks free of litter. Write a thank-you letter to a person who helps keep your environment clean.

Dear Mr. Ward,
Thank you for keeping our parks clean. It's so much more fun to play soccer when there is no litter on the field.
Your friend,
Mia

Chapter 7 Review and Test Prep

Visual Summary

Changes that people make to their environment can be helpful or harmful.

Main Ideas

1. How do people use plants? (p. C35)
2. How do people cause pollution? (p. C45)
3. What are two ways to conserve water in your home? (pp. C50–C51)
4. What is one way to reuse something? (p. C52)

Vocabulary

Choose the correct word from the box.

pollution (p. C45)
litter (p. C45)
recycle (p. C50)
reuse (p. C52)

5. Trash on the ground that causes land pollution
6. Waste that harms the land, water, or air
7. To use something again and again
8. To collect items made of materials that can be used to make new items

Test Practice

Choose a word to complete the sentence.

9. A _____ is something found in nature that people need or use.

natural resource   heat   litter   pollution

Using Science Skills

10. **Observe** What are two ways that you can observe pollution?

11. **Critical Thinking** How can you conserve the amount of paper you use in school?

Discover!

When can you see through rocks?

You can see through rocks if the rocks are made into glass. First, sand, limestone, and soda ash are mixed together. They are put in a hot furnace until they melt. Then, as the mixture cools, glass objects can be formed.

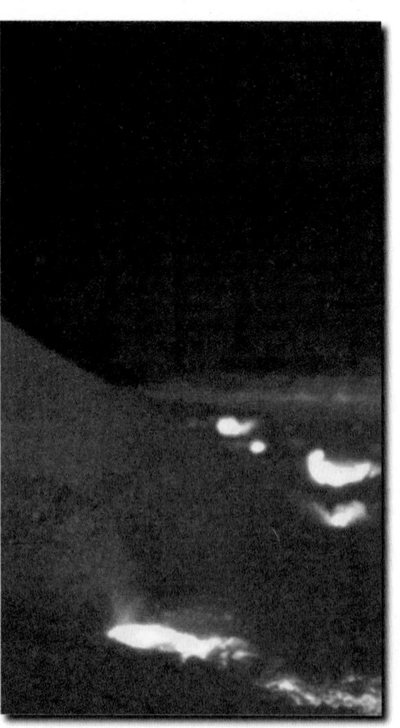

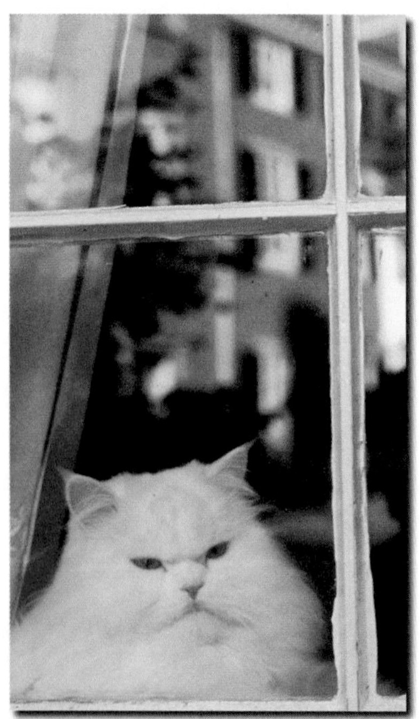

Go to **www.eduplace.com/scp/** to solve more rock riddles.

EARTH  SCIENCE

UNIT D

Patterns in the Sky

Cricket Connection

Visit www.eduplace.com/scp/ to check out *Click, Ask,* and *Odyssey* magazine articles and activities.

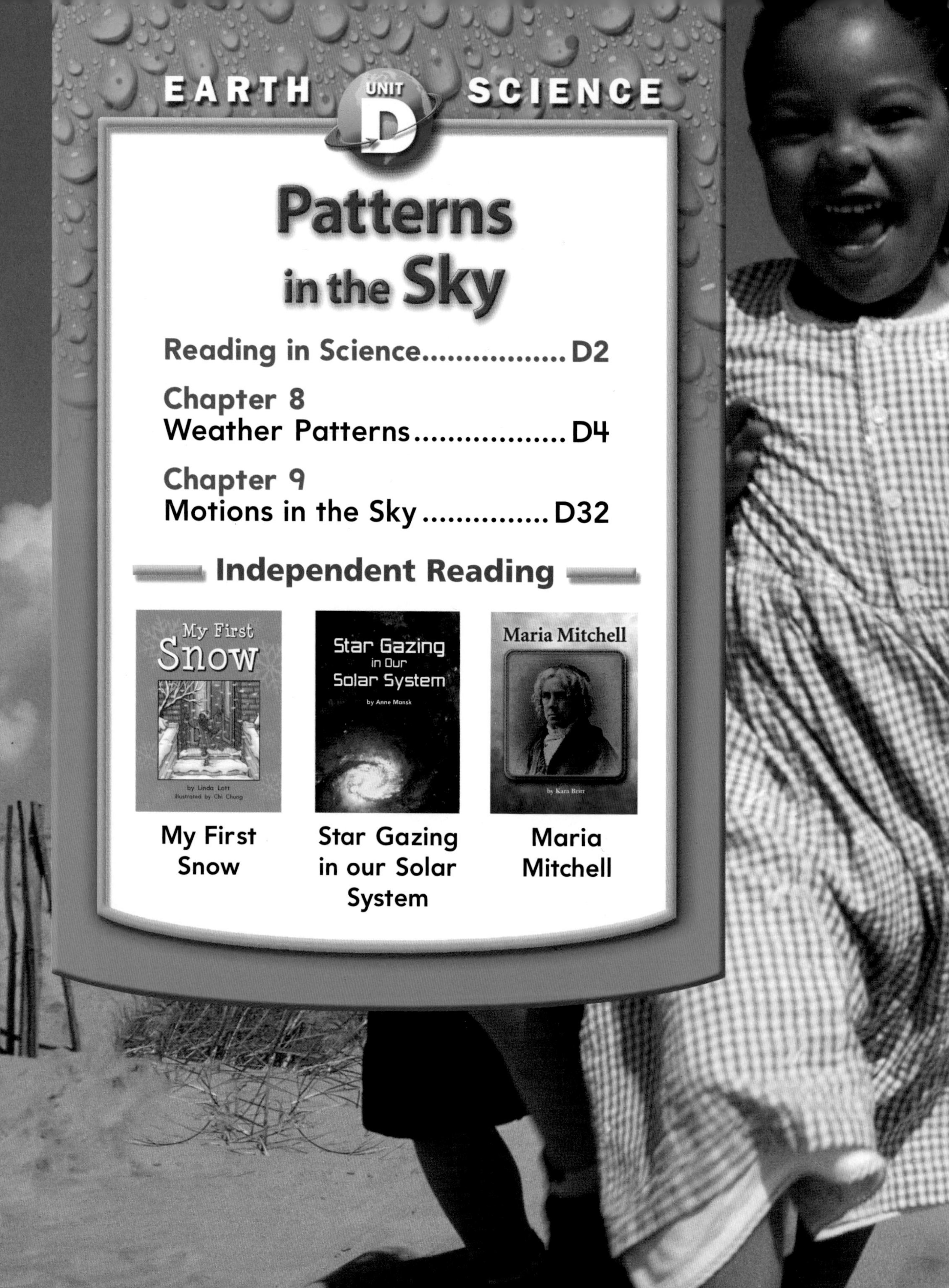

EARTH UNIT D SCIENCE

Patterns in the Sky

Independent Reading

My First Snow

Star Gazing in our Solar System

Maria Mitchell

Discover!
Why doesn't it snow
everywhere in winter?
Think about this question as you
read. You will have the answer
by the end of the unit.

Read Together

THE SUN

OUR NEAREST STAR

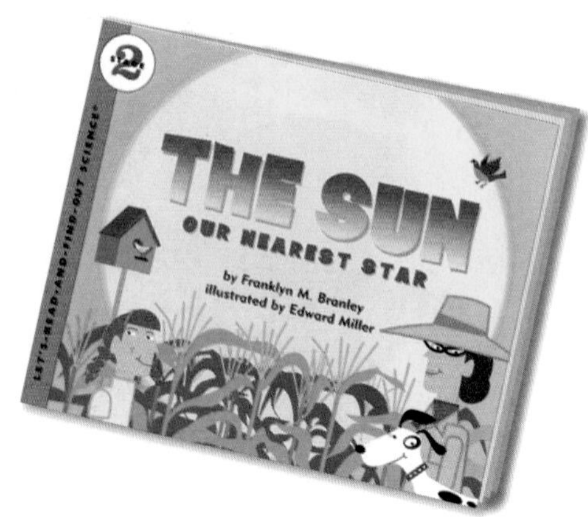

by Franklyn M. Branley
illustrated by Edward Miller

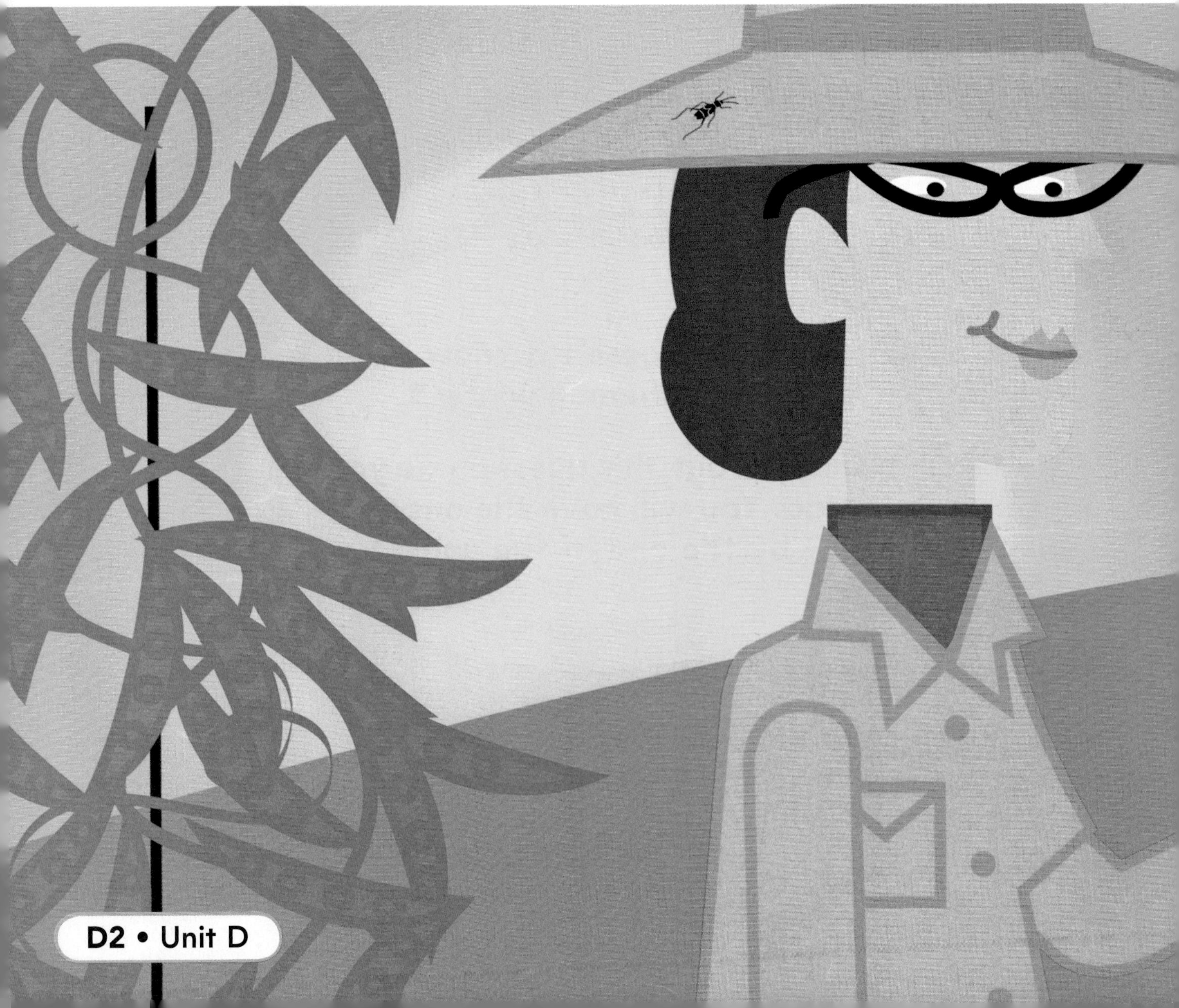

Reading in Science

Strategy: Summarize

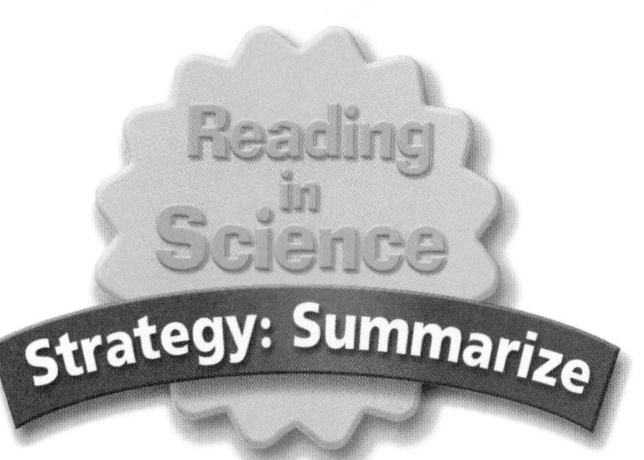

The sun is very big. It is much bigger than Earth. The sun is almost a million miles across. If Earth was the size of a pea, the sun would be the size of a beach ball.

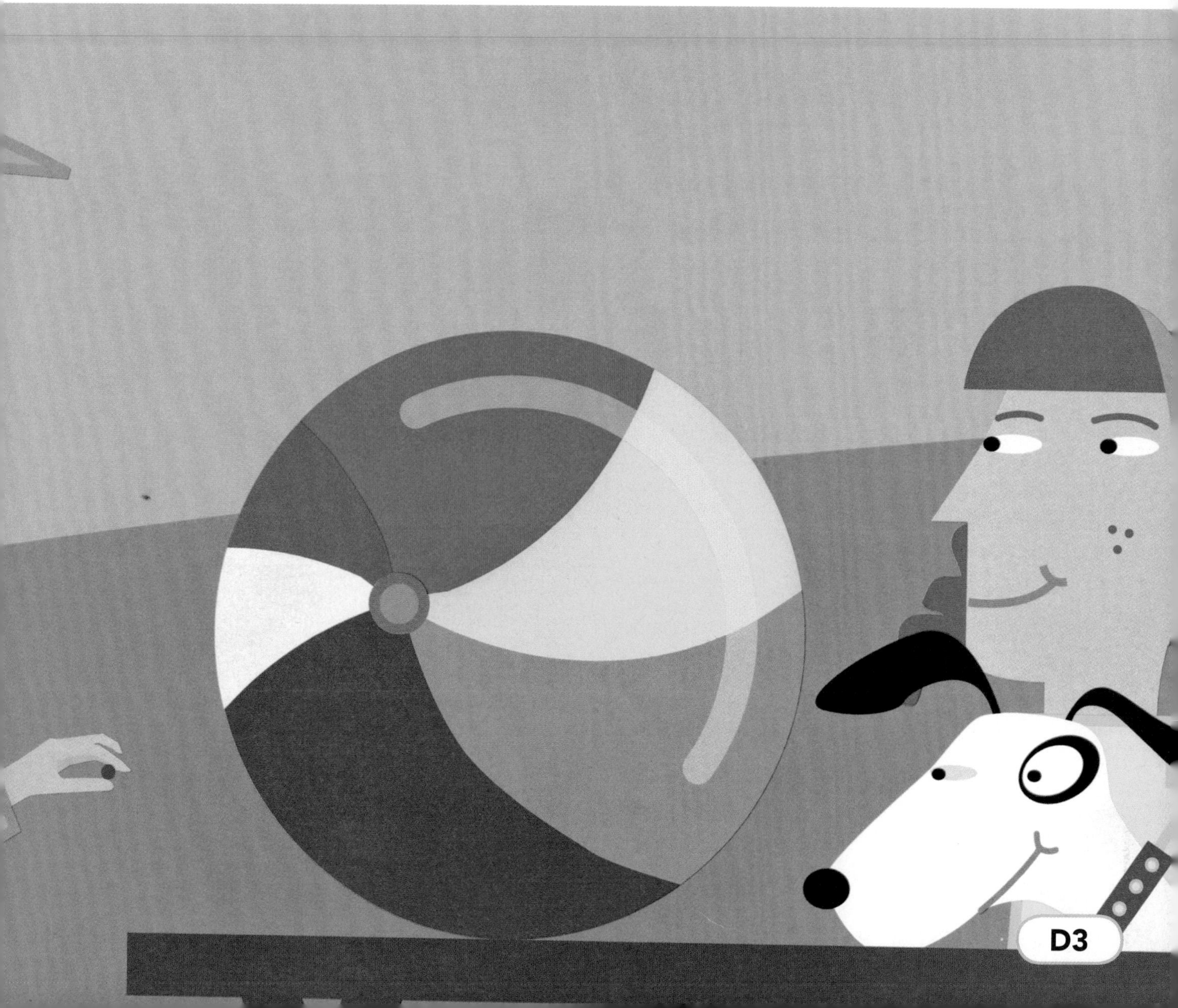

Chapter 8

Weather Patterns

Vocabulary Preview

water cycle
evaporates
water vapor
condenses
precipitation
season
hibernate
migrate

condenses

Water vapor condenses, or changes to drops of water.

precipitation

Water that falls from clouds is called precipitation.

hibernate

Some animals hibernate, or go into a deep sleep.

migrate

Some animals migrate, or move to warmer places in fall.

Lesson 1

How Does Weather Change?

Science and You

When the weather changes, you may need to change your plans for the day.

Inquiry Skill

Use Numbers You can use numbers to compare temperatures.

What You Need

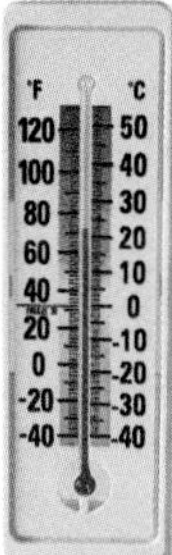

thermometer

Daily and Weekly Weather

	Monday	Tuesday	Wednesday	Thursday	Friday
Morning	Temperature ___ °F	Temperature ___ °F	Temperature ___ °F	Temperature ___ °F	Temperature ___ °F
Midday	Temperature ___ °F	Temperature ___ °F	Temperature ___ °F	Temperature ___ °F	Temperature ___ °F
Afternoon	Temperature ___ °F	Temperature ___ °F	Temperature ___ °F	Temperature ___ °F	Temperature ___ °F

weather chart

Investigate

Compare Weather

Steps

1. **Observe** See whether it is sunny, cloudy, raining, or snowing. Record what you see.

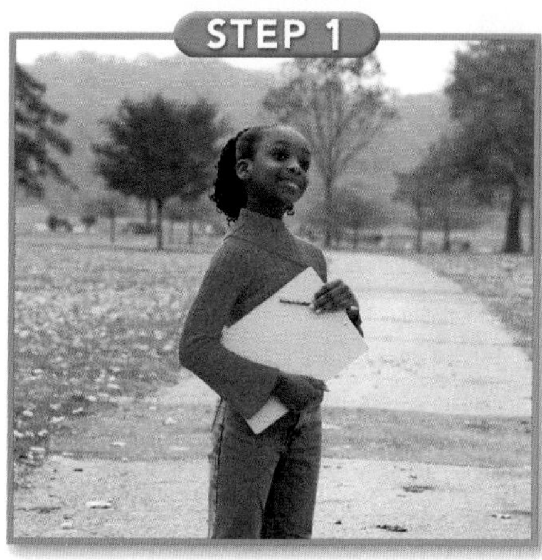
STEP 1

2. **Measure** Find the outdoor temperature. Record your findings.

STEP 2

3. **Use Numbers** Repeat steps 1 and 2 two more times during the day. Compare the temperatures you recorded.

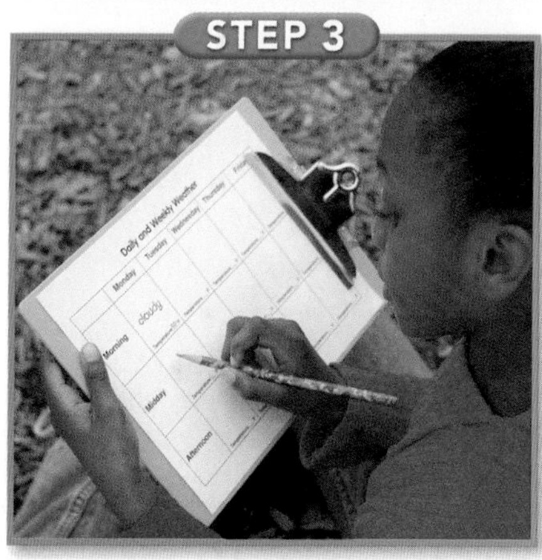
STEP 3

4. Repeat steps 1–3 for a week.

Think and Share

1. What changes did you observe during any one day?
2. **Infer** What can you infer about morning temperatures?

Investigate More!

Experiment Make a plan to measure rainfall. Talk with others about your findings.

Learn by Reading

Vocabulary

water cycle

evaporates

water vapor

condenses

precipitation

Reading Skill

Main Idea and Details

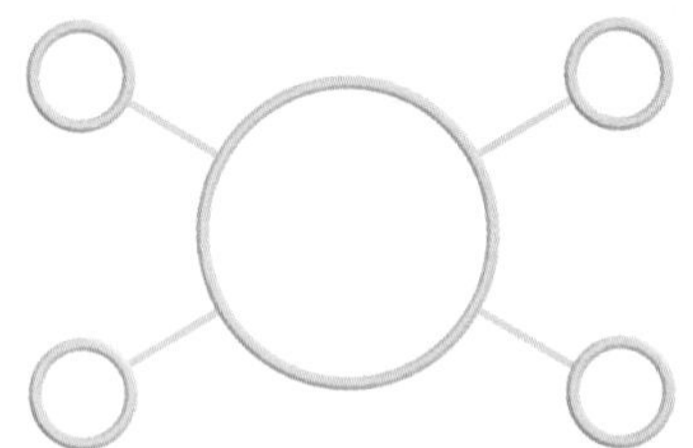

Daily Weather Patterns

Weather changes in patterns over time. Weather can change from day to day. Weather can also change throughout a day.

The air is often warmer in the afternoon than it is in the morning. The Sun warms the air during the day. Then the air gets cooler again at night. These changes in temperature are measured with a thermometer.

a storm over Tampa, Florida

Sudden Changes

Sometimes weather can change very quickly. It might be a calm and clear day. Then a storm appears, bringing rain, thunder, and lightning in the afternoon.

Scientists called meteorologists use tools to study the weather. They tell what kind of weather is coming. They use radar to keep track of weather changes.

MAIN IDEA How might weather change during a day?

The radar shows rain around the Tampa area.

The Water Cycle

Heat from the Sun warms land, water, and air. The Sun's heat causes water to change form and move. Water moving from Earth to the air and back again is called the **water cycle**.

MAIN IDEA How does the Sun change water?

2 Water as a gas is called water vapor. You cannot see it. It mixes into the air.

1 The Sun warms the water. The water evaporates, or changes to a gas.

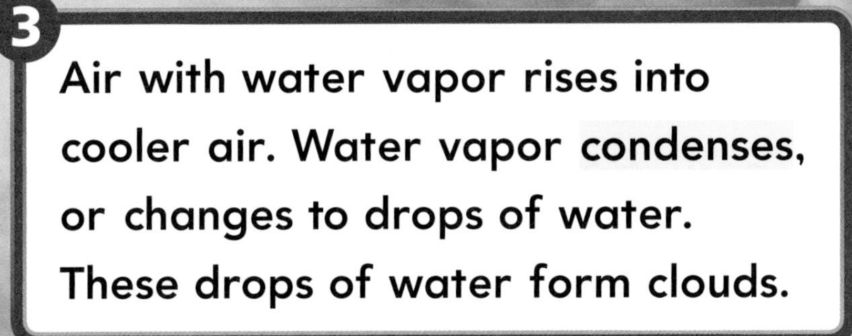

3 Air with water vapor rises into cooler air. Water vapor condenses, or changes to drops of water. These drops of water form clouds.

4 As the drops get bigger, they get heavier. The drops fall to the ground as rain, snow, sleet, or hail.

5 Rain and melted snow collect in streams, rivers, lakes, and oceans. The water cycle begins again.

Precipitation and Wind

Water that falls from clouds is called **precipitation**. Rain, snow, sleet, and hail are kinds of precipitation. When the air is warm, rain falls. When the air is cold enough, snow may fall. If falling snow melts and refreezes, it changes to sleet. When falling rain is tossed about in cold air, it freezes into balls of ice. These balls of ice are called hail. Hail often forms during thunderstorms.

◀ **hail**

Storms bring wind with rain. ▼

snowstorm with drifts

Wind is moving air. Wind can be gentle, or it can be very strong. During many storms, a strong wind blows. Strong wind can blow falling rain or snow. Wind can blow fallen snow into drifts.

MAIN IDEA What are two different kinds of precipitation?

Lesson Wrap-Up

1. **Vocabulary** What happens to water when the Sun heats it?
2. **Reading Skill** What happens to water in the water cycle?
3. **Use Numbers** A morning temperature is 50°F. What might an afternoon temperature be?

Technology Visit **www.eduplace.com/scp/** to find out more about weather.

Lesson 2

What Is the Pattern of the Seasons?

Science and You

Knowing the pattern of the seasons helps you know the best time to plant seeds.

Inquiry Skill

Communicate You can communicate by talking to others about what you find out.

What You Need

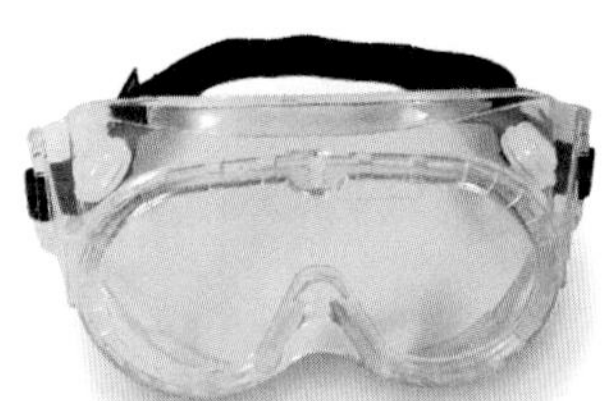
goggles

water and soil

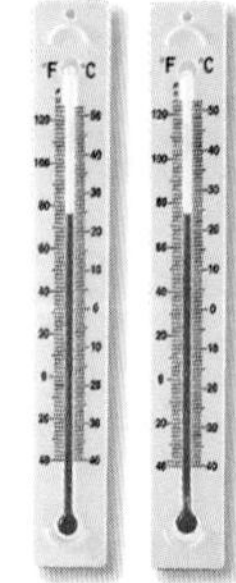
2 thermometers

Investigate

Measure Heat

Steps

1. Put the cups of soil and water in a refrigerator overnight.

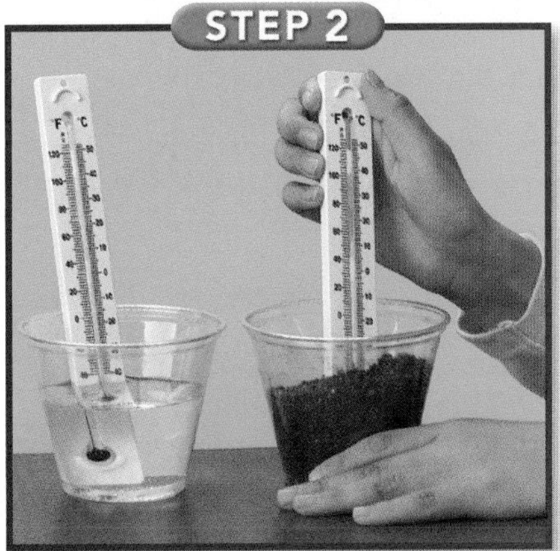

2. **Measure** Remove the cups from the refrigerator. Measure and record the temperature of each material.

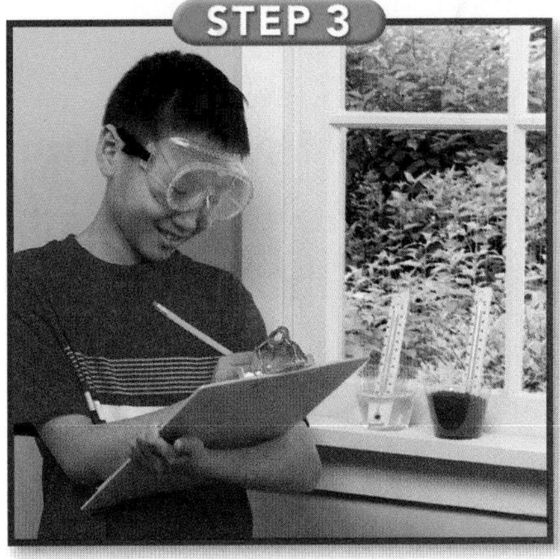

3. **Record Data** Put the cups in a warm, sunny place for 20 minutes. Record the temperature of each material again.

Think and Share

1. **Communicate** Tell how the temperature of each material changed.
2. **Infer** The thermometers measured the amount of heat absorbed. What was the source of heat?

Investigate More!

Ask Questions Think about other times when the temperatures of materials might change. What questions would you ask?

Learn by Reading

Vocabulary

season

Reading Skill

Sequence

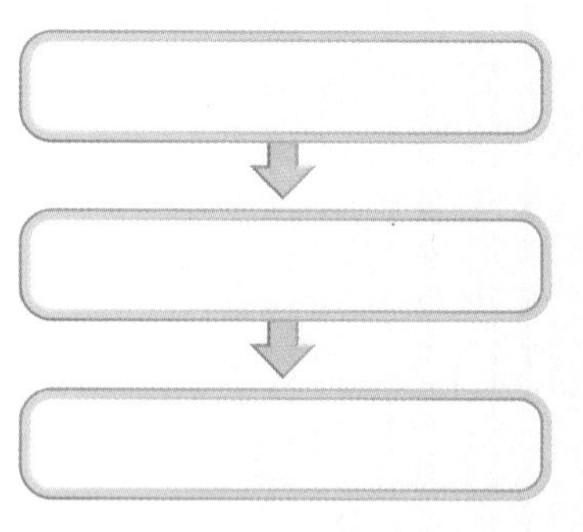

Weather Patterns of the Seasons

A **season** is a time of year. Winter, spring, summer, and fall are the four seasons. They occur in this order every year. Each season has its own weather pattern.

Air temperatures change with the seasons. Winter is the coolest. Summer is the warmest. In spring temperatures slowly rise. In fall temperatures slowly fall.

Compare the thermometers. How is the winter temperature different in these places?

Bismarck, North Dakota

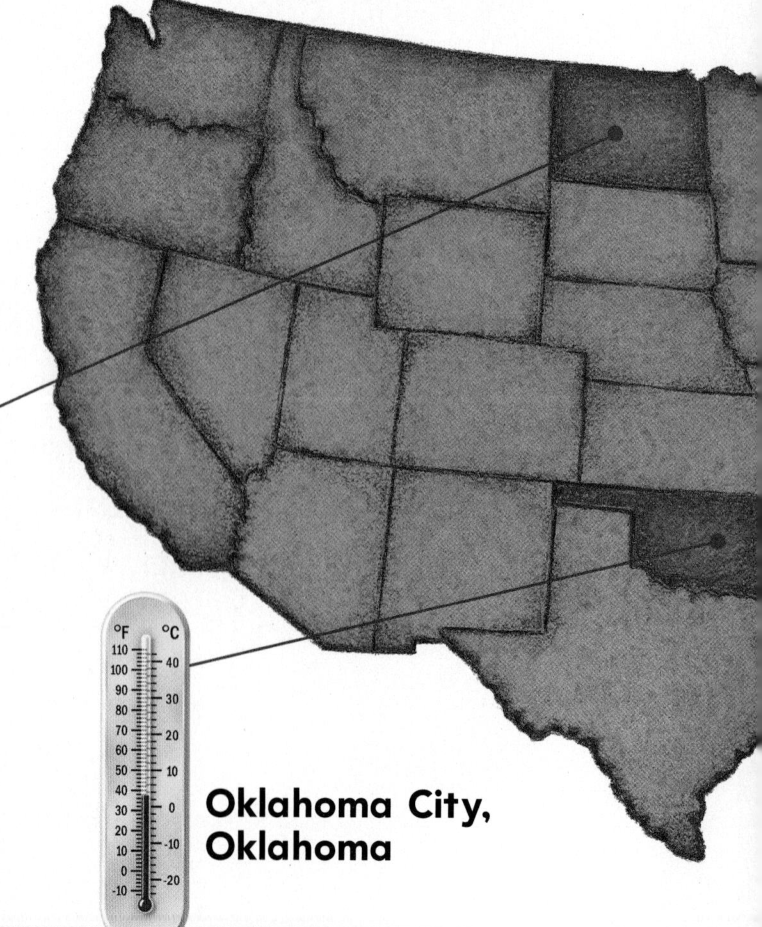

Oklahoma City, Oklahoma

Weather patterns are different from place to place. In some places, winter weather is very cold. In other places, winters are just a little cooler than summers. Some places have about the same amount of precipitation in all four seasons. In other places, one season is very wet and the others are dry.

SEQUENCE How do temperatures change as the seasons change?

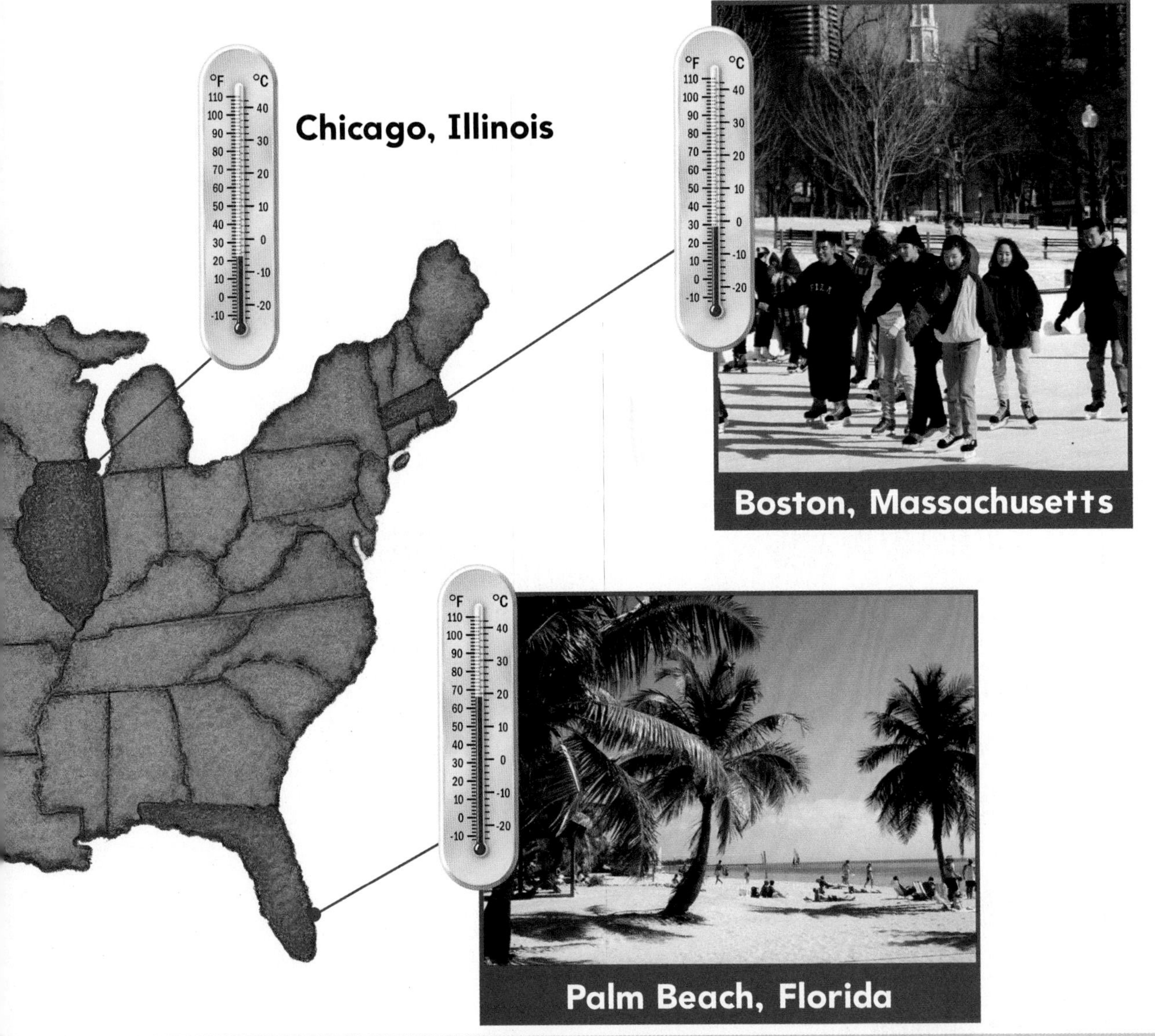

winter

Winter days have the fewest hours of daylight.

spring

In spring, daytime slowly gets longer.

Daylight Patterns

The Sun shines in the daytime. The number of daylight hours changes with the seasons. This pattern of changing daylight repeats every year.

The Sun warms Earth's land and water. Heat moves from the land and water into the air.

The land, air, and water get warmer when there are more hours of daylight. This is why summer has the warmest weather.

summer

Summer days have the most hours of daylight.

fall

In fall, the daytime slowly gets shorter.

SEQUENCE How does the number of daylight hours change as the seasons change?

Lesson Wrap-Up

1. **Vocabulary** What is a **season**?
2. **Reading Skill** Which season comes after the one with the most daylight hours?
3. **Communicate** Tell why summer has the warmest weather.

Technology Visit **www.eduplace.com/scp/** to find out more about seasons.

STAYING SAFE IN THE SUN

Too much sunlight is not healthful. It can harm your skin and damage your eyes.

You need to protect your skin and eyes from the Sun's rays in all seasons. The Sun's rays are strongest midday. If you must be outdoors at that time, try to stay in the shade. Cover your skin with tightly woven, lightweight clothing.

The Sun's rays can be harmful even when it is cold outdoors. The Sun's light can reflect off snow.

How is this child keeping safe in the Sun?

Safety in the Sun

Wear sunscreen to protect your skin. Put it on before you go outdoors.	
Wear a hat with a brim to protect your neck, ears, and face.	
Wear sunglasses to protect your eyes.	
You sweat more in warmer weather. Drink a lot of water to replace the water you lose.	

Sharing Ideas

1. **Write About It** Make a list of things you do outdoors in warm weather. Write about how you can stay safe.
2. **Talk About It** Talk with your classmates about Sun safety at school. Make a class list of ways to keep safe while outdoors.

Lesson 3

How Do Living Things Change With the Seasons?

Science and You

Knowing how living things change with the seasons helps you know when you might see baby animals.

Inquiry Skill

Compare **Tell how objects are alike or different.**

What You Need

2 cups and 2 bags

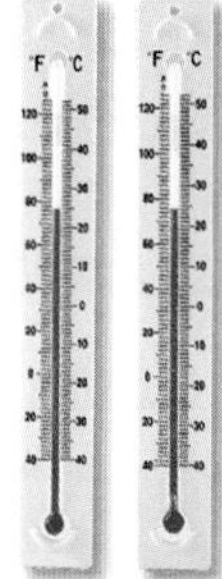

2 thermometers

ice cubes

different fabrics

Investigate

Compare Fabrics

Steps

1. Put an ice cube in each bag. Wrap a piece of fabric around each bag.

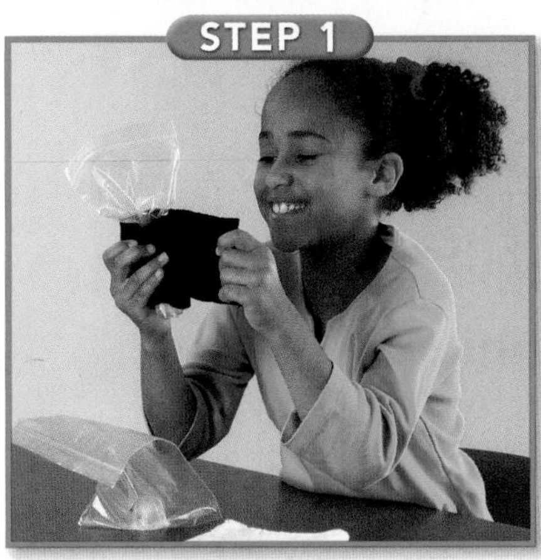

2. Place a fabric-wrapped bag in each cup. Slide a thermometer into each cup as shown.

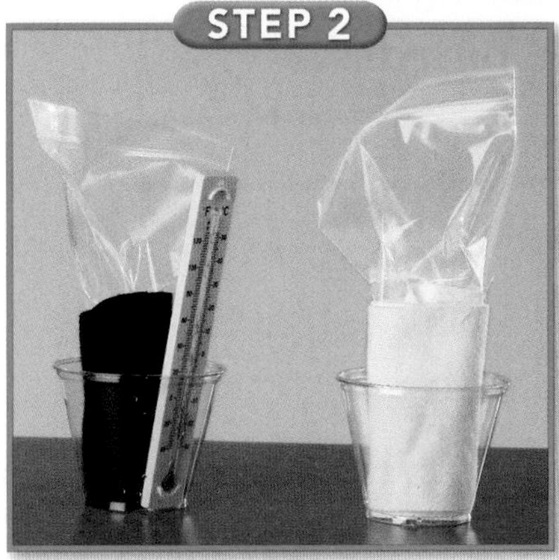

3. **Compare** Wait 15 minutes. Compare the temperatures on the thermometers. Record what you observe.

Think and Share

1. Heat moved from the air through the fabric and into the ice. Which fabric kept the air warmer?
2. **Infer** Which fabric would be good to wear in cold weather? Tell why.

Investigate More!

Be an Inventor Make a container to keep ice from melting. Tell about the materials you would use.

Learn by Reading

Vocabulary

hibernate

migrate

Reading Skill

Compare and Contrast

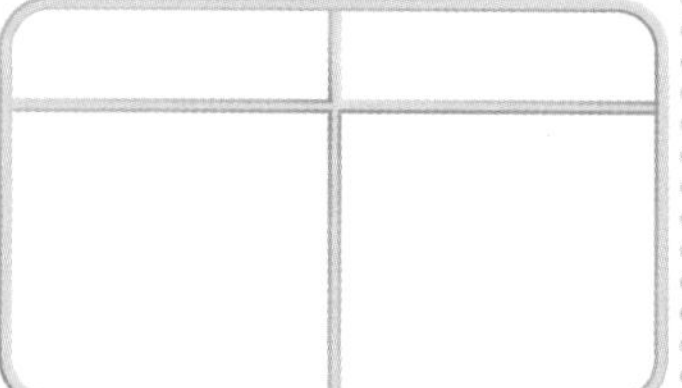

Plants and the Seasons

Changes in the seasons cause plants to change. Plants change as the air slowly warms or cools. They change as the number of daylight hours changes.

Changes with the Seasons

Season	spring
How a Sweet Gum Tree Changes	 Leaves grow and flowers bloom.

In spring, many plants flower. In summer, the fruits grow. Some plants have leaves that change color in fall. Where winters are very cold, plants stop growing.

COMPARE AND CONTRAST **How are plants different in spring and summer?**

summer	fall	winter
Spiny fruits form. Seeds form inside the fruits.	Leaves turn red and fall. Seeds spread.	Leaves and most of the fruits have fallen. The seeds rest.

Animals and the Seasons

Animals change with the seasons. Some change how they look. Most change what they do. The fur of some animals gets thicker in the fall and stays thick all winter. The fur may change color, too.

In fall, the antlers are fully grown. The deer's fur gets thicker.

In spring, a male deer's antlers begin to grow.

It is hard for animals to find food in winter. Some animals collect food in fall to store for winter. Other animals **hibernate**, or go into a deep sleep. In spring they come out of hibernation. They find food and have their young.

Some animals **migrate**, or move to warmer places in fall. The animals can find food in these warm places.

COMPARE AND CONTRAST How are a deer's antlers different in spring and fall?

▲ Ground squirrels hibernate in winter.

▲ A ground squirrel comes out of its burrow in spring.

Some monarch butterflies migrate in fall.

Dressing for the Seasons

People change the things they do with the seasons. As the weather changes, people wear different clothes.

A hat helps keep in body heat.

Layers of clothes keep heat near your body.

Socks and sturdy shoes keep your feet warm and dry.

1. **Vocabulary** What do animals do when they **hibernate**?
2. **Reading Skill** Tell how a plant is different in two seasons.
3. **Compare** Tell how an animal is different in two seasons.

Technology Visit **www.eduplace.com/scp/** to find out more about living things in seasons.

LINKS for Home and School

Math Read a Chart

The chart shows weather data for the summer months in Akron, Ohio.

Weather in Akron, Ohio			
	June	July	August
Rain	3 inches	4 inches	3 inches
Temperature	68°F	72°F	71°F
Clear Days	7	7	8
Cloudy Days	12	11	11

1. Tell about the weather in July.

2. Which month had the most clear days?

Social Studies Winter Activities

Kayla lives in Florida. Jason lives in Michigan. They drew pictures of themselves having fun in winter. Tell how winter is different in these two places. Write about winter where you live. Draw a picture of yourself having fun in winter.

Review and Test Prep

Visual Summary

Weather, plants, and animals change with the seasons.

Patterns of Change

Season	Winter	Spring	Summer	Fall
Temperature	coolest	slowly rises	warmest	slowly falls
Plants				
Animals				

Main Ideas

1. Is air temperature usually warmer in the morning or afternoon? Tell why. **(p. D8)**
2. Why does water evaporate? **(p. D10)**
3. List the seasons in the order in which they occur. **(p. D16)**
4. What do animals do in fall to get ready for winter? **(pp. D26–D27)**

Vocabulary

Choose the correct word from the box.

water cycle (p. D10)
condenses (p. D11)
precipitation (p. D12)
season (p. D16)

5. A time of year
6. When water vapor changes to drops of water
7. Water that falls from clouds
8. Water moving from Earth to the air and back again

Test Practice

Choose a word to complete the sentence.

9. Water as a gas is ____.

migrate   water vapor   water cycle   season

Using Science Skills

10. **Compare** Draw the same tree or plant in winter and spring. How are the drawings alike and different?

11. **Critical Thinking** Why would a place have fewer hours of daylight in fall than in summer?

Chapter 9

Motions in the Sky

Vocabulary Preview

- Sun
- solar system
- planet
- rotates
- revolve
- orbit
- Moon
- phases
- star
- constellation

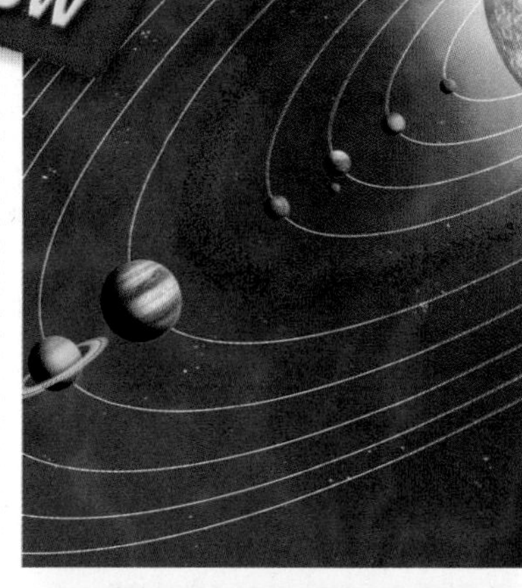

solar system

The Sun and the space objects that move around it make up our solar system.

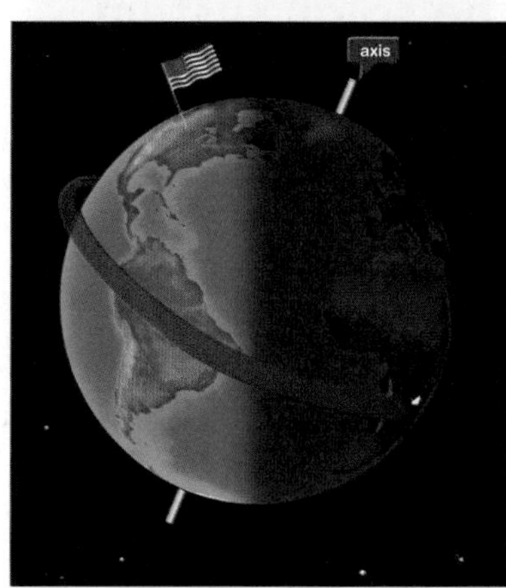

rotates

Earth rotates, or spins around an imaginary line.

phases

The different ways the Moon looks are called phases.

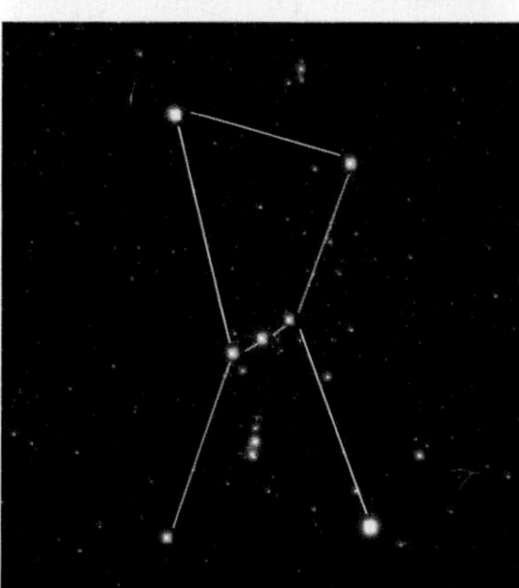

constellation

A constellation is a group of stars that forms a picture.

Lesson 1

What Makes Up the Solar System?

Science and You

Knowing about the solar system helps you see how important the Sun is to the planets.

Inquiry Skill

Predict **Use what you observe and know to tell what you think will happen.**

What You Need

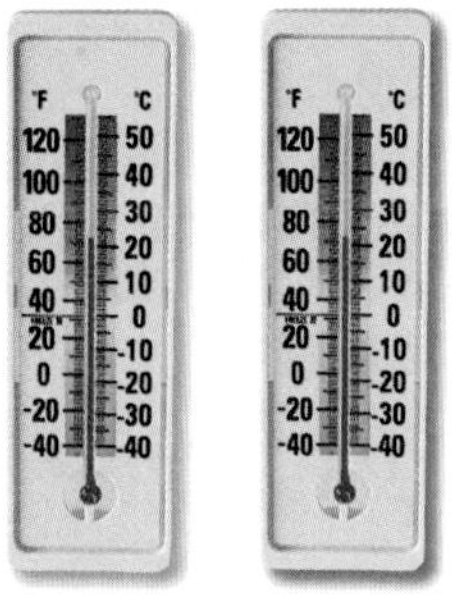

2 thermometers

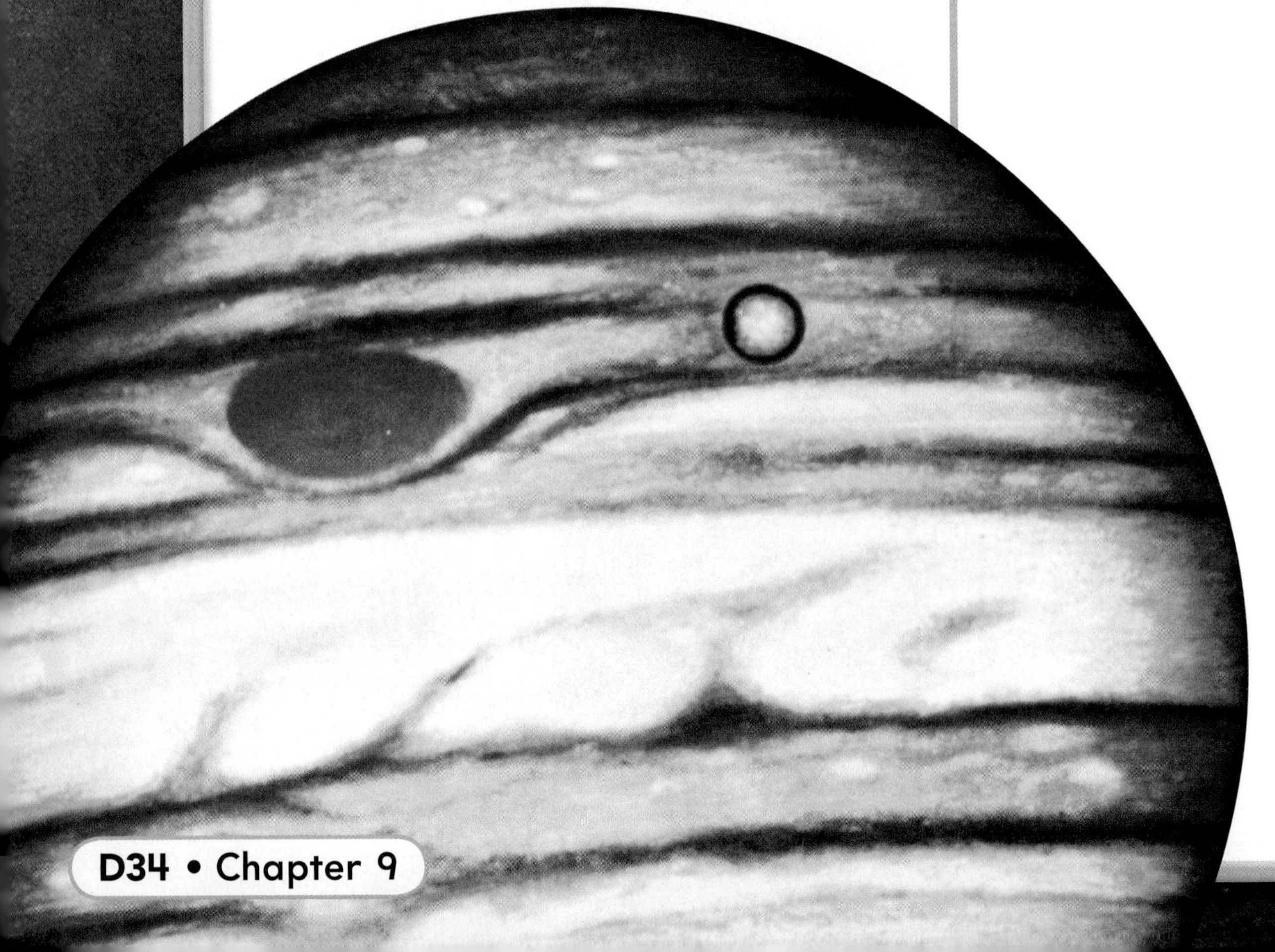

Investigate

Light and Heat

Steps

1. Put one thermometer in a sunny place. Put the other thermometer in a shaded place.

2. **Predict** Record the temperature shown on each thermometer. Predict how the temperatures will change.

3. **Record Data** Wait 15 minutes. Record the temperatures again.

STEP 1

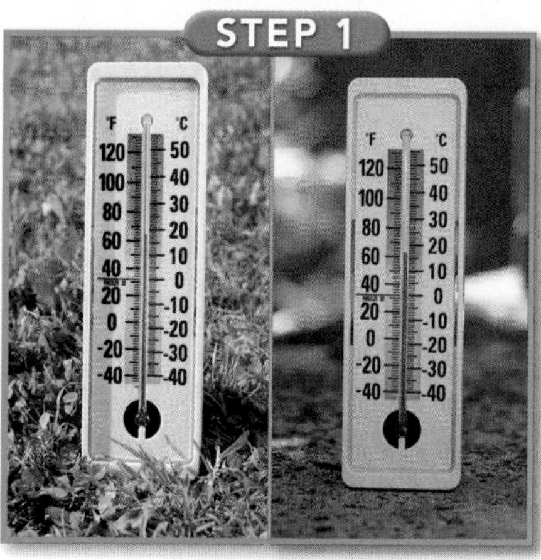

STEP 2

	First Time	Second Time
Sun	____°F	____°F
Shade	____°F	____°F

STEP 3

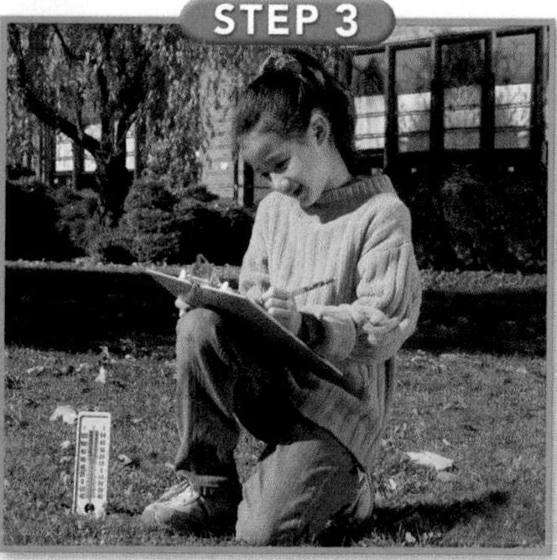

Think and Share

1. How did what you observed compare to what you predicted?
2. **Infer** How did the temperatures change? Tell why.

Investigate More!

Experiment Do the activity a few more times. Compare your findings. Were they the same each time? Tell why or why not.

Learn by Reading

Vocabulary

Sun

solar system

planet

Reading Skill

Main Idea and Details

The Sun

The **Sun** is the brightest object in the day sky. The Sun is much larger than Earth. It looks small because it is very far away. The Sun is made of hot gases that give off energy. The Sun's energy reaches Earth as light. Some of this light is changed to heat.

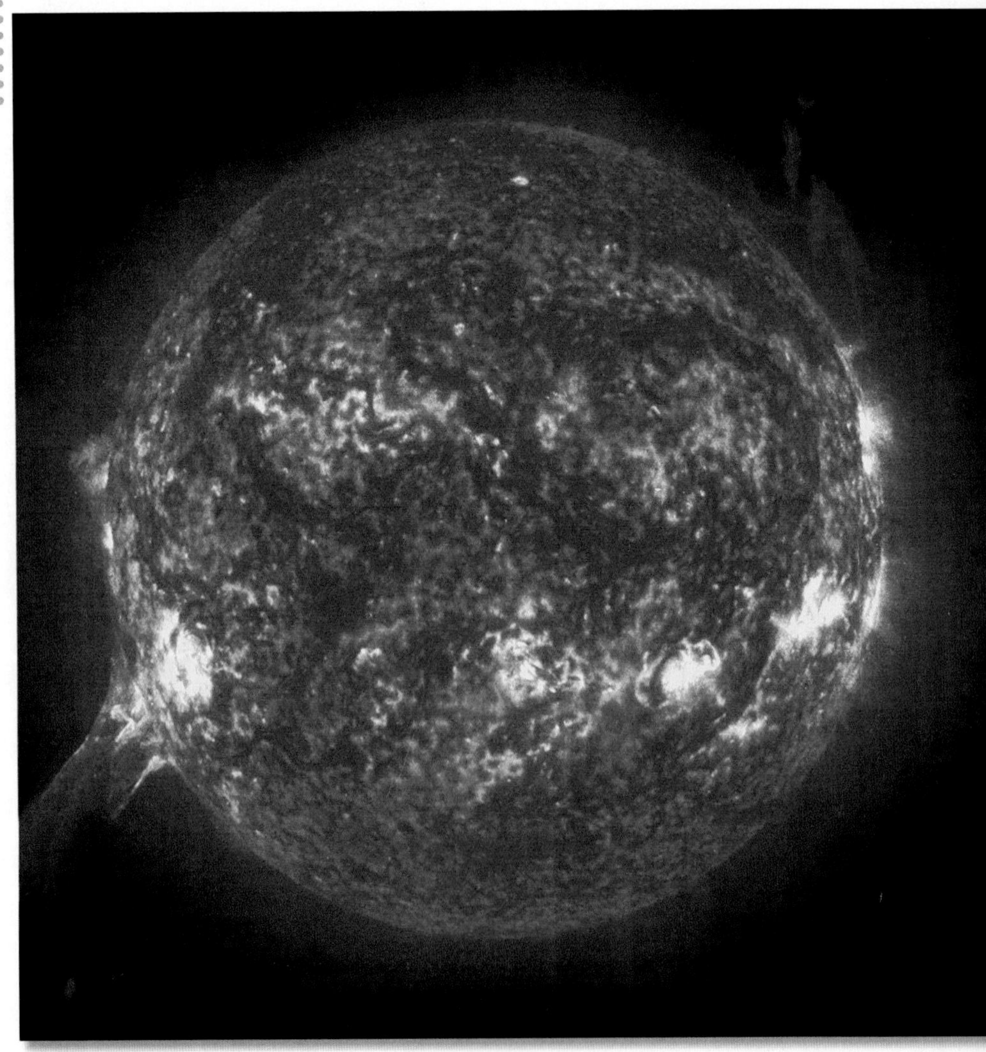

Living things on Earth use energy from the Sun. Land, air, and water are warmed by the Sun. The Sun keeps people and animals warm. Light from the Sun helps people and animals see. It helps plants live and grow.

MAIN IDEA How do living things use energy from the Sun?

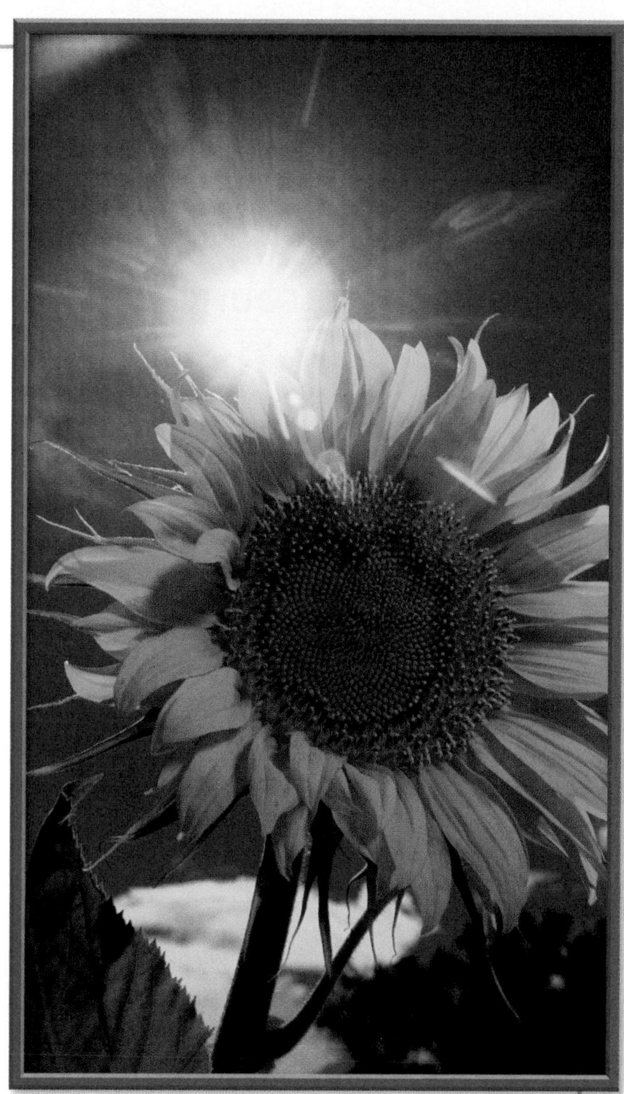

Plants use the Sun's light to make their own food.

The rocks are warmed by the Sun's heat.

The Solar System

The Sun and the space objects that move around it make up our **solar system**. There are nine planets in our solar system. A **planet** is a large object that moves around the Sun. Planets are always in the sky. Many planets have moons. Earth is a planet with one moon.

MAIN IDEA What makes up the solar system?

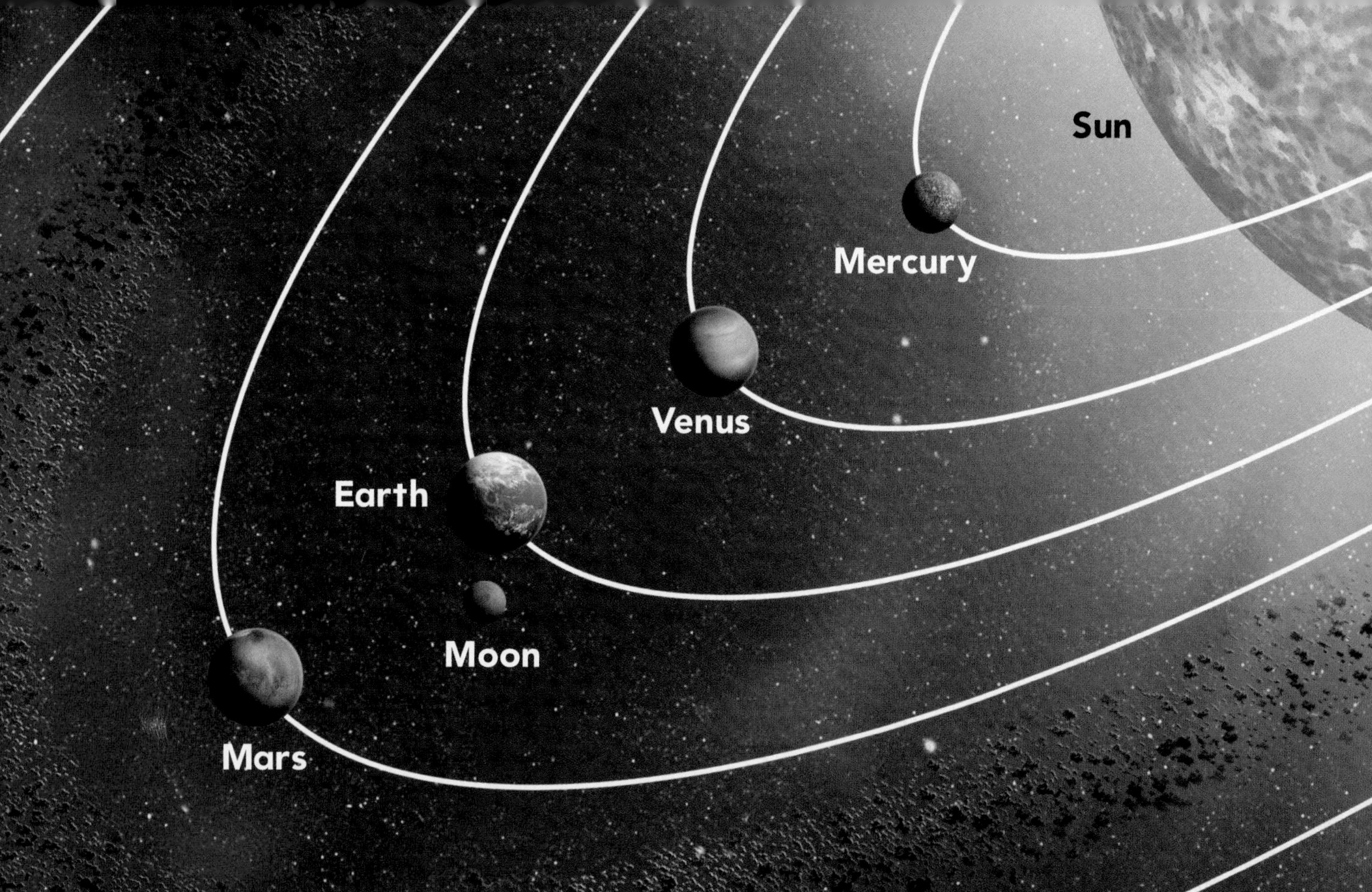

Lesson Wrap-Up

1. **Vocabulary** What is a **planet**?
2. **Reading Skill** How do living things use the Sun's energy?
3. **Predict** What might happen to a plant if it did not get enough light from the Sun? Tell why.

Technology Visit **www.eduplace.com/scp/** to find out more about the Sun.

Lesson 2

How Does Earth Move?

Science and You

Knowing how Earth moves helps you understand day and night.

Inquiry Skill

Observe Use your senses to find out about something.

What You Need

large sheet of paper

marker

ruler

Investigate

Observe Shadows

Steps

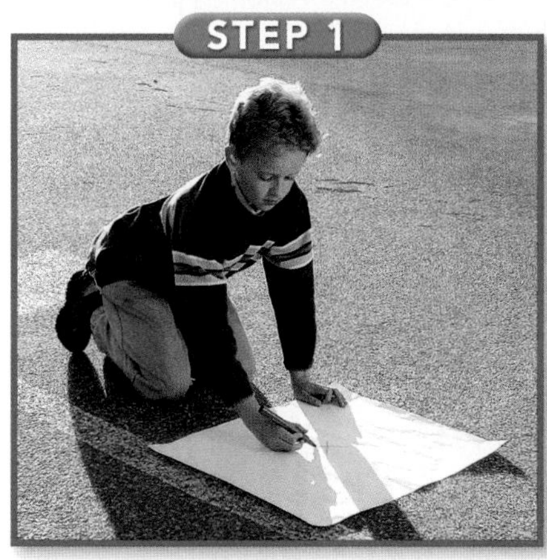

1. Go outdoors. Place a large sheet of paper on the ground. Make an X in the center of it.

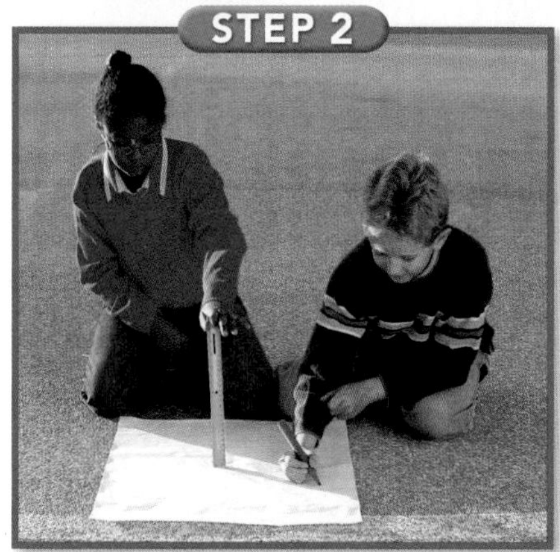

2. **Observe** Hold the ruler as shown. Trace its shadow. Write the time.

3. Put an arrow on your drawing to show where the Sun is in the sky. **Safety:** Do not look right at the Sun!
4. Repeat steps 2 and 3 two more times during the day.

Think and Share

1. How did the length and position of the shadow change during the day?
2. **Infer** What caused the shadow to change?

Investigate More!

Work Together Work with a partner. Use a flashlight and different objects to make shadows. Discuss what materials make shadows. Tell how the shadows change.

Learn by Reading

Vocabulary

rotates

revolve

orbit

Reading Skill

Draw Conclusions

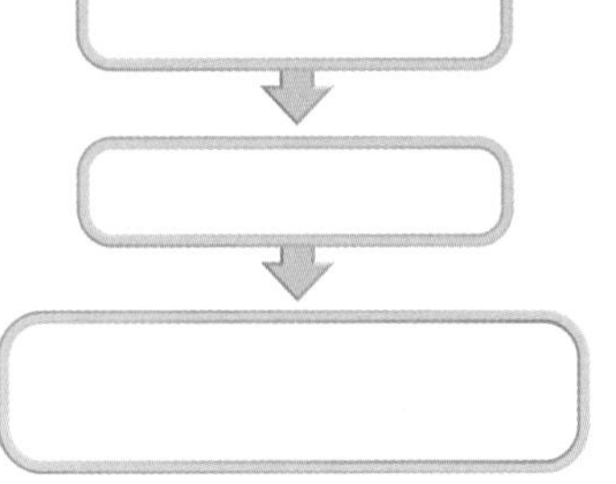

Earth Spins

Each day the Sun seems to move across the sky. But the Sun does not move. Earth **rotates**, or spins around an imaginary line. The line is called an axis. It takes Earth 24 hours, or one day, to rotate one time.

As Earth rotates, different parts face the Sun. When the part where you live faces the Sun, you have day. When the part where you live faces away from the Sun, you have night.

Where is it day in this picture?

Shadows Change

Light from the Sun shines on Earth. Shadows form when an object blocks sunlight. As Earth rotates, shadows change length and position. People can tell time by observing the Sun and shadows.

morning

In the morning, the Sun is low in the sky. Shadows are long. They grow shorter and shorter until noon.

noon

At about noon, the Sun is at its highest point in the sky. Shadows are shortest.

afternoon

In the afternoon, the Sun is low in the sky again. Shadows grow longer.

DRAW CONCLUSIONS **At what time during the day is your shadow its shortest?**

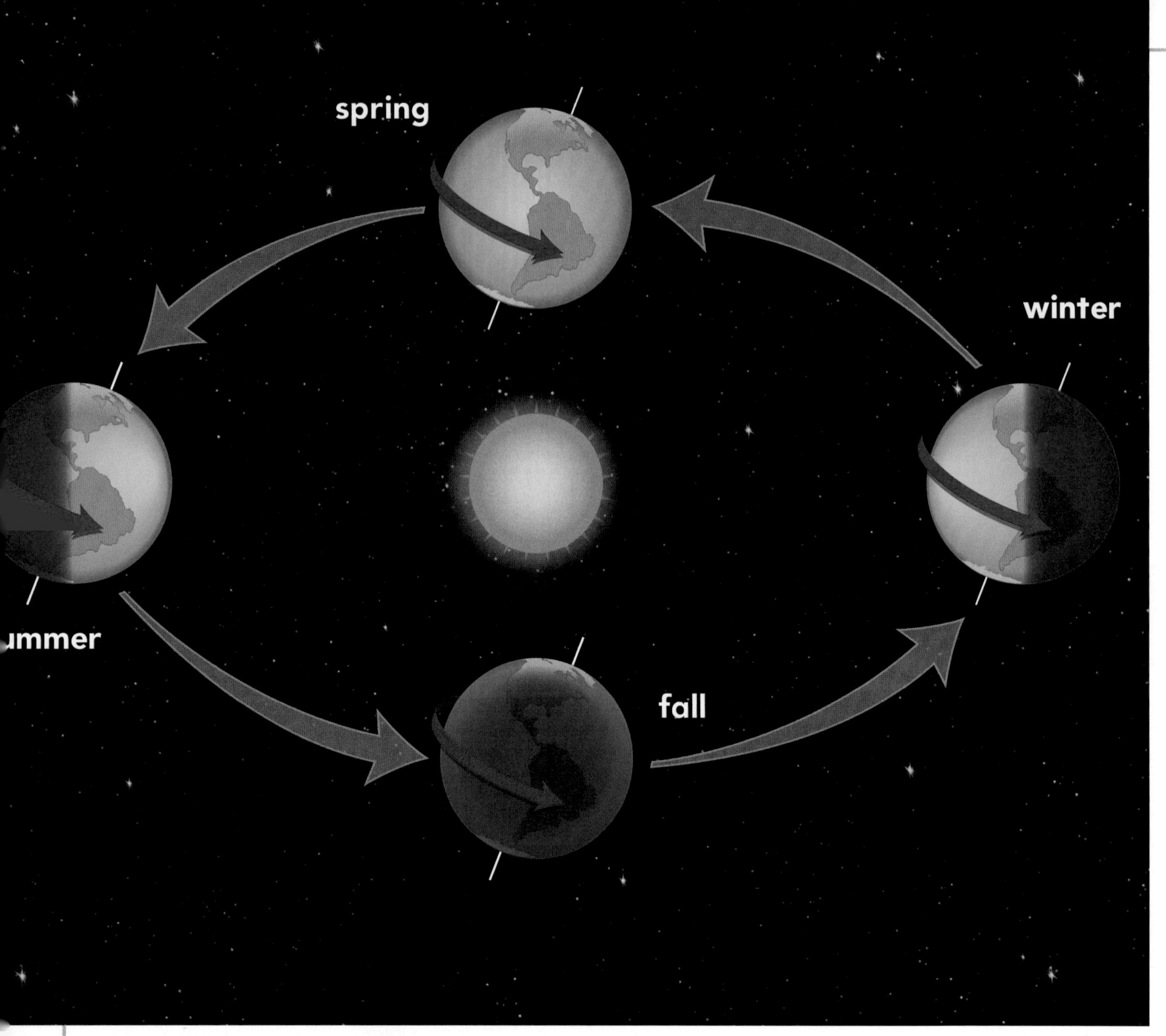

Earth Moves Around the Sun

While Earth rotates, it also moves in another way. Earth and the other planets **revolve**, or move in a path, around the Sun. The path that one space object travels around another is called an **orbit**. It takes one year for Earth to revolve around the Sun.

During Earth's orbit, the seasons change. When our part of Earth is tilted toward the Sun, we get more direct light from the Sun. It is summer. As Earth revolves around the Sun, our part of Earth tilts away from the Sun. Sunlight hits our part of Earth on a slant, so we get less light. Then it is winter.

DRAW CONCLUSIONS If it is spring, how long will it be until it is spring again?

Lesson Wrap-Up

1. **Vocabulary** Which of Earth's movements takes one year?
2. **Reading Skill** When the United States has night, where is it day?
3. **Observe** What happens to shadows throughout the day?

Technology Visit **www.eduplace.com/scp/** to find out more about Earth's movements.

Lesson 3

How Does the Moon Move?

Science and You

Knowing how the Moon moves helps you understand why it looks different each night.

Inquiry Skill

Use Models Use a model to learn about the Moon.

What You Need

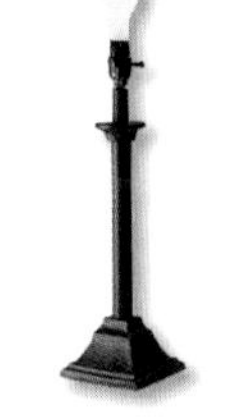

lamp

Moon model

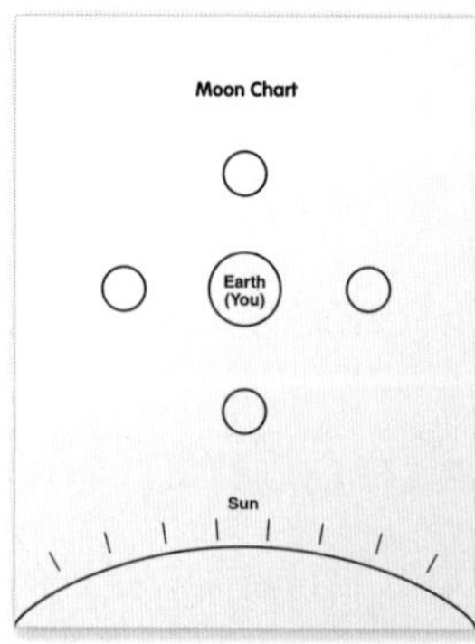

Moon chart

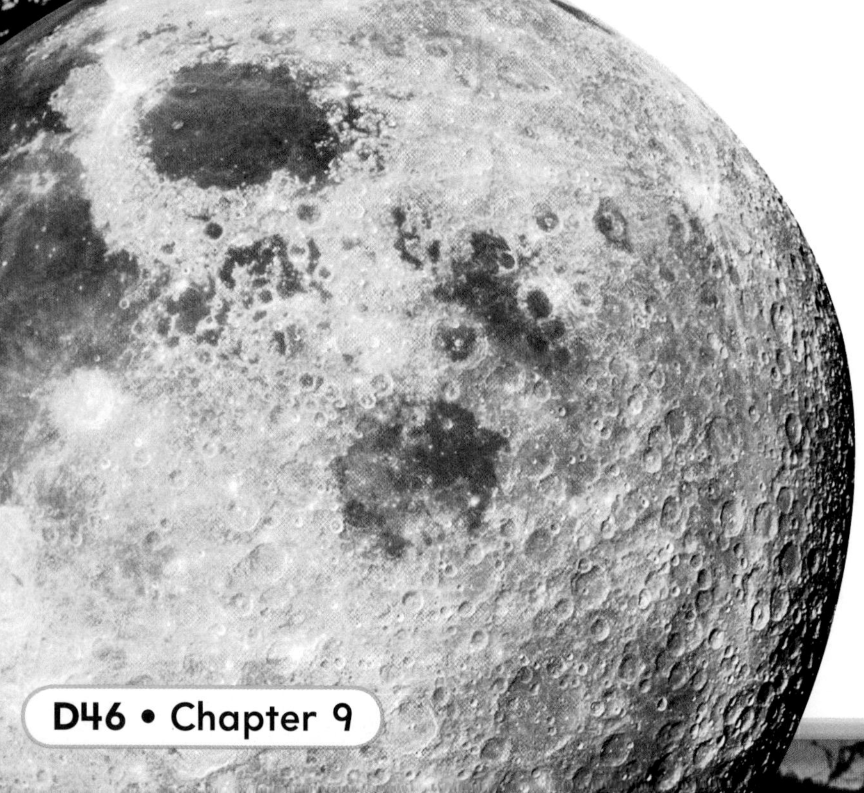

Investigate

Moon Phases

Steps

1. **Use Models** Place a lamp on a table in a darkened room. The lamp is the Sun. One child sits in a chair as Earth. One child holds a model Moon.

STEP 1

2. **Observe** The Moon slowly walks around Earth. Earth observes the changes in the amount of light on the Moon.

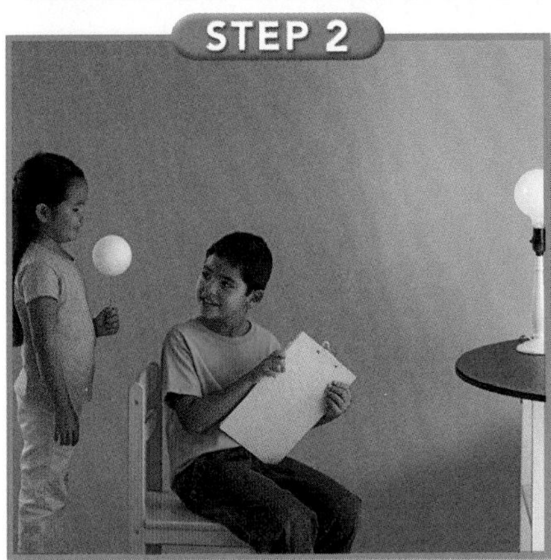
STEP 2

3. **Record Data** On the Moon chart, Earth records how the light and shadows on the Moon model change.

STEP 3

Think and Share

1. When did you see most of the Moon model?
2. What happened to the Moon model as it moved around the Earth model? Tell why.

Investigate More!

Work Together Switch roles so that everyone has a turn to be Earth. Compare your results. Talk about how the Moon seemed to change.

Learn by Reading

Vocabulary

Moon

phases

Reading Skill

Cause and Effect

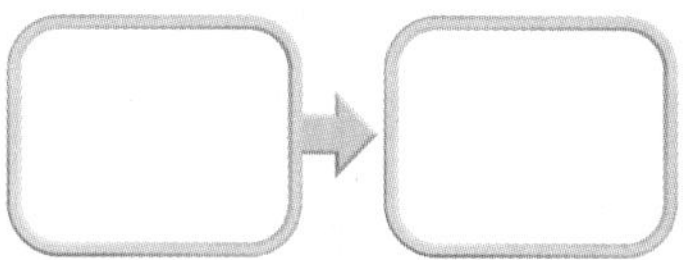

The Moon

The **Moon** is a large sphere made of rock. It is the closest large space object to Earth. As Earth rotates, the Moon seems to move across the sky at night. From Earth, you can see dark spots on the Moon. With a telescope, you can see mountains and pits, or craters, on the Moon.

Earth can be seen from the Moon.

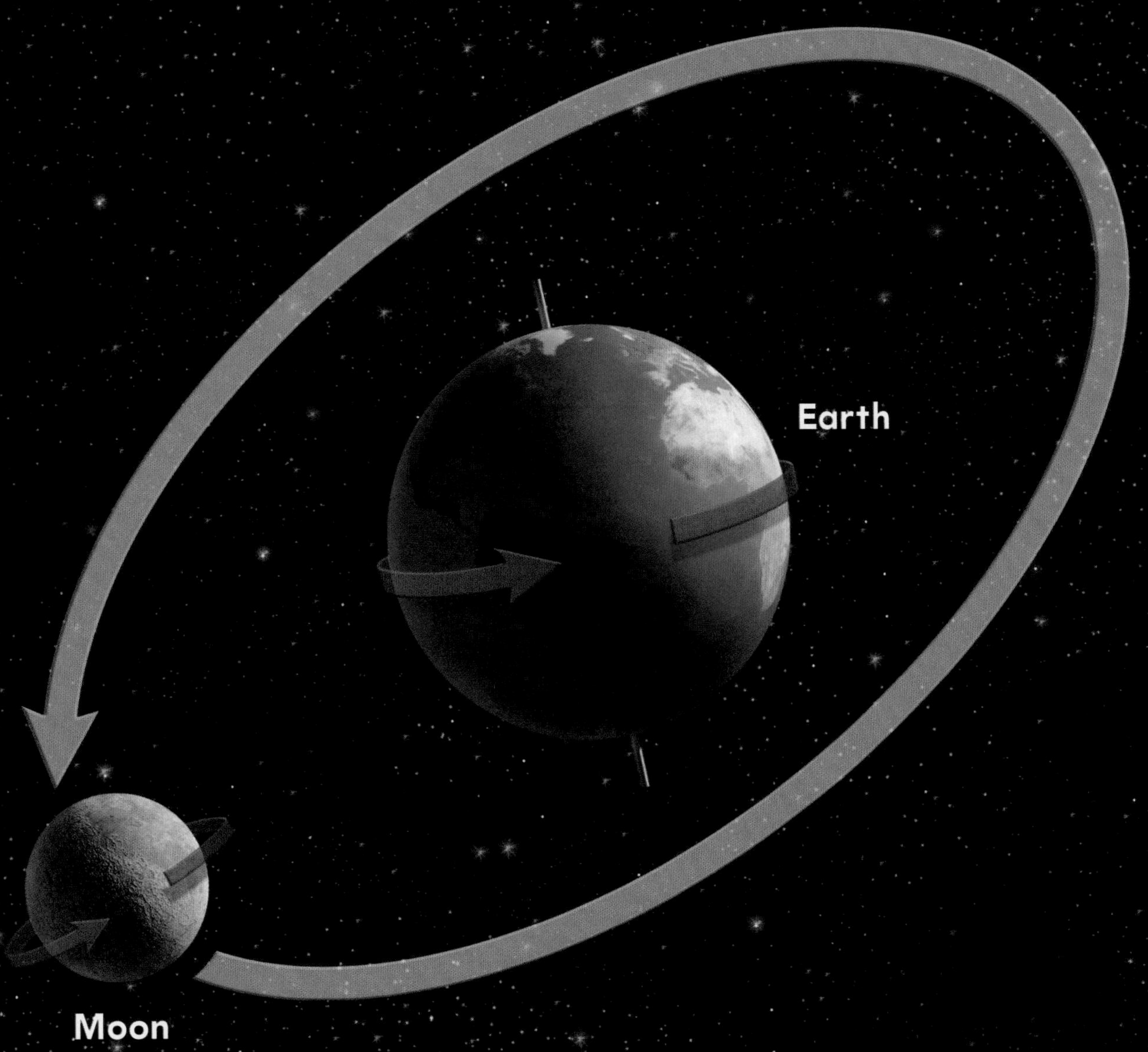

The Moon in Motion

The Moon revolves in an orbit around Earth. It takes about one month to go around one time. The pattern repeats month after month.

CAUSE AND EFFECT **Why does the Moon seem to move across the sky?**

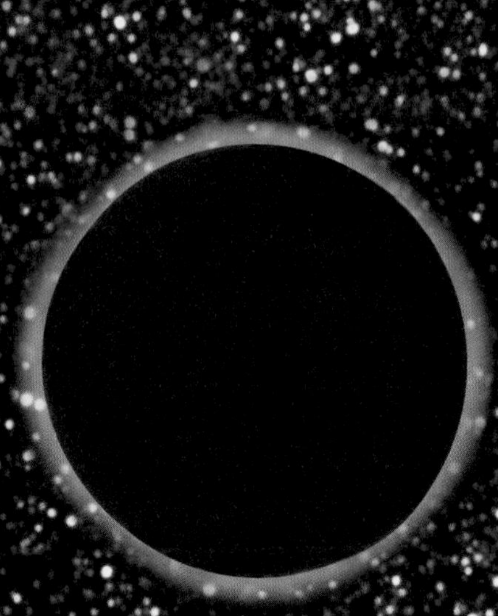

new

first quarter

The Changing Moon

The Moon does not have its own light. It reflects the Sun's light. The Sun shines on only one side of the Moon at a time. As the Moon revolves around Earth, you may see only a part of the Moon's lighted side. The Moon looks a little different every night. The different ways the Moon looks are called **phases**. The phases repeat every four weeks.

CAUSE AND EFFECT What causes the phases of the Moon?

Lesson Wrap-Up

1. **Vocabulary** What is the **Moon**?
2. **Reading Skill** Why does the Moon look bright in the night sky?
3. **Use Models** How does using models help you understand real objects?

 **Technology** Visit **www.eduplace.com/scp/** to find out more about the Moon.

Literature

Long ago, people made up stories about dark spots that they saw on the Moon. Compare one story to the facts.

The Tale of Rabbit and Coyote

by Tony Johnston
illustrated by Tomie dePaola

Now Rabbit knew of a ladder that reached into the sky. He began to climb it. Up, up, up. And he hopped all the way to the moon.

Then he hid the ladder.

Far below, he saw Coyote looking for him up in the sky. But try as he might, Coyote never found the ladder.

That is why, to this day, Coyote sits gazing at the moon.

And now and then he howls at it. For he is still *very* furious with Rabbit.

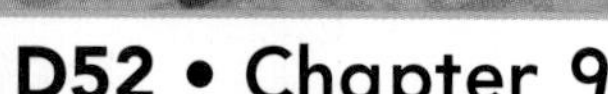

The Sun and Moon

by Patrick Moore
illustration by Paul Doherty

When you look at the moon, you can see bright and dark patches. The dark patches are called seas, but they are not real seas; there is no water in them and in fact there is no water anywhere on the moon. There are high mountains, and there are many craters, which are really holes with walls around them.

Sharing Ideas

1. **Write About It** Write a story to tell why you think there are dark spots on the Moon.
2. **Talk About It** Why do you think people made up stories about what they saw in the Moon?

Lesson 4

What Stars Can You See?

Science and You

Constellations can help you remember where some stars are in the sky.

Inquiry Skill

Compare Tell how objects or events are alike or different.

What You Need

black paper

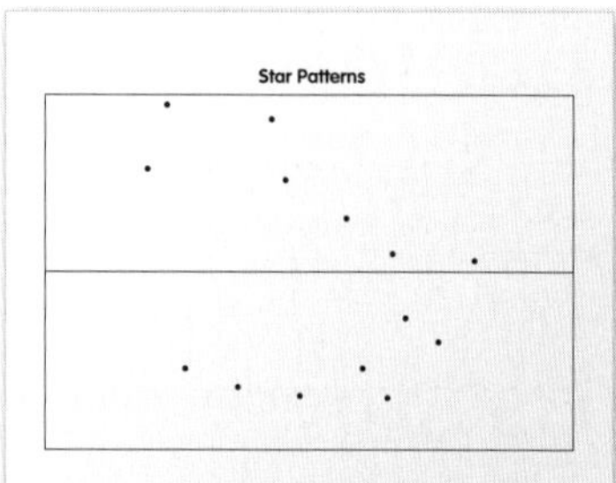

star patterns

cardboard

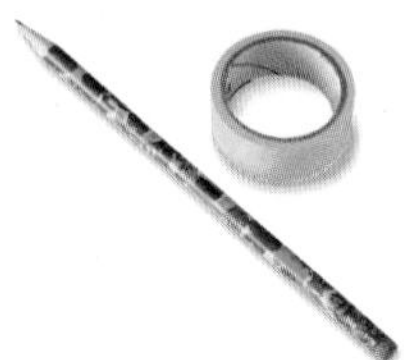

pencil and tape

Investigate

Star Pictures

Steps

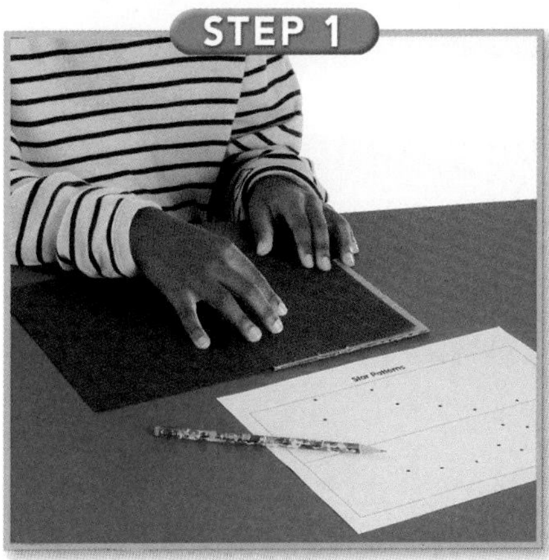
STEP 1

1. Place one half of the black paper over the cardboard. Place a star pattern over that half of the black paper.

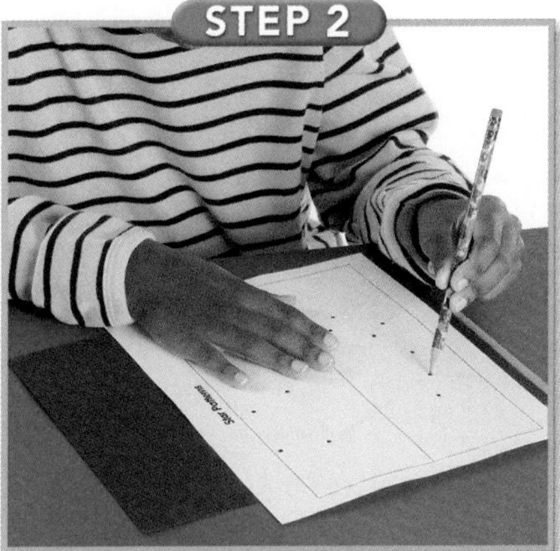
STEP 2

2. **Use Models** Make the star pattern on the black paper. Punch a hole for each dot.

STEP 3

3. Repeat steps 1 and 2 for the other star pattern. Tape the black paper to a window.

Think and Share

1. What pictures did you see?
2. **Compare** How are the star patterns alike and different?

Investigate More!

Experiment At night, go outdoors with an adult. Draw the stars that you see. Point out the brighter stars. Then look for star patterns. Share your drawings.

Learn by Reading

Vocabulary

star

constellation

Reading Skill

Compare and Contrast

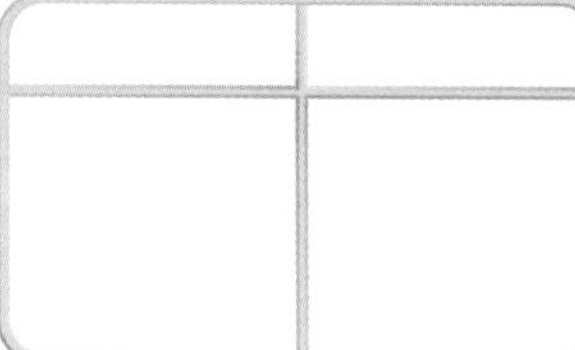

Stars

A **star** is a big ball of hot gases that gives off light. Stars are always in the sky. The Sun is a star. The Sun is the closest star to Earth. That is why living things on Earth are able to use the Sun's energy. The Sun's light is so bright that you cannot see any other stars during the day.

Stars are different colors. The Sun is a yellow star.

blue star

red star

At night, when our side of Earth faces away from the Sun, the sky is dark. Then you can see the other stars. They look like tiny points of light. There are so many that they are hard to count. Like the Sun, the other stars are very large. They look much smaller because they are farther away than the Sun. Some stars look brighter than others. Those stars may be bigger, hotter, or closer to Earth.

COMPARE AND CONTRAST **How are all stars alike?**

Star Patterns

Some stars seem to form pictures. A **constellation** is a group of stars that forms a picture. People have named the constellations. Constellations can help you find some stars. The star Polaris is in the Little Dipper. Polaris is also called the North Star. Sailors can use the North Star to help them guide their ships.

COMPARE AND CONTRAST What are two groups of stars that look alike?

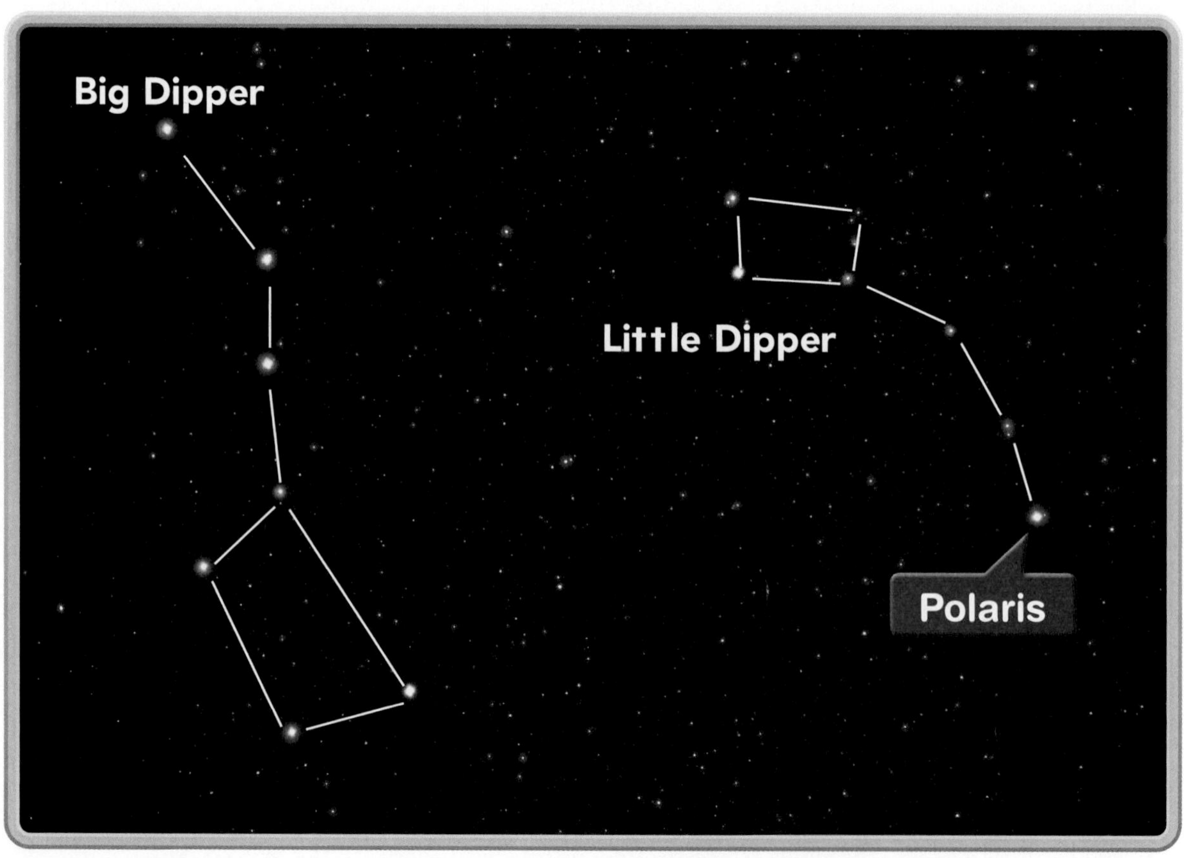

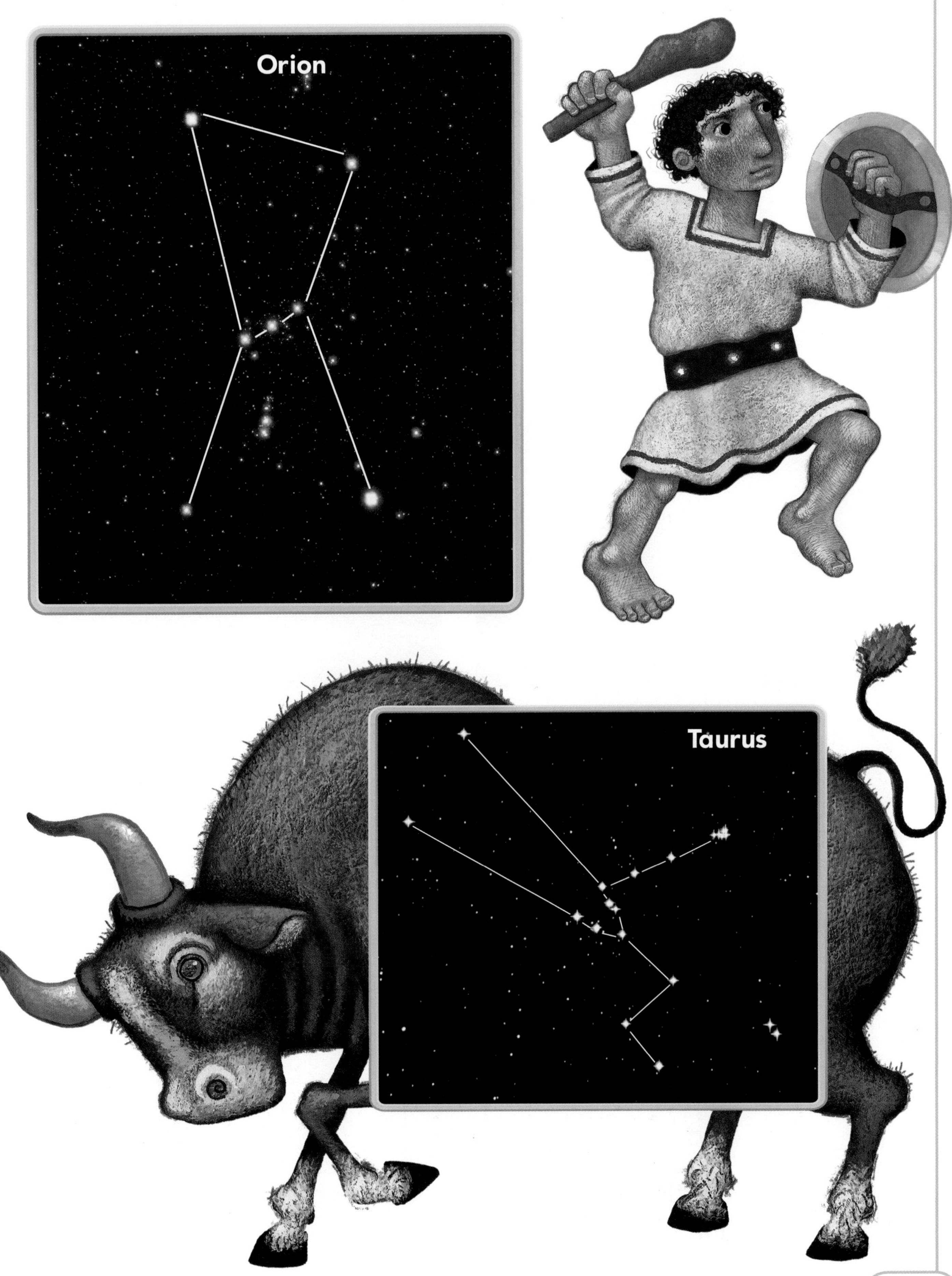
Orion
Taurus

Star Locations

Like the Moon, stars seem to move across the night sky. Earth is causing this motion. As Earth rotates, you see different parts of the night sky. You can see different stars in different seasons because Earth moves during the year.

Why does the Little Dipper seem to move?

Lesson Wrap-Up

1. **Vocabulary** What is a **constellation**?
2. **Reading Skill** How is the Sun different from other stars?
3. **Compare** How are stars different from one another?

Technology Visit **www.eduplace.com/scp/** to find out more about stars.

LINKS for Home and School

Math Use a Calendar

This calendar shows the Moon phases for a month.

March						
Sun	Mon	Tue	Wed	Thu	Fri	Sat
					1	2
3	4	5	6	7	8	9
10	11	12	13	14	15	16
17	18	19	20	21	22	23
24	25	26	27	28	29	30
31						

1. How long does it take the Moon to go from new to full?

2. Draw a picture to show how the Moon will look on April 1.

Language Arts Sky Flip Book

Make a book with four cut pages like the one shown. Label the pages in the top half **Sun, Earth, Moon,** and **star**. Write about each sky object on the bottom half of the pages. Flip pages to match each word to its description.

Chapter 9 Review and Test Prep

Visual Summary

Movements of Earth and the Moon cause patterns.

Main Ideas

1. What are some objects in the solar system? **(pp. D38–D39)**
2. What causes night and day on Earth? **(p. D42)**
3. Why does the Moon appear to change? **(p. D50)**
4. Why do some stars look brighter than others? **(p. D57)**

Vocabulary

Choose the correct word from the box.

planet (p. D38)
orbit (p. D44)
Moon (p. D48)
star (p. D56)

5. A big ball of hot gases that gives off light
6. A large object that moves around the Sun
7. A large sphere made of rock
8. The path that one space object travels around another

Test Practice

Choose a word to complete the sentence.

9. A _____ is a group of stars that forms a picture.

   planet constellation sphere phase

Using Science Skills

10. **Use Models** How can using models of the Sun and the Moon help you understand the Moon's phases?
11. **Critical Thinking** How does the Sun help living things?

Discover!

Why doesn't it snow everywhere in winter?

Because of Earth's shape and tilt, the Sun is high in the sky in places closer to the middle of Earth every day. These places get more light and heat from the Sun all year. During winter it is usually too warm to snow in these places.

winter in California

winter in Florida

Go to **www.eduplace.com/scp/** to see why it snows in some places during winter.

PHYSICAL SCIENCE

Matter and Energy

Cricket Connection

Visit www.eduplace.com/scp/ to check out *Click, Ask,* and *Odyssey* magazine articles and activities.

PHYSICAL UNIT E SCIENCE

Matter and Energy

Independent Reading

What's This Matter?

It Must Be Clay

How Does This Sound?

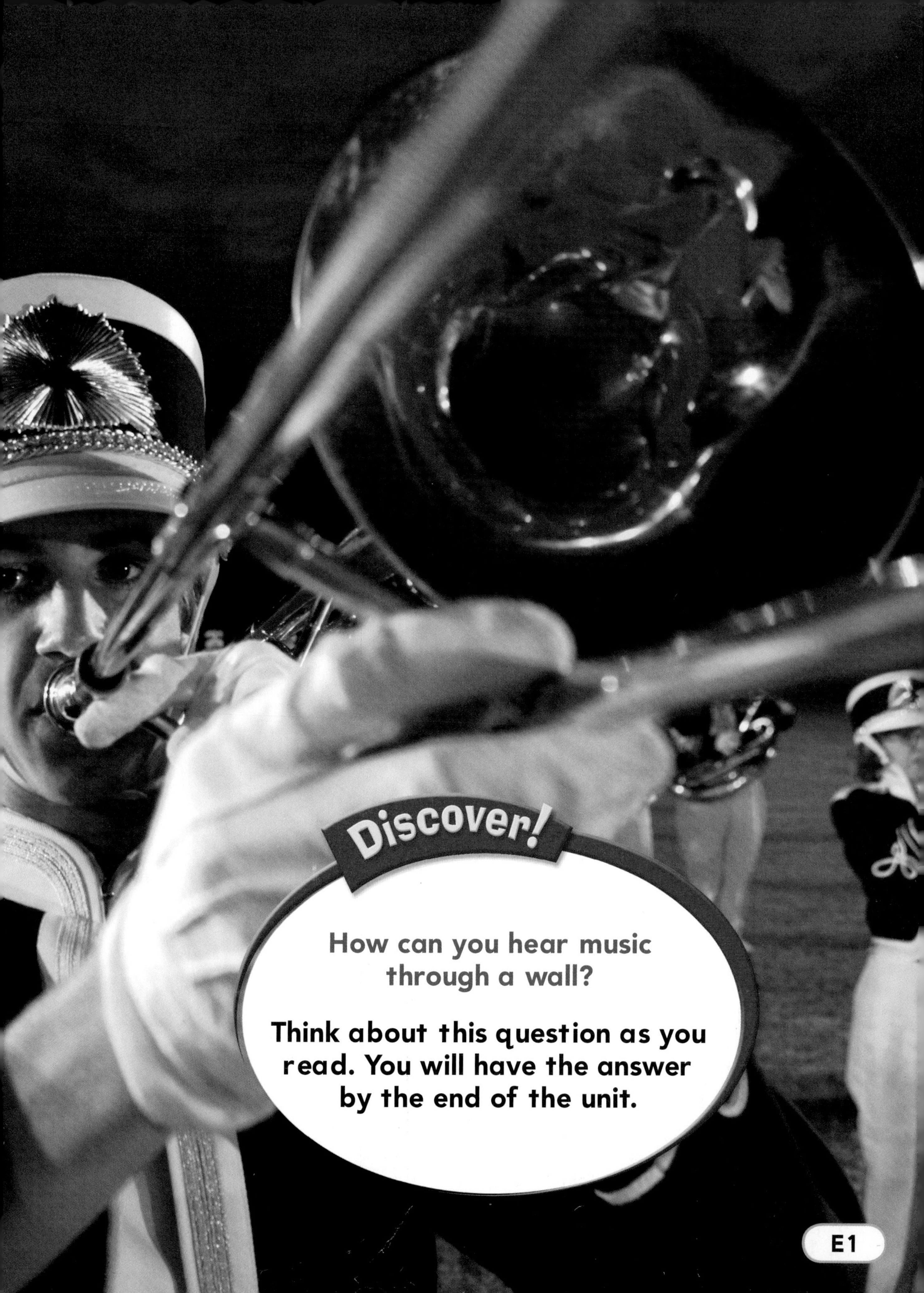
Discover!
How can you hear music through a wall?
Think about this question as you read. You will have the answer by the end of the unit.

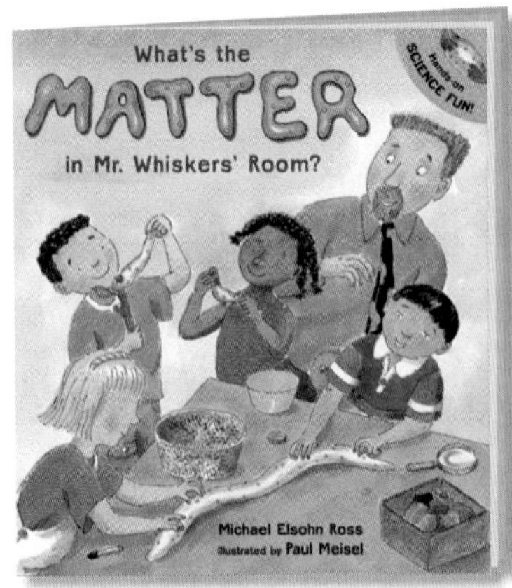

What's the Matter in Mr. Whiskers' Room?

by Michael Elsohn Ross
illustrated by Paul Meisel

"So, what you're telling me," Mr. Whiskers said, "is that matter is everywhere and everything is matter. You are matter. I am matter. Everything from Popsicles to planets is matter!"

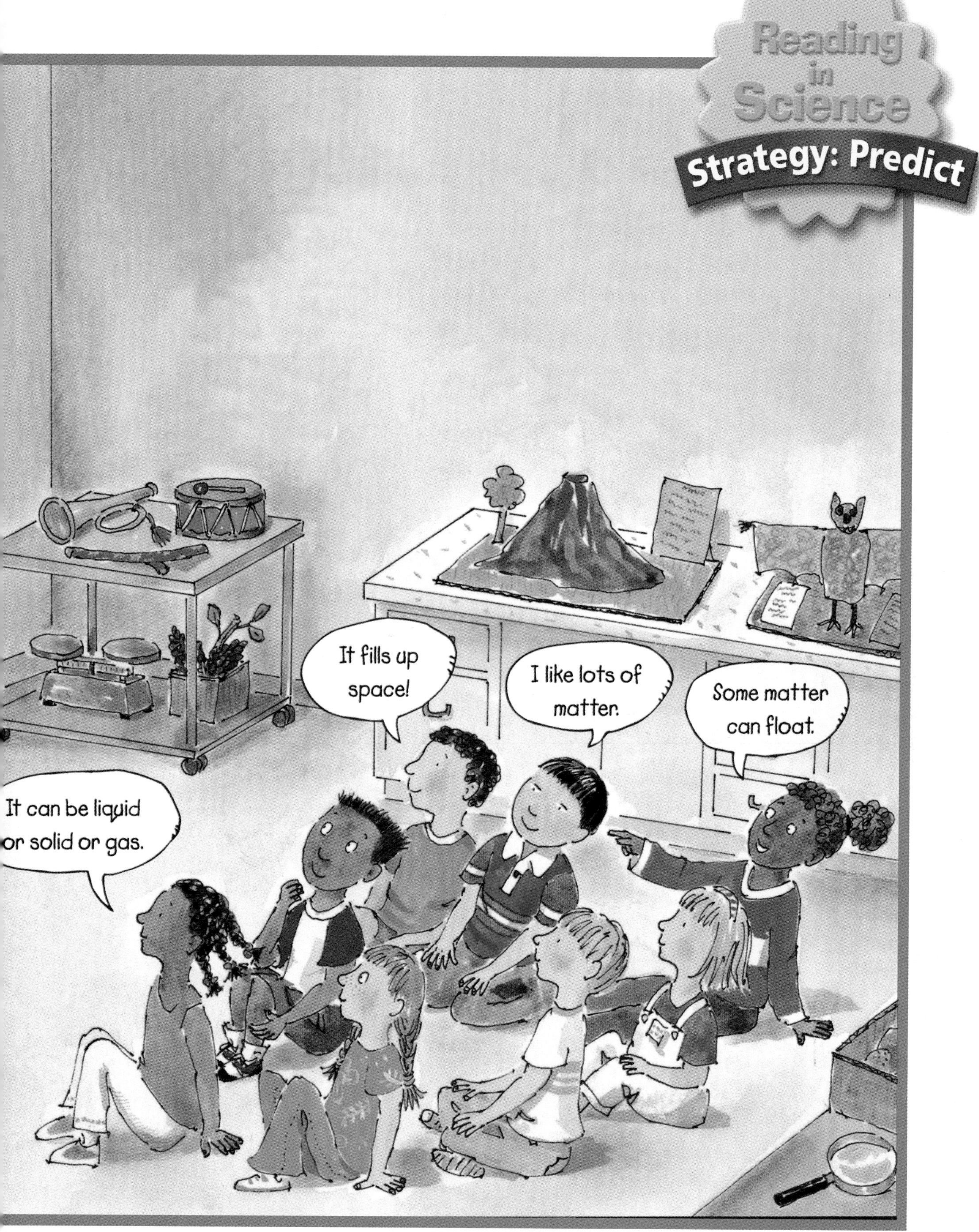
Reading in Science
Strategy: Predict
It can be liquid or solid or gas.
It fills up space!
I like lots of matter.
Some matter can float.

Chapter 10

Comparing Matter

Vocabulary Preview

properties
solid
liquid
gas
volume
mass
mixture
separate
dissolves
magnify

properties

Color, shape, size, odor, and texture are properties.

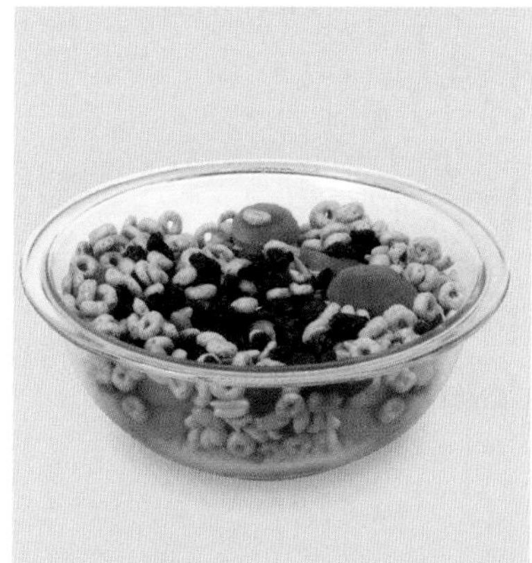

mixture

A mixture is something made of two or more things.

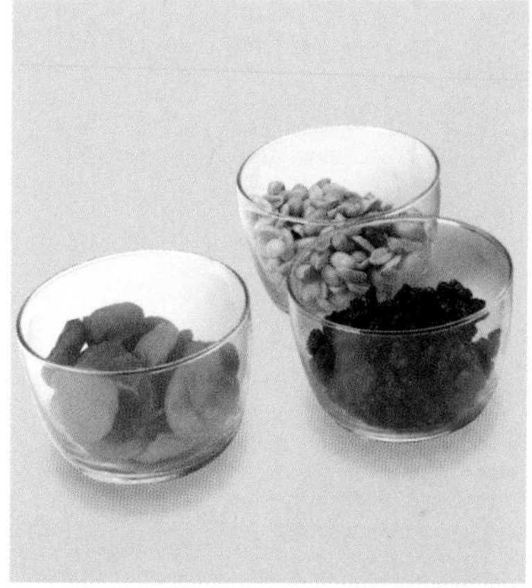

separate

You can take apart, or separate, a mixture.

magnify

Some tools can make objects look larger, or magnify them.

Lesson 1

How Can You Compare Matter?

Science and You

Knowing about matter can help you describe things.

Inquiry Skill

Measure You can use tools to measure length, volume, and mass.

What You Need

balance

gram cubes

golf ball

measuring cup and water

Investigate

Measure Matter

Steps

1. Hold a golf ball in one hand. Estimate how many gram cubes it equals.

2. **Measure** Use a balance to check your estimate.

3. **Measure** Pour water into a measuring cup to the 100-milliliter mark.

4. **Measure** Put a golf ball into the measuring cup. Measure the change in the water level.

STEP 1

STEP 2

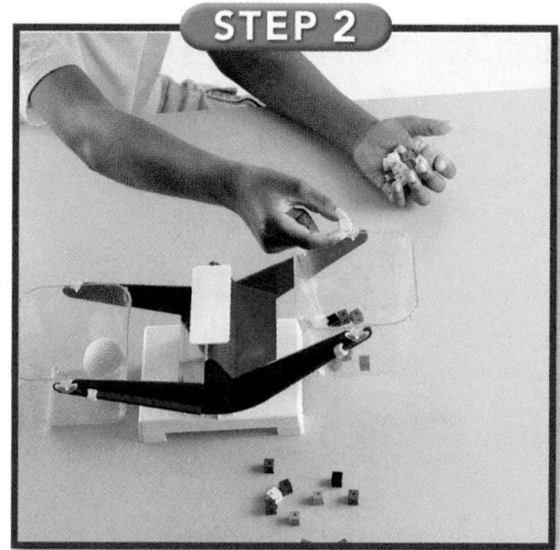

STEP 3

Think and Share

1. **Compare** How did your measurement of the ball compare to your estimate?

2. How did the number of milliliters in the cup change when you added the ball?

Investigate More!

Work Together Find other objects that can be measured on a balance. Talk about how to sort them by their measurements.

Learn by Reading

Vocabulary

properties
solid
liquid
gas
volume
mass

Reading Skill
Categorize and Classify

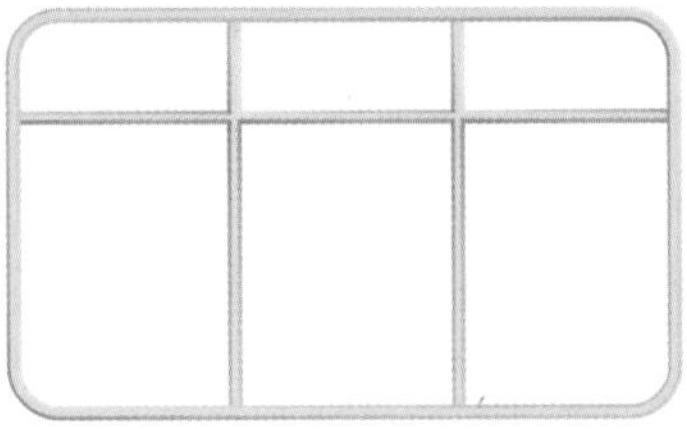

Describing Objects

You can describe objects by their properties. Color, shape, size, odor, and texture are **properties**. A balloon can be red or yellow. A slipper can be soft and fuzzy. A penny is round and flat.

You can describe objects by the materials from which they are made. A penny is made of copper. Marbles are made of glass. A spring toy can be made of plastic.

Other properties tell what objects or materials do. Some objects can bend without breaking. Others cannot. Some will stretch. Others will tear apart. Some materials will let light pass through. Others will not. A marble will roll. A rock will sink in water. A pencil will float.

CLASSIFY What are properties that you can see?

Which objects will let light pass through? Which will not?

States of Matter

All things are made of matter. The three states of matter are solid, liquid, and gas.

A **solid** is a state of matter that has its own size and shape. A toy boat is a solid. If you toss it into a pool, it will keep its size and shape.

A **liquid** is a state of matter that does not have its own shape. Water is a liquid. Liquids flow and take the shape of a container.

What are the solids, the liquids, and the gases in the picture?

A balloon holds a gas.

A **gas** is a state of matter that spreads out to fill a space. It has no shape of its own. A gas always fills a closed container and comes out when you open the container.

CLASSIFY **Is juice a solid, a liquid, or a gas?**

Using Tools to Measure

All matter takes up space. The amount of space that matter takes up can be measured. You can measure the length, width, and height of a solid object with a ruler. You can measure the amount of space that a liquid takes up, or **volume**, with a measuring cup.

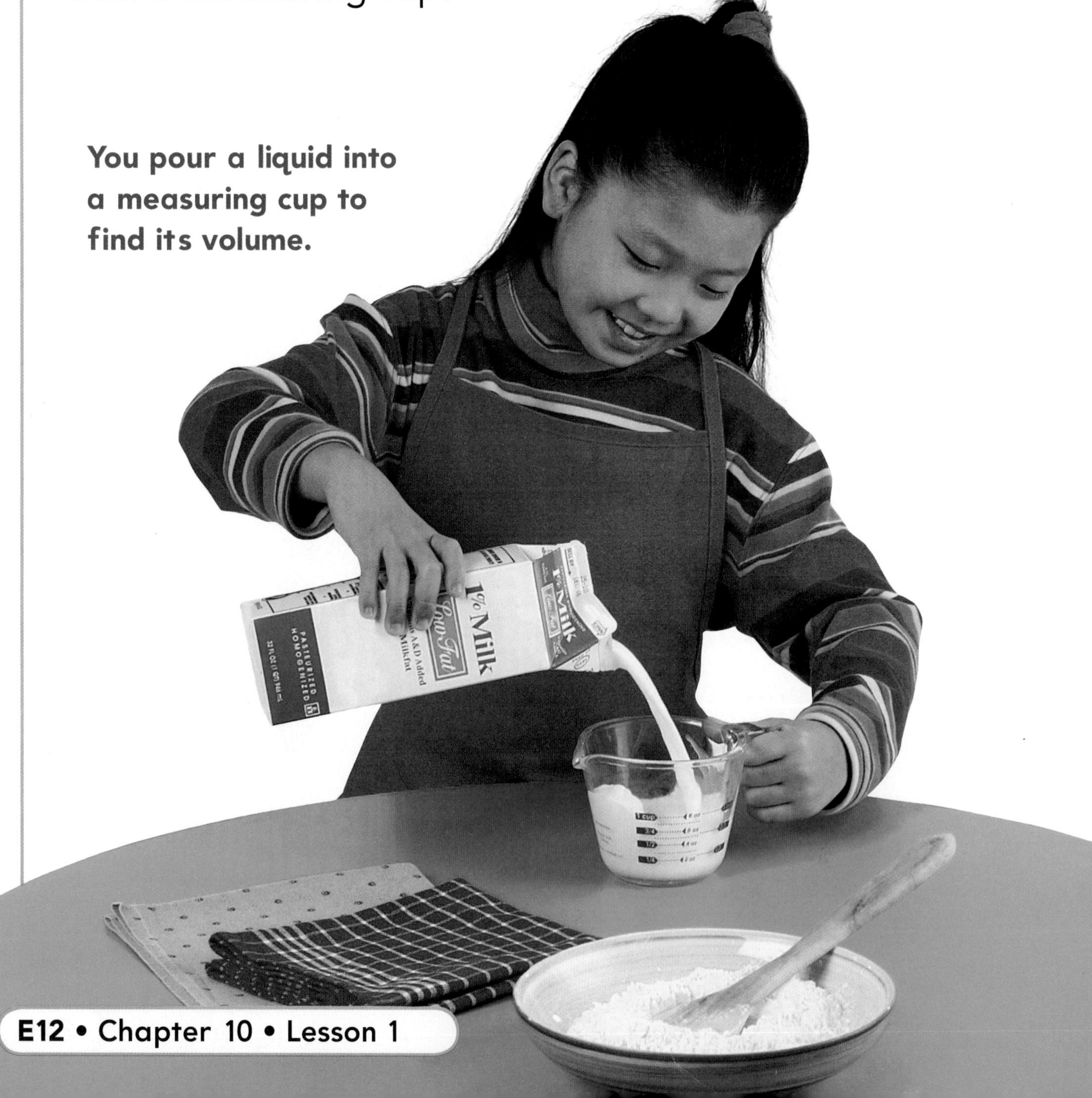

You pour a liquid into a measuring cup to find its volume.

Mass is the amount of matter in an object. All matter has mass. You can measure the mass of an object with a balance. The object sits on one side of the balance. Then you add mass units until the sides are even.

CLASSIFY Name two properties that can be measured.

Lesson Wrap-Up

1. **Vocabulary** What are color, size, shape, and texture?
2. **Reading Skill** Look at the picture. Name a solid. Name a liquid. Name a gas.
3. **Measure** What tool would you use to measure volume?

Technology Visit **www.eduplace.com/scp/** to find out more about comparing matter.

Lesson 2

How Does Matter Change?

Science and You

When glue hardens, it changes from a liquid to a solid.

Inquiry Skill

Compare Tell how objects are alike or different.

What You Need

foil

butter

wooden block

lamp

Investigate

Compare Matter

Steps

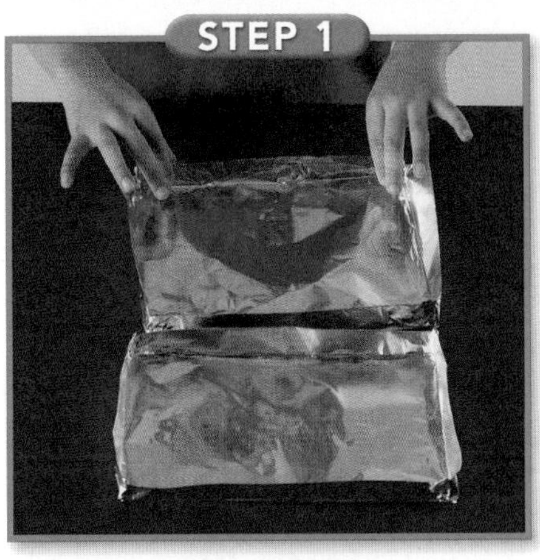

1. Make two trays from foil.

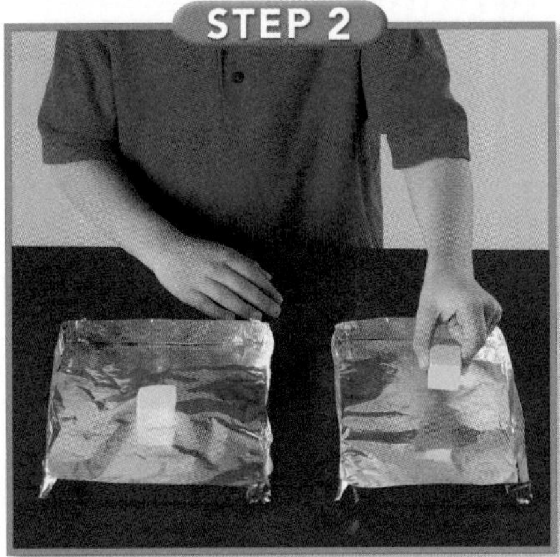

2. Put some butter on one tray. Put a block on the other tray.

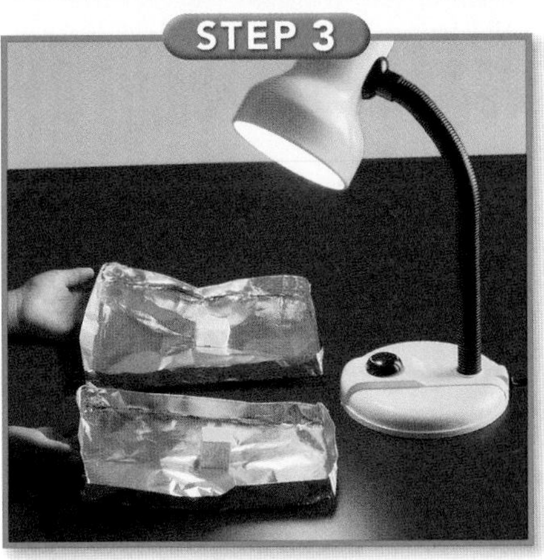

3. **Predict** Put the trays under a lamp. Tell what you think will happen after 10 minutes. Then observe. **Safety:** The lamp is hot!

4. **Compare** How did your prediction compare to your results?

Think and Share

1. **Compare** Tell how the changes to the butter and the block were alike and different.

2. **Infer** What do you think caused the changes?

Investigate More!

Experiment Repeat the activity with other solids. You might use an ice cube and a pencil. What can you infer about solids?

Learn by Reading

Mixing Matter

Vocabulary

mixture

separate

dissolves

Reading Skill

Draw Conclusions

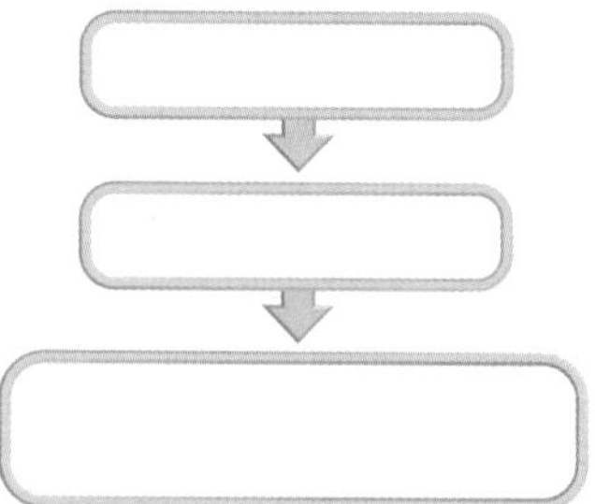

You can put matter together to make a mixture. A **mixture** is something made of two or more things.

When you make a mixture, there is no new matter. Each part is still there. You can take apart, or **separate**, a mixture.

Trail mix is a mixture that is easy to separate.

Some mixtures are easy to separate. The parts stay the same size and shape. They are easy to see.

Some mixtures are hard to separate. When you stir drink mix powder into water, it **dissolves**, or mixes completely with water. The powder breaks up into pieces too small to see. But it is still powder.

DRAW CONCLUSIONS Why are some mixtures harder to separate than others?

What is happening to the powder?

Changing Matter

You can change the properties of solid matter in many ways. You can change the shape of matter by cutting it. You can change the size or shape of matter by breaking it into smaller pieces. You can tear paper into different sizes and shapes.

cutting paper

sanding wood

You can sift sand to separate the different-sized pieces. You can pound a lump of clay until it is flat. You can sand the edges of a block of wood to make them smooth. These kinds of changes do not change the material that the matter is made of.

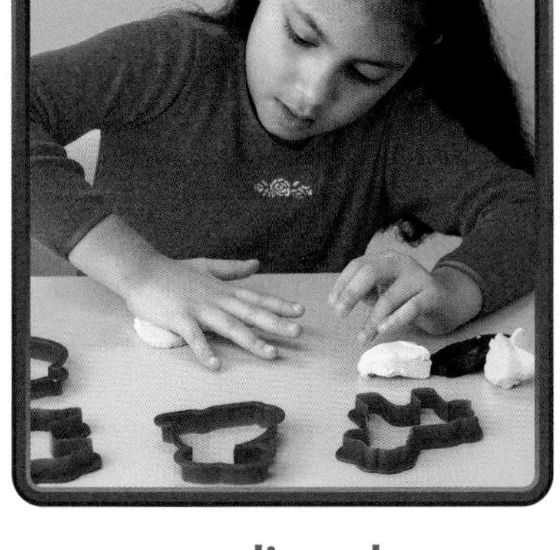
pounding clay

DRAW CONCLUSIONS How are you changing matter when you pound clay?

Changing States

Matter can change from one state to another. Taking away heat causes some liquids to change to solids. Adding heat causes some solids to change to liquids.

An ice cube is solid water. When ice is heated, it changes to liquid water. If the water is heated, it can evaporate and change to a gas, or water vapor.

How did the juice change from the pitcher to the plate?

All matter does not change the same way when heated. Some things melt quickly. Some things melt slowly. Other things do not melt at all.

DRAW CONCLUSIONS If a solid changes to a liquid, what can you say happened?

Butter melts quickly.

Lesson Wrap-Up

1. **Vocabulary** What is a **mixture**?
2. **Reading Skill** What causes matter to change state?
3. **Compare** How are butter and jelly alike and different?

Technology Visit **www.eduplace.com/scp/** to find out more about how matter changes.

Changing Matter to Make Coins

Coins are made by changing matter. It takes many steps to turn raw metal into a coin.

1

A quarter is made from two metals. The two metals begin as solids.

2

The metals are heated and change to liquids. The liquids are mixed together.

3

The mixture is cooled and becomes solid again. It is rolled out into sheets.

A new state quarter is made every 10 weeks. Five different state quarters have been made each year since 1999.

4

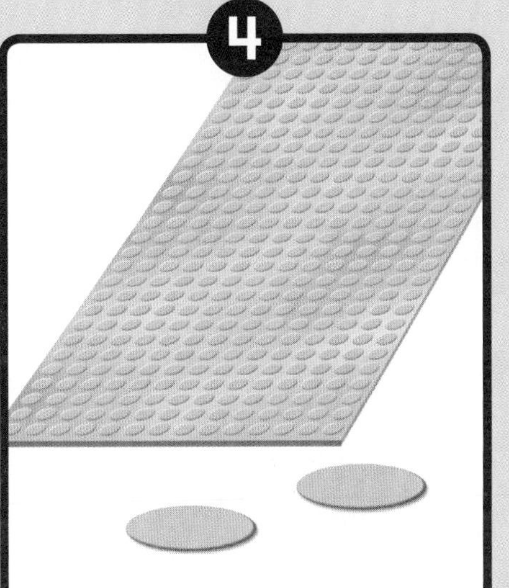

A machine cuts the metal into blank circles.

5

The pictures and words are pressed onto the coins.

Sharing Ideas

1. **Write About It** Name the ways that matter is changed to make a quarter.
2. **Talk About It** How might the quarter change after it is made?

Lesson 3

How Does Matter Look Up Close?

Science and You

A hand lens can help you learn more about the world around you.

Inquiry Skill

Observe You can use tools and your senses to find out about something.

What You Need

objects

hand lens

Investigate

Observe Objects

Steps

1. **Observe** Choose an object to observe. Write or draw what you see.
2. **Observe** Look at the same object with a hand lens. Write or draw what you see.
3. **Communicate** Show your drawings to a partner. Talk about what you saw.
4. Choose another object. Repeat the activity.

STEP 1

STEP 2

STEP 3

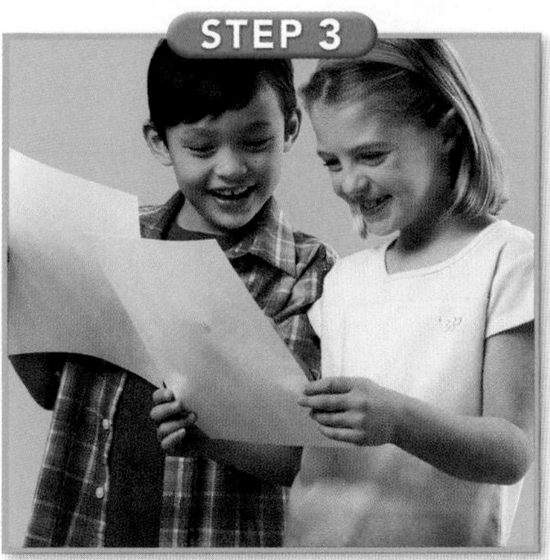

Think and Share

1. What does the hand lens do?
2. **Compare** How is what you see with the hand lens different from what you see without the hand lens?

Investigate More!

Be an Inventor A hand lens can make a task easier. Think of a task that you do at home or at school. Invent a way to use a hand lens to make the job easier.

Learn by Reading

Vocabulary

magnify

Reading Skill

Main Idea and Details

Tools that Magnify

Matter is made of parts too small to see with only your eyes. When you look at a leaf, you see a green shape with lines in it. But the leaf might have colors that you cannot see. It might have smaller lines all over it. To see these parts, you can use a tool.

Some tools can make objects look larger, or **magnify** them. You may have used a hand lens to magnify objects. Sometimes scientists use a microscope to magnify objects even more.

MAIN IDEA **Why are tools needed to see small parts of matter?**

Ants look like this without a magnifying tool.

An ant looks like this through a hand lens. ▶

◀ An ant looks like this through a microscope.

Matter Up Close

When you use a tool to magnify, you can see the small parts of matter. The pictures show how things look when magnified.

granite
feather
fish scales
sugar cube
sesame seed roll
strawberry

Lesson Wrap-Up

1. **Vocabulary** If you **magnify** something, what do you do?
2. **Reading Skill** What two tools can help you see small parts of things?
3. **Observe** What might you see if you used a hand lens to look at an ant?

Technology Visit **www.eduplace.com/scp/** to find out more about tools that magnify.

LINKS for Home and School

Math Measure Length

Choose three objects to measure. Estimate how long you think each is. Then use a ruler to measure each object. Record the measurements in a chart like the one shown. Compare the measurements.

Lengths of Objects		
Object	Estimate	Measure

Art Paint with Mixtures

Make mixtures of different colors. Add 6 teaspoons Epsom salts to $\frac{1}{4}$ cup hot water. Stir until the salts dissolve. Then add food coloring.

Use the mixtures to paint a picture. After the picture dries, use a hand lens to observe it. Tell a partner what you see.

Chapter 10 Review and Test Prep

Visual Summary

Matter is classified by its properties.

A solid has its own size and shape.	A liquid does not have its own shape.	A gas spreads out to fill a space.

Main Ideas

1. What is a solid? **(p. E10)**
2. How are gases and liquids alike? **(pp. E10–E11)**
3. What happens to some solids when they are heated? **(p. E20)**
4. Why would you use a magnifying tool? **(p. E26)**

Vocabulary

Choose the correct word from the box.

properties (p. E8)
mass (p. E13)
separate (p. E16)
dissolves (p. E17)

5. The amount of matter in an object
6. To take apart
7. Mixes completely with water
8. Color, size, shape, odor, and texture

Test Practice

Choose a word to complete the sentence.

9. Something made of two or more things is a ____.

volume   mixture   magnify   property

Using Science Skills

10. **Measure** What tools can you use to measure matter? Tell how.

11. **Critical Thinking** What changes to matter happen in nature, without help from people?

Chapter 11

Making Sound

Vocabulary Preview

sound
vibrates
sound wave
echo
pitch
volume

sound

Sound is energy that you hear.

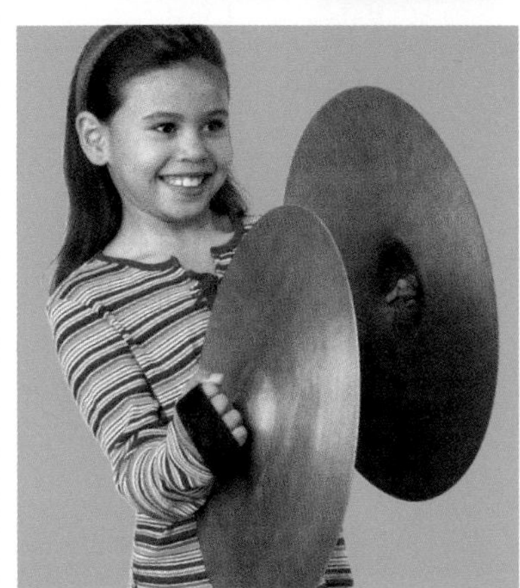

vibrates

Sound is made when matter vibrates, or moves back and forth very quickly.

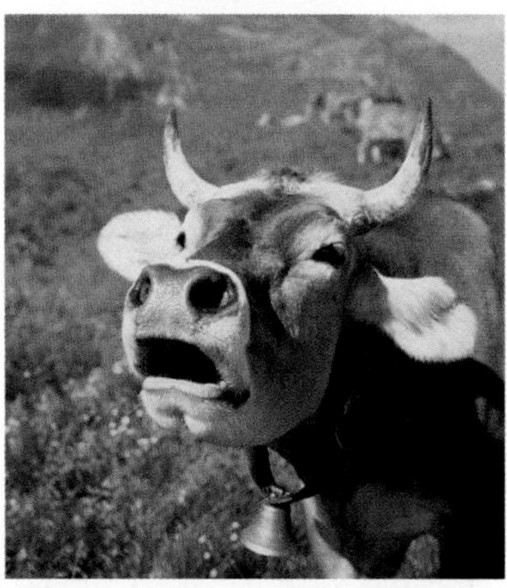

pitch

Pitch is how high or low a sound is.

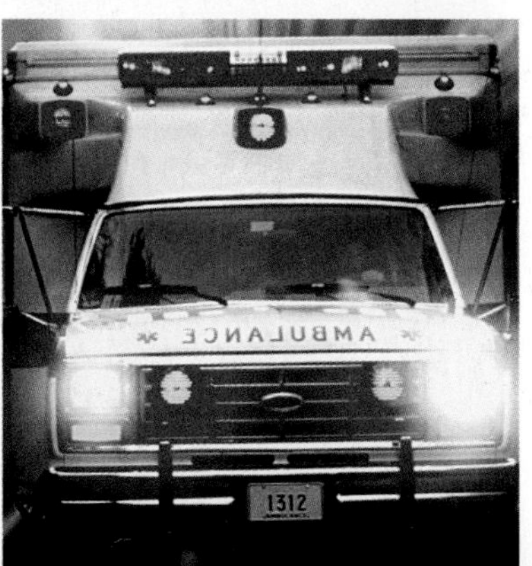

volume

Volume is how loud or soft a sound is.

Lesson 1

How Is Sound Made?

Science and You

You can use what you know about sounds to make music.

Inquiry Skill

Infer Use what you observe and know to tell what you think.

What You Need

plastic jar

wax paper and rubber band

pieces of paper

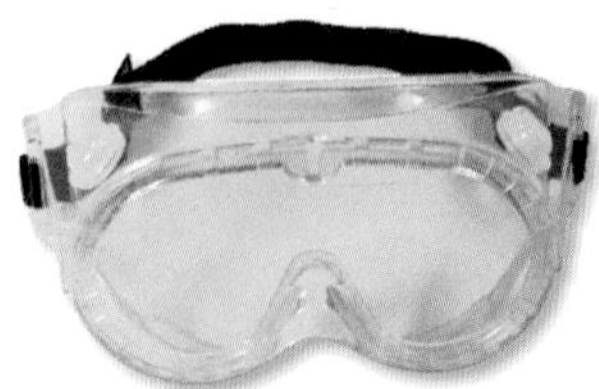

goggles

Investigate

Observe Sound

Steps

1. Stretch a piece of wax paper over the opening of a jar. Use a rubber band to hold the wax paper in place. **Safety:** Wear goggles!

2. Put paper pieces on the wax paper.

3. **Observe** Gently tap the wax paper. Tell what you see and hear.

STEP 1

STEP 2

STEP 3

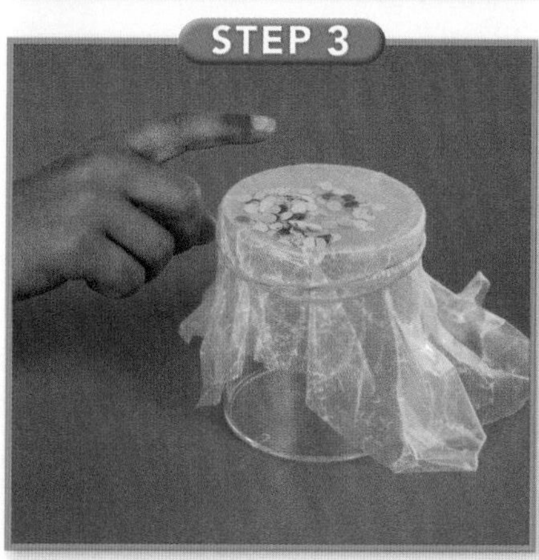

Think and Share

1. **Infer** What caused the paper to move the way it did?
2. How could you cause the paper to move differently?

Investigate More!

Experiment How can you make sound with only a jar and a rubber band? Make a plan to find out. Share your results with the class.

Learn by Reading

Vocabulary

sound

vibrates

sound wave

Reading Skill

Cause and Effect

What Makes Sound

Like heat and light, sound is a form of energy. **Sound** is energy that you hear. Sound is made when matter **vibrates**, or moves back and forth very quickly.

When you play a musical instrument, the air around it vibrates. You hear the vibrating air as sound.

shaking

hitting

You can see some things vibrate. But you cannot see air vibrate. You know that air is vibrating when you hear sound.

CAUSE AND EFFECT **What causes sound?**

How You Hear

You use your ears to hear sound. Vibrating air goes into your ear. This vibrating air is called a **sound wave**. Sound waves move through your ear. They make parts inside your ear vibrate. This causes a nerve in your ear to send a message to your brain. Your brain understands this message as sound.

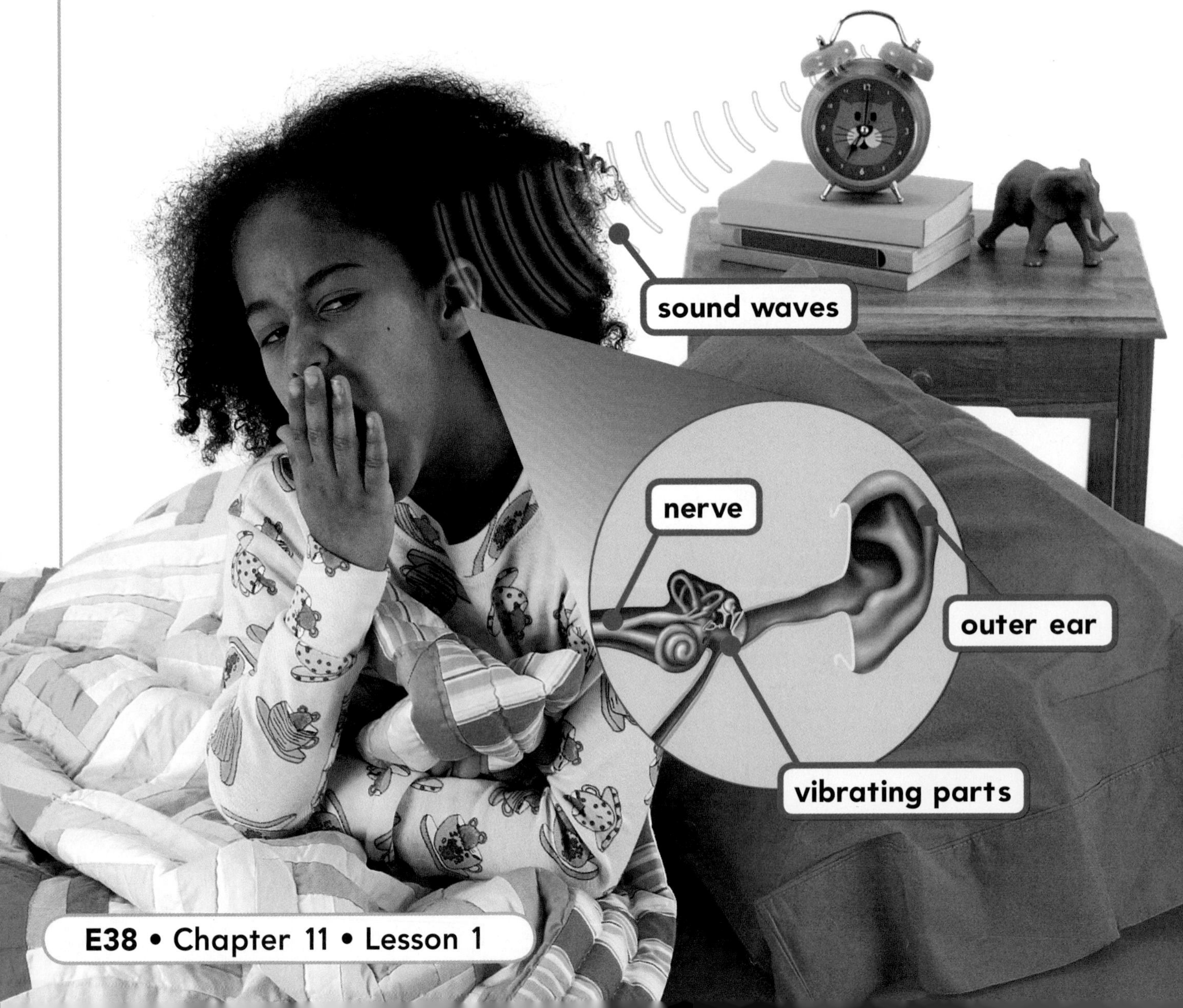

These are two different kinds of hearing aids. ▶

Some people need help to hear. They use hearing aids. A hearing aid has many parts. Some parts change sound waves to make sounds louder. Other parts help move sound waves into the ear.

CAUSE AND EFFECT What happens as sound waves move through the ear?

Lesson Wrap-Up

1. **Vocabulary** What is **sound**?
2. **Reading Skill** What causes a person to hear sounds?
3. **Infer** If you hear a person singing, what is happening to the air around the person?

Technology Visit **www.eduplace.com/scp/** to find out more about how sound is made.

Read these poems about sounds heard in different places.

Wind Song

by Lilian Moore

When the wind blows
the quiet things speak.
Some whisper, some clang,
Some creak.

Grasses swish.
Treetops sigh.
Flags slap
and snap at the sky.
Wires on poles
whistle and hum.
Ashcans roll.
Windows drum.

When the wind goes—
suddenly
then,
the quiet things
are quiet again.

My House's Night Song

by Betsy R. Rosenthal

Listen closely.
Can you hear?

Heater whooshing out
warm air.

Blinds flapping.
Floors creaking.

Clocks ticking.
Faucet leaking.

Dishwasher clicking.
Pipes pinging.

Listen closely.
My house is singing.

Sharing Ideas

1. **Write About It** Make a list of sound words from each poem. How do sounds that you have heard compare to these sounds?
2. **Talk About It** Why do you think poets write about the sounds they hear?

Lesson 2

How Does Sound Travel?

Science and You

The sounds that you hear outdoors travel through the air to your ears.

Inquiry Skill

Compare Listen carefully to tell how objects or events are alike or different.

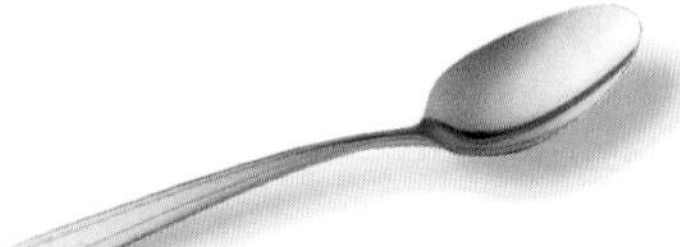

metal spoon

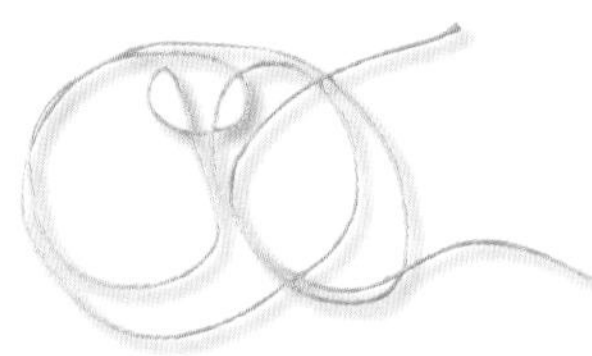

string

Investigate

Compare Sounds

Steps

1. Tie a spoon in the middle of a piece of string.

2. **Observe** Hold the ends of the string to your ears. Listen as you swing the spoon against a table edge.

3. Take the string away from your ears. Listen again as you swing the spoon against the table edge.

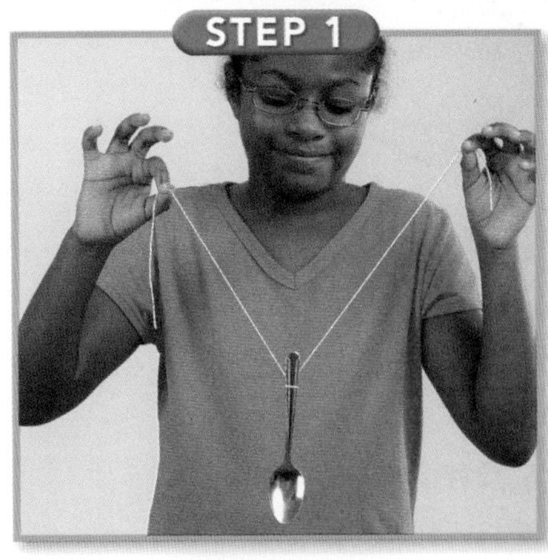
STEP 1

STEP 2

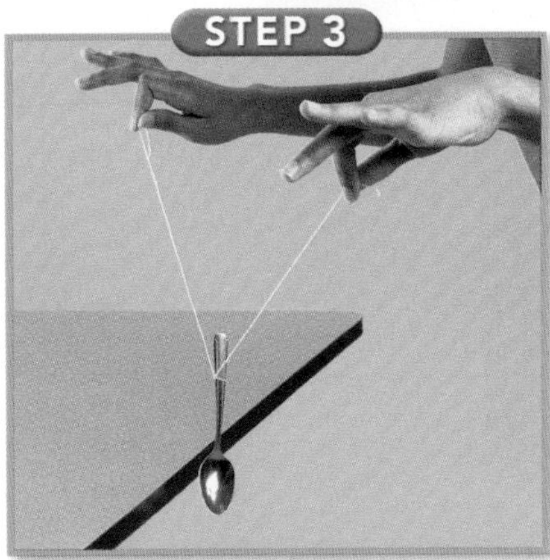
STEP 3

Think and Share

1. **Compare** How were the sounds from the spoon different?
2. **Infer** Why do you think the sounds were different?

Investigate More!

Ask Questions Think about sound as it travels through other materials. What questions would you ask?

Learn by Reading

Vocabulary

echo

Reading Skill

Compare and Contrast

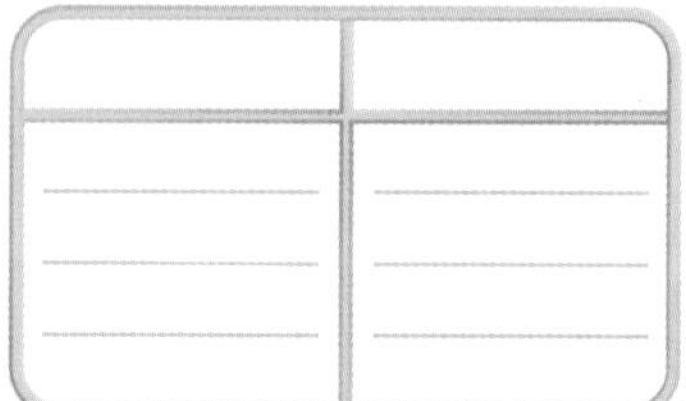

How Sound Travels

Sound travels differently through different states of matter. Most sounds travel through the air. Air is a gas. But sound can travel through liquids and solids, too.

Water is a liquid. Sounds go farther and faster in water than they do in the air. Whales make sounds to communicate with each other underwater. Scientists use an underwater microphone to listen to whale sounds.

orca whales

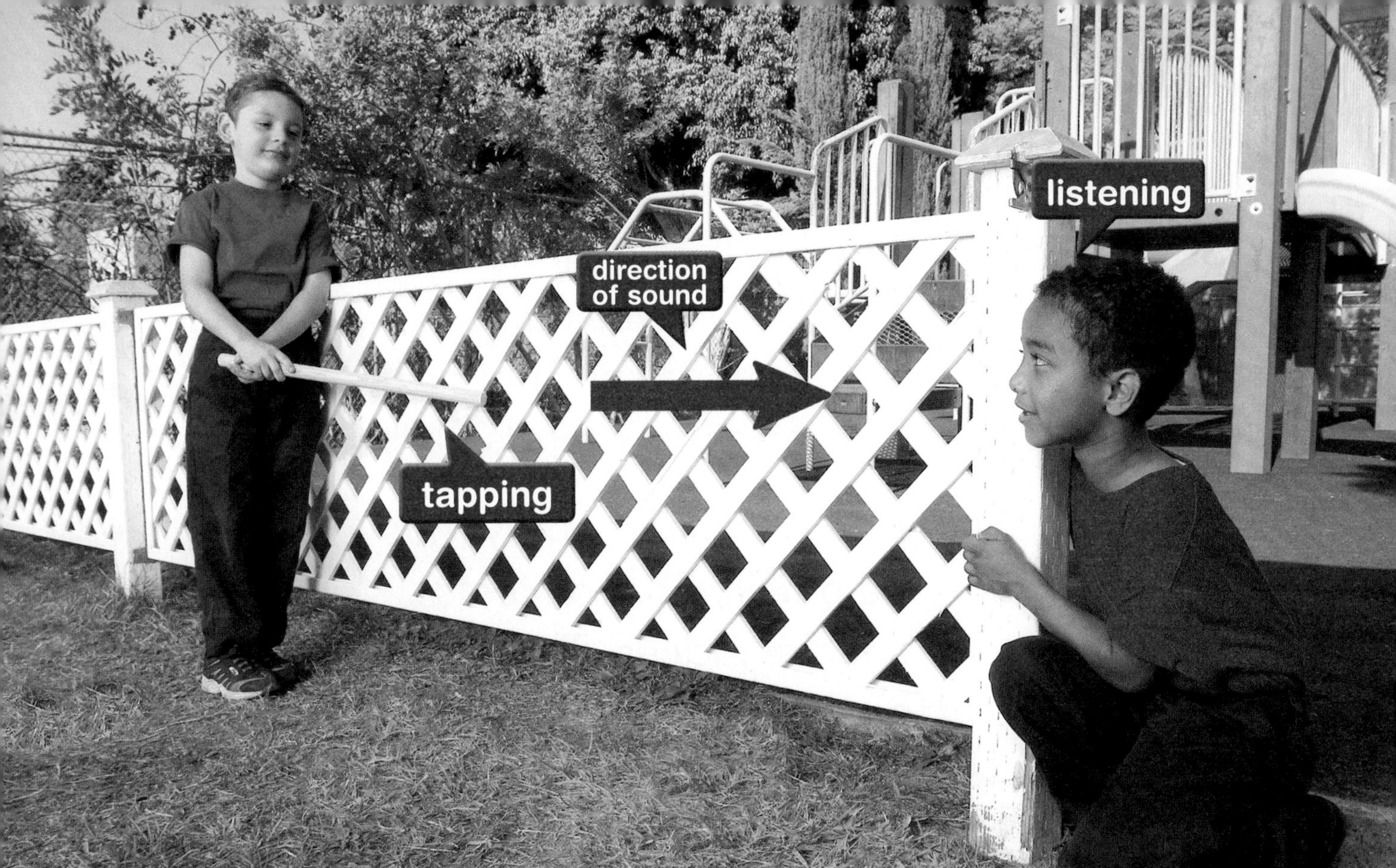

Sound travels faster through the fence than through the air.

Sound travels faster through solids than through air and water. Look at the picture. The child in blue is tapping a wooden fence with a stick. The wooden fence is a solid. The child in red has one ear against the fence. The tapping sound will reach the ear that is listening against the fence faster than it will reach the ear that is listening in the air.

COMPARE AND CONTRAST Does sound travel fastest through gases, solids, or liquids?

Directing Sound

Sound waves move in all directions from a sound. But some sound waves can be made to go in one direction. This makes it easier for people to hear the sounds.

When people go to a concert, they must be able to hear the music. So, concerts often are held in special places. These places are built to make the sound waves move from the stage to the people.

The shape of this stage helps move sound waves toward the listeners.

A bat uses an echo to find an insect. ▶

Bouncing Sound

An **echo** is a sound that repeats when sound waves bounce off a surface. Some animals, such as bats and dolphins, use echoes to find things in the dark. First, the animal makes a sound. The sound waves bouncing off an object cause an echo. The animal listens to the echo to find the object.

COMPARE AND CONTRAST How is an echo different from other sounds?

Lesson Wrap-Up

1. **Vocabulary** What is an **echo**?
2. **Reading Skill** Compare how sound travels through gases with how it travels through solids and liquids.
3. **Compare** How are sounds that travel in water different from sounds that travel in the air?

Technology Visit **www.eduplace.com/scp/** to find out more about how sound travels.

Lesson 3

How Do Sounds Change?

Science and You

Animals and people can make different sounds by changing the shape of their mouth and throat.

Inquiry Skill

Infer Use what you observe and know to tell what you think.

What You Need

8 straws

scissors

tape

Investigate

Making Sounds

Steps

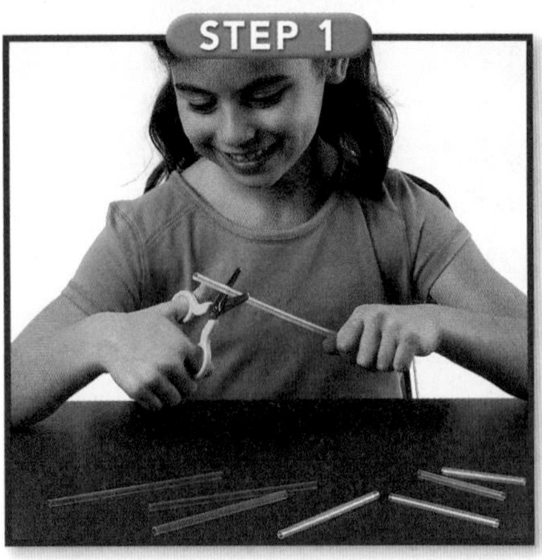

1. **Measure** Cut each straw a different length. **Safety:** Scissors are sharp!

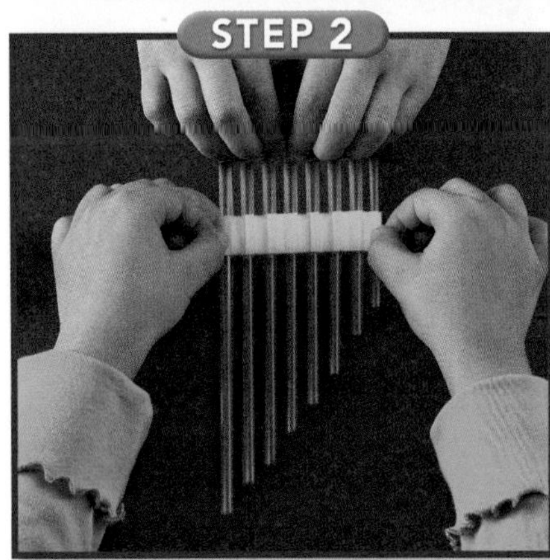

2. Put the straws in order from longest to shortest on a strip of tape. Put another strip of tape across the other side of the straws.

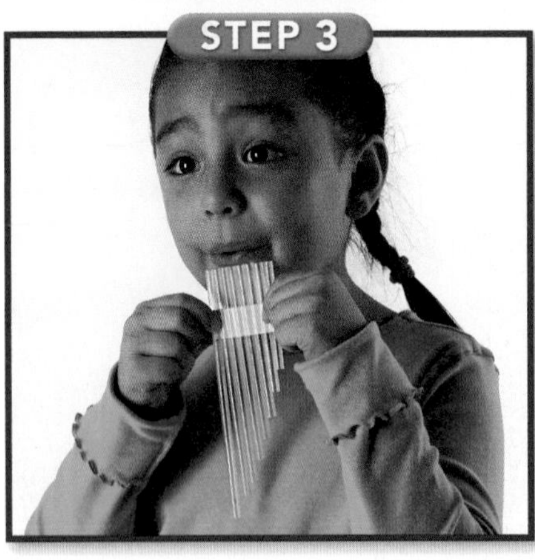

3. **Observe** Blow across the top of each straw. Decide which sounds are high and which are low.

Think and Share

1. **Infer** How does the length of the straw affect the sound it makes?
2. **Predict** If you blew across the end of a long paper tube, would it make a high sound or a low sound? Why?

Investigate More!

Be an Inventor Make an instrument, using different materials. Show others how your instrument can make high and low sounds.

Learn by Reading

Vocabulary

pitch

volume

Reading Skill

Cause and Effect

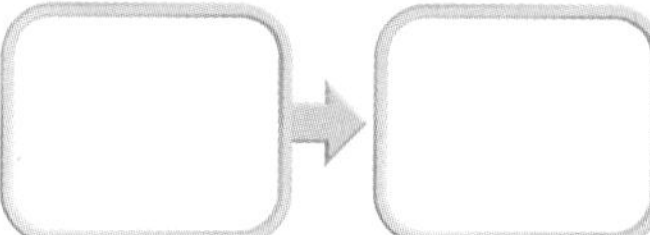

Pitch

You can describe sound by its pitch. **Pitch** is how high or low a sound is. Something that vibrates more quickly makes a sound with a high pitch. Something that vibrates more slowly makes a sound with a low pitch.

An object's size also can tell about its sound. A short or small object often makes a sound with a high pitch.

Comparing Pitch

low pitch	high pitch
flute	piccolo
cow	canary
school bell	jingle bells

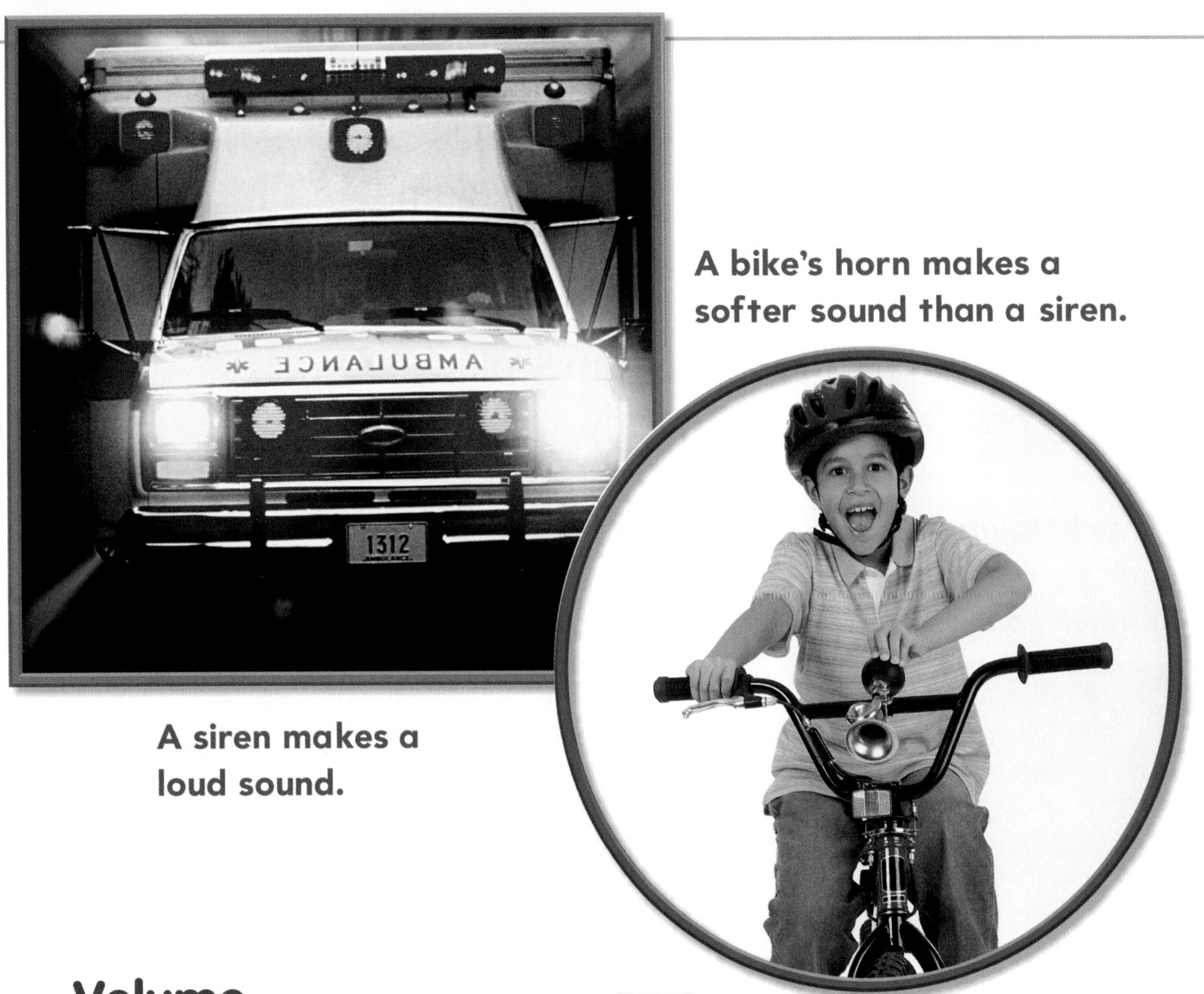

A bike's horn makes a softer sound than a siren.

A siren makes a loud sound.

Volume

Volume is how loud or soft a sound is. Like waves at the beach, sound waves can be big or small. Big sound waves carry a lot of energy. When sound waves are big, the sound is loud. Small sound waves carry less energy. The sound is softer. A sound can seem loud if it is close and soft if it is far away.

CAUSE AND EFFECT **What causes an object to make a sound with a high pitch?**

Changing Pitch and Volume

You can change the pitch and volume of a sound. To change the pitch on a guitar, you can shorten the part of the string that vibrates. To change the volume, pluck the string harder or more gently.

Short strings vibrate quickly and make a higher sound. ▼

▲ Long strings vibrate slowly and make a lower sound.

Lesson Wrap-Up

1. **Vocabulary** What is **pitch**?
2. **Reading Skill** What causes a loud sound?
3. **Infer** You hear a bark with a low pitch. Do you think it is a big dog or a small dog?

Technology Visit **www.eduplace.com/scp/** to find out more about pitch and volume.

LINKS for Home and School

Math Make a Tally Chart

Make a chart like the one shown. Go to a place where you will hear many sounds. Listen for five minutes. Record each sound. Make tally marks to show the number of times you hear each sound. Circle the sounds that you think are loud. Compare your chart with others.

Sounds I Heard	
Sounds	Tally

Music Pitch and Volume

Play different instruments. Try to change the pitch and volume. Your voice can be an instrument, too. Try to change its pitch and volume.

Chapter 11 Review and Test Prep

Visual Summary

Sound travels through different materials.

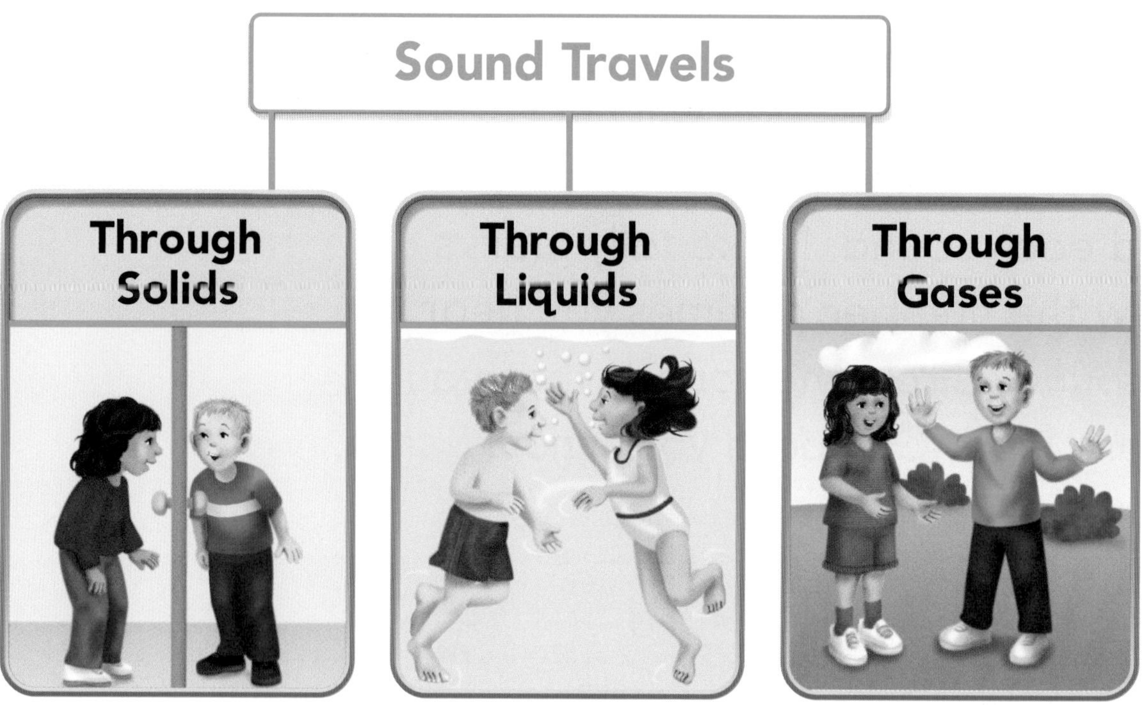

Main Ideas

1. How is sound made? **(p. E36)**
2. Explain how people hear. **(p. E38)**
3. Does sound travel faster through a liquid or a gas? **(p. E44)**
4. Describe the sound made by a slow vibration. **(p. E50)**

Vocabulary

Choose the correct word from the box.

vibrate (p. E36)
sound wave (p. E38)
pitch (p. E50)
volume (p. E51)

5. How high or low a sound is
6. To move back and forth very quickly
7. How loud or soft a sound is
8. Vibrating air

Test Practice

Choose a word to complete the sentence.

9. Energy that you hear is called ____.

   light   electricity   sound   heat

Using Science Skills

10. **Infer** A girl is swimming underwater. Her father is standing near her in the water. Who will be the first to hear a motorboat in the distance?

11. **Critical Thinking** Would you be more likely to hear an echo in a cave or an open field? Tell why.

Wrap-Up

Discover!

How can you hear music through a wall?

Sound travels through solids, liquids, and gases. Music can travel through a wall, because a wall is a solid. The music moves out from the object that made the sound. Then it moves through the air and the wall to your ear.

Go to **www.eduplace.com/scp/** to make sound waves travel.

PHYSICAL UNIT F SCIENCE

Motion and Forces

Cricket Connection

Visit www.eduplace.com/scp/ to check out *Click, Ask,* and *Odyssey* magazine articles and activities.

SCIENCE

Motion and Forces

Independent Reading

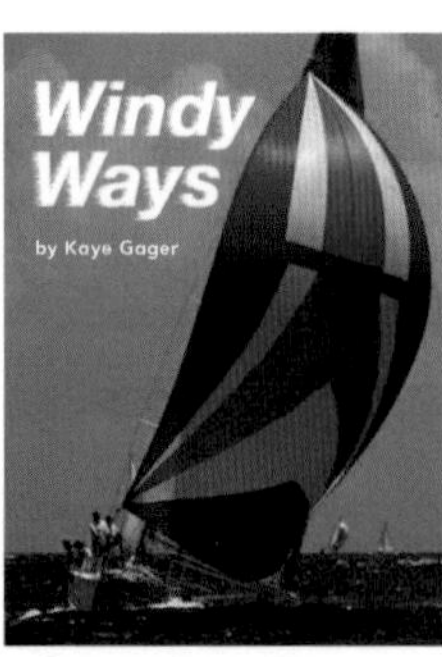

Windy Ways

Magnet Time

Push or Pull

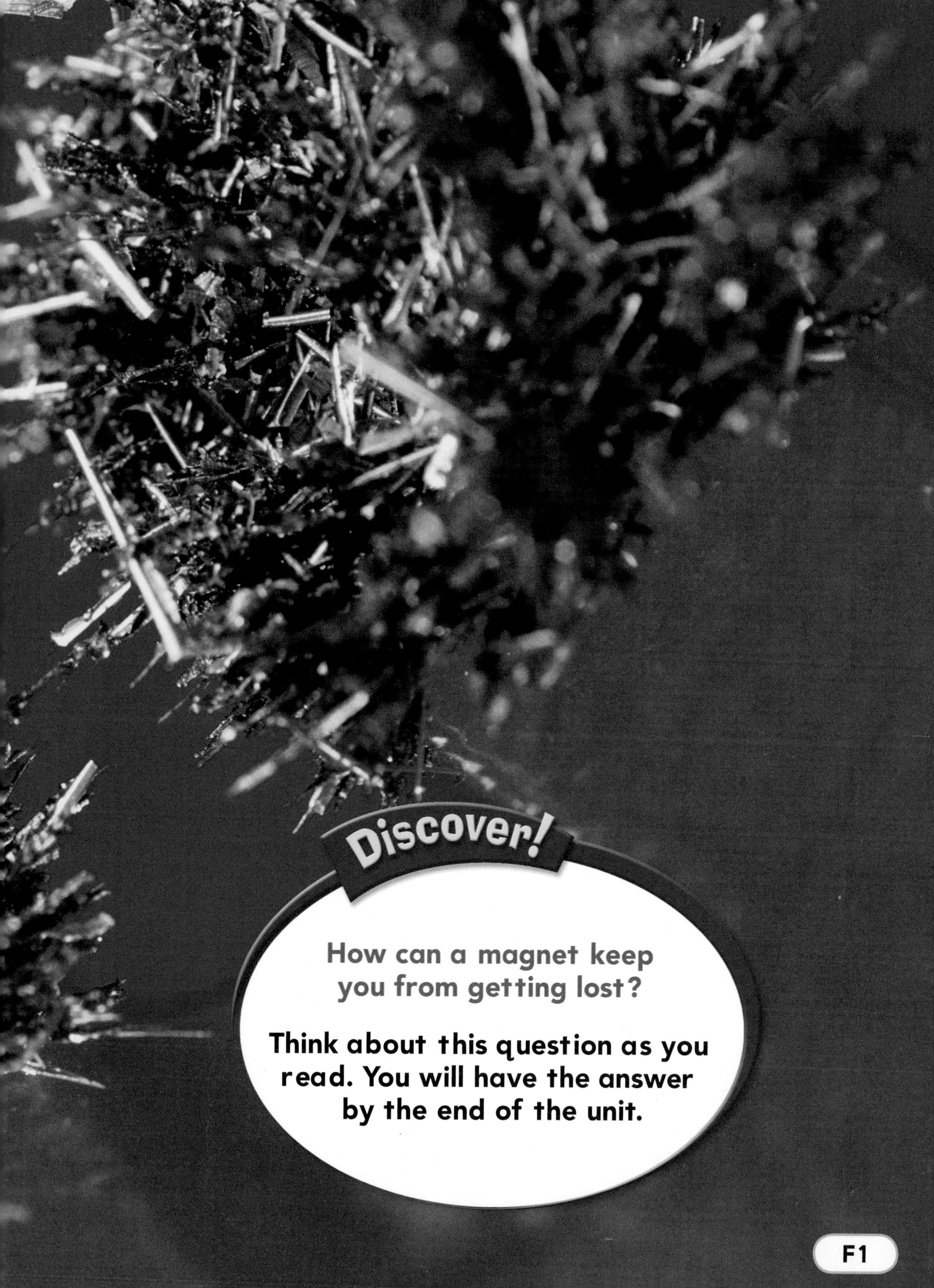
Discover!
How can a magnet keep you from getting lost?
Think about this question as you read. You will have the answer by the end of the unit.

Read Together

Motion

Push and Pull, Fast and Slow

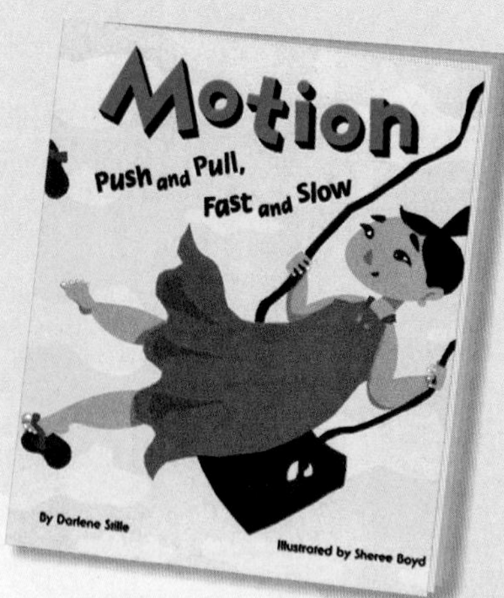

by Darlene Stille
illustrated by Sheree Boyd

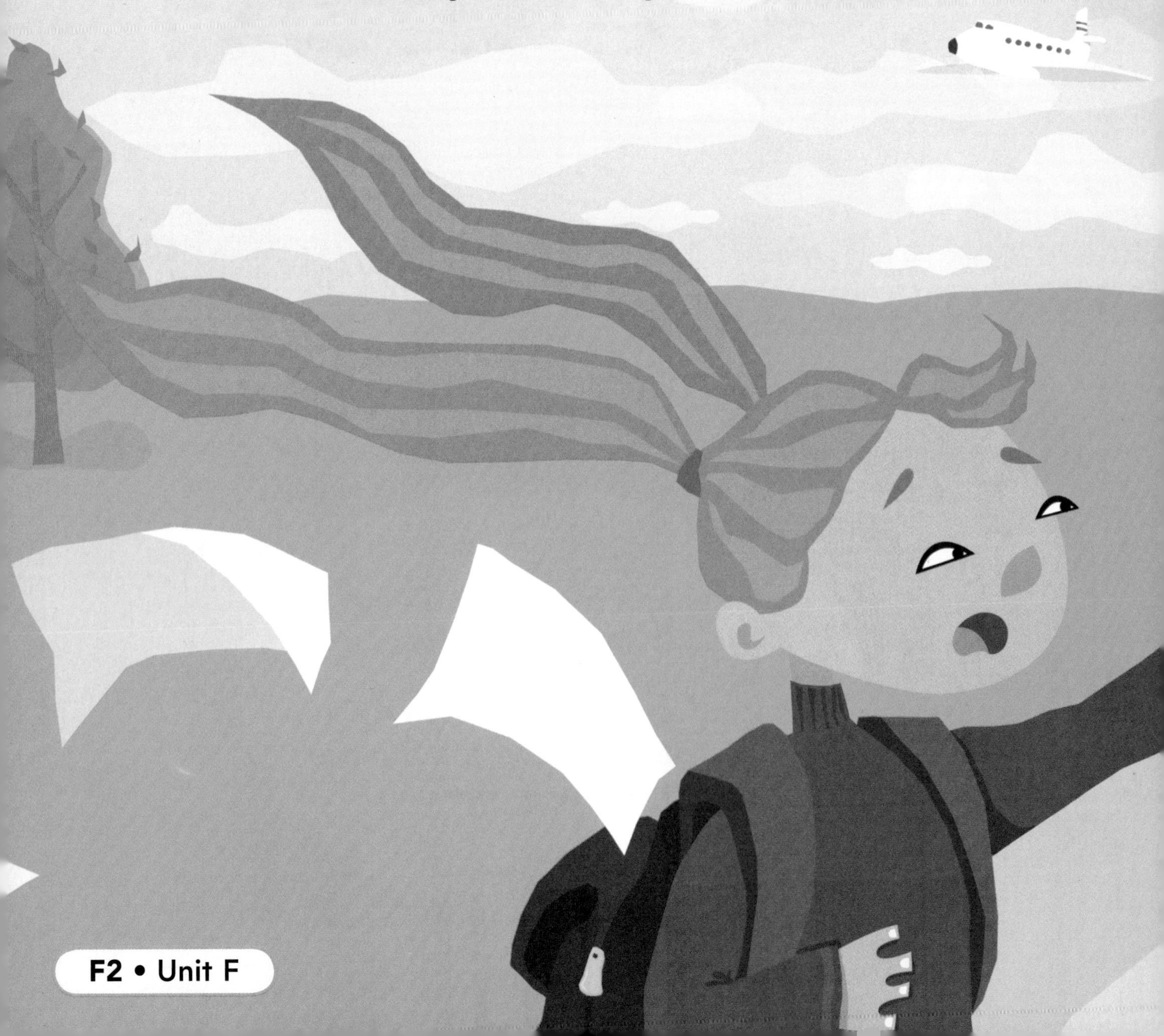

Reading in Science

Strategy: Question

You run to catch the school bus. The bus rolls down the road. Tree branches sway in the breeze. An airplane flies up into the sky. Anything that goes from one place to another is in motion.

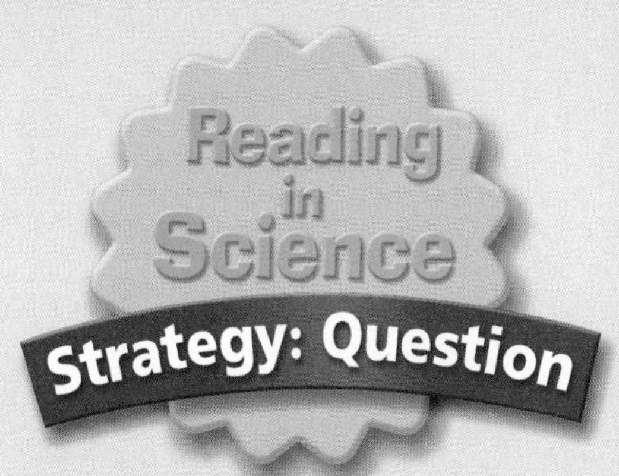

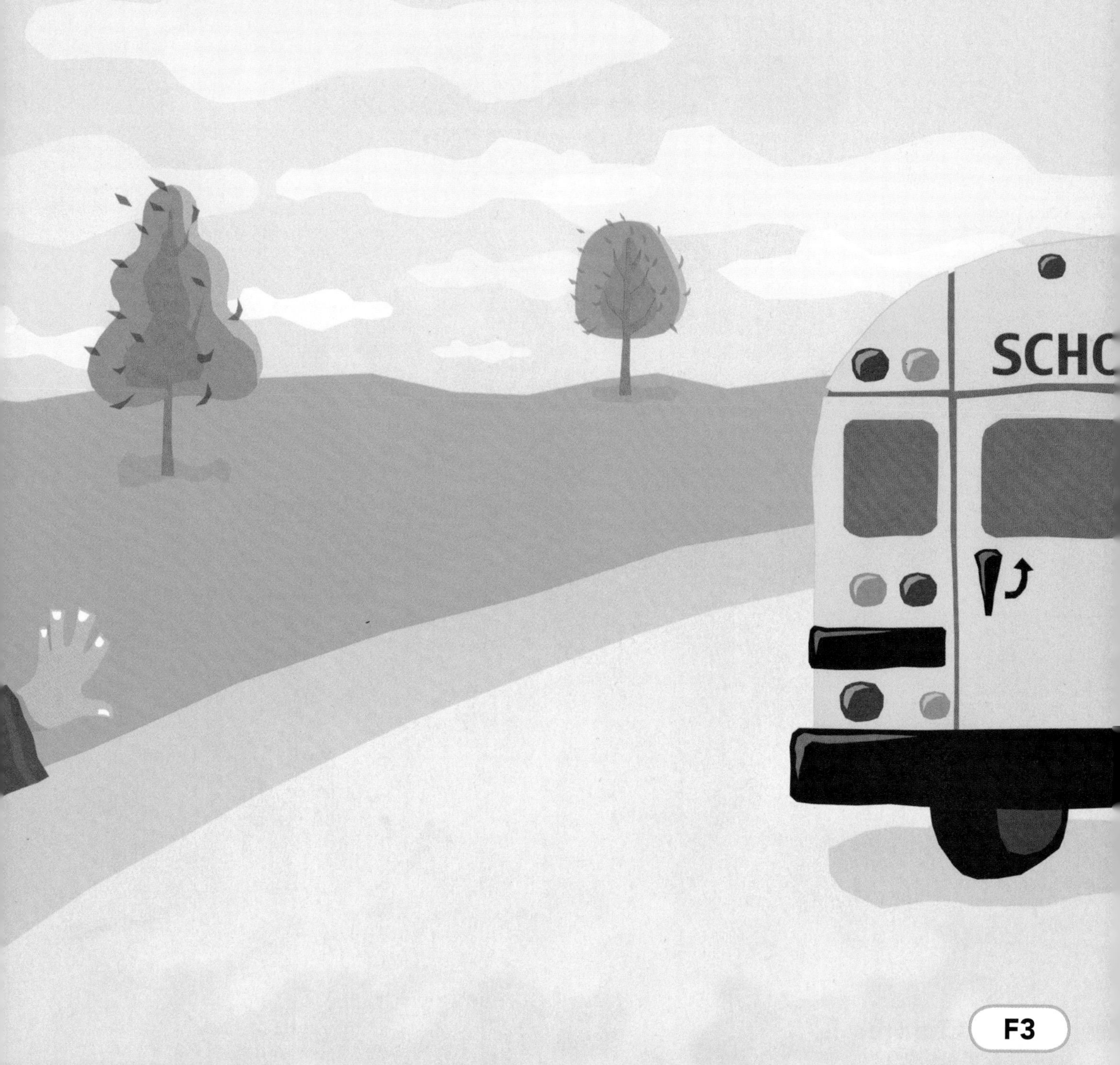

Chapter 12

Objects in Motion

Vocabulary Preview

position
motion
gravity
force
friction
simple machine
ramp
lever
pulley

motion

An object that is in motion changes its position, or moves from one place to another.

force

A force is a push or a pull.

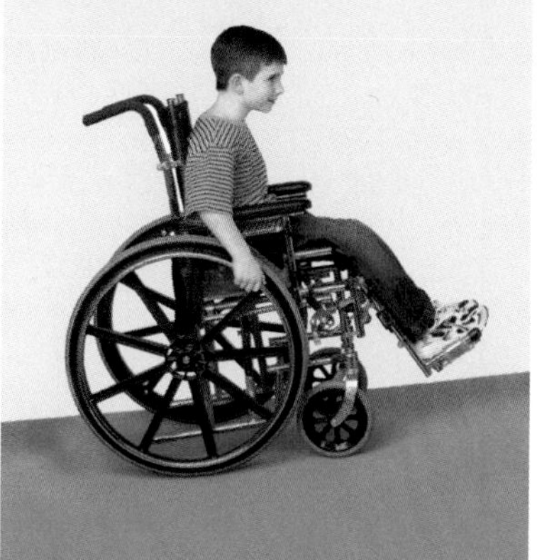

ramp

A ramp is a slanted tool used to move things from one level to another.

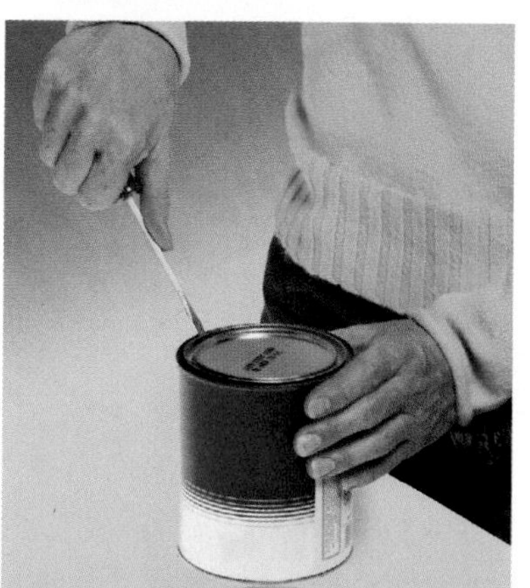

lever

A lever is a bar that moves around a fixed point.

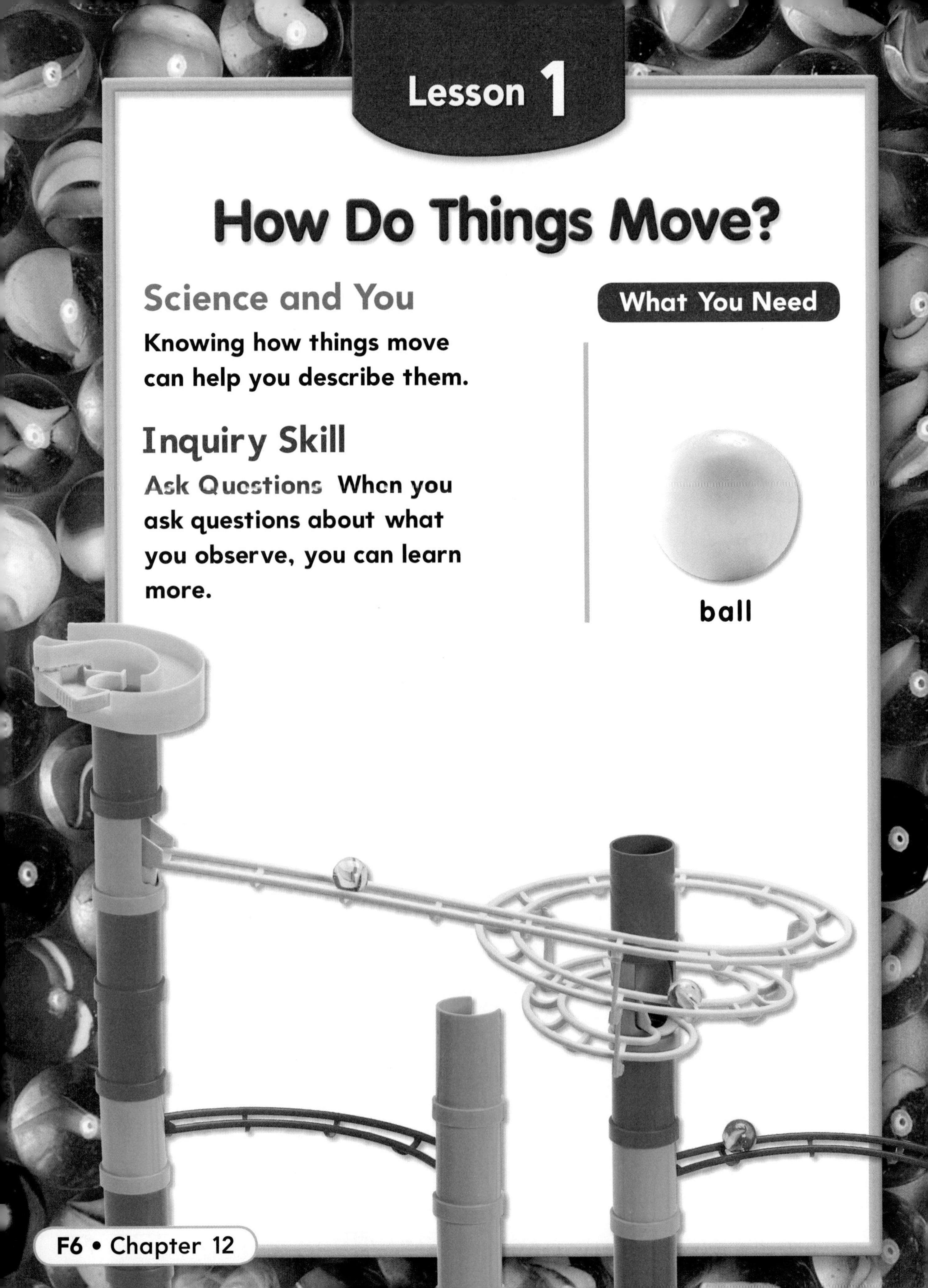

Lesson 1

How Do Things Move?

Science and You

Knowing how things move can help you describe them.

Inquiry Skill

Ask Questions When you ask questions about what you observe, you can learn more.

What You Need

ball

Investigate

Observe Motion

Steps

STEP 1

1. **Observe** Sit on the floor across from a classmate. See how many ways you can make the ball move across the floor.

STEP 2

How the Ball Moved	What I Did

2. **Record Data** Use a chart like the one shown. List the different ways that the ball moved. Write what you did to cause each motion.

STEP 3

3. **Observe** Roll the ball across a desk or table. Observe and record what happens.

Think and Share

1. What did you do to make the ball move in different ways?
2. What happened when the ball reached the edge of the desk or table? Tell why.

Investigate More!

Ask Questions What else can you do to make the ball move? Finish the question. What would happen if I ______?

Learn by Reading

Vocabulary

position

motion

gravity

Reading Skill

Draw Conclusions

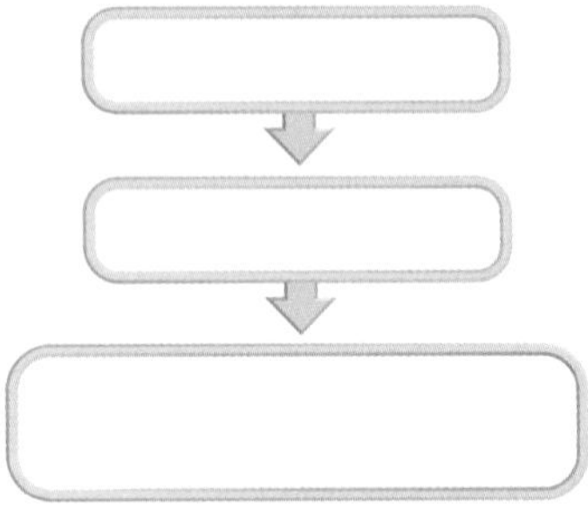

Describing Position

One way to describe an object is by its position. **Position** is a place or location.

To describe an object's position, you use position words that compare its location to other objects. You can use position words to describe the objects in this room.

DRAW CONCLUSIONS Why can more than one position word be used to describe an object?

to the left of the bank

on the desk

under the bank and over the books

above the bed
on top of
the bed
next to the bed

Changing Position

An object that is in **motion** changes its position, or moves from one place to another. One way to tell if an object is moving is to compare its position to objects around it. There are different kinds of motion. An object can move in a straight line, back and forth, or even in a circle.

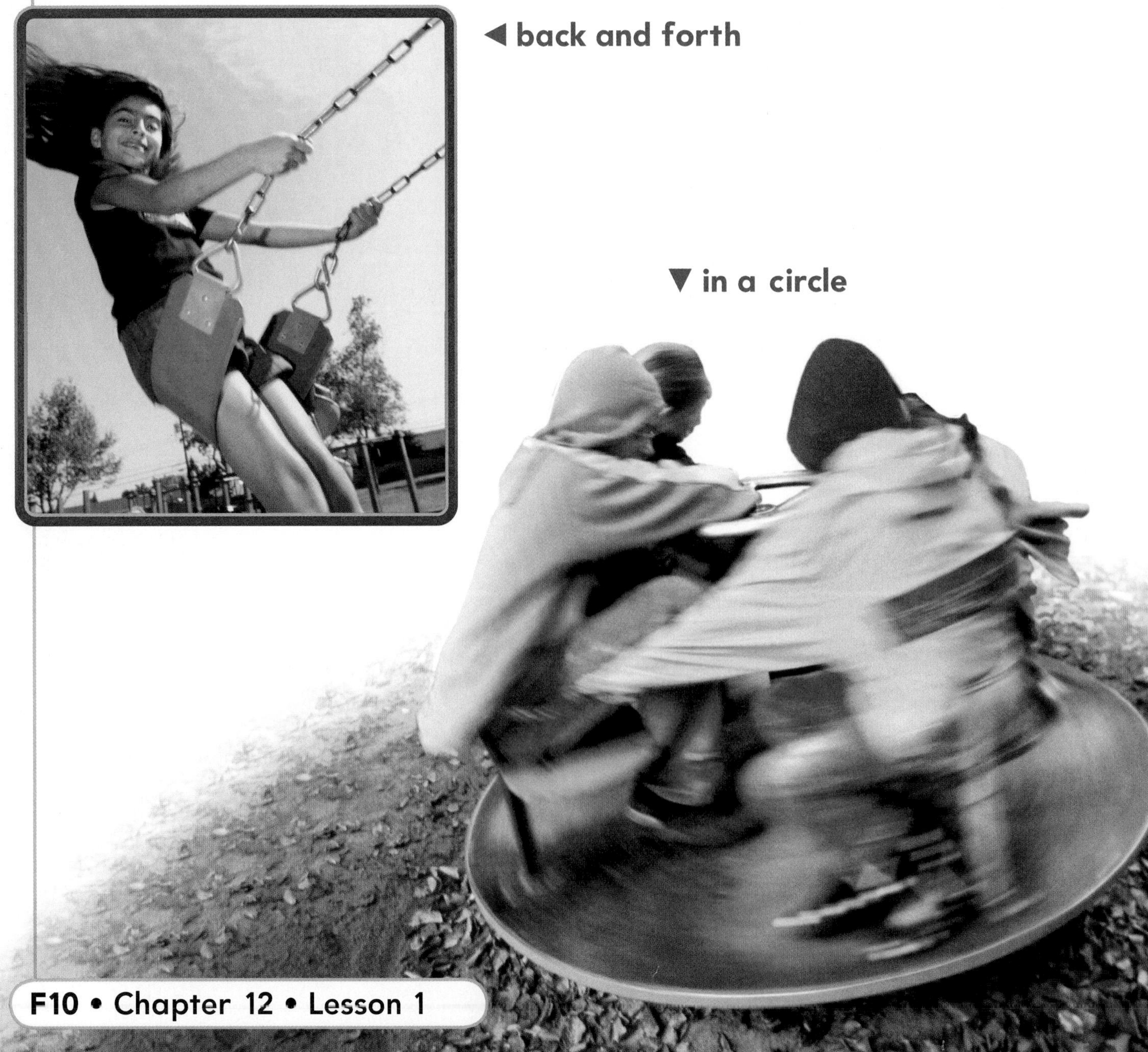

◀ back and forth

▼ in a circle

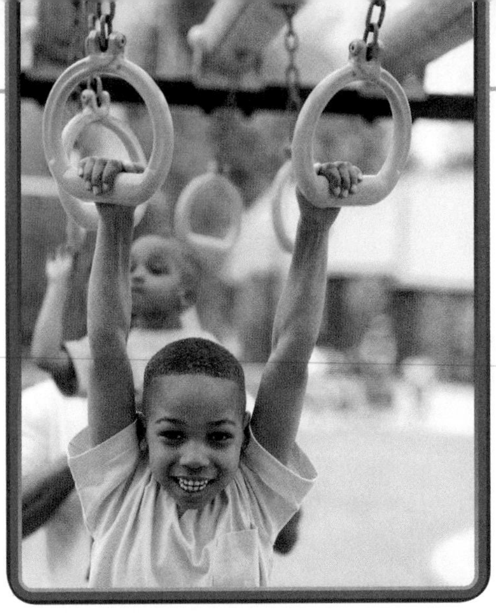

◀ in a straight line

▼ How will this ball move next?

An object can also move up and down. Objects drop to the ground unless something holds them up. This change in position is caused by gravity. **Gravity** is a pull toward the center of Earth.

DRAW CONCLUSIONS Does a baseball move in a straight line or a circle when hit?

Lesson Wrap-Up

1. **Vocabulary** How do you describe the **position** of an object?
2. **Reading Skill** Why is the ground beneath a tree often covered with leaves in fall?
3. **Ask Questions** What else do you want to know about how things move?

Technology Visit **www.eduplace.com/scp/** to find out more about motion.

Lesson 2

What Do Forces Do?

Science and You

Knowing about forces can help you know how to move something.

Inquiry Skill

Compare Tell how objects or events are alike and different.

What You Need

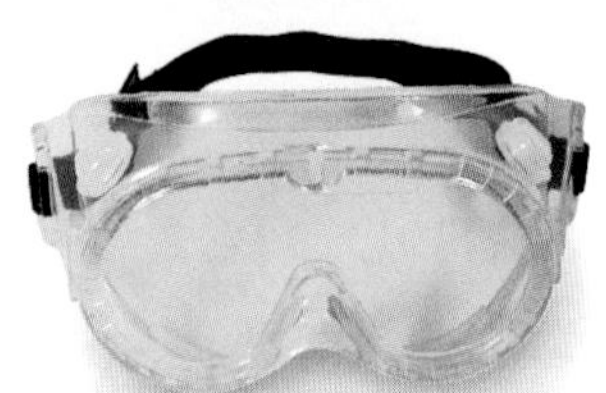
goggles

chair

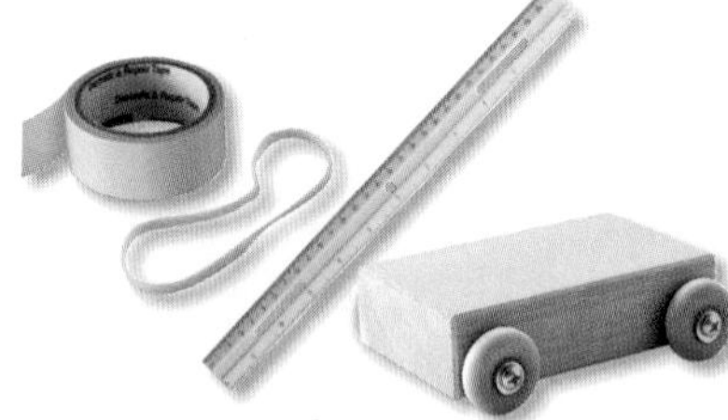
cart, rubber band, tape, and ruler

classroom objects

Investigate

Make Things Move

Steps

1. **Measure** Place two strips of tape 15 centimeters apart. Put a chair leg next to one strip of tape. Put a rubber band around the chair leg. Stretch the rubber band. **Safety:** Wear goggles!

2. **Observe** Place a cart against the band. Pull the cart back to the second line. Let it go. Use tape to mark where the cart stops.

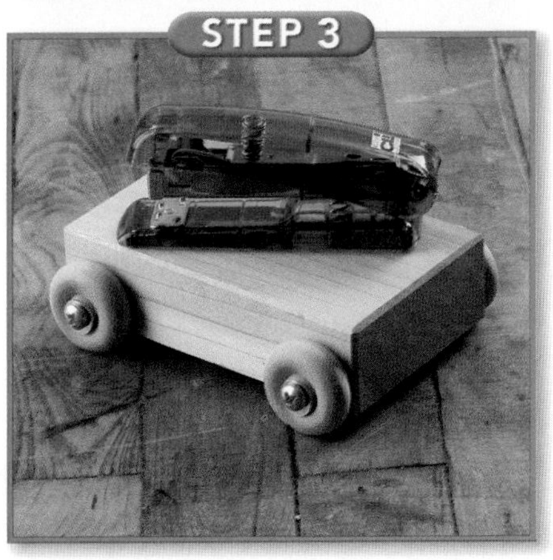

3. **Compare** Put an object on the cart. Repeat step 2. Compare the distances.

Think and Share

1. Why do you think the cart went different distances?
2. **Predict** How could you make the heavier cart go the same distance as the lighter cart?

Investigate More!

Experiment Put other objects on the cart. Compare the distances that the cart moves.

Learn by Reading

▶ Vocabulary

force

friction

▶ Reading Skill

Cause and Effect

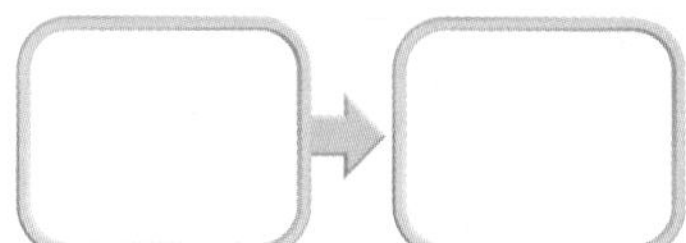

Forces and Motion

To move an object, you use force. A **force** is a push or a pull. A large force is needed to move a heavy object. A smaller force can move lighter objects.

When you push or pull an object, you give the object energy. The amount of energy depends on the size of the force.

▼ large push

▼ small push

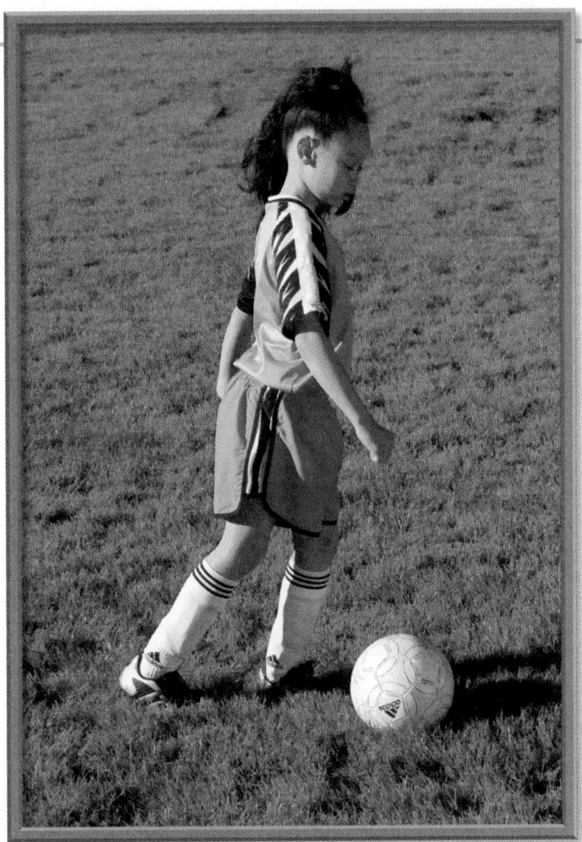

Which kick will make the ball move farther?

A large force gives an object more energy. If you kick a ball with a lot of force, the ball moves fast and goes far. If you kick the same ball with less force, the ball moves more slowly for a shorter distance.

CAUSE AND EFFECT If you kick a ball with a little force, what will happen?

▼ **pull**

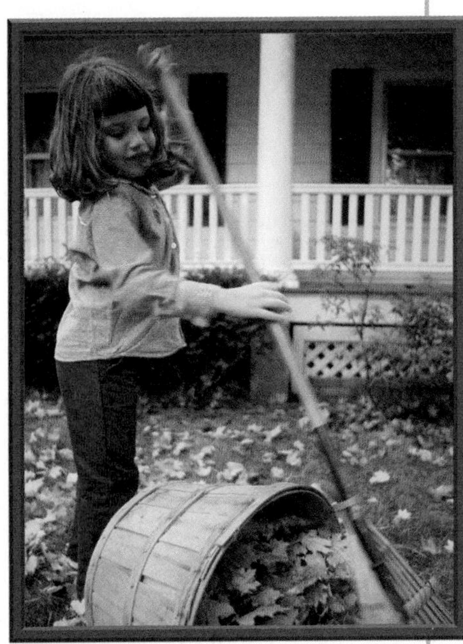

Friction and Motion

Friction is a force that makes an object slow down when it rubs against another object. When the tires on your bike rub against the road, the rubbing causes friction. Riding on a rough surface causes more friction than riding on a smooth surface. You have to pedal harder when there is more friction.

Friction between the brakes and the wheel stops the bike.

less friction

more friction

Changing Direction

Forces can change the direction of a moving object. When you bounce a ball, you push it with your hand. It keeps moving down until it hits the ground. Then it changes direction and bounces back up. You push the ball again. The direction of the ball keeps changing.

CAUSE AND EFFECT What will happen to the basketball if you push harder on it?

Lesson Wrap-Up

1. **Vocabulary** What is a **force**?
2. **Reading Skill** What happens when a bicycle moves from a smooth surface to a rough surface?
3. **Compare** Is it easier to lift a backpack filled with books or an empty backpack? Tell why.

Technology Visit **www.eduplace.com/scp/** to find out more about forces.

Safety in Motion

How can science help you stay safe? Let the Safety Team tell you all about it!

Cast

Narrator
Joan
Miguel
Sue
Leon

Narrator: The Safety Team uses what they know about science to stay safe while they have fun. Listen to what they have to say.

Joan: When I roller skate, I am in motion. I wear a helmet to protect my head. If I fall, the helmet will hit the ground before my head does and take in most of the force.

Miguel: Don't forget knee pads, elbow pads, and wrist guards. If you fall, your knees, elbows, wrists, and hands will be protected, too.

Narrator: The Safety Team thinks about science and safety on the playground, too.

Miguel: Playground swings move back and forth. I never walk in front of, or behind, a moving swing. If I did, I could get knocked over!

Joan: A push is a force. When you push someone, even for fun, the person will move. Gravity might pull the person to the ground. That can really hurt! I find it is best to follow the No Pushing rule.

Readers' Theater

Narrator: Understanding science can help keep you safe at home.

Leon: I like to play with toys that have wheels. I push or pull them in different directions, both indoors and outdoors.

Sue: Me too! And wheels move fastest on a smooth surface because there is less friction.

Leon: But, if a toy with wheels is left out, someone might step on it. The toy's wheels could make it move, and the person could fall and get hurt.

Sue: So, remember to put away wheeled toys after playing with them.

Narrator: Science and safety matter in the car too. In fact, they can save your life!

Sue: I always wear a safety belt. A moving car might stop suddenly or hit something. That force can make you move inside the car. A safety belt helps keep you in your seat. It can stop you from banging into a window or other things in the car.

Narrator: Time is up. We have to put on the brakes. We hope you will be part of the Safety Team.

All: And use science to stay safe!

1. **Write About It** Tell about a time when you should have been more careful and why.
2. **Talk About It** Share ideas about things you do at home to keep you and your family members safe.

Lesson 3

What Can You Do with Motion?

Science and You

You can move things more easily when you know about simple machines.

Inquiry Skill

Measure Use tools to find out how far and how much time.

What You Need

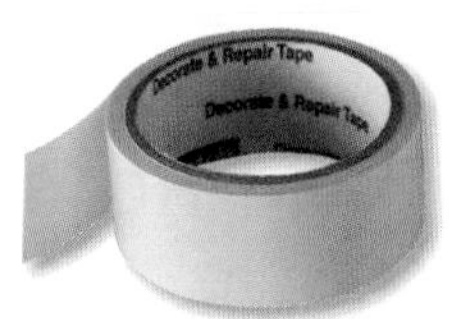

masking tape

2 toy cars

meter stick

stopwatch

Investigate

Measure Motion

Steps

1. Mark a start line on the floor with tape. Put one toy car on the start line.
2. **Measure** Push the car forward. Measure the time from when it starts to when it stops.
3. **Measure** Use a meter stick to see how far the car moved.
4. Repeat steps 1–3 with the other car. Use the same force. Compare the results.

STEP 1

STEP 2

STEP 3

Think and Share

1. **Use Data** Which car went farther? Which car took more time?
2. **Infer** What can you infer about going a longer distance?

Investigate More!

Experiment Plan ways to make the car move farther. Test your ideas. Tell which idea worked the best. Tell why you think so.

Learn by Reading

Vocabulary

simple machine

ramp

lever

pulley

Reading Skill
Compare and Contrast

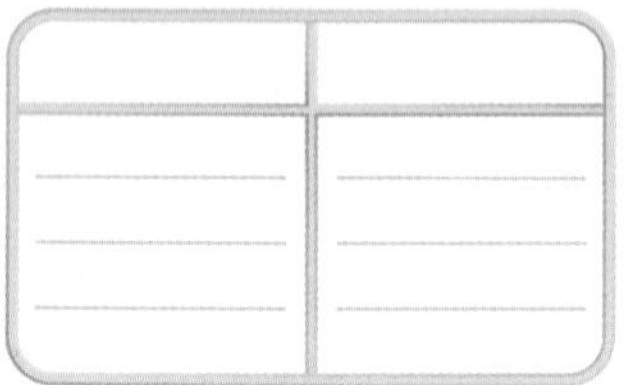

Measuring Motion

Motion can be measured in different ways. You can measure how far something travels. A swimmer may travel a distance of 50 meters or 100 meters.

You also can measure the time it takes to go a certain distance. In a swimming race, a stopwatch is used to find the time it takes each swimmer to go a certain distance.

Fastest Swimming Times

Distance	Time
50 meters	about 22 seconds
100 meters	about 48 seconds
200 meters	about 1 minute 44 seconds
400 meters	about 3 minutes 40 seconds

It takes more time to go a longer distance.

The swimmer who finishes first moves at a faster speed than the others. The rate at which that swimmer is kicking may be faster than the rates of others. Moving at a faster rate usually means that it will take less time to go a certain distance.

Which swimmer moved faster?

COMPARE AND CONTRAST

What is the difference between a fast swimmer and a slow swimmer?

Using Ramps

A **simple machine** is a tool that can make it easier to move objects. A **ramp** is a slanted tool used to move things from one level to another. Movers must move heavy objects from the ground into a truck. It takes less force to move things up a ramp than to lift them straight up off the ground.

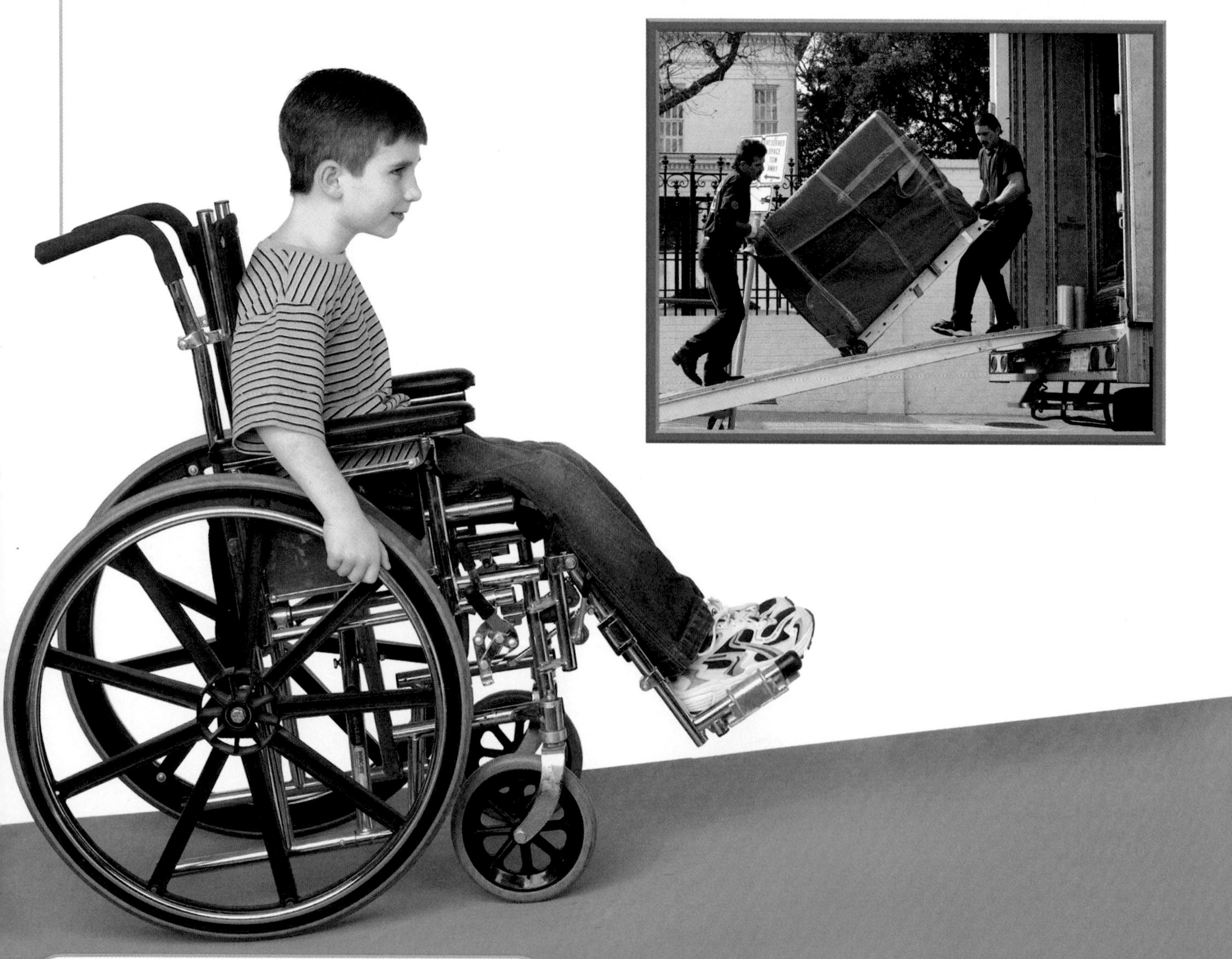

Using Levers

A **lever** is a bar that moves around a fixed point. A lever can change the direction of a motion. Different kinds of levers are used for different jobs.

▲ When you lift one end of a can opener, the other end pushes down on the can.

COMPARE AND CONTRAST
How are a ramp and a lever alike?

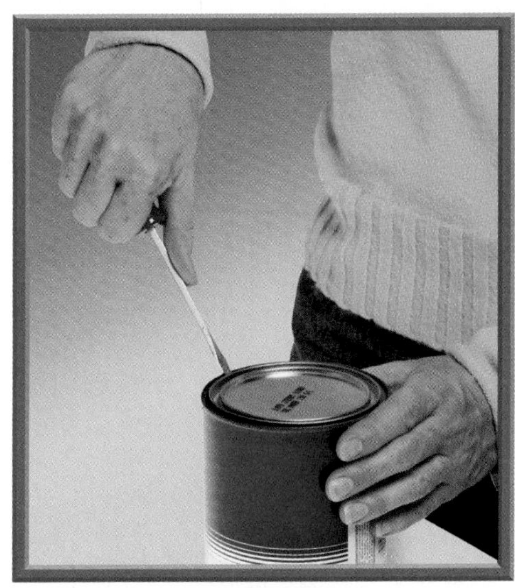

▲ You push down on one end of a screwdriver and the other end lifts off the lid.

A heavier object on one side of a balance will lift the lighter object on the other side. ▼

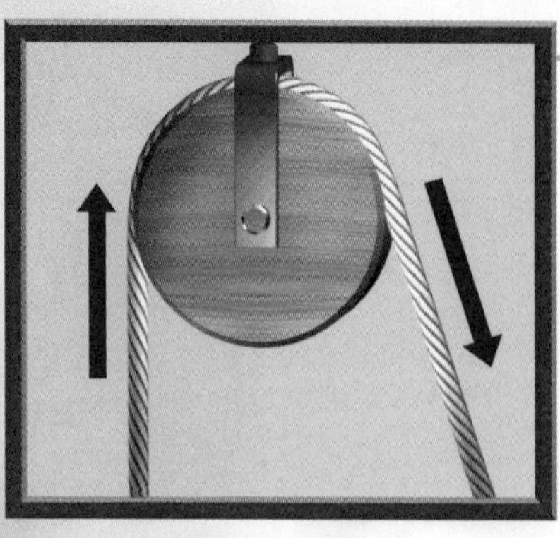

pulley

Using Pulleys

Another machine used to lift objects is a pulley. A **pulley** is a wheel with a groove through which a rope or chain moves. When you raise a flag, you pull down on the rope on one side of the pulley. The rope on the other side goes up. A pulley changes the direction of a force.

Lesson Wrap-Up

1. **Vocabulary** What is a bar that moves around a fixed point?
2. **Reading Skill** How are all simple machines alike?
3. **Measure** How can you measure the distance that a ball rolls?

Technology Visit **www.eduplace.com/scp/** to find out more about simple machines.

LINKS for Home and School

Math Measure Distances

Estimate the distance from your desk to the chalkboard. Record your estimate in a chart like the one shown. Then use a measuring tool to find the actual distance. Repeat for two other distances. Compare the measurements.

Classroom Distances			
Starting Point	Ending Point	Estimated Distance	Actual Distance
desk	chalkboard		

Social Studies Moving Through Time

Today trucks, trains, ships, and planes move goods from place to place. Find out what people long ago used to move goods. Draw pictures or make models to show what you learned.

Chapter 12 Review and Test Prep

Visual Summary

Forces cause objects to move.

Main Ideas

1. What is the position of an object? **(p. F8)**
2. How can gravity make something move? **(p. F11)**
3. How will an object move when a large force is used? **(p. F15)**
4. What is a tool that makes it easier to move objects? **(pp. F26–F28)**

Vocabulary

Choose the correct word from the box.

motion (p. F10)
force (p. F14)
ramp (p. F26)
pulley (p. F28)

5. A push or a pull
6. A wheel with a groove through which a rope or chain moves
7. A slanted tool used to move things from one level to another
8. To move from one place to another

Test Practice

Choose a word to complete the sentence.

9. _____ is a force that makes an object slow down when it rubs against another object.

Position   Friction   Push   Pulley

Using Science Skills

10. **Compare** Is more force needed to move a heavy object or a lighter object?

11. **Critical Thinking** What are some levers used at home or at school?

Chapter 13

Magnets

Groceries
eggs
milk
bread

Baseball
Game at
6:00 PM

Vocabulary Preview

pole
attracts
repels
magnetic
nonmagnetic
magnetic field

pole

A pole is the place on a magnet where the force is the strongest.

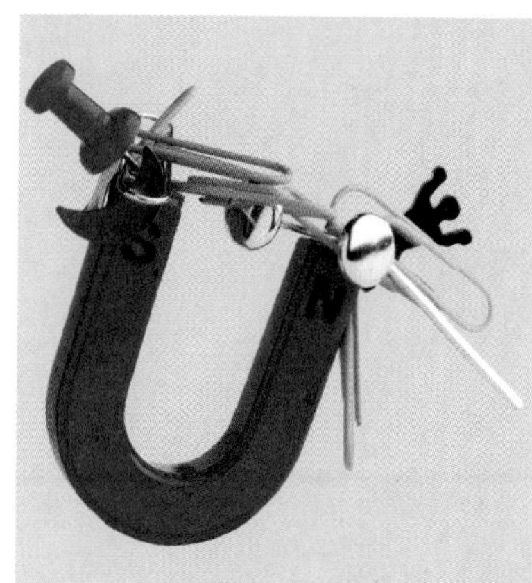

attracts

When a magnet attracts, it pulls an object toward itself.

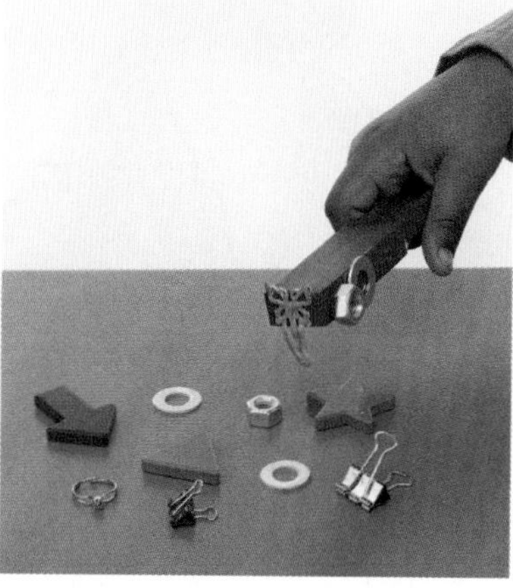

magnetic

If an object is attracted by a magnet, the object is magnetic.

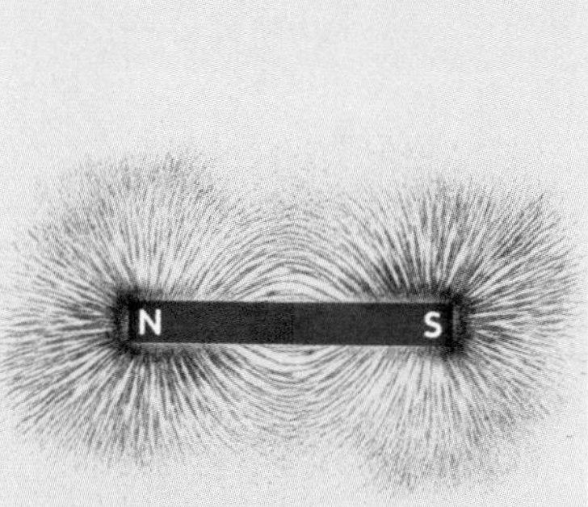

magnetic field

The area around a magnet where the magnet's force acts is a magnetic field.

Lesson 1

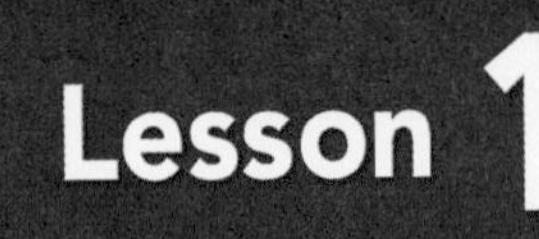

What Can Magnets Do?

Science and You

Magnets can be used to push and pull some objects.

Inquiry Skill

Observe Use your senses to find out about something.

What You Need

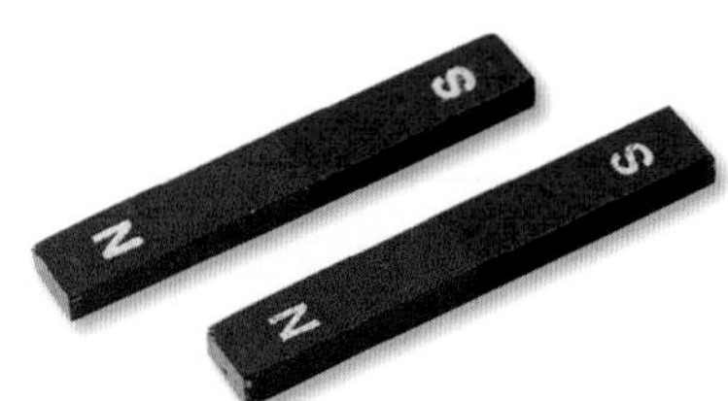

2 bar magnets

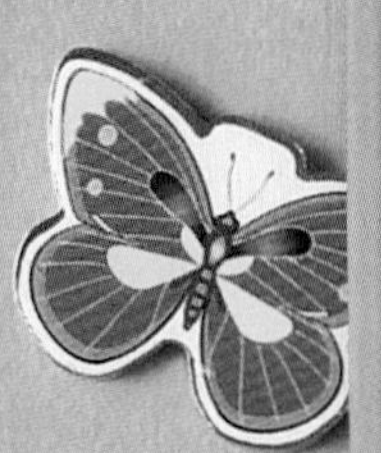

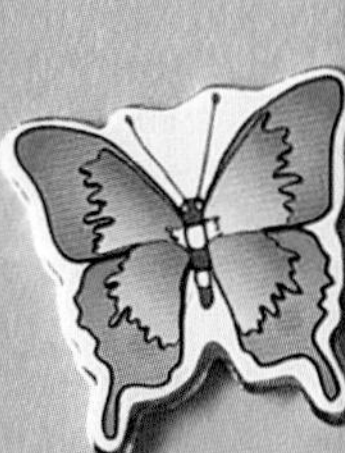

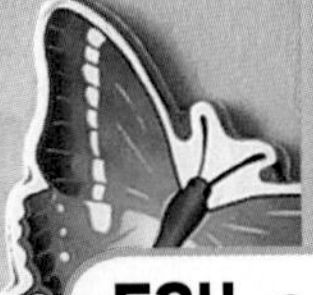

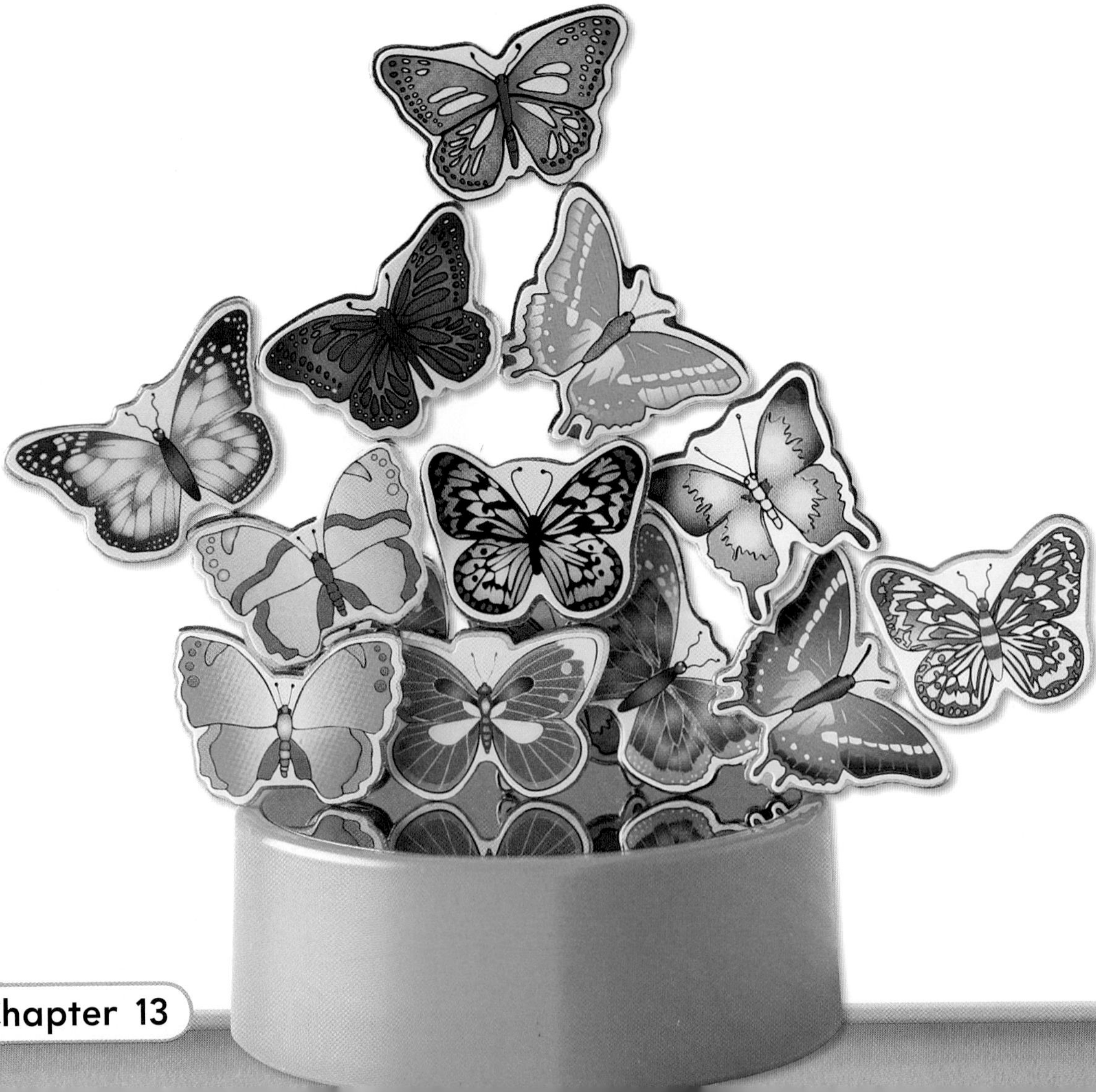

Investigate

Test Magnets

Steps

1. **Observe** Hold an end of one magnet near an end of the other magnet. Observe what happens.

2. **Record Data** Record your observations on a chart like the one shown.

3. Turn one magnet around. Hold it near the other magnet. Record your observations.

STEP 1

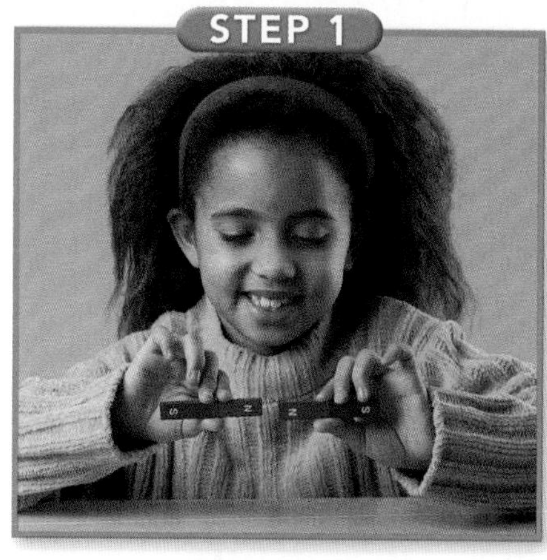

STEP 2

Testing Magnets

Position of the Magnets	What Happened

STEP 3

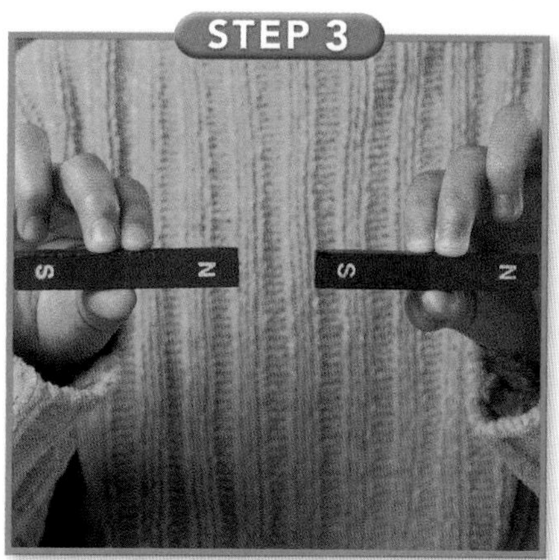

Think and Share

1. **Compare** What difference did you observe?
2. **Infer** What do you think caused the difference?

Investigate More!

Experiment Work with others to repeat the activity with other magnets. Find out which part of each magnet causes the other magnet to move.

Learn by Reading

Vocabulary

pole

attracts

repels

Reading Skill

Cause and Effect

Magnets Push and Pull

Magnets come in many shapes and sizes. Some magnets are flat and straight. Others are curved or round. All magnets can push or pull some objects. Pushes and pulls are forces.

▼ bar magnets

horseshoe magnet ▼

ring magnets ▲

Magnets Have Poles

All magnets have two poles. A **pole** is the place on a magnet where the force is the strongest. The poles are in different places on different magnets. On a bar magnet, one pole is labeled N for north pole. The other pole is labeled S for south pole.

COMPARE AND CONTRAST How are magnets alike and different?

Where is the force of the bar magnet strongest?

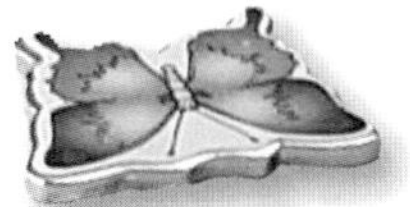

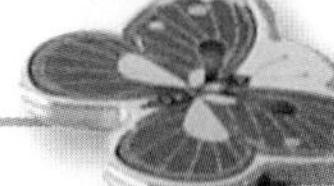

Magnets Act on Each Other

All magnets have forces that act on other magnets. The force between two magnets can be either a push or a pull.

If the north pole of one magnet is near the south pole of another magnet, the magnets attract. When a magnet **attracts**, it pulls an object toward itself. Unlike poles attract each other.

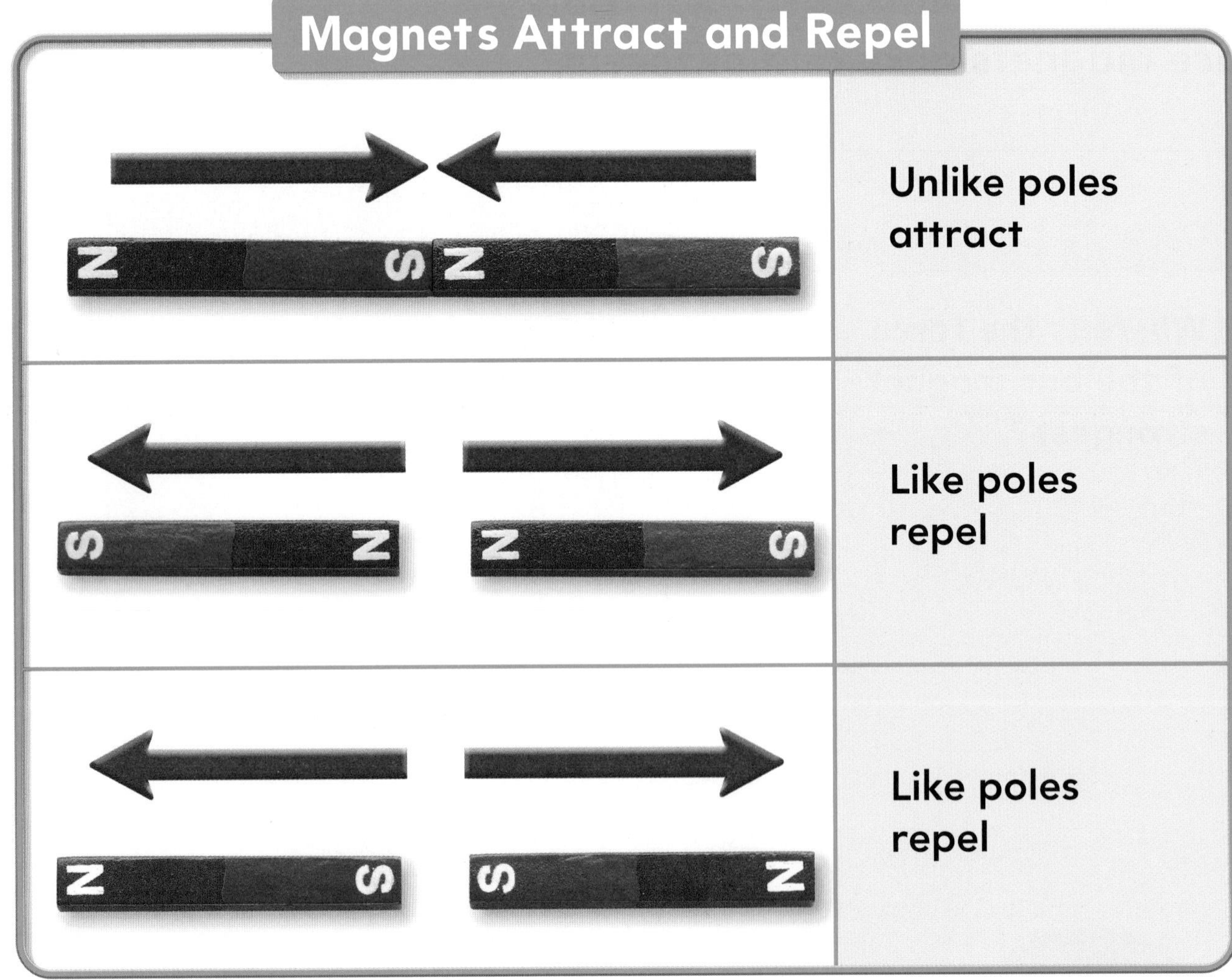

If two north poles are near each other or two south poles are near each other, the magnets repel. When a magnet **repels**, it pushes an object away from itself. Like poles repel each other.

CAUSE AND EFFECT What happens when like poles are near each other?

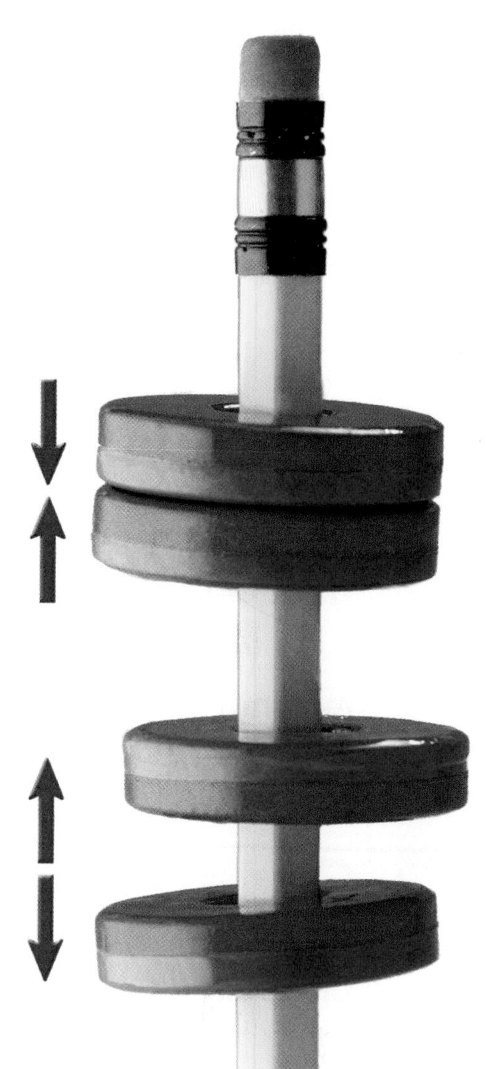

What causes the magnets to be in this position? ▶

Lesson Wrap-Up

1. **Vocabulary** What is important about a **pole** of a magnet?
2. **Reading Skill** What causes two magnets to push away from each other?
3. **Observe** How can you find the poles of a magnet if they are not labeled?

Technology Visit **www.eduplace.com/scp/** to find out more about magnets.

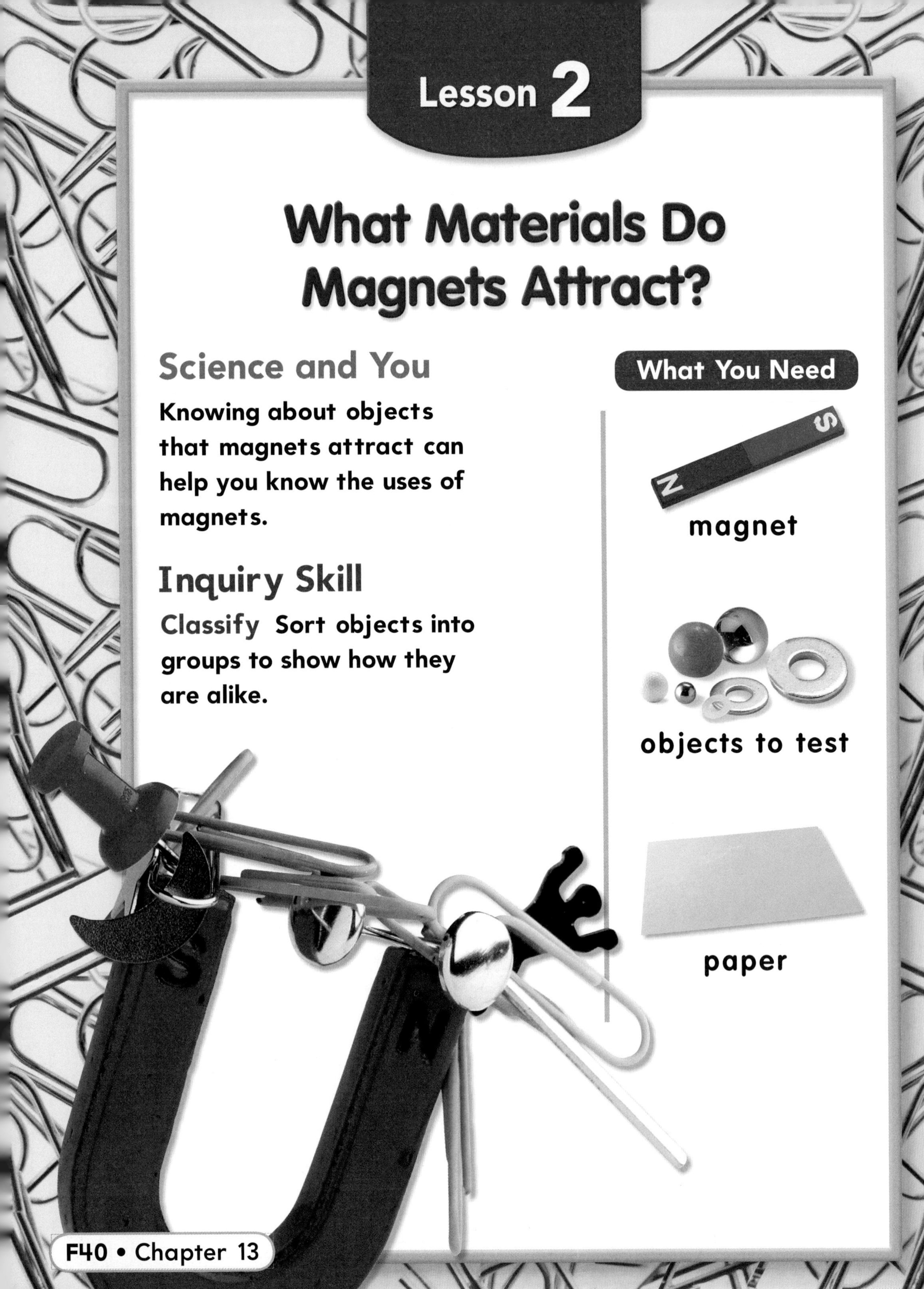

Lesson 2

What Materials Do Magnets Attract?

Science and You

Knowing about objects that magnets attract can help you know the uses of magnets.

Inquiry Skill

Classify Sort objects into groups to show how they are alike.

What You Need

magnet

objects to test

paper

Investigate

Classify Objects

Steps

1. **Predict** Decide if a magnet might attract each object. Record your predictions on a chart like the one shown.

2. **Observe** Hold the magnet near each object. Observe and record what happens.

3. **Classify** Sort the objects into two groups called **Attracted** and **Did Not Attract**.

STEP 1

Testing Objects

Object	Prediction	What Happened

STEP 2

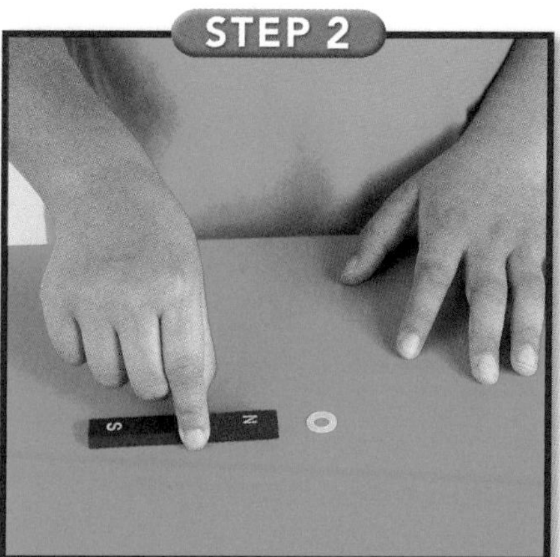

STEP 3

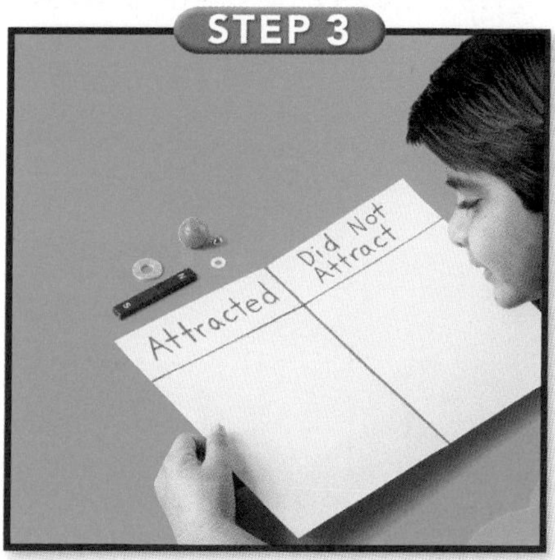

Think and Share

1. **Infer** What kinds of objects do magnets attract?
2. What are some clues you used to make your predictions? Tell why.

Investigate More!

Ask Questions Think about items that you might want to attract with a magnet. Make a list of questions to ask. Make a plan to find answers.

Learn by Reading

Vocabulary

magnetic

nonmagnetic

Reading Skill

Compare and Contrast

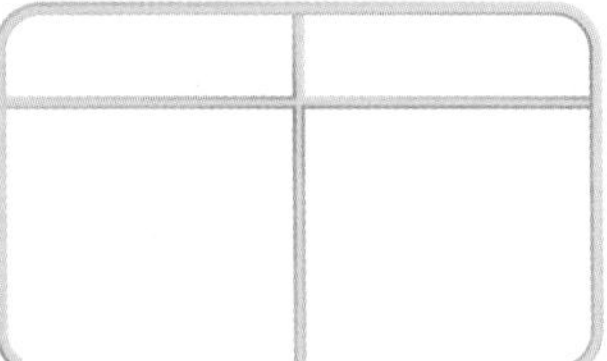

Magnetic Objects

You have learned that magnets can attract other magnets. Magnets can attract other objects, too. If an object is attracted by a magnet, the object is **magnetic**. Most magnetic objects have a metal in them called iron.

Objects a Magnet Attracts

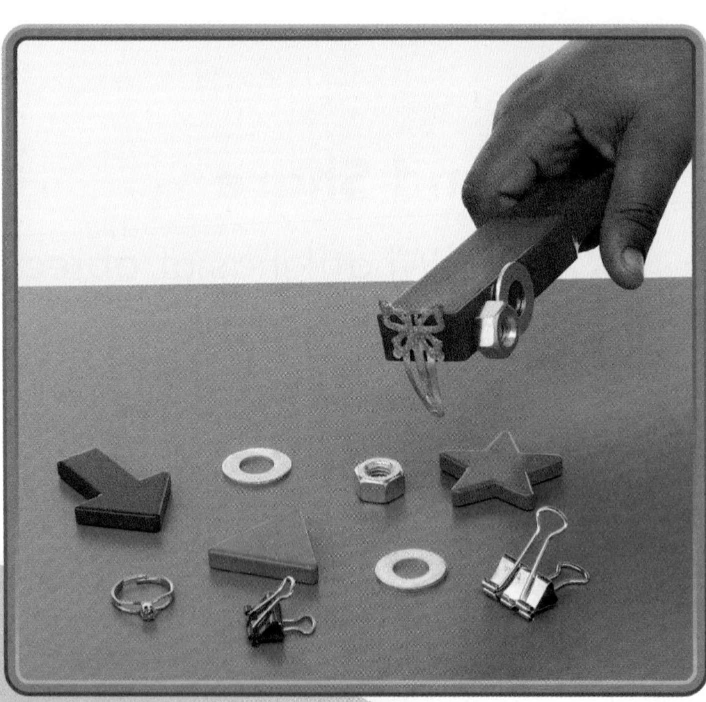

Nonmagnetic Objects

Some objects are not attracted by magnets. If an object is not attracted by a magnet, the object is **nonmagnetic**. Objects made from glass, paper, wood, or plastic are nonmagnetic.

COMPARE AND CONTRAST How are magnetic and nonmagnetic objects different?

Objects a Magnet Does Not Attract

Everyday Magnets

Many common objects use magnetic force to help them work. Videotapes and computer games have magnets inside. Some toy cars use magnets to make their motors run. Magnets help keep refrigerator doors closed.

A magnet at the end of this crane lifts heavy metal objects.

A magnet lifts the cut lid out of the can. ▶

compass ▶

People often use a compass when they are hiking in the woods. Ships at sea use a compass. A magnet in a compass helps you find direction. The needle always points north.

COMPARE AND CONTRAST How are the magnets on a crane and a can opener alike?

Lesson Wrap-Up

1. **Vocabulary** What are two **nonmagnetic** materials?
2. **Reading Skill** How is a metal paper clip different from a plastic paper clip?
3. **Classify** Is a toothpick magnetic or nonmagnetic? Why?

Technology Visit **www.eduplace.com/scp/** to find out more about magnetic materials.

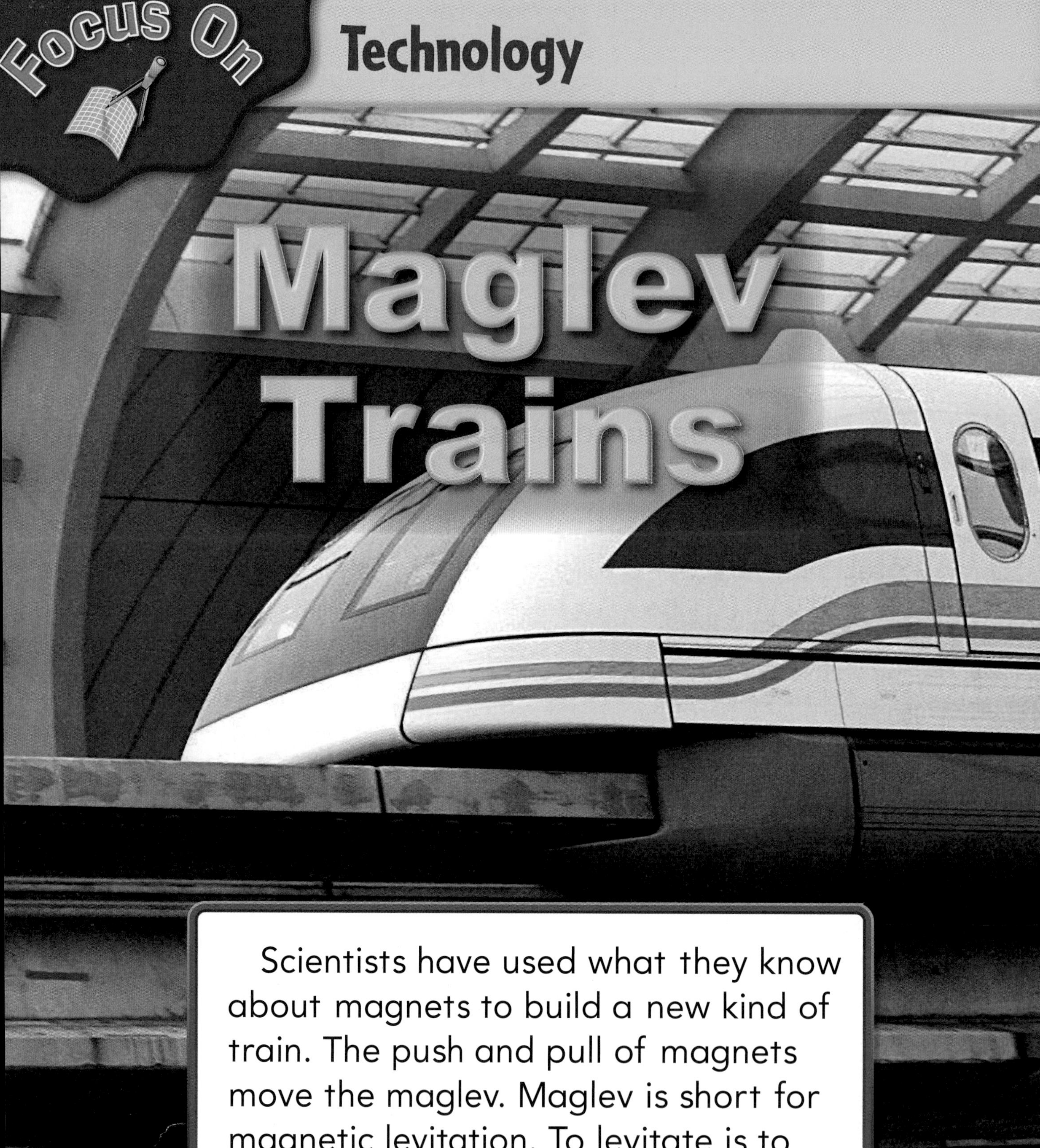

Maglev Trains

Scientists have used what they know about magnets to build a new kind of train. The push and pull of magnets move the maglev. Maglev is short for magnetic levitation. To levitate is to rise into the air and float. The pushing force causes the train to float as much as four inches above the track!

After the maglev is in the air, other magnets cause it to move forward. Magnets in the front of the train pull it. Magnets behind the train push it. Together, these forces cause the maglev to move twice as fast as the fastest regular trains.

Coils along the track repel magnets on the maglev.

Sharing Ideas

1. **Write About It** The magnetic coils in the track repel the magnets on the bottom of a maglev. What does this tell you about the poles of the magnets?
2. **Talk About It** How did scientists help people by inventing the maglev?

Lesson 3

What Is a Magnetic Field?

Science and You

Knowing about a magnet's force can help you know where magnets can be used.

Inquiry Skill

Predict Use what you know and observe to tell what you think will happen.

What You Need

magnet

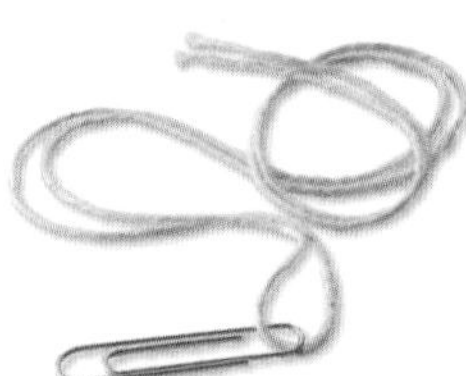

paper clip on a string

tape

test objects

Investigate

Observe Force

Steps

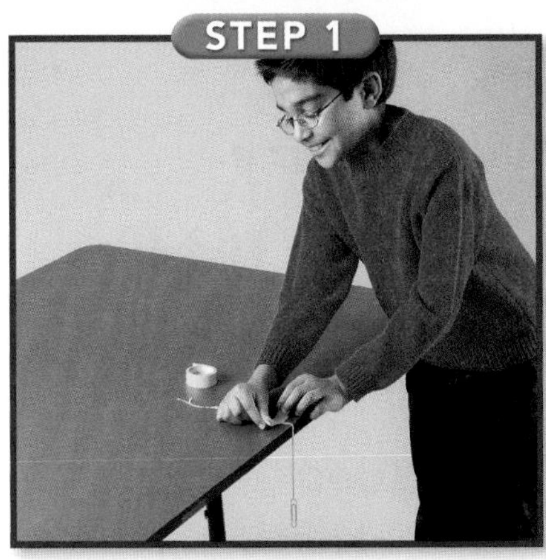

1. Hang a paper clip from a table edge with string and tape.

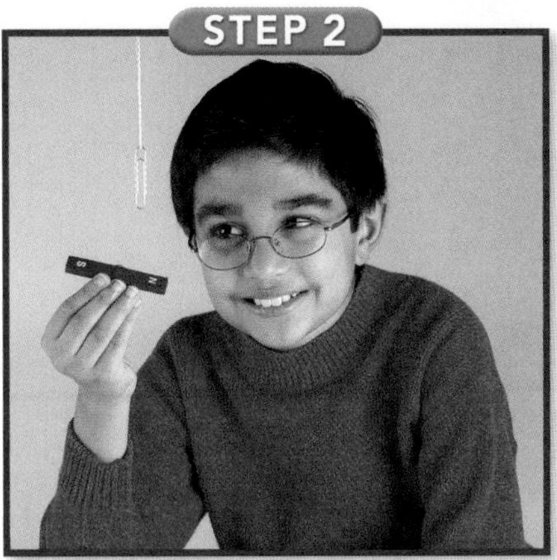

2. **Observe** Wave a magnet under the clip. Observe the magnet's force.

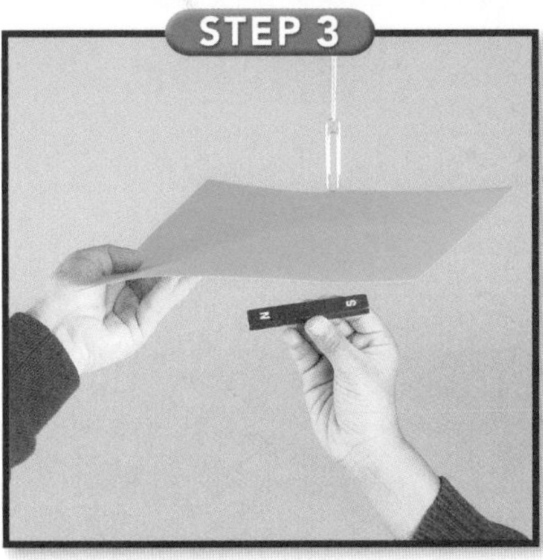

3. **Observe** Have a partner slide an object between the magnet and the clip. Wave the magnet again.

4. Test the other objects.

Think and Share

1. Which objects did the magnet's force pass through?
2. **Predict** What other objects do you think the magnet's force will pass through? Tell why you think so.

Investigate More!

Experiment Make a plan to find out if a magnet's force can pass through water. Test your plan. Share your results.

Learn by Reading

Vocabulary

magnetic field

Reading Skill
Main Idea and Details

Magnetic Fields

A magnet's force is different around different parts of the magnet. It is strongest near the poles of the magnet. It gets weaker as you move away from the poles.

The area around a magnet where the magnet's force acts is a **magnetic field**. A magnet can attract or repel only objects in its magnetic field.

The iron filings show that the magnetic field is strongest at the poles.

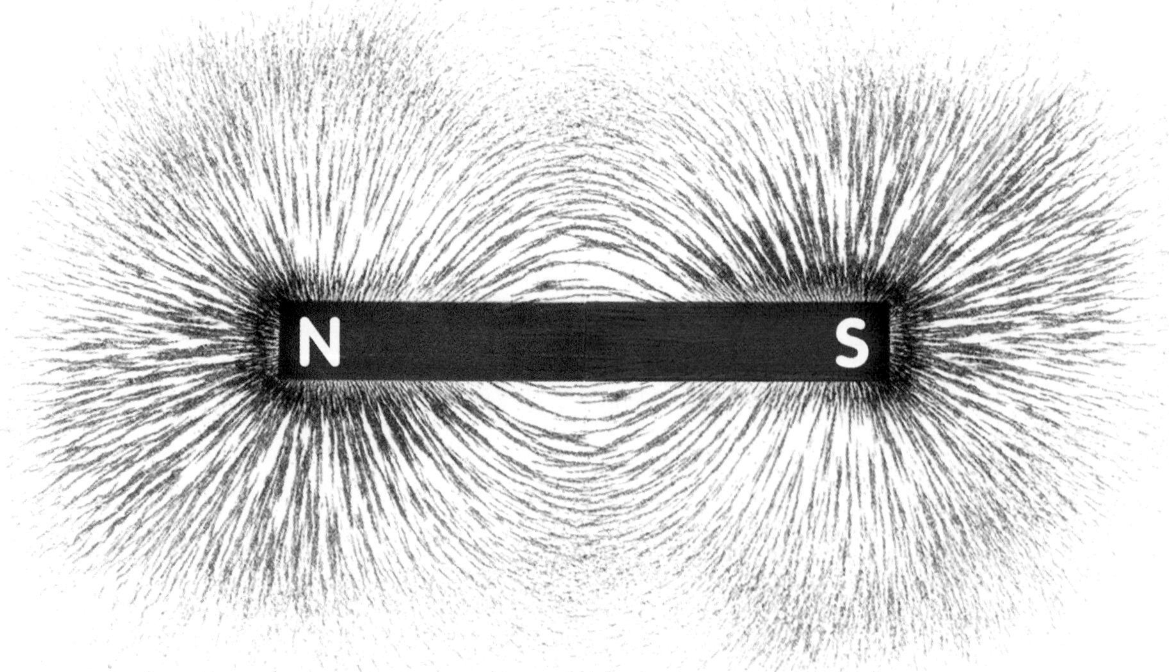

Magnets Work Through Materials

A magnet can make an object move without being touched. A magnet's force works through paper, glass, plastic, water, and air. These kinds of matter do not stop a magnet's force. If paper comes between a magnet and a magnetic object, the object will still move toward the magnet.

MAIN IDEA What are three materials that magnets can work through?

Magnets work through plastic. ▼

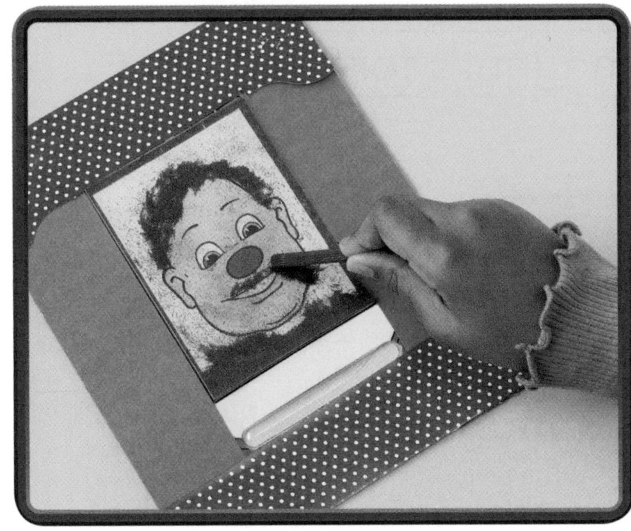

Magnets work through glass and water. ▶

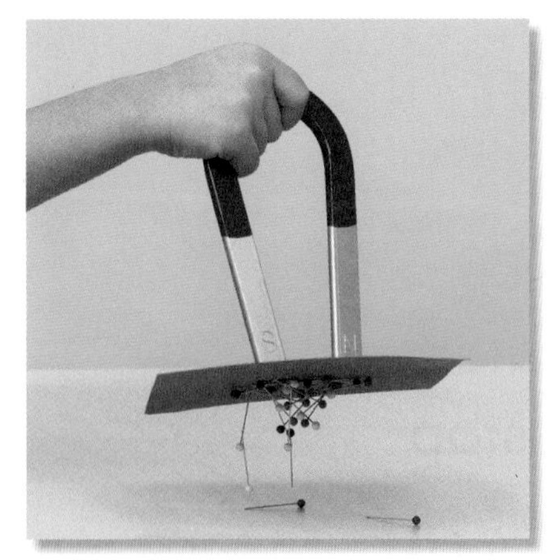 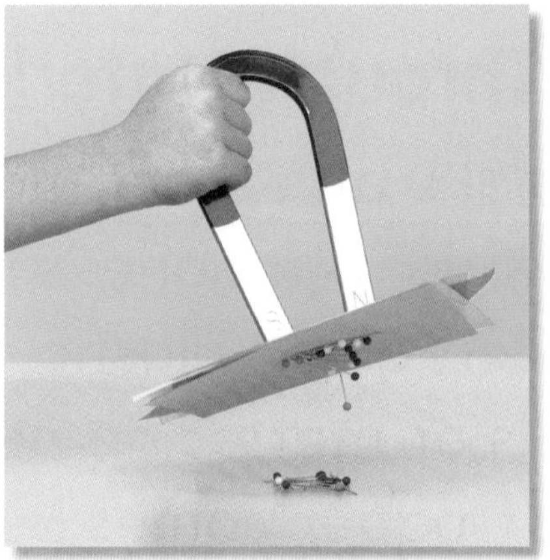 

Weakening a Magnet's Force

A magnet's force can easily move through one sheet of paper and attract many pins. As more sheets of paper are added, the magnet attracts fewer pins. The pins are farther away from the magnetic field of the magnet, so the magnet's force is weaker.

Lesson Wrap-Up

1. **Vocabulary** What is a **magnetic field**?
2. **Reading Skill** Where is the magnetic field the strongest?
3. **Predict** How can you use what you observe to make a prediction at another time?

Technology Visit **www.eduplace.com/scp/** to find out more about magnetic fields.

LINKS for Home and School

Math Measure Magnetic Fields

Measure and compare the magnetic fields of three different magnets. Place a paper clip next to a pole of a magnet. Move the clip away from the pole until the magnet no longer attracts the clip. Measure and record that distance. Decide which magnet has the strongest force based on your measurements.

Magnet	Distance

Art Magnetic Theater

Make a cardboard puppet theater. Use a thin sheet of cardboard for the stage. Attach paper characters to paper clips. Hold a magnet under the stage to move the characters.

Chapter 13 Review and Test Prep

Visual Summary

Magnets have many different properties.

Properties of Magnets

- Attract and Repel
- Attract Magnetic Objects

- Work Through Plastic

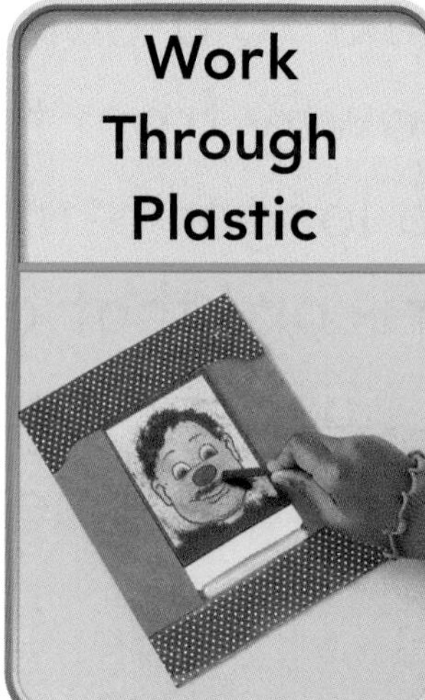

- Strongest at the Poles

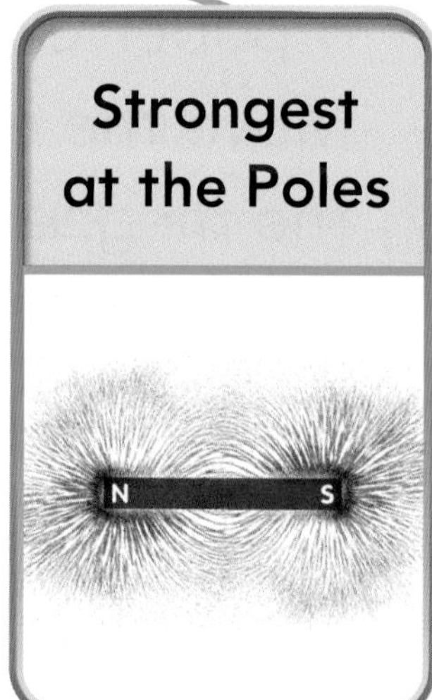

Main Ideas

1. What can all magnets do? **(p. F36)**
2. What happens when you put the north pole of one magnet near the south pole of another magnet? **(p. F38)**
3. What is something that is nonmagnetic? **(p. F43)**
4. What are four materials through which a magnet will work? **(p. F51)**

Vocabulary

Choose the correct word from the box.

pole (p. F37)
repels (p. F39)
magnetic (p. F42)
magnetic field (p. F50)

5. An object that is attracted by a magnet
6. The place on a magnet where the force is the strongest
7. The area around a magnet where the magnet's force acts
8. Pushes an object away from itself

Test Practice

Choose a word to complete the sentence.

9. An object that is not attracted by a magnet is _____.

   magnetic   pole   attracted   nonmagnetic

Using Science Skills

10. **Predict** Suppose two horseshoe magnets are repelling each other. What would happen if one of the magnets were flipped over?
11. **Critical Thinking** Tell why a magnet can hold a photograph to a refrigerator door but cannot hold a picture frame to the door.

Wrap-Up

Discover!

How can a magnet keep you from getting lost?

If the magnet is a compass, it can keep you from getting lost. A compass needle is a small magnet. Earth gives off a magnetic force at the North Pole. A compass needle always points north because it is attracted by Earth's magnetic force.

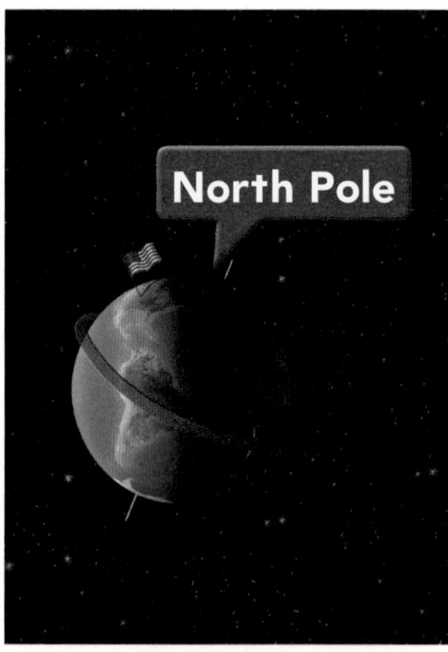

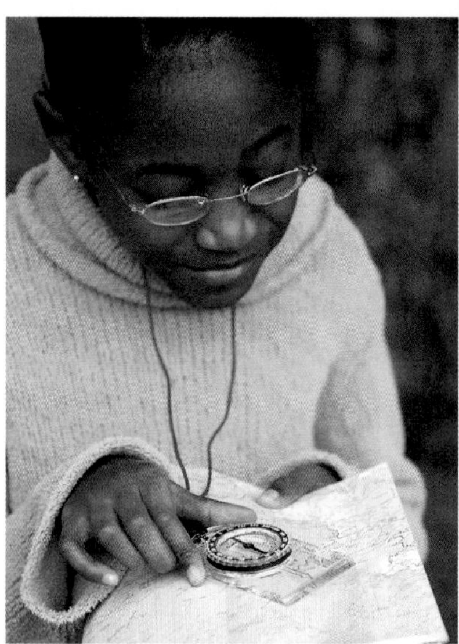

Go to **www.eduplace.com/scp/** to explore using a compass.

Science and Math Toolbox

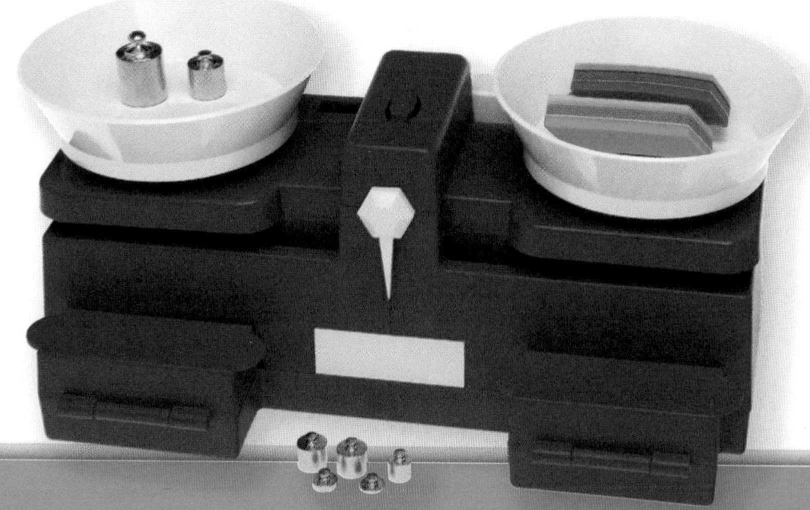

Using a Hand Lens

A hand lens is a tool that makes objects look bigger. It helps you see the small parts of an object.

Look at a Coin

1. Place a coin on your desk.

2. Hold the hand lens above the coin. Look through the lens. Slowly move the lens away from the coin. What do you see?

3. Keep moving the lens away until the coin looks blurry.

4. Then slowly move the lens closer. Stop when the coin does not look blurry.

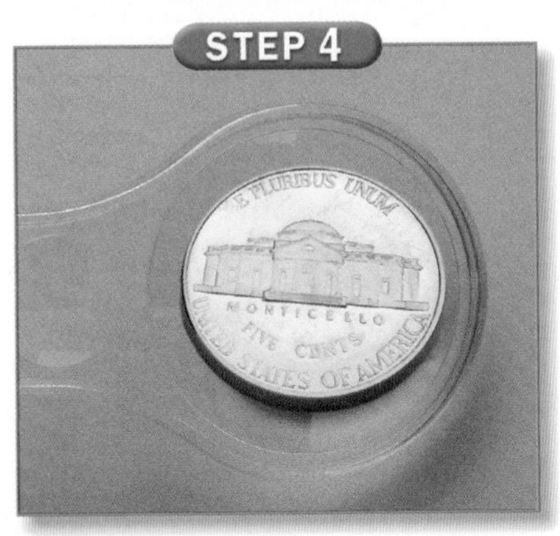

Using a Thermometer

A thermometer is a tool used to measure temperature. Temperature tells how hot or cold something is. It is measured in degrees.

Find the Temperature of Water

1. Put water into a cup.
2. Put a thermometer into the cup.
3. Watch the colored liquid in the thermometer. What do you see?
4. Look how high the colored liquid is. What number is closest? That is the temperature of the water.

Using a Ruler

A ruler is a tool used to measure the length of objects. Rulers measure length in inches or centimeters.

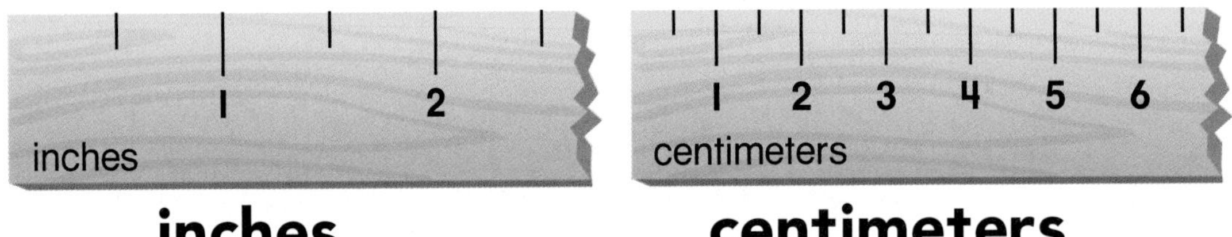

inches **centimeters**

Measure a Crayon

1. Place the ruler on your desk.

2. Lay your crayon next to the ruler. Line up one end with the end of the ruler.

3. Look at the other end of the crayon. Which number is closest to that end?

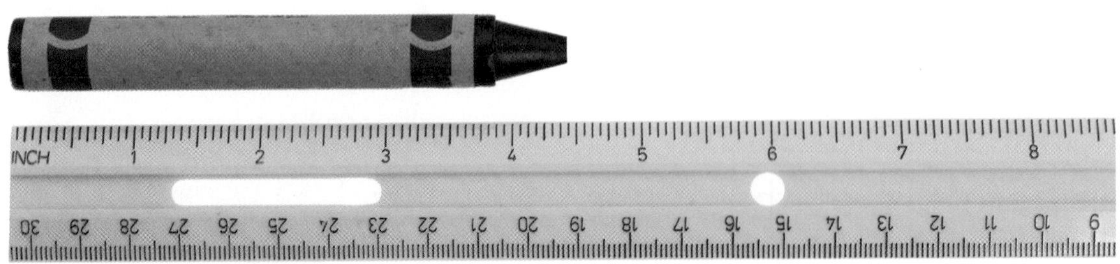

Using a Calculator

A calculator is a tool that can help you add and subtract numbers.

Subtract Numbers

1. Tim and Anna grew plants. Tim grew 5 plants. Anna grew 8 plants.

2. How many more plants did Anna grow? Use your calculator to find out.

3. Enter **8** on the calculator. Then press the **–** key. Enter **5** and press **=**.

What is your answer?

Using a Balance

A balance is a tool used to measure mass. Mass is the amount of matter in an object.

Compare the Mass of Objects

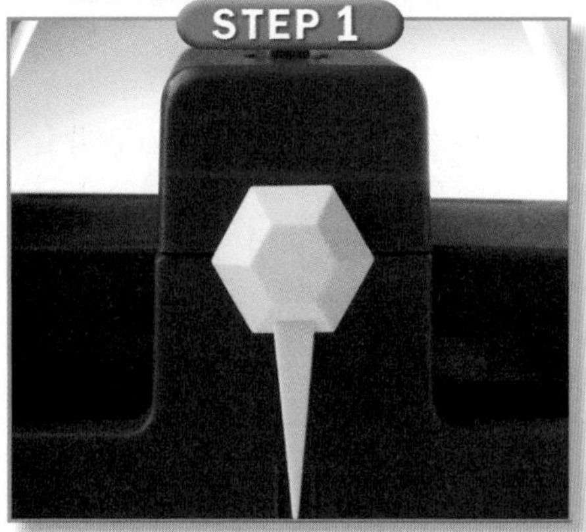

1. Check that the pointer is on the middle mark of the balance. If needed, move the slider on the back to the left or right.

2. Place a clay ball in one pan. Place a crayon in the other pan.

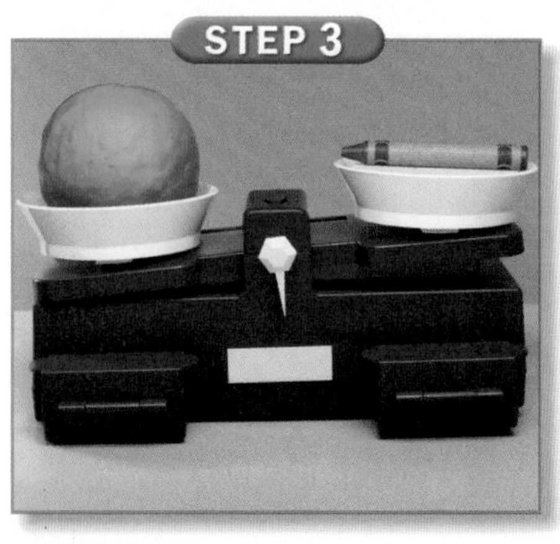

3. Observe the positions of the two pans.

Does the clay ball or the crayon have more mass?

Making a Chart

A chart can help you sort information, or data. When you sort data it is easier to read and compare.

Make a Chart to Compare Animals

1. Give the chart a title.
2. Name the groups that tell about the data you collect. Label the columns with the names.
3. Carefully fill in the data in each column.

How Animals Move

Animal	How it Moves
fish	swim
dog	walk, swim
duck	walk, fly, swim

Which animal can move in the most ways?

Making a Tally Chart

A tally chart helps you keep track of items as you count.

Make a Tally Chart of Kinds of Pets

Jan's class made a tally chart to record the number of each kind of pet they own.

1. Every time they counted one pet, they made one tally.
2. When they got to five, they made the fifth tally a line across the other four.
3. Count the tallies to find each total.

How many of each kind of pet do the children have?

Kinds of Pets

Pet	Tally
cat	卌 ||
dog	卌 |||
hamster	|||

Making a Bar Graph

A bar graph can help you sort and compare data.

Make a Bar Graph of Favorite Pets

You can use the data in the tally chart on page H8 to make a bar graph.

1. Choose a title for your graph.
2. Write numbers along the side.
3. Write pet names along the bottom.
4. Start at the bottom of each column. Fill in one box for each tally.

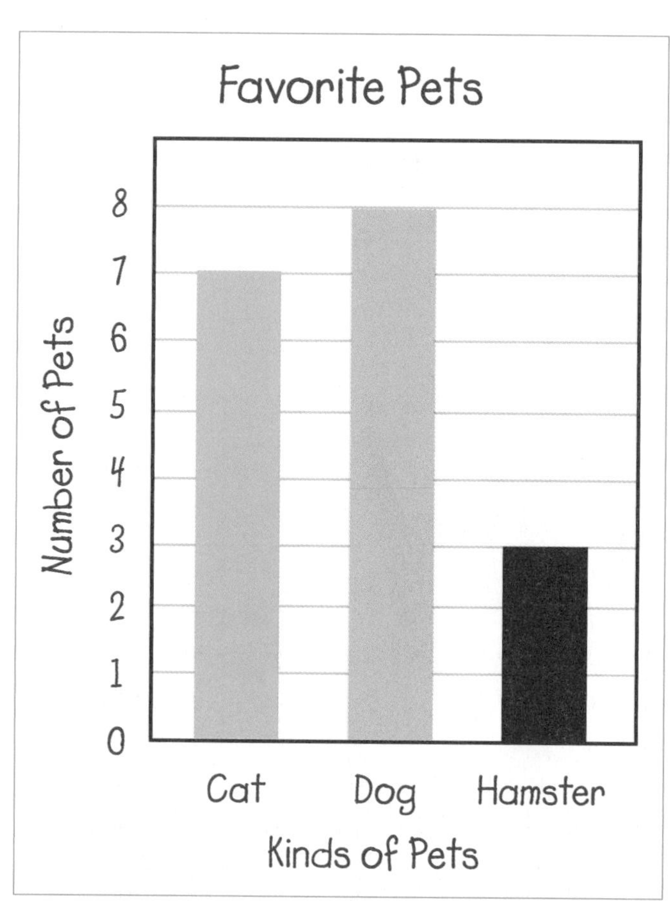

Which pet is the favorite?

Health and Fitness Handbook

When your body works well, you are healthy. Here are some ways to stay healthy.

- Know how your body works.
- Follow safety rules.
- Dance, jump, run, or swim to make your body stronger.
- Eat foods that give your body what it needs.

Your Senses

Your five senses help you learn about the world. They help you stay safe.

Sight

Light enters the eye through the pupil. The iris controls how much light comes in. Other parts of the eye turn the light into messages that go to the brain.

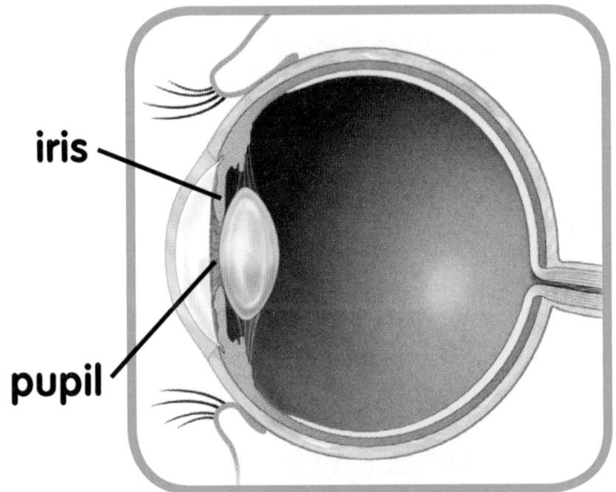

The iris is the colored part of the eye.

Hearing

The ear has three main parts. Most of your ear is inside your head. Sound makes some parts of the ear move back and forth very fast. The inner ear sends information about the sound to the brain.

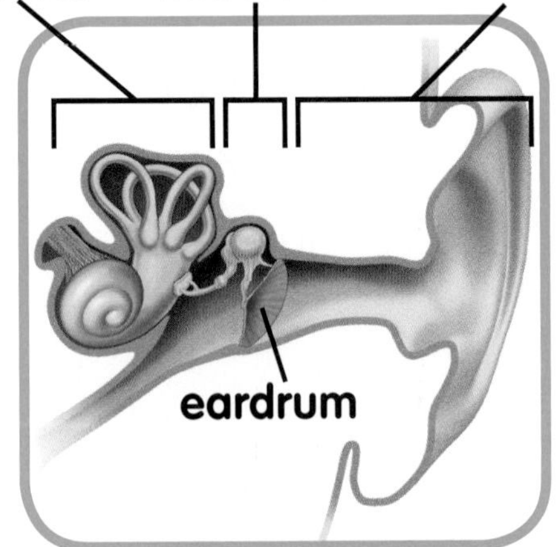

The eardrum is easily injured. Never stick anything in your ear.

Taste

Your tongue is covered with thousands of tiny bumps called taste buds. They help you taste sweet, salty, sour, and bitter things. Some parts of the tongue seem to sense some flavors more strongly. The whole tongue tastes salty foods.

bitter
sour
sour
sweet

Your body makes a new set of taste buds about every two weeks.

Smell

All kinds of smells travel through the air. These smells enter your nose. Your nose sends messages to your brain about them.

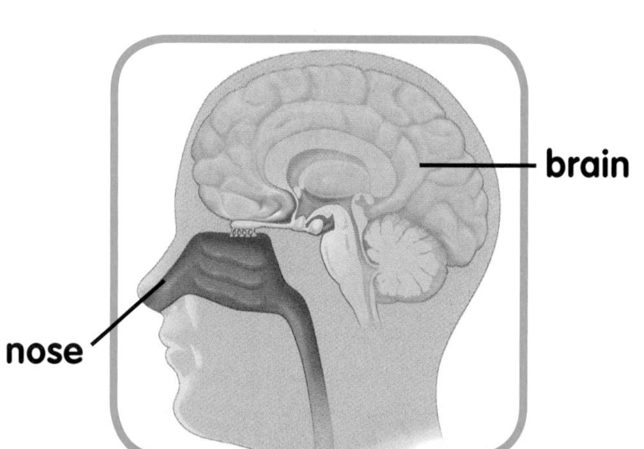

Your sense of smell also helps you taste.

Touch

Touch a tree trunk, and it feels rough. A kitten feels soft. Your skin senses all this information. Then the brain decides how to respond.

Your skin is your body's largest organ.

Protect Eyes and Ears

You use your eyes and ears to see and hear. You can protect your eyes and ears.

Protect Your Eyes

- Keep sharp things away from your eyes.
- Wear sunglasses when you are outside. They protect your eyes from the Sun's rays.

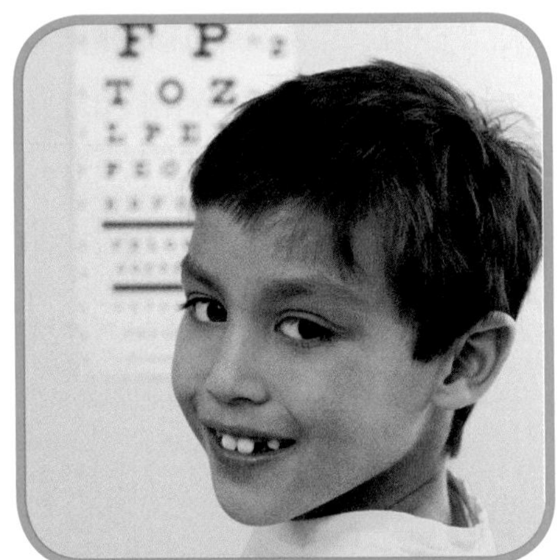

An eye test can help tell if a person needs glasses.

Protect Your Ears

- Wear a helmet when you play baseball or softball.
- Loud noises can damage your ears. Keep music at a low volume.

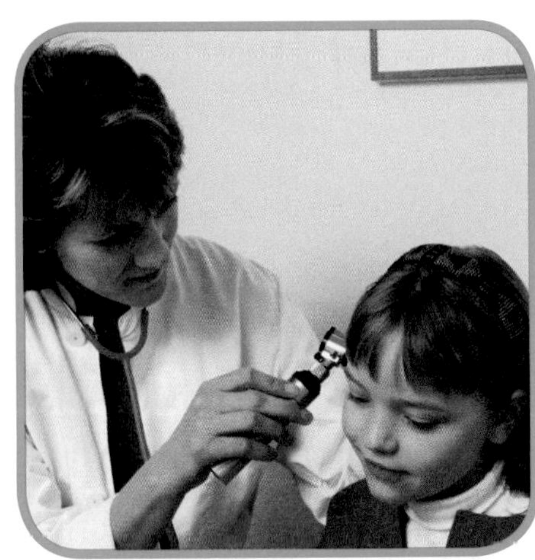

A hearing test tells if a person has a hearing loss.

Staying Safe on the Road

How do you get to school or a playground? Here are ways to help you stay safe.

Walk Safely

- Stay on the sidewalk.
- Walk with a friend or trusted adult.
- Cross at crosswalks. Look both ways before you cross!
- Don't run between parked cars. Drivers might not see you.

Car and Bus Safety

- If a bus has seat belts, wear one.
- Stay seated and talk quietly so the driver can pay attention to the road.
- Cross the street in front of a bus after all traffic stops.

Only cross when the "walk" sign is lit.

Obey crossing guards.

Always wear your seat belt in a car.

Move Your Muscles!

All kinds of things can be exercise. Here are some ways you can make your muscles stronger.

By Yourself

- Kick a ball as far as you can. Chase it and kick it back.
- Ride your bike.
- Jump rope.
- Do jumping jacks.
- Put on music and dance.

With Others

- Play ball!
- Play tag. Run!
- Go for a hike.
- Play hopscotch.
- Play with a flying disk.

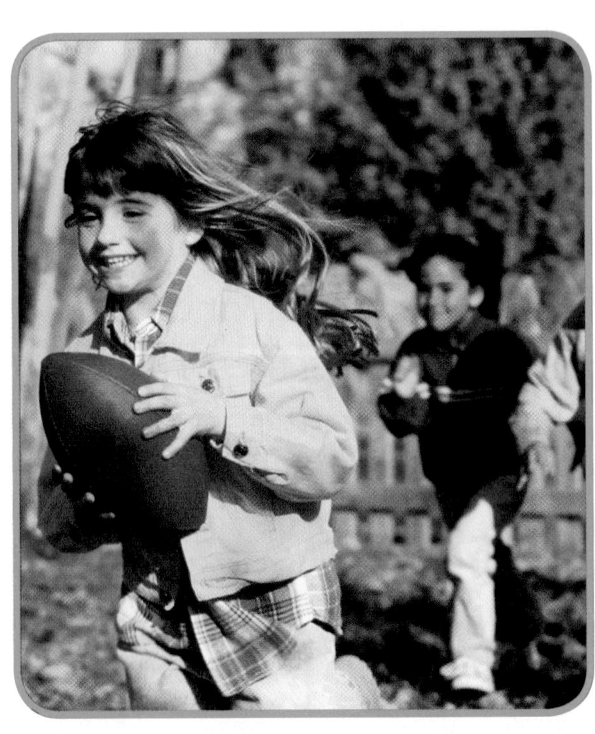

Food Groups

Food gives your body energy and what your body needs to grow. Foods in different groups help you in different ways.

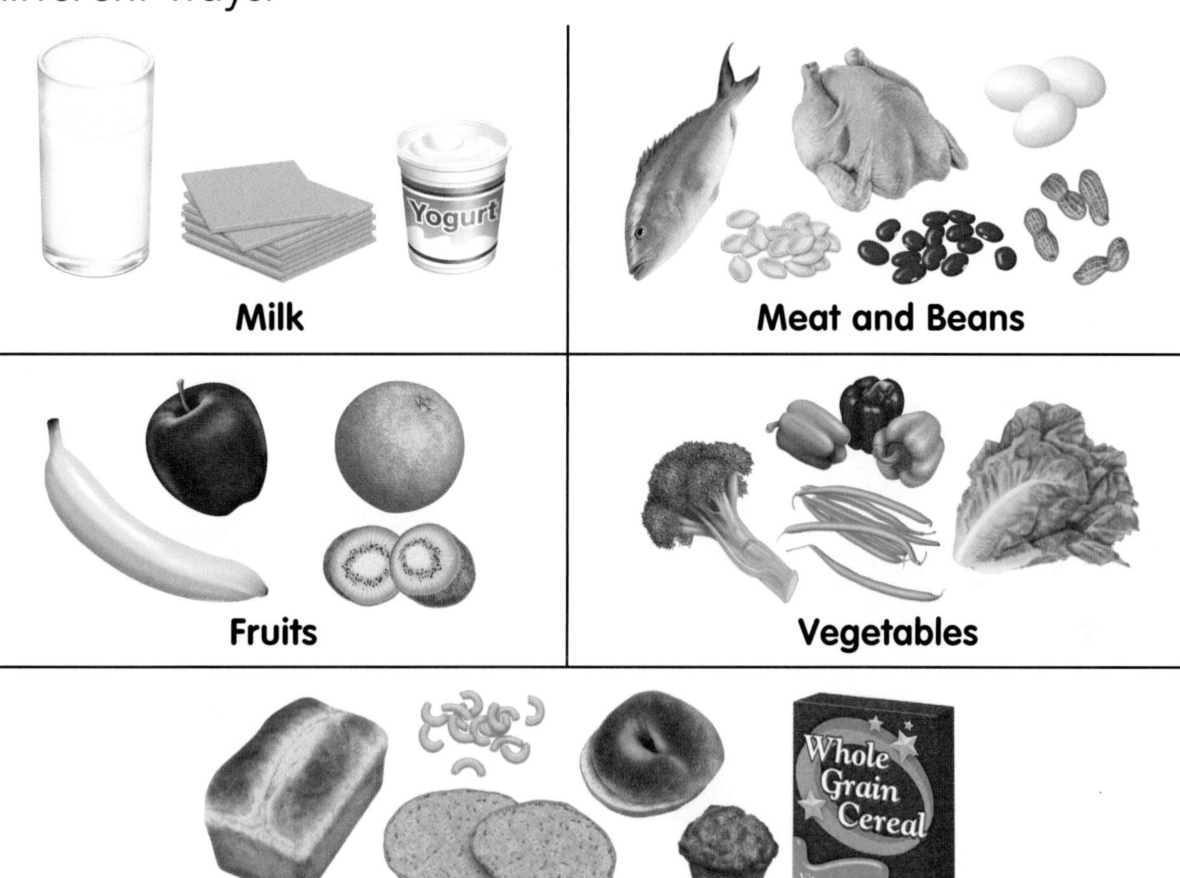

Milk

Meat and Beans

Fruits

Vegetables

Grains

Pizza includes the Milk group (cheese), the Grains group (crust), and the Vegetable group (tomatoes).

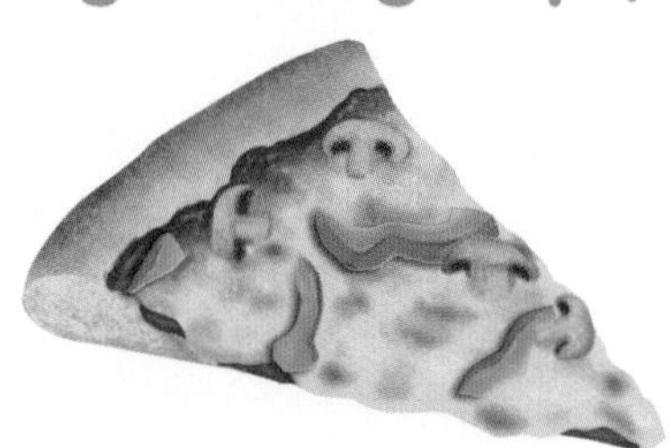

What groups are in this bowl of cereal?

Picture Glossary

adaptation
A body part or action that helps a living thing meet its needs where it lives. (A54)

amphibian
An animal that lives part of its life in water and part of its life on land. (A44)

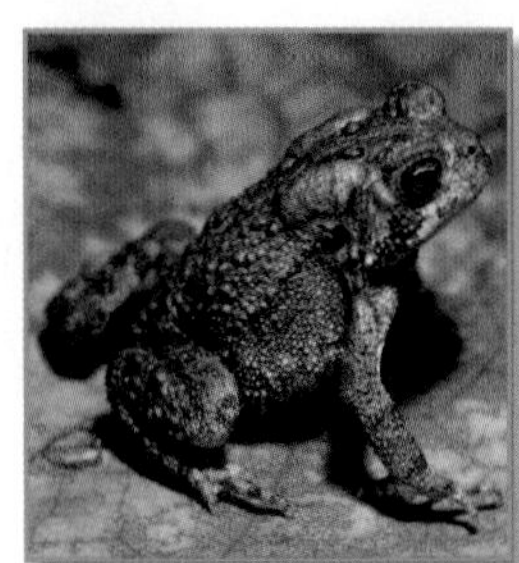

ask questions
Learn more about what you observe by asking questions of yourself and others.

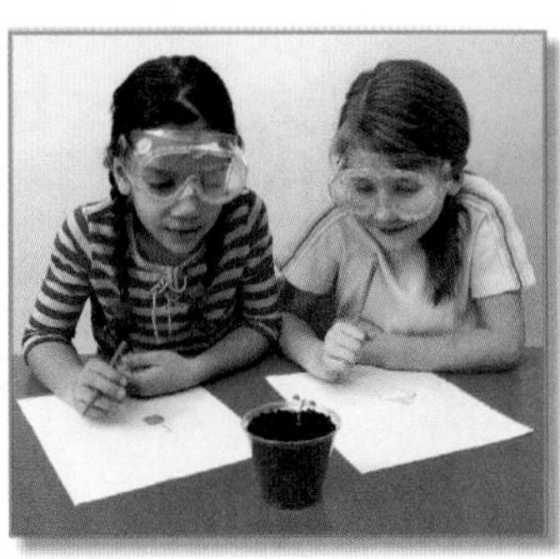

attracts
When a magnet pulls an object toward itself. (F38)

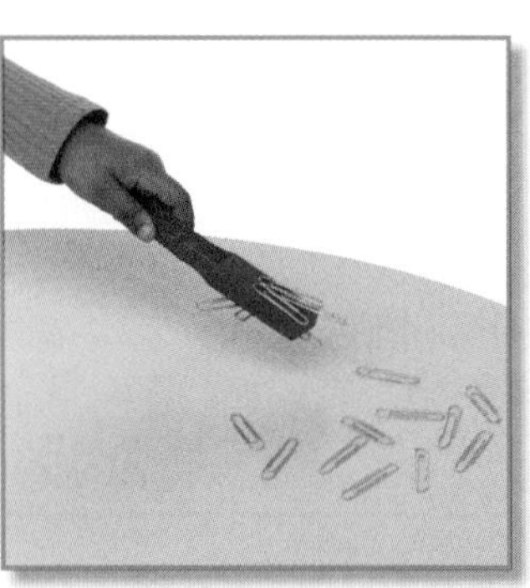

B

bird
An animal that has feathers and wings. (A38)

classify
Sort objects into groups that are alike in some way.

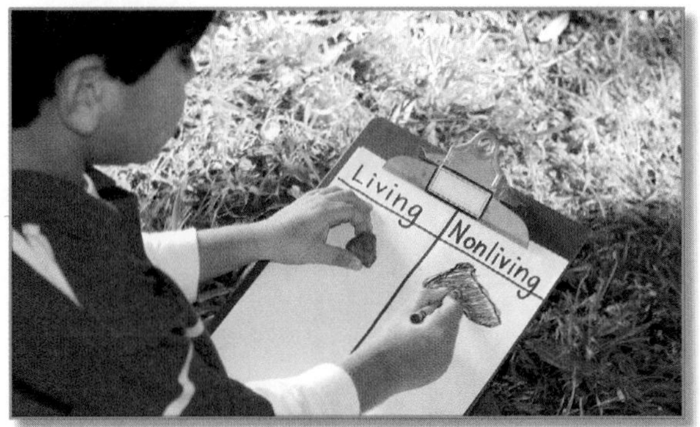

communicate
Share what you learn with others by talking, drawing pictures, or making charts and graphs.

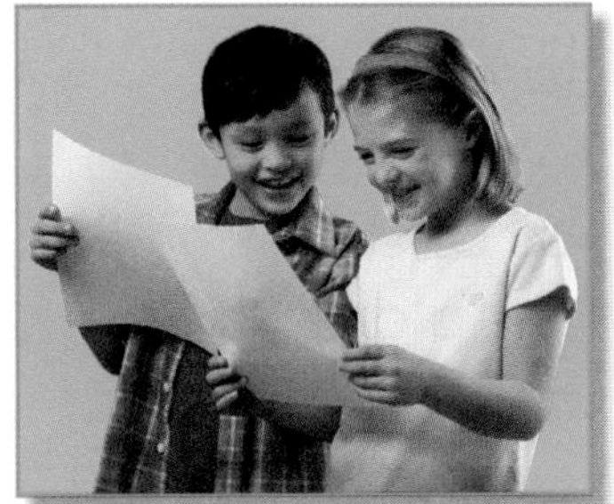

compare
Look for ways that objects or events are alike or different.

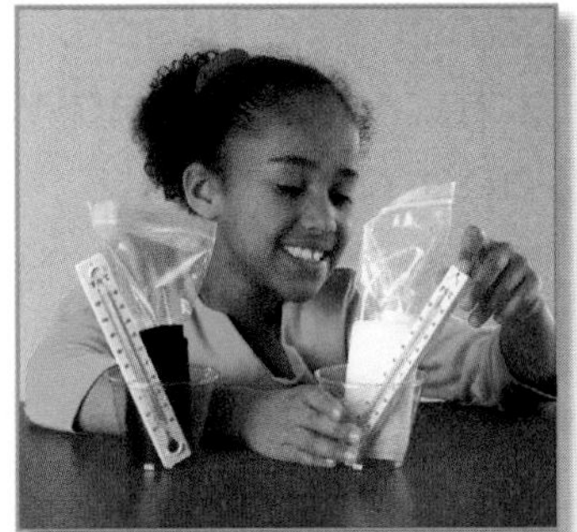

condenses
Changes from water vapor to drops of water. (D11)

cone
Part of a nonflowering plant where seeds form. (A20)

conserve
To use less of something to make it last longer. (C50)

constellation
A group of stars that forms a picture. (D58)

D

dissolves
Mixes completely with water. (E17)

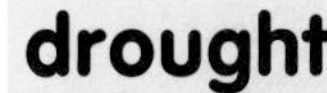

drought
A long time with little or no rain. (B28)

Picture Glossary

echo
A sound that repeats when sound waves bounce off a surface. (E47)

energy
The ability to do things. Living things get energy from food. (B38)

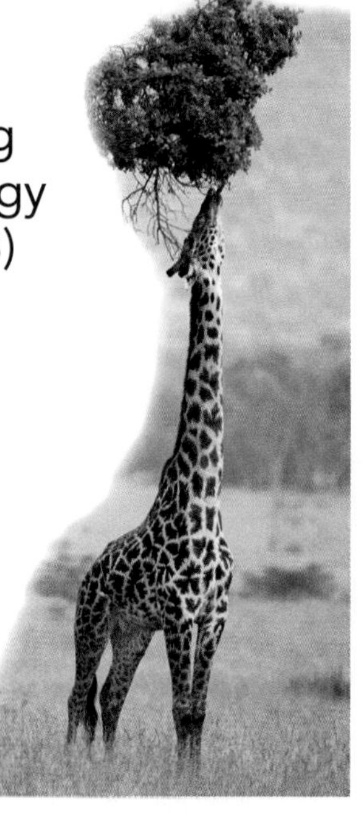

environment
All of the living and nonliving things around a living thing. (B8)

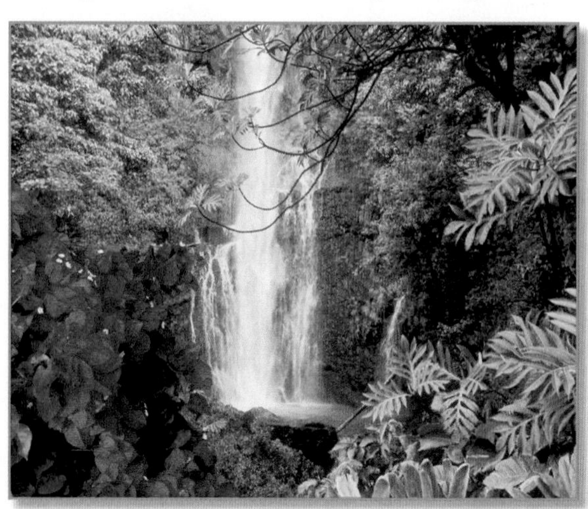

erosion
The carrying of weathered rock and soil from place to place. (C18)

evaporates
Changes to a gas. The Sun warms water, and water evaporates. (D10)

experiment
Make a plan to collect data and then share the results with others.

Testing Magnets	
Position of the Magnets	What Happened

fibrous root
A root that has many thin branches. (A22)

fish

An animal that lives in water and has gills. (A46)

flower

The plant part where fruit and seeds form. (A14)

food chain

The order in which energy passes from one living thing to another. (B40)

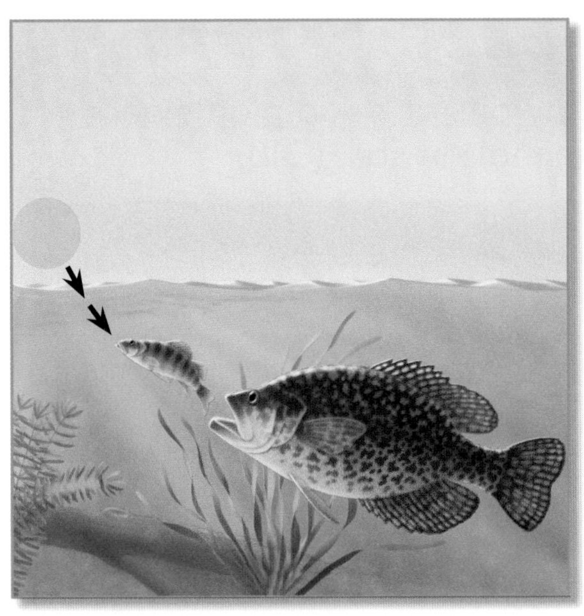

food web

A model that shows how different food chains are related. (B42)

force

A push or a pull. (F14)

fossil

Something that remains of a living thing from long ago. (C22)

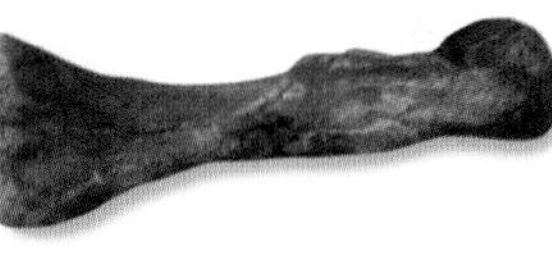

friction

A force that makes an object slow down when it rubs against another object. (F16)

fruit
The part of a flower that grows around a seed. (A14)

gas
A state of matter that spreads out to fill a space. A gas fills the inside of a balloon. (E11)

gravity
A pull toward the center of Earth. Objects fall to the ground unless something holds them up. (C18, F11)

habitat
The part of an environment where a plant or an animal lives. (B10)

healthful food
A food that is good for your body. (B50)

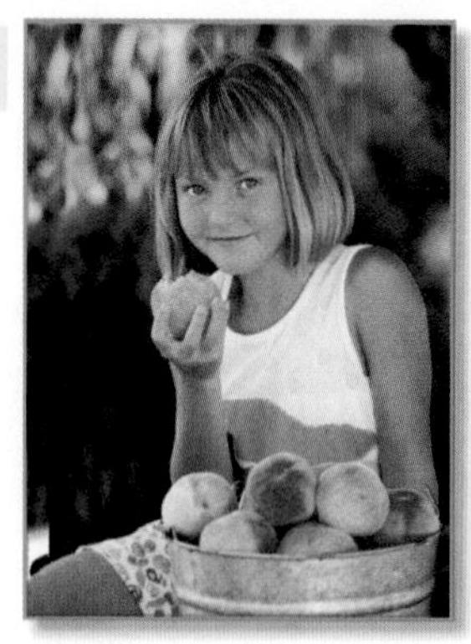

healthful meal
A meal with foods from the different food groups. (B52)

hibernate
To go into a deep sleep. (D27)

humus
Tiny bits of dead plants and animals in soil. (C10)

imprint
The shape of a living thing found in rock. (C22)

infer
Use what you observe and know to tell what you think.

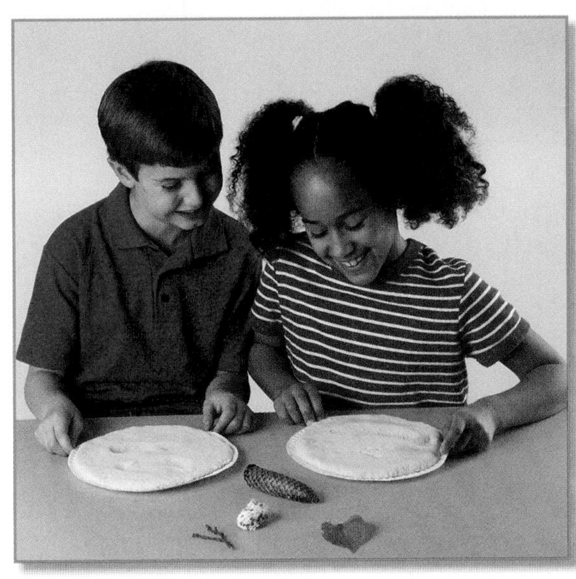

L

larva
A wormlike thing that hatches from an egg. (A74)

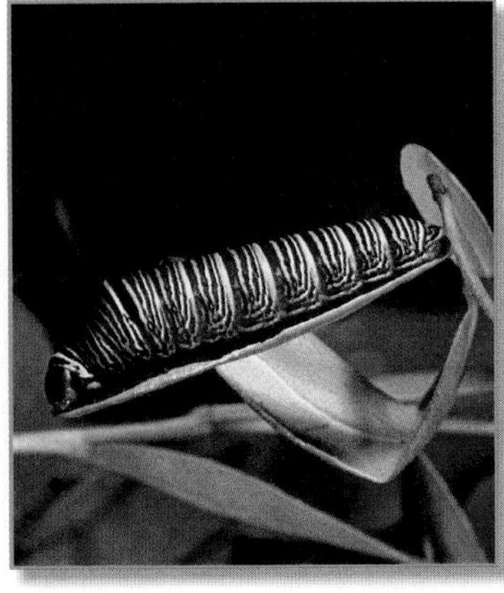

lever
A bar that moves around a fixed point. (F27)

life cycle
The series of changes that a living thing goes through as it grows. (A26)

liquid
A state of matter that does not have its own shape. (E10)

litter
Trash on the ground. (C45)

living thing
Something that grows and changes. (A8)

magnify
To make objects look larger. (E26)

magnetic
An object that is attracted to a magnet. (F42)

magnetic field
The area around a magnet where the magnet's force acts. (F50)

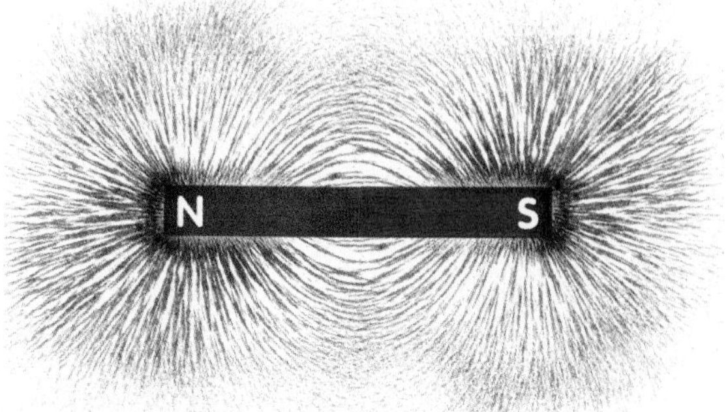

mammal
An animal that has fur or hair and makes milk to feed its young. (A36)

mass
The amount of matter in an object. You can measure mass with a balance. (E13)

measure
Use different tools to collect data about the properties of objects.

migrate
To move to warmer places in fall. (D27)

mineral
A nonliving solid found in nature. One or more minerals form rocks. (C8)

mixture
Something made of two or more things. (E16)

Moon
A large sphere made of rock. (D48)

motion
Moving from one place to another. (F10)

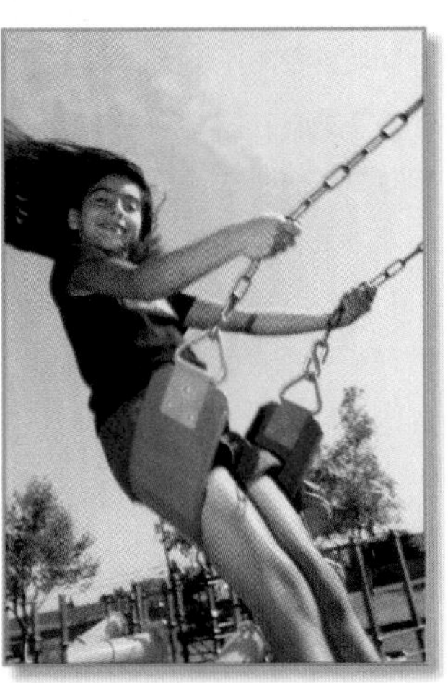

N

natural resource
Something found in nature that people need or use. (C34)

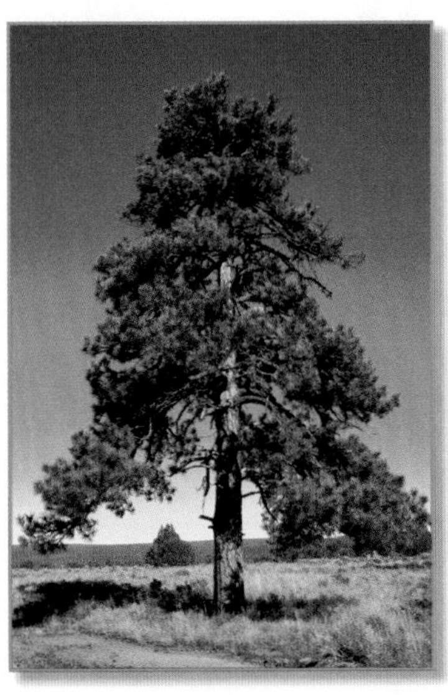

nonmagnetic
An object that is not attracted to a magnet. (F43)

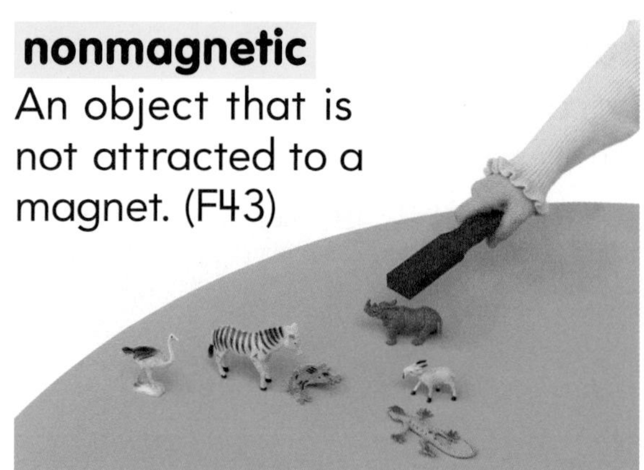

nutrient
A material in soil that helps a plant live and grow. Roots take in water and nutrients from the soil. (A11)

observe
Use tools and the senses to learn about the properties of an object or event.

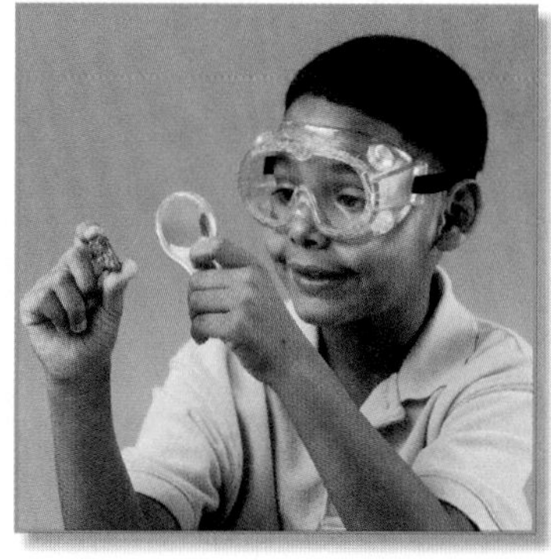

offspring
The group of living things that come from the same living thing. (A64)

orbit
The path that one space object travels around another. (D44)

P

phases
The different ways the moon looks. (D50)

pitch
How high or low a sound is. Cymbals have a low pitch. (E50)

planet
A large object that moves around the Sun. (D38)

precipitation
Water that falls from clouds. (D12)

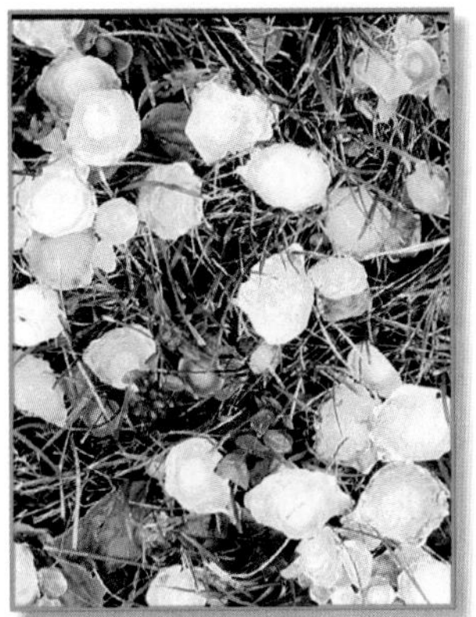

pole
The place on a magnet where the force is the strongest. (F37)

predict
Use what you know and patterns you observe to tell what will happen.

Testing Objects		
Object	Prediction	What Happened

pollution
Waste that harms the land, water, or air. (C45)

properties
Color, shape, size, odor, and texture. A penny is small and round. (E8)

position
A place or location. The bird is on top of the cactus. (F8)

pulley
A wheel with a groove through which a rope or chain moves. (F28)

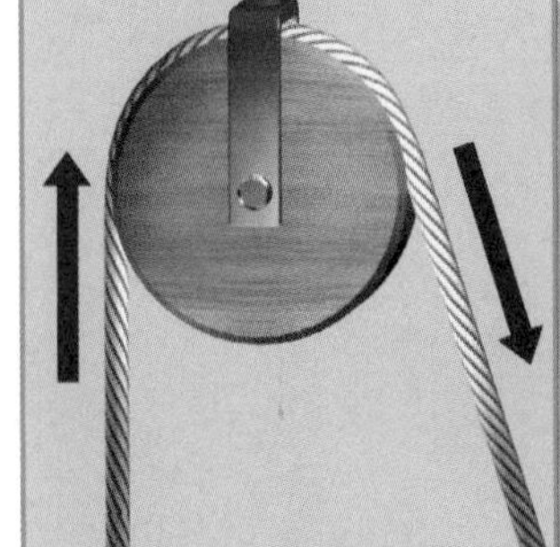

pupa
The stage between larva and adult when an insect changes form. (A75)

ramp
A slanted tool used to move things from one level to another. (F26)

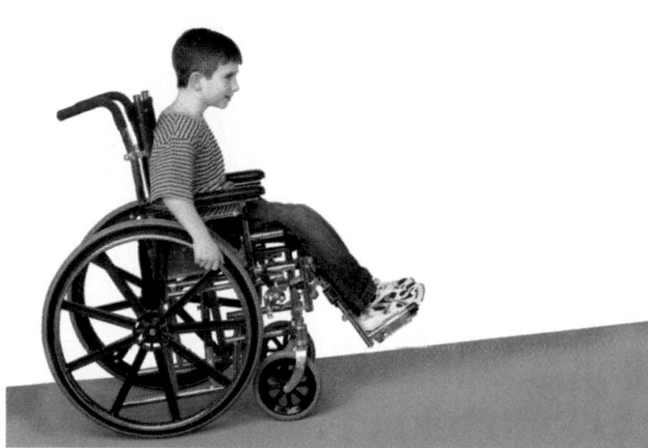

record data
Write or draw to show what you have observed.

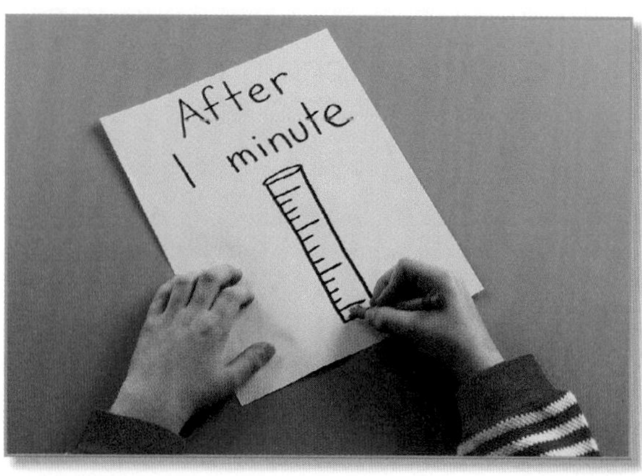

recycle
To collect items made of materials that can be used to make new items. (C50)

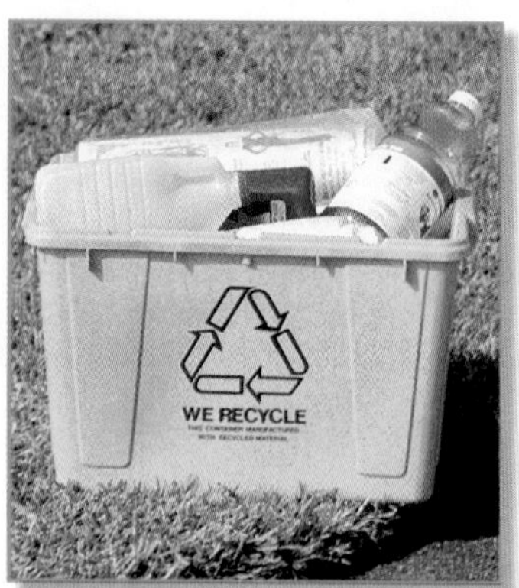

repels
When a magnet pushes an object away from itself. (F39)

reproduce
To make more living things of the same kind. (A64)

reptile
An animal whose skin is covered with dry scales. (A42)

resource
Something that plants and animals use to live. (B22)

reuse
To use again and again. Old tires can be reused on a playground. (C52)

revolve
To move in a path around an object. (D44)

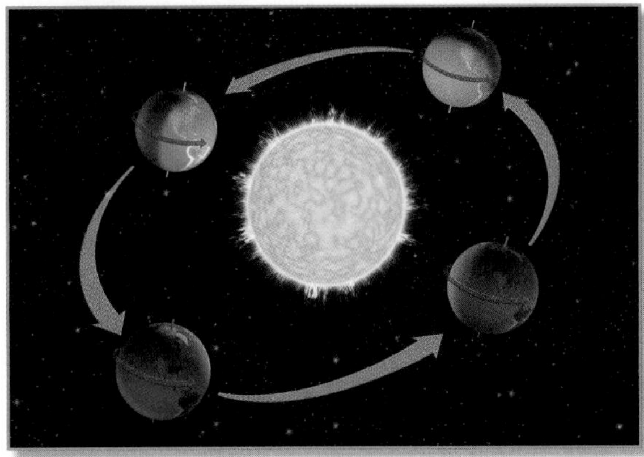

rock
A solid made of one or more minerals. (C8)

rotates
Spins around an imaginary line. (D42)

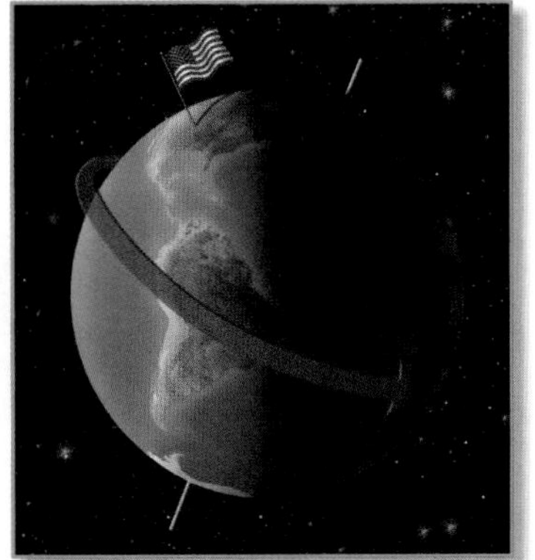

S

season
A time of year. (D16)

seed
The part from which a new plant grows. (A14)

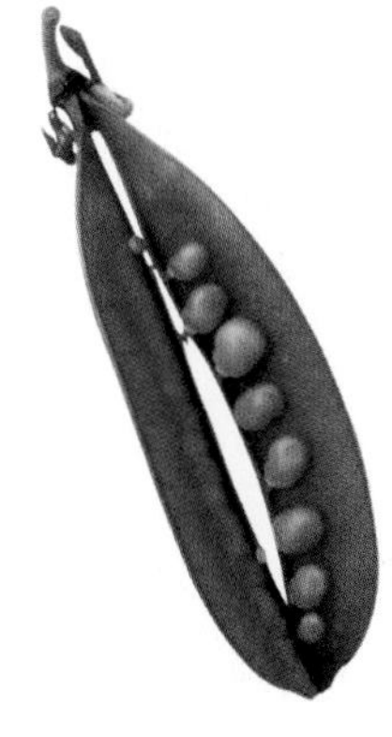

seedling
A young plant that grows from a seed. (A26)

separate
To take apart. (E16)

shelter
A place where a living thing can be safe. (A9)

simple machine
A tool that can make it easier to move objects. (F26)

soil
The loose material that covers Earth's surface. (C10)

solar system
The Sun and the space objects that move around it. (D38)

solid
A state of matter that has its own size and shape. (E10)

sound
Energy that you hear. (E36)

sound wave
Vibrating air. (E38)

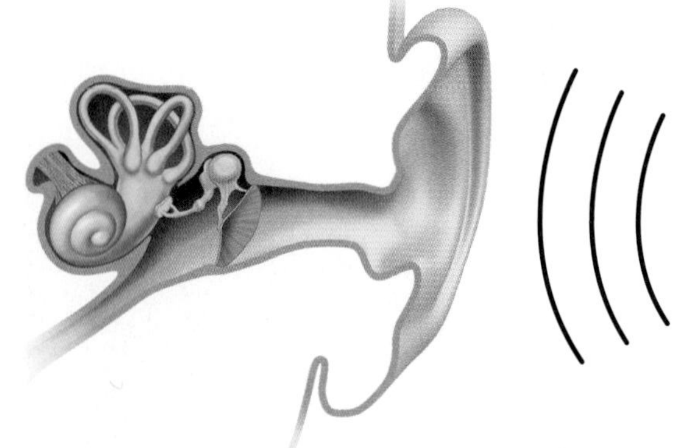

star
A big ball of hot gases that gives off light. (D56)

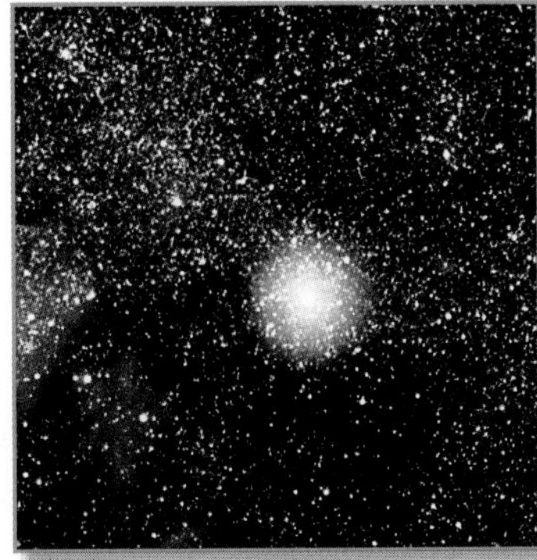

stream
A small river. (B14)

Sun
The brightest object in the day sky. (D36)

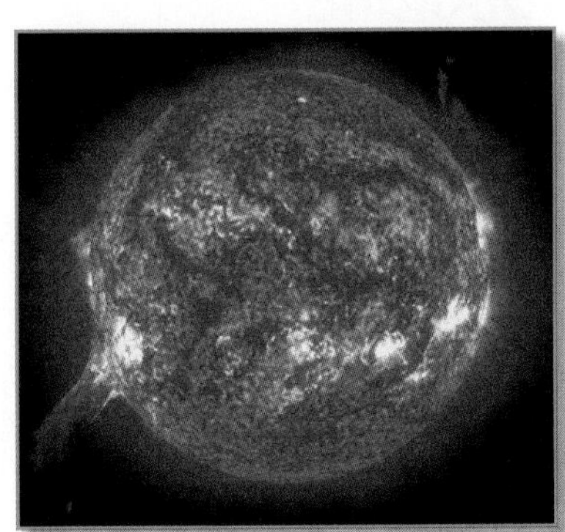

T

taproot
A root that has one main branch. (A22)

U

use data
Use what you observe and record to find patterns and make predictions.

use models
Use something like the real thing to understand how the real thing works.

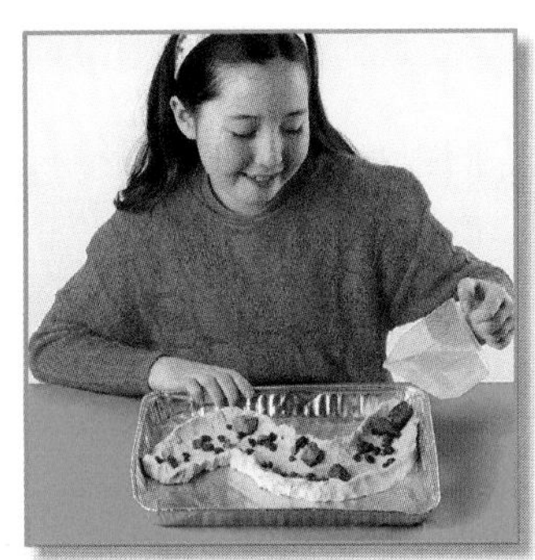

use numbers
Count, measure, order, or estimate to describe and compare objects and events.

Length of Triops	
Day 1	about ________ cm
Day 2	about ________ cm
Day 3	about ________ cm
Day 4	about ________ cm
Day 5	about ________ cm

vibrates
Moves back and forth very fast. A guitar string vibrates to make a sound. (E36)

volume
1. The amount of space a liquid takes up. (E12)

2. How loud or soft a sound is. A siren is loud. (E51)

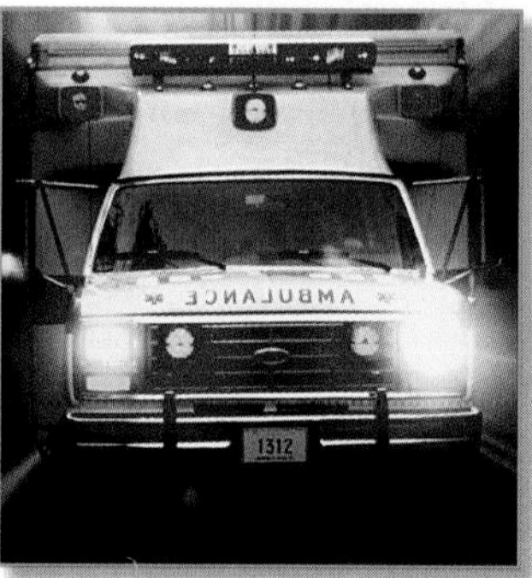

water cycle
Water moving from Earth to the air and back again. (D10)

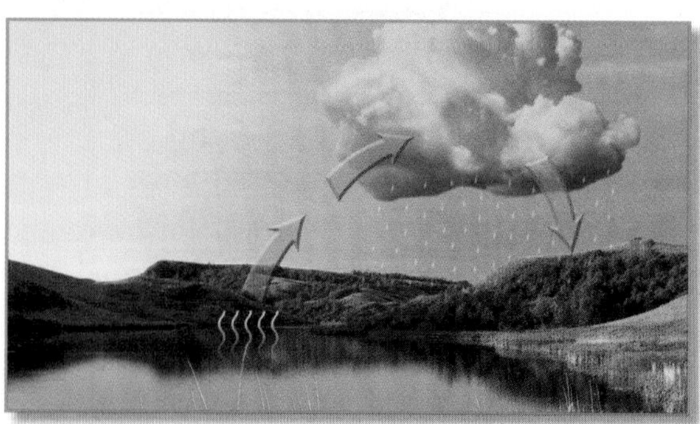

water vapor
Water as a gas. You cannot see water vapor. (D10)

weathering
The wearing away and breaking apart of rock. (C16)

woodland
A place with many trees and bushes. (B20)

work together
Work as a group to share ideas, data, and observations.

Credits

Permission Acknowledgements

Excerpt from The Tale of Rabbit and Coyote, by Tony Johnston, illustrated by Tomie de Paola. Text copyright © 1998 by Roger D. Johnston and Susan T. Johnston as Trustees of the Johnston Family Trust. Illustrations copyright © 1998 by Tomie de Paola. Used by permission of G.P. Putnam's Sons, a Division of Penguin Young Readers Group, A Member of Penguin Group (USA) Inc., 345 Hudson Street, New York, NY 10014, the author and Writers House LLC, acting as agent for the author. All rights reserved. Excerpt from Motion: Push and Pull, Fast and Slow, by Darlene Stille, illustrated by Sheree Boyd. Copyright © 2004 by Picture Window Books. Reprinted by permission of Picture Window Books. Excerpt from Let's Go Rock Collecting, by Roma Gans, illustrated by Holly Keller. Text copyright © 1984, 1997 by Roma Gans. Illustrations copyright © 1997 by Holly Keller. Reprinted by permission of HarperCollins Publishers. Excerpt from From Seed to Pumpkin, by Wendy Pfeffer, illustrated by James Graham Hale. Text copyright © 2004 by Wendy Pfeffer. Illustrations copyright © 2004 by James Graham Hale. Reprinted by permission of HarperCollins Publishers. Excerpt from River of Life, by Debbie S. Miller, illustrated by Jon Van Zyle. Text copyright © 2000 by Debbie S. Miller. Illustrations copyright © 2000 by Jon Van Zyle. Reprinted by permission of Clarion Books, an imprint of Houghton Mifflin Company. Excerpt from Crawdad Creek, by Scott Russell Sanders, illustrated by Robert Hynes. Text copyright © 1999 by Scott Russell Sanders. Illustrations copyright © 1999 by Robert Hynes. Reprinted by permission of National Geographic Society. Excerpt from The Starry Sky: The Sun and Moon, by Patrick Moore, illustrated by Paul Doherty. Copyright © 1994 Aladdin Books Limited. Text copyright © 1994 by Patrick Moore. Revised edition © 2000. Reprinted by permission of Aladdin Books Limited. Excerpt from The Sun: Our Nearest Star, by Franklyn M. Branley, illustrated by Edward Miller. Text copyright © 1961, 1988, 2002 by Franklyn M. Branley. Illustrations copyright © 2002 by Edward Miller III. Reprinted by permission of HarperCollins Publishers. Excerpt from My House's Night Song from My House is Singing, by Betsy R. Rosenthal. Copyright © 2004 by Betsy R. Rosenthal. Reprinted by permission of Harcourt, Inc. This material may not be reproduced in any form or by any means without the prior written permission of the publisher. *Wind Song* from *I Feel The Same Way*, by Lilian Moore. Copyright © 1967, 1995 by Lilian Moore. Reprinted by permission of Marian Reiner Literary Agency.
Excerpt from What's the Matter in Mr. Whisker's Room, by Michael Elsohn Ross, illustrated by Paul Meisel. Text copyright © 2004 by Michael Elsohn Ross. Illustrations copyright © 2004 by Paul Meisel. Reproduced by permission of the publisher Candlewick Press Inc., Cambridge, MA.

Cover

(bear cub) (Spine) Daniel J. Cox/Getty Images.(Back cover bears) Tom Walker/Getty Images. (landscape) Panoramic Images/Getty Images.

Photography

Unit A Opener Martin Harvey/Wild Images. **A1** Dave Watts/Dave Watts Photography. **A4–A5** Robert W. Ginn/Photo Edit, Inc. **A5** (tc) Colin Keates/DK Images. (bc) © Dwight Kuhn. (t) Gary VestalPhotographer's Choice/Getty Images. **A6** (bl) Robert A. Ross/Color Pic, Inc. **A6–A7** (bkgd) Andrew Brown/Ecoscene/Corbis. **A9** (tr) Bob & Clara Calhoun/Bruce Coleman, Inc. (br) Jeff Foott/Bruce Coleman, Inc. **A10** (inset) Nigel Cattlin/Photo Researchers, Inc. **A10–A11** (bkgd) Michael Busselle/Taxi/Getty Images. **A12–A13** (bkgd) Kathy Atkinson/Osf/Animals Animals. **A14** (l) Philip Dowell/DK Images. (r) © Dwight Kuhn. **A16** (t) Photo 24/Brand X Pictures/Getty Images. (b) N. Et Perennou/Photo Researchers, Inc. **A17** (t) M. Loup/Peter Arnold. (b) Matthew Ward/DK Images. **A18** (b) Alan & Linda Detrick/Photo Researchers, Inc. **A18–A19** (bkgd) Adam Jones/Osf/Animals Animals. **A20** (c) Matthew Ward/DK Images. (b) Colin Keates/DK Images. **A21** (tl) William Leonard/DRK Photo. **A21** (tr), (bl), (br) Matthew Ward/Dk Images. A22 (tl), (tr) © Dwight Kuhn. **A23** (tl) Ace Stock/Alamy Images. (r) Lani Howe/Photri. (bl) Jan Stromme/Bruce Coleman, Inc. **A24–A25** (bkgd) Michael B. Gadomski/Photo Researchers, Inc. **A28** (tr) © Dwight Kuhn. **A30** (l)© E.R. Degginger/Color–Pic, Inc. (lc) M. Loup/Peter Arnold. (c) © Dwight Kuhn. (rc) Colin Keates/DK Images. (r) Matthew Ward/DK Images. **A32–A33** (bkgd) Stephen J. Krasemann/DRK Photo. **A33** (t) Brain Stablyk/Photographer's Choice/Getty Images. (tc) Skip Moody/Dembinsky Photo Associates. (bc) John Cancalosi/DRK Photo. **A33** (b) G. Staebler/Masterfile. **A34–A35** (bkgd) Leslie Newman & Andrew Flowers/Photo Researchers, Inc. **A36** Brian Stablyk/Photographer's Choice/Getty Images. A37 (cl) Alan & Sandy Carey/Photo Researchers, Inc. (br) Tom Brakefield/DRK Photo. **A38** (t) K. McGougan/Bruce Coleman, Inc. (bl) Skip Moody/Dembinsky Photo Associates. **A39** Norman Owen Tomalin/Bruce Coleman, Inc. **A40** (bl) Frans Lantig/Minden Pictures. **A40–A41** (bkgd) Maresa Pryor/Earth Scenes/Animals Animals. **A42** Rod Planck/Photo Researchers, Inc. **A43** (tr) John Cancalosi/DRK Photo. (b) S.Gatzen/EyePress/Photri. **A44** (r) Sharon Cummings/Dembinsky Photo Associates. (bl) Gay Bumgarner/Index Stock Imagery. (frog) Skip Moody/Dembinsky Photo Associates. **A45** (tr) Frans Lanting/Minden Pictures. (tl) Michael & Patricia Fogden/Minden Pictures. (cr) Scott Camazine/Photo Researchers, Inc. (b) Dwight Kuhn/Bruce Coleman, Inc. **A46** (tl) William Leonard/DRK Photo. **A46** (cl) Marilyn Kazmers/Dembinsky Photo Associates. **A46–A47** (bkgd) Avi Klapfer/Mo Yung Productions/Norbert Wu Productions. **A47** (tr) Hans Reinhard/Bruce Coleman, Inc. (cr) © E. R. Degginger/Color Pic, Inc. **A52** (bl) Medford Taylor/National Geographic Image Collection. (bkgd) David Sanger/Alamy Images. **A54** (cr) G. Staebler/Masterfile. (b) Gregory G. Dimijian/Photo Researchers, Inc. **A55** (c) P. Kobeh/Peter Arnold. (bkgd) Tobias Bernhard/Oxford Scientific Library. **A56** © E.R. Degginger/Color Pic, Inc. **A58** (tl) Brian Stablyk/Photographer's Choice/Getty Images. (tlc) Skip Moody/Dembinsky Photo Associates. (tc) Rod Planck/Photo Researchers, Inc. (tcr) Skip Moody/Dembinsky Photo Associates. (tr) Marilyn Kazmers/Dembinsky Photo Associates. (bl) Alan & Sandy Carey/Photo Researchers, Inc. (blc) K. McGougan/Bruce Coleman, Inc. (bc) S.Gatzen/EyePress/Photri. (bcr) Dwight Kuhn/Bruce Coleman, Inc. (br) © E.R. Degginger/Color Pic, Inc. **A60–A61** (bkgd) John Cancalosi/Nature Picture Library. **A61** (t) Don & Pat Valenti/DRK Photo. (tc) John Daniels/Ardea. (bc) E.R. Degginger/Color Pic, Inc. (b) Eric Lindgren/Ardea. **A62** (bl) Nigel Cattlin/Photo Researchers, Inc. **A62–A63** (bkgd) Nigel Cattlin/Photo Researchers, Inc. **A64** John Daniels/Ardea. **A65** Dick Luria/Taxi/Getty Images. **A66** (tl) David R. Frazier/Photo Researchers, Inc. (tr) Don & Pat Valenti/DRK Photo. (cl), (cr) © Dwight Kuhn. **A67** (tl) J.L. Lepore/Photo Researchers, Inc. (tr) Anthony Mercieca/Photo Researchers, Inc. (cl) © Dwight Kuhn. (cr) DK Images. **A68** (tl) The Granger Collection, New York. (b) Academy of Natural Sciences of Philadelphia/Corbis. (frame) Image Farm. **A68–A69** (b) Merian, Maria Sibylla Graff (1647–1717)/Fitzwilliam Museum, University of Cambridge, UK/The Bridgeman Art Library. **A70** (bl) Gary Meszaros/Dembinsky Photo Associates. (br) Bob Jensen/Bruce Coleman, Inc. **A70–71** (bkgd) Michael Hubrich/Dembinsky Photo Associates. **A72** (c) E.R. Degginger/Bruce Coleman, Inc. (b) © E.R. Degginger/Color Pic, Inc. (r) Gary Meszaros/Bruce Coleman, Inc. **A72–A73** (bkgd) Marion Owen/Alaska Stock.com. **A73** (l) E.R. Degginger/Bruce Coleman, Inc. (r) John Shaw/Bruce Coleman, Inc. **A74** (l), (c), (r) © E.R. Degginger/Color Pic, Inc. **A74–A75** (bkgd) Garry Black/Masterfile. **A75** (l), (r) © E.R. Degginger/Color Pic, Inc. A76 (l), (c) © Dwight Kuhn. (r) Gary Meszaros/Dembinsky Photo Associates. **A78** (tl), (tcl), (tcr), © Dwight Kuhn. (tr) DK Images. **A78** (bl), (bcl), (bcr), (br) © E.R. Degginger/Color Pic, Inc. **A80** (l), (c) Ron Sanford/Corbis. (r) Caudia Adams/Dembinsky Photo Associates. Unit B Opener Rod Williams/Nature Picture Library. **B1** Denver Bryan Photography. **B4–B5** (bkgd) Tim Davis/Corbis. **B5** (t) Jeff Hunter/Getty Images. (tc) John Shaw/Bruce Coleman, Inc. (b) Nigel Cattlin/Photo Researchers, Inc. (bc) Garry Black/Masterfile. **B6** (bl) Fritz Polking/Peter Arnold. **B6–B7** (bkgd) Terry W. Eggers/Corbis. **B8** Tom Soucek/AlaskaStock.com. **B9** (t) Bill Brooks/Masterfile. **B9** (b) Ric Ergenbright/Corbis. **B10** (t) Jeff Hunter/Photographer's Choice/Getty Images. (b) Zigmund Leszczynski/Animals Animals. **B11** (t) David Fritts/Stone/Getty Images. (cr) Wayne Lynch/DRK Photo. B**12–B13** (bkgd) Darrell Gulin/DRK Photo. **B12** (bl) David T. Roberts/ Nature's Images/Photo Researchers. **B14–B15** (bkgd) John Shaw/Bruce Coleman, Inc. **B15** (tr) Stephen J. Krasemann/DRK Photo. **B16** (tl) Joe McDonald/Visuals Unlimited. (bl) Gary Meszaros/Bruce Coleman, Inc. (r) Edward Kinsman/Photo Researchers, Inc. **B17** (tl) M.P. Kahl/Photo Researchers, Inc. (tr) Naturfoto Honal/Corbis. (cr) Jim Battles/Dembinsky Photo Associates. B18 (bl) © Gary Meszaros/Dembinsky Photo Associates. **B18–B19** (bkgd) Douglas Faulkner/Corbis. **B20** Colin Varndell/Nature Picture Library. **B21** Jim Zipp/Photo Researchers, Inc. B22 (l) Scott Camazine/Photo Researchers, Inc. (c) Jim Battles/Dembinsky Photo Associates. **B23** (tl) Wayne Bennett/Corbis. (tr) Bill Marchel/Outdoor's Finest Photography. **B24** (bl) Todd Stailey/Courtesy of Tennessee Aquarium. **B24–B25** (bkgd) Tennessee Aquarium. **B26** (bl) Gary Gray/DRK Photo. **B26–B27** (bkgd) Art Wolfe/ Imagebank/Getty Images. **B28** Nigel Cattlin/ Holt Studio International/Photo Researchers, Inc. **B29** (tr) Breck Kent/Animals Animals. (b) J. E. Swedberg/Bruce Coleman, Inc. **B30** DRK Photo. **B32** (lc) Bill Marchel/Outdoor's Finest Photography. (cr) Zigmund Leszczynski/Animals Animals. (l) Edward Kinsman/Photo Researchers, Inc. (r) David Fritts/ Stone/Getty Images. **B34–B35** (bkgd) Kevin Dodge/Masterfile. **B35** (t) Jean–Michael Cornet/Stock Image/Pixland/Alamy Images. (b) Richard Hutchings/Photo Edit, Inc. (bc) C Squared Studios/Photodisc/Getty Images. **B36** (bl) Laura Riley/Bruce Coleman, Inc. **B36–B37** (bkgd) Johnny Johnson/DRK Photo.**B38** Harry Rogers/Photo Researchers, Inc. **B39** (l) Bill Beatty/Visuals Unlimited. (r) Anup Shah/ Taxi/Getty Images. **B41** (t) Peter Finger/Corbis. (c) Lynn Stone/Index Stock Imagery/PictureQuest. (b) Superstock/PictureQuest. **B46** (br) Brian Sytnyk/Masterfile. **B46–B47** (bkgd) Cosmo Condina/Getty Images. **B48** (c) J. C. Carton/Bruce Coleman, Inc. (bl) VCL/Taxi/Getty Images. **B48–B49** (b) David P. Hall/Masterfile. **B49** (tr) Judd Piloss of FoodPix. **B50** Ross Whitaker/Imagebank/Getty Images. **B52** (t) Richard Hutchings/Photo Edit, Inc. (blc) Burke/Triolo/Brand X/PictureQuest. (bl), (brc) Photodisc/Getty Images. (br) Comstock Images. **B54** (tr) Lynn Stone/Index Stock Imagery/PictureQuest. (bl) Laura Riley/Bruce Coleman, Inc. (br) Brian Sytnyk/Masterfile. **B56** (l) Mike Kelly/The Image Bank/Getty Images. (c) John Downer/Taxi/Getty Images. (r) Frank Krahmer/The Image Bank/Getty Images. Unit C Opener (bkgd) Index Stock Imagery/Alamy Images. **C1** Gary Ladd Photography. **C4–C5** (bkgd) Arthur M. Greene/Bruce Coleman, Inc. **C5** (t) Tony Freeman/Photo Edit, Inc. (tc) David Young–Wolff/Photo Edit, Inc. (bc) Rod Planck/Photo Researchers, Inc. (b) Tom Bean/DRK Photo. **C6–C7** (bkgd) Jeff Foott/Bruce Coleman, Inc. **C8–C9** (bkgd) Dennis MacDonald/Photo Edit Inc. **C9** (tl), (tc) Tony Freeman/Photo Edit Inc. (tr) Larry Stepanowicz/Visuals Unlimited. (bl) Roger Wood/Corbis. (bc) Phil Degginger/Color Pic, Inc. (br) Owen Franken/Corbis. **C11** (tl) John William Banagan/ The Image Bank/Getty Images. (tc) E.R. Degginger/Color Pic, Inc. (tr) David Young–Wolff/Photo Edit Inc. **C12** (tl) Hulton Archive/ Stringer/Getty Images. (b) Bettmann/Corbis. **C12–C13** (bkgd) Brian K. Miller/Animals Animals/Earth Scenes. **C13** (t) YardDoctor.com/Briggs and Stratton. (lc) F. Damm/Masterfile. (rc) Jane Grushow/Grant Heilman Photography. **C14–C15** (bkgd) © Susan E. Degginger/Color Pic, Inc. **C16** J. David Andrews/Masterfile. **C17** (tl) E.R. Degginger/Color–Pic, Inc. (tr) Rod Planck/Photo Researchers, Inc. (b) Tom Bean/DRK Photo. **C18** Stephen J. Krasemann/DRK photo. **C19** (t) Brian Miller/Bruce Coleman, Inc. (cr) Thomas Dressler/DRK Photo. **C20** (bl) Francois Gohier/Photo Researchers, Inc. **C20–C21** (bkgd) Kazimieras Mizgiris/AFIAP/Mizgiris Amber Museum. **C23** (tr) Alvis Upitis/Superstock. (cr) William P. Leonard/DRK Photo. (br) Mindy McNaugher/Stock Photo Archives/Carnegie Museum of Natural History. **C24–C25** (c) DK Images. **C25** (t) Bob Jensen/Bruce Coleman, Inc. (br) Frank Staub/Index Stock Imagery. **C26** (tr) Francois Gohier/Photo Researchers, Inc. (cr) Tom bean/DRK Photo. (br) T. A. WieWandt/DRK Photo. **C27** (br) Bill Aaron/Photo Edit, Inc. **C28** (tr) J. David Andrews/Masterfile. (tl) Rod Planck/Photo Researchers, Inc. (bl) Thomas Dressler/DRK Photo. (br) Brian Miller/Bruce Coleman, Inc. **C30–C31** (bkgd) ©Dwight Kuhn. **C31** (t) Buddy Mays/Corbis. (tc) E.R. Degginger/Color Pic, Inc. (bc) Arnold John Kaplan/Photri. (b) Corbis. **C32** (bl) Jock Montgomery/Bruce Coleman, Inc. **C32–C33** (bkgd) Jonathan Nourok/Photo Edit Inc. **C34** David Young–Wolff/Photo Edit, Inc. **C35** (tl) Susan Van Etten/Photo Edit, Inc. (tr) Ingram Publishing/Index Stock/Alamy Images. (c) Buddy Mays/Corbis. (br) Michael D. L. Jordan/Dembinsky Photo Associates. (bl) C Squared Studios/Getty Images. **C36** (tl) Michael E. Lubiarz/Dembinsky Photo Associates. **C36–C37** (bkgd) Jeremy Woodhouse/DRK Photo. **C37** (tr) Andrew Rakoczy/Bruce Coleman, Inc. (cr) ©Phil Degginger/Color Pic, Inc. **C42** (bl) Joe Macdonald/Bruce Coleman, Inc. **C42–C43** (bkgd) E.R. Degginger/Bruce Coleman, Inc. **C44** Paul Conklin/Photo Edit, Inc. **C45** (t) Jonathan Nourok/Photo Edit, Inc. (br) © E.R. Degginger/Color Pic, Inc. **C46** Jim West/The Image Works. **C47** (l) Steven C Kaufman/DRK Photo. **C47** (r) Darrell Gulin/DRK Photo. **C50** Arnold John Kaplan/Photri. **C51** (tl) Superstock. (tr) Charles Orrico/Superstock. (br) Myrleen Ferguson Cate/Photo Edit, Inc. **C52** Richard Hutchings/Photo Edit, Inc. **C54** (tl) © E.R. Degginger/Color Pic, Inc. (tr) Jim West/The Image Works. (cl) Jonathan Nourok/Photo Edit, Inc. (cr) Steven C Kaufman/DRK Photo. (bl) Emmanuel Faure/SuperStock. (br) Darrell Gulin/DRK Photo. **C56** (l), (c) Courtesy of Spectrum Glass. (r) Kevin Fleming/Corbis. Unit D Opener NTPL/Ian Shaw/The Image Works. **D1** Image Source/PictureQuest. **D4–D5** (bkgd) Warren Faidley/Weather Stock. **D5** (t) Andy Crawford/DKImages. (tc) Gary Meszaros/Photo Researchers, Inc. (bc) Jeff Foott/PictureQuest. (b) Jacana/Photo Researchers, Inc. **D6** (bl) Frank LaBua/Photri. **D6–D7** (bkgd) Corbis. **D8–D9** (bkgd) Don Nauman. **D9** (bc) Tom Warner/Noaa. **D10–D11** (bkgd) Jim Steinberg/Photo Researchers, Inc. **D12** (cl) Gary Meszaros/Photo Researchers, Inc. (b) Scott Smith/Index Stock Imagery. **D13** (t) Jim Mone/AP Wide World Photo. **D14** (bl) Kike Calvo/Bruce Coleman, Inc. **D14–D15** (bkgd) Carol Mallory/Dembinsky Photo Associates. **D15** (inset) Alison Barnes Martin/Masterfile. **D16** (bl) Dawn Charging/Bismark – Mandan CVB. **D17** (cr) Kindra Clineff/Index Stock Imagery. (b) Ralph Krubner/Mira. **D22** (bl) Sid & Shirley Rucker/DRK Photo. **D22–D23** (bkgd) Maslowski Photo/Photo Researchers, Inc. **D24** (t) Bill Beatty. (b)Fred Habegger/Grant Heilman Photography. **D25** (tl) Harry Rogers/Photo Researchers, Inc. (tc) Thase Daniel/Bruce Coleman Inc. (tr) Edward L. Snow/Bruce Coleman Inc. (bl) Fred Habegger/Grant Heilman Photography. (bc) Geoff Bryant/Photo Researchers, Inc. (br) Fred Habegger/Grant Heilman Photography. **D26** (bl) Photri. (b) Daniel J Cox/Natural Selection Stock Photography. **D27** (tr) Jeff Foott/PictureQuest. (tcr) S. Charles Brown; Frank Lane Picture Agency/Corbis. (cr) Bill Beatty/Animals Animals. (b) Fred Bruemmer/DRK Photo. **D30** (tr) Thase Daniel/Bruce Coleman, Inc. (tl) Edward L. Snow/Bruce Coleman Inc. (tcl) Bill Beatty. (tcr) Harry Rogers/Photo Researchers, Inc. (bcl) S. Charles Brown; Frank Lane Picture Agancy/Corbis. (bcr) Bill Beatty/Animals Animals. (bl) Jeff Foott/PictureQuest. (br) Fred Bruemmer/DRK Photo. **D32–D33** (bkgd) John Henry Williams/Bruce Coleman, Inc. **D33** (bc) John Sanford/Photo Researchers, Inc. (b) Roger Ressmeyer/Corbis. **D34** (bl) Nasa/Photri. **D34–D35** (bkgd) Nasa/Photri. **D36** Nasa/Science Photo Library/Photo Researchers, Inc. **D37** (t) © Eric O'Connell/Iconica/Getty Images. **D40** (bl) World Perspectives/Photographer's Choic/Getty Images. **D40–D41** (bkgd) Bill Aron/Photo Edit, Inc. **D46** (bl) World Perspectives/Stone/Getty Images. **D46–D47** Steven Satushek/Botanica/Getty Images. **D48** World Perspectives/Stone/Getty Images. **D50–D51** (bkgd) John Sanford/Photo Researchers, Inc. **D54–D55** (bkgd) Bill Frymire/Masterfile. **D56** (cl) Eckhard Slawick/Photo Researchers, Inc. **D56–D57** (bkgd) Michael Simpson/ Taxi/Getty Images. (cr) Photri. **D57** (cl) Susan McCartney/Photo Researchers, Inc. (br) Photri. **D58** Roger Ressmeyer/Corbis. **D59** (tl) Roger Ressmeyer/Corbis. (br) John Sanford & David Parker/ Science Photo Library/Photo Researchers, Inc. D64 (l) Owaki–Kulla/Corbis. (r) Tony Arruza/Corbis. Unit E Opener Thinkstock/PictureQuest. **E1** Thinkstock/PictureQuest. **E4–E5** (bkgd) Everett Kennedy Brown, Staff/ European Press Photo Agency, EP/AP Wide World Photo. **E5** (b) Iverson/Folio Inc. **E6** (bl) Gusto/Photo Researchers, Inc. **E6–E7** (bkgd) Thom Lang/Corbis. **E13** (br) G K & Vikki Hart/Getty Images. **E23** (c) Image Courtesy of the United States. **E24** (bl) Skip Moody/Dembinsky Photo Associates, Inc. **E24–E25** (bkgd) George D. Lepp/Corbis. **E26** Ralph A. Clevenger/Corbis. **E27** (t) Jose Luis Pelaez, Inc./Corbis. (lc) Jim Zuckerman/Corbis. (rc) Iverson/Folio Inc. (b) Greg Wahl–Stephens/AP Wide World Photo. **E28** (tl) Mark A. Schneider/Dembinsky Photo Associates. (tr) Darrell Gulin/Corbis. (tc) Skip Moody/Dembinsky Photo Associates. (bc), (bl) Iverson/Folio Inc. (br) Clouds Hill Imaging Ltd./Corbis. **E32–E33** (bkgd) Daniel Bosler/Stone/Getty Images. **E33** (b) Gabe Palmer/Corbis. (bc) Premium Stock/Corbis. **E34–E35** (bkgd) Image100/Alamy Images. **E39** Michael Newman/Photo Edit, Inc. **E42** (bl) A. Ramey/Photo Edit, Inc. **E42–E43** David Madison/Photodisc/Getty Images. **E44** Flip Nicklin/Minden Pictures. **E45** Michael Newman/Photo Edit, Inc. **E46** Michael Newman/PhotoEdit, Inc. **E48–E49** Howie Garber/Animals Animals. **E50** (tl), (br) C. Squared Studios/Photodisc/Getty Images. (tr), (bl) PhotoDisc/Getty Images. (cl) Premium Stock/Corbis. (cr) Cyril Laubscher/DK Images. **E51** (tl) Gabe Palmer/Corbis. **E53** (t) C Squared Studios/Getty Images. (l) Photodisc/Getty Images. (r) Steve Cole/Getty Images. (b) David Murray/DK Images. Unit F Opener Tek Image/Photo Researchers Inc. **F1** (bkgd) Steve Taylor/Stone/Getty Images. **F4–F5** (bkgd) Joe McBride/Photgrapher's Choice/Getty Images. **F5** (t) Tony Freeman/Photo Edit, Inc. (b) © Phil Degginger/Color–Pic, Inc. **F6–F7** (bkgd) Thinkstock/Getty Images. **F10** (cl) Tony Freeman/Photo Edit, Inc. (br) Picture Plain/Photo Library.com. **F11** (tl) John Fox/Alamy Images. (br) RubberBall Productions/Getty Images. **F12–F13** (bkgd) Rolf Bruderer/Corbis. **F15** (br) Barry Runk/Grant Heilman Photography. **F16** (tl) Philip Gatward/DK Images. **F17** Rubberball Productions/Getty Images. **F24–F25** David Madison/Stone/Getty Images. **F25** (tr) Alan Thornton/Stone/Getty Images. **F26** (cr) Bob Daemmrich/Corbis Sygma. **F27** (tr) © E.R. Degginger/Color–Pic Inc. (cr) © Phil Degginger/Color–Pic Inc. F28 (l) Kimberly Robbins/Photo Edit, Inc. **F30** (tc) Barry Runk/Grant Heilman Photography. (tr) Philip Gatward/DK Images. (bl) John Fox/Alamy Images. (bc) Picture Plain/Photo Library.com. (br) Tony Freeman/Photo Edit, Inc. **F33** (tc) Michael Newman/Photo Edit, Inc. **F40** (bl) Michael Newman/Photo Edit, Inc. **F40–F41** (bkgd) Image Source Limited/Index Stock Imagery. **F44** (cr)Tom Pantages. (bl) © E.R. Degginger/Color Pic, Inc. **F45** (tr) © Phil Degginger/Color Pic, Inc. **F46–47** (bkgd) LIU Jin/AFP/Getty Images. **F48** (bl) Tim Pannell/Corbis. **F56** (r) David Young–Wolf/Photoedit, Inc.

Assignment

A6, A7 © HMCo./Ken Karp Photography. **A12, A13, A18** © HMCo./Richard Hutchings Photography. **A19** © HMCo./Lawrence Migdale Photography. **A24** (tc),(bc) © HMCo./Ken Karp Photography. **A24** (t),(br) © HMCo./Richard Hutchings Photography. **A25** (t) © HMCo./Ken Karp Photography. **A34, A35** © HMCo./Richard Hutchings Photography. **A40, A41, A48, A49, A52, A53, A62, A63** © HMCo./Ken Karp Photography. **A70** (bc) © HMCo./Richard Hutchings Photography **A70** (t),(tc),(b) **A71** © HMCo./Ken Karp Photography. **B6** (t) © HMCo./Richard Hutchings Photography. **B7** © HMCo./Lawrence Migdale Photography. **B12, B13, B18, B26, B27, B36, B37, B46, B47** © HMCo./Richard Hutchings Photography. **C6, C7, C14, C15, C20, C21, C32, C33** © HMCo./Richard Hutchings Photography. **C38** © HMCo./Ken Karp Photography. **C42, C43, C48, C49** © HMCo./Richard Hutchings Photography. **D6, D7** © HMCo./Richard Hutchings Photography. **D14** (c) © HMCo./Ken Karp Photography. **D14** (t) © HMCo./Richard Hutchings Photography. **D15,D20** © HMCo./Ken Karp Photography. **D22, D23, D28, D34, D35, D40, D41** © HMCo./Richard Hutchings Photography. **D43** © HMCo./Bud Endress Photography. **D46, D47, D54** (t), (bc), (b) © HMCo./Coppola Studios Inc. **D54** (bl) © HMCo./Ken Karp Photography. **D55** © HMCo./Richard Hutchings Photography. **E5** © HMCo./Ken Karp Photography. **E6** (t), (tc), (bc) © HMCo./Richard Hutchings Photography. **E6** (b) © HMCo./Ken Karp Photography. **E7** © HMCo./Richard Hutchings Photography. **E10–E11** © HMCo./Bud Endress Photography. **E12** © HMCo./Richard Hutchings Photography. **E13** © HMCo./Ken Karp Photography. **E14, E15** © HMCo./Richard Hutchings Photography. **E16, E17, E18, E19, E20, E21** © HMCo./Ken Karp Photography. **E24, E25, E33** (t) © HMCo./Richard Hutchings Photography. **E33** (tc), **E34** (bl) © HMCo./Ken Karp Photography. **E34** (t), (tc), (bc), (b), **E35, E36–E37, E38, E42, E43, E48, E49, E51, E52** © HMCo./Richard Hutchings Photography. **F5** (tc) © HMCo./Lawrence Migdale Photography. **F5** (bc), **F6** (b) © HMCo./Ken Karp Photography. **F6** (tr), **F7** © HMCo./Richard Hutchings Photography. **F8–F9** © HMCo./Ken Karp Photography. **F12, F13** HMCo./Richard Hutchings Photography. **F14** © HMCo./Ken Karp Photography. **F15, F16** © HMCo./Lawrence Migdale Photography. **F18, F20** © HMCo./Ken Karp Photography. **F22** © HMCo./Richard Hutchings Photography. **F22** (bkgd) © HMCo./Ken Karp Photography. **F23** © HMCo./Richard Hutchings Photography. **F26** © HMCo./Ken Karp Photography. **F30** © HMCo./Ken Karp Photography. **F33** (t) © HMCo./Richard Hutchings Photography. **F33** (bc) © HMCo./Ken Karp Photography. **F34, F35, F36, F37** © HMCo./Richard Hutchings Photography. **F38** © HMCo./Ken Karp Photography. **F39, F40, F41,** © HMCo./Richard Hutchings Photography. **F42, F43, F48** (bl) © HMCo./Ken Karp Photography. **F48** (t), **F49** © HMCo./Richard Hutchings Photography. **F51, F52** © HMCo./Ken Karp Photography.

Illustration

A5 Wendy Smith. **A8** Jeff Wack. **A15, A26–A27** Wendy Smith. **A28** Lori Anzalone. **A48–A51** Liz Conrad. **B16–B17** Luigi Galante. **B20–B21** Michael Maydak. **B22–B23** Patrick Gnan. **B35** © Lelend Klanderman. **B40–B4**3 © Leland Klanderman. **B51** Argosy Publishing. **B54** © Leland Klanderman. **C10** Richard Orr. **C22–C23** Michigan Science Art. **C26** Michael Maydak. **C38–C41** Theresa Smythe. **C48** Tim Johnson. **C50–C51** Digital Dimensions. **D16–D17** Robert Schuster. **D16–17** (map) Annette Cable. **D18–D19** Kristin Barr. **D21** Mark & Rosemary Jarman. **D20–D21** (bkgd) JoAnn Adinolfi. **D33** (t) Bob Kayganich. **D33** (tc) Patrick Gnan. **D38–D39** Bob Kayganich. **D42** Patrick Gnan. **D44** Argosy. **D49** Patrick Gnan. **D59** Matthew Trueman. **D60** Argosy Publishing. **E14–E15, E18–E19** Tim Johnson. **E22–E23** Robert Schuster. **E30** Terri Chicko **E33, E38** Sharon and Joel Harris. **E40** Laura Ovresat. **E41** Shane McGowan. **E47** Patrick Gnan. **E54** Terri Chicko. **E56** David Klug. **F18–F21** John Berg. **F28** George Baquero. **F47, F56** Patrick Gnan.

Nature of Science

PHOTOGRAPHY: (solar disc) © Brand X Pictures/The Stocktrek Corp/Alamy Images. **S1** © Jose Luis Pelaez, Inc./CORBIS. **S2-3** JSC/NASA. **S4-5** © Ernest Manewal/Superstock. **S5** (br) © HMCo./Ed Imaging. **S6-7** Stephen Dalton/NHPA. **S7** (r) © HMCo./Ed Imaging. **S8-9** © HMCo./Joel Benjamin Photography. **S10-1** Lloyd C. French/JPL/NASA. **S11** (r) © Reuters/CORBIS. **S12-3** (bkgd) © David Martyn Hughes/Alamy Images. **S12-3** (l) (m) (r) © HMCo./Bruton Stroube. **S14-15** © Craig Steven Thrasher/Alamy Images. **S16** © HMCo./Richard Hutchings Photography.

Health and Fitness Handbook

PHOTOGRAPHY: **H10** © Ariel Skelley/Corbis. **H13** George Shelley/Masterfile. **H14** (t) Picturequest. (b) Photodisc/Getty Images. **H15** (t) Brad Rickerby/Getty Images. (m) Rubberball/Getty Images. (b) Photodisc/Getty Images. **H16** (t) Dex Image/Getty Images. (b) Ariel Skelley/Corbis. ILLUSTRATION: **H18–H19** William Melvin. **H23** Linda Lee.

Science and Math Toolbox

H7 (t) John Giustina/Getty Images. (m) Georgette Douwma/Getty Images. (b) Giel/Getty Images. **H8** Photodisc/Getty Images.